THE PLAYING CURE

CHILD THERAPY SERIES

A SERIES OF BOOKS EDITED BY CHARLES SCHAEFER

Cognitive-Behavioral Play Therapy
Susan M. Knell

Play Therapy in Action: A Casebook for Practitioners
Terry Kottman and Charles Schaefer, Eds.

Family Play Therapy
Lois Carey and Charles Schaefer, Eds.

The Quotable Play Therapist
Charles Schaefer and Heidi G. Kaduson, Eds.

Childhood Encopresis and Enuresis
Charles Schaefer

The Therapeutic Powers of Play
Charles Schaefer, Ed.

Play Therapy Techniques
Donna Cangelosi and Charles Schaefer, Eds.

Children in Residential Care: Critical Issues in Treatment
Charles Schaefer and Arthur Swanson, Eds.

Therapeutic Use of Child's Play
Charles Schaefer, Ed.

Clinical Handbook of Sleep Disorders in Children
Charles Schaefer, Ed.

Clinical Handbook of Anxiety Disorders in Children and Adolescents
Andrew R. Eisen, Christopher A. Kearney, and Charles Schaefer, Eds.

Practitioner's Guide to Treating Fear and Anxiety in Children and Adolescents:
Cognitive-Behavioral Approach
Andrew R. Eisen and Christopher A. Kearney

Words of Wisdom for Parents: Time-Tested Thoughts on How to Raise Kids
Charles Schaefer, Ed.

The Playing Cure: Individualized Play Therapy for Specific Childhood Problems
Heidi G. Kaduson, Donna Cangelosi, and Charles Schaefer, Eds.

101 Favorite Play Therapy Techniques
Heidi G. Kaduson and Charles Schaefer, Eds.

THE PLAYING CURE

Individualized Play Therapy
For Specific Childhood Problems

Edited by

Heidi G. Kaduson
Donna Cangelosi
Charles E. Schaefer

JASON ARONSON INC.
Northvale, New Jersey
London

This book was set in 10 pt. Goudy by TechType, Inc. of Ramsey, New Jersey and printed and bound by Book-mart Press of North Bergen, New Jersey.

The editors gratefully acknowledge permission to reprint excerpts from the *Diagnostic and Statistical Manual of Mental Disorders, Fourth Edition.* Copyright 1994 American Psychiatric Association.

Library of Congress Cataloging-in-Publication Data

The playing cure : individualized play therapy for specific childhood
   problems / [edited] by Heidi G. Kaduson, Donna Cangelosi, Charles E.
   Schaefer.
       p. cm.
   Includes bibliographical references and index.
   ISBN 0-7657-0021-2 (alk. paper)
   1. Play therapy. 2. Child psychotherapy.   I. Kaduson, Heidi.
   II. Cangelosi, Donna M.   III. Schaefer, Charles E.
   [DNLM: 1. Play Therapy—in infancy & childhood. WS 350.2 P723 1996]
   RJ505.P6P58   1996
   618.92'891653—dc20
   DNLM/DLC
   for Library of Congress   96-22725

Manufactured in the United States of America. Jason Aronson Inc. offers books and cassettes. For information and catalog write to Jason Aronson Inc., 230 Livingston Street, Northvale, New Jersey 07647.

Contents

Contributors

Helen E. Benedict, Ph.D.

Professor of Psychology and Director of Clinical Training, Department of Psychology and Neuroscience, Baylor University, Waco, TX.

James N. Bow, Ph.D.

Director of Psychiatry, Hawthorn Center and Wayne State University School of Medicine, Detroit, MI.

James M. Briesmeister, Ph.D.

Staff psychologist at Family Development Service, Bloomfield Hills, MI; psycho-diagnostician and counselor for vocational rehabilitation for the state of Michigan; private practice, Shelby Township, MI.

Neil Cabe, M. Div., M.A.

Clinician, Rainbeau Northfield Counseling Center, Northfield Center, OH; private practice, Northfield Center, OH.

Donna M. Cangelosi, Psy.D.

Private practice, Teaneck, NJ.

Jo Ann L. Cook, Ed.D.

Private practice, Winter Park, FL.

Pamela E. Hall, Psy.D.

Adjunct Associate Professor of Psychology, Pace University, New York City; private practice, Summit, NJ.

Heidi Gerard Kaduson, Ph.D.

Co-Director of Play Therapy Training Institute, Hightstown, NJ; private practice, Hightstown, NJ.

Terry Kottman, Ph.D.

Associate Professor of Counseling, University of Northern Iowa, Cedar Falls, IA.

D'Arcy Lyness-Richard, Ph.D.

Clinical Assistant Professor of Family and Community Medicine, Director of Behavioral Medicine, The Reading Hospital and Medical Center, Reading, PA.

Lisa Binz Mongoven

Post-doctoral Fellow at Dallas Child Guidance Clinic, Dallas, TX.

Janine Shelby, Ph.D.

Director of Child Trauma Clinic, Harbor-UCLA Medical Center, Torrance, CA.

Risë VanFleet, RPT-S

President, VanFleet Associates Family Enhancement and Play Therapy Center, Mechanicsburg, PA.

Preface

Sigmund Freud described psychotherapy with adults as the "talking cure" since he believed verbal interaction between therapist and patient to be the main vehicle for therapeutic change. With children, however, the "playing cure" seems a more fitting description since young people interact with adults more readily vis-à-vis play behavior than through talk. Erik Erikson (1979) noted, "To play it out is the most natural self-healing measure childhood affords" (p. 475). Likewise, Haim Ginott (1994) wrote: "Through the manipulation of toys, the child can show more adequately than through words how he feels about himself and the significant persons and events in his life" (p. 33). Ginott proposed that "A child's play is his talk and toys are his words" (p. 33). Along the same line, Ruth Hartley (1994) wrote: "To read the language of play is to read the hearts and minds of children" (p. 37).

Play therapy is by no means a new school of thought. It has, in fact, been the most popular and widely used form of child therapy in the United States for at least fifty years. However, it has only been in recent times that clinicians and researchers in this field have looked at specific qualities inherent in play behavior that make it a therapeutic agent for change. Schaefer (1993) introduced a taxonomy in which he outlined fourteen "therapeutic powers" of play that have one or more curative functions. These therapeutic powers, often referred to

Therapeutic Factors of Play

Therapeutic Factor	Beneficial Outcome
Overcoming resistance	Working alliance
Communication	Understanding
Competence	Self-esteem
Creative thinking	Innovative solutions to problems
Catharsis	Emotional release
Abreaction	Adjustment to trauma
Role play	Practice/acquiring new behaviors, empathy
Fantasy/visualization	Fantasy comprehension
Metaphoric teaching	Insight
Attachment formation	Attachment
Relationship enhancement	Self-actualization, self-esteem, closeness to others
Positive emotion	Ego boost
Mastering developmental fears	Growth and development
Game play	Ego strength, socialization

From Schaefer (1993).

as "therapeutic factors," frequently overlap. The above table illustrates Schaefer's therapeutic factors along with their likely benefits.

This book introduces a prescriptive model of play therapy that applies these factors in the conceptualization and treatment of children who present with a variety of psychological disorders and adjustment difficulties. While prescriptive treatments have been used effectively in the fields of medicine (Fredin 1989), nutrition (Wurtman 1987), and special education (Kirk et al. 1985, Rappaport 1991), the use of such techniques has been limited in the field of child clinical psychology and in the area of play therapy in particular. The major goal of this book is to introduce a broad-spectrum model of prescriptive play therapy that takes into consideration

1. the psychological issues that are commonly seen in specific childhood disorders;
2. biopsychosocial variables that are unique to individual children;
3. immediate, short-term, and long-term needs of children with specific presenting problems;
4. play therapy treatment planning that integrates and applies those therapeutic factors that relate to a child's needs;
5. skillful application of interventions that address play therapy goals and objectives.

Within this prescriptive approach, psychological techniques and interventions are prescribed based on the characteristics and needs of individuals from specific clinical populations. Research shows that certain techniques work better with some psychological disorders than with others. For instance, it has been argued that behavioral techniques are the most effective treatment for autism

(Lovaas 1980); cognitive behavioral approaches are most effective for alleviating depression (Beck 1983); and psychodynamic interventions are the treatment of choice for personality disorders (Kohut and Wolf 1978). Similarly, some approaches coincide more closely with the biopsychosocial profiles and needs of certain individuals than do others. Psychodynamic interventions are most effective in the treatment of neurotic disorders among bright, verbal individuals, while behavioral interventions work best with less verbal, more action-oriented persons.

The use of prescriptive treatments challenges the clinician to examine the strengths and weaknesses of specific theoretical orientations for treating various disorders. Research indicates that treatment strategies are needed to address specific client characteristics due to the amount of heterogeneity and variability that exists among individuals in the same diagnostic groups (Barlow 1981, Burke and Silverman 1987, Rappaport 1991). However, it is often very difficult for clinicians to move outside of their theoretical orientation in conceptualizing the needs of clients and in devising treatment plans.

There is an unfortunate tendency for professionals with a strong theoretical bent to apply personally preferred techniques despite the fact that some children may not benefit from them. Gupta and Coxhead (1990) note that this tendency is perpetuated as even authors of textbooks have a tendency to "eloquently defend a particular remediation technique yet fail to offer (any) empirical evidence of its real superiority over other techniques" (p. 2). Thus, new and seasoned clinicians are at risk for developing and perpetuating professional blind spots regarding client needs, which can result in ineffective treatment.

A prescriptive approach to play therapy challenges the clinician to weave together a variety of interventions in formulating one comprehensive treatment program that is tailor-made for a particular child. Although many of the therapeutic factors of play that are listed above originated in specific schools of thought, they can be integrated into one cohesive treatment plan. For instance, role play techniques, which are rooted in the principles of Gestalt and behavior therapy, can be effectively adapted and applied to cognitive (Goldstein and Glick 1987) and psychodynamically oriented (Levenson and Herman 1993) play therapy.

This approach of integrating techniques reflects what Norcross (1987) calls "synthetic eclecticism" since it stresses applying various theories into one interactive and coordinated modality of treatment. This is quite different from "kitchen-sink eclecticism," which Norcross cautions is an atheoretical treatment modality. In the latter, clinicians apply techniques from various schools of thought in a manner that ignores the theory that underlies them. Such an approach is haphazard and ineffective at best and may, in fact, be harmful to some children.

The broad-spectrum approach to play therapy advocated in this book considers the immediate, short-term, and long-term needs of the child. The therapeutic factors described above are applied at various points in the therapy

---

xii Preface

depending on the specific treatment plan. For instance, if it is believed that achild's immediate need is to acquire skills for confronting a current or impending life situation, role-playing techniques would be incorporated into the treatment. Likewise, metaphoric teaching may be used to increase insight when this is deemed an important goal of treatment.

Each of the therapeutic factors is useful with children from diverse backgrounds and clinical populations, as will be shown in the chapters that follow. However, there are several important issues that should be considered when applying any intervention. The most important issues relate to the child's needs and ability to use and benefit from the approach or technique. Therapist factors such as knowledge base, training, competence, and comfort with using various interventions will need to be considered as well. Lastly, situational variables such as parent involvement, the child's living situation, and resources available for treatment will play a significant role in the development and implementation of an effective treatment plan.

The primary goal of this book is to illustrate how therapeutic factors that are inherent in play behavior can be prescribed for children with a variety of psychological disorders and presenting problems. This book describes how this approach can be adapted in the treatment of children who internalize (Part I), children who present with stress reactions (Part II), children who externalize (Part III), and children who experience difficulties related to other circumstances (Part IV). Case illustrations demonstrate how techniques are utilized in a manner that effectively applies one or more therapeutic powers of play.

References

Barlow, D. H., ed. (1981). *Behavioral Assessment of Adult Disorders*. New York: Guilford.

Beck, A. T. (1983). *Cognitive Therapy of Depression: New Perspectives*, ed. P. Crayton. New York: Raven.

Burke, A. E., and Silverman, W. K. (1987). The prescriptive treatment of school refusal. *Clinical Psychology Review* 7:353–362.

Erikson, E. (1979). Play and cure. In *Therapeutic Use of Child's Play*, ed. C. E. Schaefer, pp. 475–485. New York: Jason Aronson.

Fredin, J. (1989). New hope for people with epilepsy. *Journal of Orthomolecular Medicine* 1:193–204.

Ginott, H. (1994). In *The Quotable Play Therapist*, ed. C. E. Schaefer and H. Kaduson, p. 33. Northvale, NJ: Jason Aronson.

Goldstein, A. P., and Glick, B. (1987). *Aggression Replacement Training: A Comprehensive Intervention for Aggressive Youth*. Champaign, IL: Research Press.

Gupta, R. M., and Coxhead, P., eds. (1990). *Interventions with Children*. London: Routledge.

Hartley, R. (1994). In *The Quotable Play Therapist*, ed. C. E. Schaefer and H. Kaduson, p. 37. Northvale, NJ: Jason Aronson.

Kirk, S., Kirk, W., and Minskoff, E. (1985). *Phonic Remedial Reading Lessons*. Nocato, CA: Academic Therapy.

Kohut, H., and Wolf, E. (1978). The disorders of the self and their treatment. *International Journal of Psycho-Analysis* 59:413–425.

Levenson, R., and Herman, J. (1993). Role playing. In *Play Therapy Techniques*, ed. C. E. Schaefer and D. M. Cangelosi, pp. 225–236. Northvale, NJ: Jason Aronson.

Lovaas, O. I. (1980). *Teaching Developmentally Disabled Children: The ME Book*. Baltimore: University Park Press.

Norcross, J. (1987). *Casebook of Eclectic Psychotherapy*. New York: Brunner/Mazel.

Rappaport, S. R. (1991). Diagnostic-prescriptive teaming: the road less traveled. *Journal of Reading, Writing and Learning Disabilities* 7:183–199.

Schaefer, C. E. (1993). *The Therapeutic Powers of Play*. Northvale, NJ: Jason Aronson.

Wurtman, R. (1987). Circulating nutrients and neurotransmitter symptoms. *Journal of Applied Nutrition* 1:7–28.

Part I

INTERNALIZERS

1

Play Therapy with Depressed Children

James M. Briesmeister

Background and Historic Antecedents

The concept of depression has a long and controversial past. Since earliest recorded times the presence of depressive disorders has plagued mankind and occupied the attention of physicians and laymen alike. The term has assumed much of the diagnostic burden that was once carried by the notion of melancholia (Gray 1978). Indeed, the troubled state of the psyche known as melancholia has been documented in ancient Egyptian, Greek, and Hebrew literature (Beck and Brady 1977). A review of the writings of Hippocrates and Galen reveals the great lengths to which these early healers sought to explain what they perceived to be the link between melancholia and the imbalance of bodily humors (Madden 1966).

By the time the Kraepelinian system of categorizing mental disorders evolved, melancholia had been divided into types. Melancholia simplex, melancholia with delusions, and melancholia attonities are but a few representations of this early categorization system (Gray 1978). In 1899, when Kraepelin's diagnostic synthesis was published into a sixth edition, melancholia was included with anxious depression of the involutional (menopausal) period and was grouped with senile deteriorations. Depression that occurred in the earlier years of life was associated with dementia praecox or manic-depressive disorders (Gray 1978).

It is noteworthy that none other than the founder of psychoanalysis shed light upon the concept of depression. In *Mourning and Melancholia* (1917) Freud compared and contrasted melancholia with the normal emotion of grief. He proposed that depression is analogous to the process of mourning in that both were responses to the loss of a loved object. Pioneer psychoanalytic formulations of depression were further espoused by Karl Abraham (Gray 1978). Abraham proposed that aggressive impulses felt toward the loved object are repressed and directed toward the ambivalent introject. As a consequence of this process, the person phenomenologically experiences self-reproach and depression. Historically, a multitude of impressive and influential researchers and clinicians have been influenced by Freud's conceptualization of the concept of depression. A substantial psychoanalytically oriented body of literature emerged with each subsequent contributor extending beyond Freud's original formulations. Extensive records that include the historic structure and conceptualization of the depressive process, including the nature, etiology, and treatment of this disorder, can be reviewed and studied in the works of Bleuler (1911), Fenichel (1926, 1941, 1945), Rado (1928), Deutsch (1933), Klein (1935), Bibring (1953), and Ostow (1970), to name but a representational few.

There is little doubt that the concept of depression has been amply and ably represented within the historic documents of psychology and psychopathology. These original conceptualizations, however, focused exclusively on depression as experienced by adults. Depression, in both its primary and secondary manifestations, has been unquestionably recognized, diagnosed, and treated in adults. Indeed, the acknowledgment that depression occurs so frequently in adults has merited the disorder the dubious distinction of being dubbed "the common cold" of psychology. Historically, however, and up to as recently as the past fifteen years, the notion of depression in children has been riddled with skepticism, confusion, and controversy (Arieti 1962, Arieti and Bemporad 1978, Asch 1966, Bemporad and Wilson 1978, Cytryn and McKnew 1981, Lefkowitz and Burton 1978).

Childhood depression as a clinical construct was not included in the World Health Organization's 1974 *Glossary of Mental Disorders* or in the second edition of the *Diagnostic and Statistical Manual of Mental Disorders* (1968). It is listed in the third edition of the *Diagnostic and Statistical Manual of Mental Disorders* (1980), but not under the heading "Disorders first evident in infancy, childhood, or adolescence." This reluctance to acknowledge that the diagnostic category of depression may include and impact upon children is not without precedence. One need only remember that a diagnosis of schizophrenia in children, which is now so readily accepted, was also met with initial skepticism and controversy (Toolan 1981). The fourth edition (1994) stipulation that the separation of disorders into distinct sections based on age is merely for convenience rather than any clear distinction between "childhood" and "adult" disorders.

Typically, in the not so distant past, it was held that children do not have the ego capacities or cognitive abilities necessary to experience depression. In an early paper, Bibring (1953) reduced the multiplicity of depressive conditions to what he considered their lowest common denominator, namely, a loss of self-esteem. He suggested that children (prior to adolescence) have not yet developed enough self and self-differentiation to experience a loss in this realm. Sperling (1959) wrote that children lack the adequate criteria for a "full" depressive illness; instead, they may experience "depressive equivalents." Rie (1966) concurs with Loevinger's (1959) observations that the "ability to concep-tualize one's self " does not fully occur before early adolescence. It should be noted that Loevinger does acknowledge that the beginnings of this capacity may emerge as early as 8 years of age in *some* children. In essence, these theorists have suggested that the fully differentiated and generalized primary affects character-izing depression, namely, an experienced sense of loss to the self, despair, and hopelessness, are not within the experiential repertoire of the majority of children prior to the end of the latency years.

In 1946 Spitz published a paper on the reaction of infants to maternal separation. In addition to opening avenues of productive research that continue today, Spitz made an invaluable contribution to the concept of "depression-like episodes" in infancy. In describing his observations of 6-month-old infants and their subsequent separation from their respective maternal figures, Spitz re-ported that these infants responded with weepy, complaining behavior that eventually gave way to withdrawal and lethargy. He coined the term *anaclitic depression* to define and describe this phenomenon. While recognizing some similarities between his syndrome of analytic depression and Abraham's (1911) and Freud's (1917) classical theories concerning depression, Spitz pointed out some essential differences. He cautioned that while the syndrome manifested by these infants may be similar to adult depression, they differ from the adult episodes in that infantile "depression-like" episodes lack the major factor of the adult disorder, namely, the formation of a cruel and self-punitive superego.

John Bowlby was one of many prolific theorists who was influenced by René Spitz's research regarding the appearance of depression-like episodes in the early years of life. Bowlby studied and documented the process of infantile attachment to, and separation from, the maternal figure. In "Grief and Mourning in Infancy and Early Childhood" (1960), Bowlby proposed concepts that are particularly relevant to the study of infant and childhood depression. Bowlby (1969) asserted that three stages occur within the separation process. In the initial stage, protest, the infant is very upset and tries to reinitiate contact with the other by crying. In the second stage, despair, the infant still appears to seek reunion with the mother. At this point, however, the infant is quieter and less constant. By the third and last stage, detachment, the infant seems to have overcome his sense of loss and will respond to other adults. However, the infant no longer exclusively selects out the mother. Bowlby's research not only described this three-stage process of reacting to loss and separation but also suggested that if the mother–child attachment was prematurely disrupted or not formed in the first place depression-like symptoms resulted. He was also optimistic in proposing that the negative and disabling impact of rifts in the mother–child bond were not irreversible. Fortunately, healthy development can be reinstated by correcting the problematic situation. Therapeutic intervention is possible and offers hope for the resolution of the existing problems.

The Nature and Prevalence of Depression in Children

Researchers have gradually moved from a stance that adamantly denied the possibility of depression in infants and preadolescent children to a position that at least allows for "depression-like equivalents" in this population. Currently, among professionals there is a recognition that depression per se can certainly be present in children. Youngsters can and do experience the symptoms, troublesome affect, sense of loss, and overwhelming negative consequences that typically accompany a depressive syndrome. The pervasive impact of this disorder on the physical well-being, cognitive functioning, emotional status, and behavioral expressions of the preadolescent child has been acknowledged, and the body of research studies regarding this clinical issue continues to grow exponentially. Those researchers and clinicians who still preclude the possibility of childhood depression form a relatively small segment of today's professional community. The existence of this painful disorder prior to adolescence is well documented.

In the fourth edition of the *Comprehensive Textbook of Psychiatry*, in his discussion of affective disorders, Puig-Antich writes, "All types of affective disorders described in adult patients are also found in children and adolescents" (1985, p. 1851). This researcher then goes on to illustrate some of the various potential forms and categories that childhood depression may take, including major depressive episodes, such as endogenous subtypes of melancholia and psychotic depressions; dysthymic disorders; schizoaffective disorders; and adjustment reactions with depressive symptoms and features. Indeed, in the *Concise Guide to Child and Adolescent Psychiatry*, Dulcan and Popper (1991) point out that the prevalence of major depression in children has been estimated at 2 percent in prepubertal youngsters and approximately 4.7 percent in adolescents. The fourth edition of the *Diagnostic and Statistical Manual of Mental Disorders* (1994) does allow for the inclusion of children in the diagnostic category of mood disorders. The manual states that "The core symptoms of a Mood Depressive Episode are the same for children and adolescents, although there are data that suggest that the prominence of characteristic symptoms may change with age" (*DSM-IV* 1994, p. 324).

Childhood Depression and the Risk for Suicide

Not only is there a general acceptance of childhood depression among mental health and medical professionals, but few would deny the harrowing incidence of suicidal impulses and ideation among children and preadolescents. In the United States, the annual admission rate to psychiatric facilities for children between the ages of 5 and 14 who have made suicide attempts amounts to 12,000. Many professionals feel that this is a significant underestimation (Shamoo and Patros 1990). Recent statistics regarding suicide suggests that it is the tenth leading cause of death in children 1 to 14 years of age (Centers for Disease Control 1985). There is also evidence suggesting that between 27 and 52 percent of child clinic samples meet the criteria for depressive disorders (Asarnow et al. 1987).

Although the rates of completed suicide are relatively low prior to 14 years of age, suicidal ideation, impulses, and nonfatal suicide attempts are not uncommon in preadolescent children. The occurrence of these factors has been noted to be in evidence prior to fatal suicides. Still further, they often occur in the context of clinical depression (Pfeffer et al. 1979). The specific relation between depression and suicidal attempts remains unclear. Although there is significant overlap, there is a substantial occurrence of depressed, nonsuicidal youngsters as well as suicidal children who are not necessarily depressed (Carlson and Cantwell 1982). It has become increasingly clear, however, that depression can be experienced by preadolescent children, and in some cases the depression may place the children at risk for suicide. The concept of childhood depression and suicide merits ongoing research. The experience of childhood depression in all its various guises warrants clinical concern and psychotherapeutic intervention.

Description of Depression: Symptomatology in the Context of the Developmental Process

It is not easy to diagnose depression in children (Kerns and Lieberman 1993). The diagnosis of depression or a related mood disorder is established when a child presents sufficient evidence of a persistent depressive mood or almost total inability to derive pleasure from the usual rewards and reinforcements in life. The child exhibits a loss of interest in those activities that previously elicited a sense of pleasure, excitement, or curiosity (Puig-Antich 1985). The DSM-IV (1994) criteria for a major depressive disorder requires that five or more symptomatological characteristics from an extensive list of potential symptoms and features must be present for at least a two-week period or more. These symptoms must also represent a change from previous functioning. Furthermore, at least one of the symptoms must include either a depressed mood or a significant loss of interest or pleasure (DSM-IV 1994). The list encompasses such qualifying symptoms as subjectively reported mood changes or sadness, diminished interests, significant changes in normal eating habits and normal weight maintenance, sleep disorders, psychomotor agitation, fatigue, a pervasive sense of worthlessness or guilt, diminished cognitive functioning, difficulties maintaining attention or concentration, and thoughts of death or suicide.

These qualifying diagnostic symptoms must be interpreted with extreme caution when assessing and evaluating children. Any consideration of the diagnosis and treatment of depression from the pediatric age group to the preadolescent age group must consider the psychopathological symptoms against the backdrop of the developmental process. Jules Bemporad points out that "the clinical manifestations, causes, and therapeutic options vary greatly with age and one has to be flexible both in terms of understanding the disorder and in the therapeutic course of action" (Arieti and Bemporad 1978, p. 344). Not only are the developmental differences and stages relevant, but the astute practitioner must also be alert for the multitude of manifestations and expressions that may occur in children. Although the criteria for mood disorders are essentially similar for children as for adults, the behaviors may certainly be expressed in different ways at different developmental epochs (Dulcan and Popper 1991). It should be noted that children in their naïveté may frequently hide their depressive affect and features behind more easily discernible problems such as school failure, shyness and social withdrawal, or subtle manifestations of self-doubts and low self-esteem.

The presence of depression in a child can be frightening to concerned parents and family members. It may also be disguised and, as such, offer diagnostic challenges to even the most experienced clinician. Too often the depressed child goes undiagnosed or misdiagnosed. The child is often thought to simply have a behavior problem. However, behaviors such as sadness, weepiness, acting out, withdrawal, low self-esteem, and a loss of interest and/or pleasure in the usual activities of the youngster's life should be considered a cry for help.

The clinical manifestations of childhood depression can be direct or indirect (masked). The symptoms of depression in all its vicissitudes can certainly assume a myriad of unexpected forms. Younger children, for example, may exhibit symptoms of separation anxiety, fear of strangers, and phobic avoidance. Latency-age children may show a change in characteristic behavior patterns. Typically gregarious, friendly, and social youngsters may rather suddenly respond in a shy and withdrawn manner. The school grades and overall academic performance of bright children may take a noticeable decline. Normally well-behaved children may start to act out; temper outbursts may become more prevalent. They may become significantly more verbally combative and abusive with parents, peers, and teachers. Children who are not characteristically physically aggressive may transform into playground bullies. In contrast, children who have been outgoing and popular with their peers may become sullen and socially withdrawn; they may refuse to participate in normal play. Girls and boys who are age-appropriately independent and assertive in their styles of self-expression may become sullen and reticent. Adults in the youngsters' lives may begin to notice a marked diminished capacity for attention and concentration. Children who usually are able to play, read, watch television, or communicate for relatively long and age-appropriate time durations may decline to engage in these activities for any reasonable length of time. They bore quickly. These specific symptoms, for instance, may be confused with an attention-deficit hyperactivity disorder and the underlying depression may be ignored or dismissed. These various behavioral, cognitive, emotional, and social symptoms and features may be directly expressed or they may be more covert and disguised. In addition, they may present in isolation or in a multitude of combinations. In any case, they must be assessed, diagnosed, understood, and treated against the backdrop of appropriate developmental stages and processes.

It is important to note that research studies on depression in pre–latency-age children indicate that the symptoms of depression may coexist with other childhood disorders. A significant body of research and therapeutic intervention modalities have addressed this issue as well as the problematic features and consequences of childhood affective disorders. There is evidence that the risks for conduct disorders as well as depression increases in children with significant developmental lags or deficits in social skills. Likewise, research indicates that youngsters with symptoms associated with oppositional defiant disorders may be at risk for low-grade depressive illnesses and related affective disorders (Wenning et al. 1993).

Whatever the configuration of disruptive and disabling features, depression does not present as an isolated symptom. It is a syndrome and there are innumerable ways in which children experience and express the emotional, behavioral, cognitive, and social consequences of this persistent and pervasive disorder. Although a dysphoric (sad) mood is not necessarily specific to childhood depression (Carlson and Cantwell 1979, Stark 1990), it is usually the primary and most evident hallmark of the affective disturbance. The evidence indicates that the dysphoria usually coalesces with a combination of several related characteristics, such as weepiness, anhedonia, lethargy, low self-esteem, self-pity, self-negation, withdrawal, eating or sleeping disorders, suicidal ideation, and the like.

Whatever the unique symptom constellation, the phenomenological experience of sadness is unquestionably one of the main indicators of the severity of the disorder. Children who experience a more severe and clinically relevant level of depression are more likely to be experiencing an endogenous depression. On the other hand, those whose depression is rather mild may be reacting to a short-term unpleasant experience or a relatively current loss. The severity of the symptoms of sadness or dysphoria is primarily a function of two variables, both of which define a dimension of time. The first variable considers the amount of time each day that the child feels sad. This may vary from rather brief and fleeting to an overwhelming sense of sadness that encompasses the entire day. The second variable refers to the duration of the dysphoric episode. Do the sad feelings last for a day, a week, a month, or a year? In evaluating the severity of the affective disorder the longer the time span of both dimensions, the more severe, persistent, and chronic the symptom.

In addition to remaining alert to the various combinations the symptoms of depression may assume, it is important for the therapist to consider the age-appropriateness of a child's behavior. Any formulation of a therapeutic structure or therapeutic goals must be developed within the framework of the child's developmental level. Few therapists would expect a pre–latency-age child to have the hypothetical reasoning powers of an adolescent. Similarly, a clinician would not expect a normal pubescent youngster to be comfortable playing with the toys of a toddler. However, with all due appreciation of developmental levels and age-appropriateness, it is equally important to consider the unevenness of the child's developmental achievements and progress across the areas assessed in therapy. Indeed, development does not always follow a smooth and rigidly predictable course.

Children evolve at different rates in different areas of functioning. Circumstances may catapult some youngsters into inappropriate roles and place atypical expectations and demands on them. The old adage that every rule has its exception definitely holds when considering the rules of child development and the unique forms and detours that human development may assume. O'Connor (1991) illustrates this point in his discussion of the characteristics of pseudomature children and the impact these features have on these youngsters and others in their environment. Typically, in these youngsters the depressive underpinnings result in the loss of physical energy, motoric skills, and psychological-emotional stamina. They are markedly slowed down in their movements and responses. Consequently, their behavior may appear more controlled and more mature (pseudomature) than that of other children in their age category. They may, for example, become consistently quiet and withdrawn. Over time, parents, teachers, and peers come to expect that these children will be adultlike in all situations at all times. If and when they do act out in what is actually an age-appropriate manner, others appear surprised. People may become overly harsh and critical. They do not expect, nor do they allow for, any deviations from the pseudomature style. In this situation the adultlike behaviors and reactions actually mask the nature and severity of the depression. Unfortunately, since others gradually come to expect and demand these pseudomature behaviors, these youngsters are, in essence, discouraged from acting like children. Play therapy may be of particular relevance for them. It offers an opportunity to ventilate, act out, and react in a manner that is consistent with their chronological age.

In view of the various and hidden ways in which the syndrome of depression can be expressed and the complexity of the developmental process, it is not surprising that depressed children are underidentified. We must also keep another major factor in mind. There is a commonly held belief in our culture that childhood is a time of innocence and bliss. This cultural myth precludes the existence of serious depression in childhood. Oftentimes, the depression is dismissed as "a phase" the child is going through. Many adults who did not have the advantage of a happy childhood prefer to think of themselves as the exception rather than the rule (Stark 1990). The repression or denial of any unhappiness in the early years of life tends to perpetuate the myth of a spontaneous and carefree childhood. Too often depression in children is considered to be a temporary slump, a moody or negative phase. It will pass, or so we like to believe. This belief fails to recognize the intensity and impact of the depressive symptoms and features. It also denies and undermines the child's very genuine pain and distress. It may leave the child feeling that no one understands. More to the point, he may think, "No one really believes how sad I am." We can only hope that the child does not conclude that no one really cares.

We must also be aware of the tendency to assume that if depression is present in childhood, it is not only atypical but probably a temporary reaction to some existing event. Consequently, we assume that simply altering the unpleasant event will eliminate the depression. While this may, indeed, be an effective solution in some instances, there are those children for whom even a positive or constructive environmental intervention is not enough to provide a cure. Bemporad (Arieti and Bemporad 1978) suggests that with very young children the depressive state is usually a reaction to some readily discernable stress in the environment. He holds that young children are usually upset over an illness or being criticized or ignored by a parental figure. However, this is not always the case. The depression is not always a reactive disorder. Furthermore, the causes of depression are not always so easily discernable. Children of all ages are certainly capable of experiencing an adjustment reaction. They can encounter difficulties in coping with existing stressors in their lives. It should also be noted that children of all ages are also capable of experiencing genuine depression in all its various and convoluted forms. We must exercise caution and avoid dismissing the very real possibility of existing depression simply because everything in the child's world appears to be going fine. Once again, we are reminded that childhood depression can be quite insidious. Not only is it difficult to recognize, its roots cannot always be traced to identifiable unpleasant events or losses.

Traditional Treatment Strategies

There are numerous forms of therapeutic intervention that have been designed to address and counter clinical depression. Play group psychotherapy (PGP) has been suggested as a viable strategy for addressing depression and reducing risk factors (Kernberg and Chazan 1991). Likewise, art therapy has been reported as a useful technique to diagnose and remedy depression in a young boy who presented problem behaviors following the accidental death of his sibling

(Cohen 1971). Therapists have attempted to alter the negative self-talk (Meichenbaum 1977, Meichenbaum and Goodman 1971), the destructive and distorted perceptions of the self and one's abilities (Beck 1976, 1983), and the self-blaming and pessimistic attributional styles (Seligman 1974) that research indicates are usually associated with the syndrome of depression in adults as well as children. In addition, a review of the literature unearths many studies that employ theoretical and clinical applications of psychoanalytic principles to assess and intervene in cases of childhood depression. The writings of Spitz (1946), Mahler (1961), and Jacobson (1971) represent but a small sampling of psychodynamically oriented approaches that have been applied to the treatment of direct and indirect expressions of depression in children. These interventions have met with various degrees of success and failure. Some approaches have been successful in enhancing self-esteem, positively restructuring self-negating tendencies, and facilitating healing.

Rationale for Play Therapy

In treating children who suffer from depression, the therapist must consider a myriad of relevant factors in making treatment selections and adaptations. The modalities that are enlisted must be suited to the individual child's needs, circumstances, and idiosyncratic configuration of symptoms. Consequently, the clinician must be aware of the child's prevailing ecosystem. The impact from immediate and extended family members, playmates, school, and teachers cannot be overemphasized. The youngster's total environment and perception of that environment must be considered. Still further, since depression is a multifarious disorder, the unique ways in which the child experiences the symptoms, including their intensity and duration, must be evaluated and reevaluated prior to, and within the context of, treatment. The prescriptive approach also sets viable long- and short-term goals that are relevant to the target child. Since dysphoria is the major and most characteristic symptom of depression, short-term goals usually focus on an immediate reduction of the sad affect and emotional tone.

The greater portion of the psychotherapeutic strategies that have been developed to alleviate adult depression can be adopted for use with children within a play therapy format. It should be noted, of course, that the bulk of the adult approaches rely heavily on cognitive and verbal skills. They require the designated patient to identify and verbalize the disruptive and disturbing feeling, thoughts, and behaviors that negatively impact on their functioning and their enjoyment of daily life. Words are used to express the problems, and words frame and facilitate the curative process. In the preface of this book we are reminded that none other than Freud referred to therapy with adults as the "talking cure."

Depending on their developmental level and their individual abilities, children, especially very young children, usually have not yet developed an adequate capacity for verbalizing feelings. Given their lack of language and verbal proficiency, they are usually unable to verbalize the complexity and intensity of dysfunctional affect and symptoms. As previously mentioned, the syndrome of depression frequently coexists with other problems and diagnostic disorders. The combination of symptoms is staggering. Furthermore, the symptoms are so subtle, varied, disguised, and idiosyncratic that even trained physicians and mental health professionals risk ignoring or misdiagnosing them. How much more difficult, if not improbable, it would be for a child to be able to verbally disclose, explain, and express the intense phenomenologically felt affect that is associated with depression in a clear and comprehensible manner.

Although they may lack verbal proficiency and a full development and grasp of verbal-linguistic abstractions, most children are capable of, and competent at, play. Play is not only one of the most tangible manifestations of a child's ego functioning (Waelder 1933), it is the mode through which children communicate and express themselves. Erikson (1979) asserted that play was a natural form of self-expression and self-healing for children. Anna Freud (1965) postulated the notion that the fantasy involved in play can be highly adaptive and may function as a form of regression in the service of the ego. Both Freud (1917) and Erikson (1950) emphasized the child's inherent drive to achieve internal mastery. Similarly, the child must come to master external objects and situations in the world. From infancy through maturity we are called upon to gain control over ourselves and situations around us and to master specific developmental tasks at each stage of transition and growth.

Schaefer's (1993) systematic taxonomy and analysis of the therapeutic factors in play reaffirm the notion that play therapy is much more than child playing within a session. Play as therapy consists of an integrated configuration of various treatment modalities of highly developed theoretical perspectives and clinical techniques. These theoretical orientations and technical strategies must be implemented in relation to developmental theories. This merger serves one major purpose: to reinstate the child's age-appropriate and natural "right" to be a child. One of the primary goals of play therapy focuses on helping the child engage in fun. Play therapy seeks to reestablish what Erikson (1979) defined as "natural self-expression" and "natural self-healing" in childhood.

Therapeutic Powers of Play Involved in Treating Depressed Children

Depressed children have difficulties in establishing a sense of control and mastery. The symptoms of depression, especially the dysphoric mood, inhibit any sense of achievement and competency. In each situation and in each stage of development, the child gradually gains a sense of mastery in the world through successful interactions and negotiations with parents, siblings, teachers, and peers. The social withdrawal, sense of pessimism and futility, and learned helplessness that usually accompany clinical depression significantly diminish successful social interactions and, in turn, successful mastery. In attempting to establish a sense of mastery and control, depressed children may exhibit too much control, as in the case of pseudomature children, or too little control, as is often seen in impulsive and agitated children. The disabling symptoms of depression severely restrict one's ability to cope with the external world and all its demands. It also profoundly limits one's ability to gain control over the intensity of internal processes.

A factor such as role playing, for instance, encourages the acquisition of new and constructive behaviors and empathy within the child. The games that form an essential part of play therapy not only enhance ego strength but also develop mutuality and reciprocity and, in general, promote positive social and interpersonal skills. The catharsis that is so crucial in working with depressed children is yet another therapeutic factor. This release of emotion is particularly important for the depressed child in whom intense affect serves as the foundation and core features of the disturbance. These are but a few examples of the many benefits inherent within the play therapy framework.

Too often depressed children have forgotten how to play. The dysphoria and anhedonia preclude any sense of natural and spontaneous fun. They may be constricted and inhibited in their potential to experience joy and pleasant feelings. Indeed, successful play therapy is defined by the child's ability to recapture a sense of natural joy, a personally experienced pleasure that is not self-conscious, contrived, or stunted by overwhelming and persistent sadness or difficulties in coping with life's challenges. The predominant goal of play therapy is to overcome those behaviors that prevent the youngster from enjoying life and to establish the kinds of coping skills, interpersonal relationships, self-assessments, and ego strengths that assist the child in functioning optimally in the world.

Approach: The Application of Cognitive-Behavioral Strategies within a Play Therapy Format

Although several overlapping and interwoven therapeutic strategies have been implemented to treat depression and its symptoms, there is evidence that cognitive-behavioral approaches have proven particularly effective in alleviating this disorder in adults (Beck 1983). Likewise, cognitive-behavioral play therapy appears to be particularly relevant in eliminating the complex symptoms of depression in children. In addition to the painful emotions associated with depression, children cannot focus on the symptoms for any reasonable length of time or express the intensity of the affect. They cannot clarify or verbalize the overwhelming feelings. Frequently when asked how they feel, they respond with a generic, but age-appropriate, single word, such as "yukky" or "bad" or "sad." These are hardly clear and discernable descriptions that explain the complexity, intensity, or duration of affect. Play therapy affords the child an opportunity to express through the actions of play that which cannot be expressed verbally. By integrating the principles of cognitive-behavioral strategies into a play therapy format, we merge major theoretical and clinical perspectives, which have been repeatedly researched and proven highly effective, with a therapy structure that is sensitive to the specific developmental levels and age-appropriate needs and abilities of childhood.

Children with depression prove a special challenge for the cognitive-behavioral therapists. Since the symptoms of depression tend to aggregate in various combinations and can be so readily disguised, they have an adverse impact on intervention strategies (Kendall 1991). The cognitive-behavioral approach requires that the child be an active participant in the treatment process. Cognitive-behavioral therapy is essentially a collaborative venture. The depressed child who is passive, socially withdrawn, experiencing psychomotor agitation or inhibition, and exhibiting inhibited verbal responses tends to resist therapeutic participation and interaction. Of course, this penchant for resisting interaction further maintains and exacerbates the dysphoric mood. It also intensifies the sense of hopelessness. The depressed child may think, "Why bother, nobody can help me" or "I feel so sad, it's useless." These negative cognitions and symptoms further impede the child's readiness and willingness to take an active role in therapy. Typical cognitive-behavioral tasks such as homework assignments, social skills training, or role playing require an active involvement on the part of the child. In addition, the depressed child often finds intense interpersonal contacts and involvements too difficult, confusing, and threatening to sustain for any reasonable length of time.

Faltering concentration is another all too common symptom of depression. As such, the child may find traditional "talking cures" too boring, too verbal. Play therapy has the advantage of being more engaging and having a more pleasant affective tone than some other forms of intervention. Kendall (1991) suggests that a heightened and pleasant emotional tone has a positive impact on cognitive processes. Therapy techniques that are naturally fun and engaging for the youngster will have a greater likelihood of succeeding in the development and facilitation of cognitive restructuring. Intervention strategies that are enjoyable will meet with less resistance on the child's part. Fears of interpersonal contacts will erode more readily. Since play therapy appeals to the child's natural propensity for engaging in pleasurable activities, and it addresses the developmental needs of the child, even depressed children may be more receptive to the intervention and more willing to participate in the collaborative process of the "playing cure."

Techniques

Preassessments and the Formation of Play Therapy Goals and Objectives

Prior to the onset of play therapy, it is crucial to meet with the child and his or her family. This initial collateral intake gives the therapist an occasion to preview the child's interactions with the parents as well as the family dynamics. This is also a chance to administer some types of self-reports, parent reports, or interviews. Assessment is an essential part of the therapeutic process. It impacts on the diagnosis, the structure and content of therapy, the therapeutic goals and objectives, and all aspects of the therapeutic endeavor. Depending on the presenting problems and the individual needs of the child and family, the initial evaluations may focus on determining the child's developmental level, cognitive processes, interrelational patterns, ego strengths, reactions to stress, and the like. One might, for example, elect to administer the Marschak Interactional Method (MIM; Jernberg et al. 1980) to evaluate complex interactional styles. Similarly, various measures for determining cognitive, emotional, social, academic, and coping strategies might be employed. It is also important to have a thorough and recent physical/medical update on the child. The kinds of prescription medicines that the child is taking are also important. This is particularly relevant if a referral is made for psychopharmacological intervention. All information about the child must be interpreted against the backdrop of the child's developmental level. All treatment plans and evaluations should be designed with full consideration of these developmental issues.

It is equally important to assess the type, intensity, and duration of the depressive symptoms. A variety of measurements of childhood depression might be used. Depending upon the child's age and cognitive and verbal levels, the Depression Adjective Check List (DACL; Lubin 1967) could be administered. A semistructured interview such as the Schedule of Affective Disorders and Schizophrenia for School-Age Children (Kiddie SADS; Puig-Antich and Ryan 1986) could be part of the initial interview. Another valuable assessment tool is the Children's Depression Inventory (CDI; Kovacs 1983). This self-rating measure incorporates the essential elements of the Beck Depression Inventory (BDI; Beck et al. 1980), which is used with adults. The structure and content of the CDI statements are modified for children. The initial intake and preassessments with the child and family offer an indication of the child's functioning, level of development, and the persistence of the symptoms of depression. Diagnosis, the structure and content of the play therapy sessions, and the therapeutic goals and objectives are all grounded in the preassessment. It is intimately linked to differential diagnoses (major depression, dysthymia, bipolar, adjustment reaction with depressed mood, etc.) and to the determination of the predominant symptoms and their duration.

Prognosis for change can be evaluated based on certain factors in the child, the parents, and the child's total gestalt. If, for instance, the family members are engaging in maladaptive interactions or harmful verbal exchanges, will they be willing and able to make positive changes? Will the child and family be able to follow through and comply with the basic requirements of play therapy? Are the therapeutic modalities, techniques, and format suited to the child and the family? Thorough and relevant assessments will determine the answers to these and other pertinent questions.

The goals of play therapy must also be established. First and foremost, play therapy should afford the child a chance to be a child; it should facilitate natural play. Therapy also needs to create a corrective experience for the youngster. Furthermore, it needs to provide creative ways for engaging the child in the collaborative process of therapy. The specific problem issues, experiences, and needs of the child determine the goals. These certainly must incorporate ways of providing an inviting setting for the therapy sessions. The establishment and maintenance of the therapy setting are necessary but not sufficient conditions for the healing process (O'Connor 1991). Therefore, other factors, such as establishing rapport with the child, gaining the trust and cooperation of the family, the need for limits, and techniques for engaging the child in interactive play and games, are but a few of the issues that must be addressed.

It is also crucial that we remain alert to the child's perceptions regarding the purpose of therapy. The goals must be established and presented to the child in a manner that does not risk misinterpretation. We do not want the child to feel that therapy is a punishment for overly inhibited, maladaptive, or bad behaviors. In this regard play therapy has a marked advantage over other treatment formats since play by its very nature is pleasurable, engaging, and fun for the child, it is less likely to be misconstrued as punitive. The goals should be established and presented with the collaborative nature of play therapy in mind. The child and the therapist are both active participants in this curative venture. The child should not be made to feel that she *must* perform in a certain way or play required games or hide certain thoughts or feelings. The child and the family are cotherapists in the sense that they along with the clinician form viable intervention strategies and objectives. If the goals are formulated with the child's specific needs, strengths, and developmental level in mind, the process, structure, and content of therapy will feel natural to the child, the family, and the therapist. Every attempt should be made to establish goals that ensure that the child is not only an active participant in the therapy but also the central focus of therapy. Play therapy is for, and about, the well-being and the healing of the child.

Treatment Techniques

Cognitive-behavioral play therapy incorporates a variety of techniques that can be highly effective in treating childhood depression. This approach typically involves cognitive restructuring in which the child is taught methods for replacing maladaptive thoughts and perceptions with adaptive cognitions. Social skills training, modeling, and role playing are some of the techniques that can help the child relate to peers and adults in a more appropriate manner. These therapeutic gamuts can reduce social withdrawal and destructive behavior patterns and teach new and more constructive behaviors and interactional styles. Positive changes become solidified and strengthened through the process of behavioral reinforcements. Through the use of these modalities and daily activity schedules, the youngster can be taught how to self-monitor. In this way positive behaviors can be rewarded even in the absence of the therapist or a parent figure.

Case Illustration of Play Therapy with a Depressed Child

A comprehensive treatment program that integrated cognitive-behavioral strategies within the structure and format of play therapy was applied in the case of Robbie, a 7-year-old child. Robbie's mother brought him to the initial intake and assessment session. She was concerned because Robbie had been listless and unmotivated for an extensive period of time. Although he was not shy, Robbie had a tendency to avoid other children. He withdrew socially in school and he made minimal contact with other children. During play time, for instance, he would sit alone or would prefer to sit with the teacher. When he did interact with his peers, he would become quite domineering and bossy. Robbie insisted on having his own way. If he received any opposition or challenge from the other youngsters, he would simply walk away and become sullen, withdrawn, and refuse to play anymore. This, of course, fed the cycle of social isolation. Robbie avoided other children and because of his maladaptive interactional patterns, they avoided him. He was an only child. Furthermore, the apartment complex that the family lived in was occupied predominantly by retired adults. He had virtually no occasions to interact with other children his own age once he was home from school.

Robbie's mother had been diagnosed with breast cancer about three years earlier. She underwent a radical mastectomy when Robbie was 4 years old. Despite a grueling routine of chemotherapy, a second mastectomy was performed about a year and a half later. At the time Robbie entered treatment, the cancer appeared to be controlled. However, his mother ruminated a good deal about the risks of the cancer's return and she harbored a fatalistic dread that, in her words, "It's probably just a matter of time before they find the cancer spreading someplace else." Whenever Robbie engaged in undesirable or negative behaviors, his mother had a tendency to remark, "You know Mommy is sick. If you really loved me you would be a good boy." She particularly made these comments when Robbie was withdrawn, refused to engage in play or communications with the family or was reluctant to talk. She would add, "You know Mommy worries about you when you act like this." The mother was in treatment for her own depression and to help her cope with the debilitating effects of cancer. Due to the long duration of the illness, the family had been financially as well as emotionally drained. Consequently, Robbie's father worked an extra part-time job to pay mounting medical costs and to maintain the family. He had a good relationship with his son and Robbie looked forward to the time he could spend with his father. However, due to the circumstances, those occasions were relatively rare.

Robbie's behaviors and comments were an interesting paradox. For the most part, he would act in a pseudomature style. He imagined himself his mother's caregiver and protector. His comments also suggested that he tried to be a "good boy." Unfortunately, his way of being good was to become quiet, sullen, and unresponsive. He would not engage in play or communication. Robbie enjoyed passive activities such as watching television and playing electronic games. He came to all the first few sessions with his hand-held "Gameboy." There were occasions, however, when he dropped his pseudomature facade and become quite manipulative and demanding. He would pout and whine when he did not get his way (or a new electronic game) and his comments were analogous to his mother's. He would remark, "If you loved me, you would let me have it."

Given his pseudomature features, Robbie preferred the company of adults to that of other children. He also sought a lot of attention from adults and was eager to please them. Therefore, it was not particularly challenging to engage him in interactions with the therapist. In the initial stages of therapy the electronic game was used as a springboard for facilitating mutual interests and interactions. Erikson (1979) proposed that the child's play life is often disrupted by internal conflicts that are linked to stressful and traumatic situations. This appeared to be the case with Robbie. Even in play he remained pseudomature. He *allowed* the therapist to play with the game. He also attempted to determine his own rules for the game and would decide the time duration for each game. However, by around the third or fourth session Robbie became more responsive to the therapist, the therapeutic setting, and other toys in the room. A therapeutic alliance was formed and he would leave his electronic game for substantial amounts of time and play with the "therapist's toys." As the sessions progressed, he also expressed various negative and dysfunctional perceptions of himself and his responsibility to his mother. His comments clearly exposed his assumption that his role was to be good in order that his mother may live. To fulfill this role and expectation, he adopted the parental and caregiver role.

Cognitive restructuring procedures were implemented within a play therapy framework in order to counter and change Robbie's negative thoughts such as "My mother may die if I'm not a good boy" or "If I love my mother, I would always do what she wants." Accompanying these thoughts were the underlying assumption and attitude that he must act in a pseudomature manner. All attempts were made to remain quiet and out of sight (invisible) as he was encouraged to do while his mother was recuperating from both surgeries. This proved his love for his mother and his concern for her well-being. Even further, in his distorted view, he played an active and essential role in making his mother better. Indeed, if he could only be good enough, love her enough, and remain sufficiently well behaved (pseudomature), his mother would be completely cured. By isolating himself from the company of children he could also be close at hand in case his mother needed something or suddenly became ill. It should be noted that these interpretations were discussed with his parents. However, they were not presented to Robbie. Erikson (1950) cautioned against a direct interpretation of an impulse or intense affect for fear that it might increase anxiety and regression or disrupt play.

Robbie's symptoms appeared to be related to an interaction of dysfunctional cognitive patterns (including negative self-statements) and deficits in social skills. These hybrid factors maintained the dysphoria, isolation, poor self-esteem, psychomotor listlessness and inhibition, and age-inappropriate pseudomature characteristics. Keeping in mind the developmental level, specific skills and needs of this youngster, and the importance of making him an active and collaborative partner in the therapy, cognitive-behavioral strategies were formulated within a play therapy context. For example, puppet play was used to foster cognitive restructuring. The puppets were placed in imaginary scenarios by Robbie. In these situations the "child puppet" was told that its behaviors were making another puppet ill. At these times, the therapist would also engage in puppet play and would counter with adaptive cognitive and verbal responses. The therapist would remark, "Someone might be upset if I don't do what they want me to do but that can't make them seriously sick" or "Just because you (child puppet) won't talk or play with me (other puppet) that doesn't mean you don't love me and I can still love you."

The play also implemented and integrated constructive modeling in which the therapist would offer alternative ways of interpreting others' negating statements. Depressed children often have a very difficult time reinforcing and rewarding themselves (Lewinsohn and Graf 1973). One of the devastating facts about depression is that the depressed person experiences negative perceptions of the self, the world around him, and any potential for change within the future (Beck 1983). Since the depressed person expects that nothing can help, he usually lacks the motivation for change. This, of course, precludes the experience of pleasure or reinforcement. Robbie felt that he did not deserve pleasurable feelings. After all, in his distorted perception he did not love his mother enough to cure her. If he complied with her wishes and became more outgoing and social, she would worry less. Furthermore, even though he was aware of the circumstances, he still resented his father's long work hours and wanted to spend more time with him. While creating various scenarios in puppet play, Robbie reenacted his own situation. He was reminded that it is understandable and permissible for a child to miss his parents and want to spend more time with them under any and all circumstances. Alternative self-statements, especially self-evaluative statements, were offered within the context of puppet play, role playing, and modeling. Appropriate strategies and comments that reward and reaffirm the self were introduced. He was also taught how to evaluate his own behaviors on a scale from very bad to very good. A point system was introduced in which 1 corresponds to very bad behavior and 5 to very good behavior. He and his parents were instructed in the use of a daily activity schedule. They were also taught how to evaluate and reinforce good and very good behaviors with positive comments, self-statements, and self-evaluations.

Similarly, Robbie was taught to gauge the intensity of his affect. Most children know what a thermometer is and what purpose it serves. A large thermometer was constructed out of cardboard. A red strip of poster board was inserted in a slot in the cardboard thermometer. The red strip was mobile and able to slide up or down a gauge from the lowest point, number 1, up through 2, 3, 4, and the highest point, number 5. Whenever one of the puppets had a strong feeling, good or bad, Robbie was asked to move the red strip on the "feeling thermometer" to evaluate the intensity of the feeling. Was it just a little feeling or was it very strong? The ploys used in play were also instrumental in teaching him how to identify feelings and differentiate between positive (good, pleasurable) feelings and negative (bad, unpleasant) feelings. In time, he was able to understand that feelings are not an all-or-nothing experience. Instead, they exist on a continuum from good to bad feelings, and the intensity of affective experiences also varies. This training helped counter the tendency of depressed individuals to think and evaluate in generalizations, to maximize or minimize, and to make all-or-nothing assumptions (Beck et al. 1980). Robbie's parents were also instructed in this self-monitoring procedure and he was able to use a daily mood schedule at home. In this way the positive benefits of therapy were able to continue at home and, it is hoped, generalize outside of the playroom. Since feelings are subjectively felt, his parents were not asked to evaluate the intensity of Robbie's feelings.

A second large cardboard thermometer was also constructed. This one had a blue sheet of movable paper in the insert to avoid confusion. It was dubbed the "doing thermometer." In a similar manner, Robbie was taught how to evaluate his behaviors and interactional styles. He first evaluated the behaviors and social styles of the puppets and representative figures within the role-playing skits, and then, in time, his own actions. He was able to discern very good behaviors from very bad. In addition to this self-monitoring, his parents were also asked to offer Robbie evaluations of his behaviors since these have consequences for others. Hence, Robbie was offered some feedback and a means of comparing his interpretations of his actions to the interpretations of others. He was better able to understand the impact that his behaviors may have on other people. The presentation of alternative behaviors also increased the repertoire of his responses.

Puppet play, role playing, games, and modeling were also employed to help remedy social skill deficits. Mutuality, fair play, and reciprocity were strongly emphasized in the games and in the context of role playing. Within the context of role playing, Robbie was offered alternative ways of interacting in social situations. For example, the therapist played the role of Robbie and the youngster, in turn, played the role of one of his classmates. In this play technique Robbie was able to appraise his interrelational patterns from the perspective of another child. This empathy and perspective training proved very valuable for this youngster. Robbie was asked how a reenactment of his interpersonal styles, including bossiness and sullen pouting, made him feel. At one point, he admitted, "That kind of stuff [his own behaviors with other children] isn't good if you want to be a friend." Alternative and constructive relational patterns were also reenacted in role playing and in puppet play.

After approximately twelve sessions, with his parents' consent, Robbie was placed with two other children in a small group play therapy program. This gave all three children a chance to interrelate, practice their new, adaptive social-interpersonal skills, and engage in games of reciprocity. The children were also asked to evaluate their own social-interpersonal patterns. They were not asked to evaluate the styles of the other two youngsters. Instead, they were asked to share how the other children's behaviors and interactions made them feel. Therefore, all three children received relevant feedback on how their patterns affected their peers without any negative comparisons or unfavorable judgments.

In his formulation of the principle of reciprocal determinism, Bandura (1977) proposed that behavior is a product as well as an initiator of cognitions and environmental factors. This principle explains the mutual interconnectedness among cognitions, social relationships, and behaviors. The family is certainly a major social structure in which we see the impact of this principle. A great many of Robbie's responses and comments, for instance, reflected his mother's statements and styles. Any form of therapy with children must always involve the family. The family is the major source of socialization, and actions within the family directly affect the child. Family therapy has been proven to be a powerful and well-accepted form of therapeutic intervention within the family system. The impact of the family dynamics on healthy as well as problematic behaviors has been reviewed (e.g., Schaefer and Briesmeister 1989).

Robbie's symptoms could not be adequately understood, addressed, or remedied without intervening within the family and changing some of the dysfunctional cognitions, statements, and interactional patterns. Robbie's mother was strongly advised to continue with her own course of individual psychotherapy. At the same time, she and the father agreed to biweekly meetings with the therapist to facilitate Robbie's treatment process. His mother was able to alter her emotionally laden comments to Robbie in a positive direction. She stopped prefacing every statement and every request with, "If you loved me, then you would comply with my wishes." She also discussed cognitive processes and attributional styles with her own therapist. She made dramatic progress in a relatively brief period of time. The greater challenge was to remedy the father's absence from the home due to his overwhelming work schedule. Nevertheless, he was eager to resolve the family's dysfunctional patterns, spend more time with Robbie, and facilitate major reductions in depressive affect in his wife and son. He was able to attend family sessions twice a month. He, too, made significant progress.

Robbie remained in play therapy for about eleven months. During the last four months of treatment, sessions were decreased to once every two weeks. Throughout the entire course of therapy, the family sessions continued on a biweekly basis. The play group sessions also continued on the same biweekly schedule. At the time treatment was terminated, Robbie's self-reports, his parents' reports, and objective assessments indicated a significant drop in dysphoric mood, improved social contacts, and a dramatically enhanced sense of self and self-worth. More importantly, his behaviors, cognitive schemes, self-statements, social relationships, coping, and overall functioning became markedly improved, more positive, and more adaptive.

Follow-up sessions were scheduled four months after the last treatment session and, again, six months after the last treatment session. All reports and observable evidence suggested marked increases in energy levels, improvements in social contacts, and more positive and age-appropriate cognitions and self-statements. Despite what his father described as "one or two small setbacks," Robbie no longer manifested pseudomature behaviors or features. He stopped parenting, withdrawing, and isolating himself physically, socially, and emotionally. The new and healthy adaptive patterns that were established during the course of play therapy were maintained and generalized to many areas of Robbie's life and functioning. His parents also benefited from their cotherapist roles. His mother, in particular, was able to appreciate the link between her behaviors and comments and Robbie's condition. In a very real sense, Robbie was also a cotherapist for his mother. He enabled her to see the impact that her depressive patterns had upon the entire family. Through helping him, she also helped herself. Play therapy effectively eliminated many of the symptoms of the syndrome of childhood depression and allowed Robbie to return to his rightful and appropriate status of being a child.

Summary

This chapter has reviewed some of the major historical trends regarding the concept and existence of childhood depression. The possibility that this clinical disorder could be present in a preadolescent population was initially met with skepticism and opposition. The very notion was contrary to the accepted position that children have not yet developed the cognitive and ego faculties necessary for the phenomenologically felt experience of depression. Gradually, due to a wealth of research and a substantial body of clinical and practical evidence, the concept of childhood depression gained acceptance as a viable and prevalent clinical disorder. Within recent decades there has been a growing recognition that the symptoms of depression that plague adults can also be present in very young children and preadolescents. There is also an acknowledgment that the expressions and manifestations of the symptoms of depression are quite different for adults and children.

Any symptomatic disorder of childhood must be assessed, understood, and interpreted against the backdrop of the developmental process. Empirical research and clinical procedures intertwine with established developmental theories to effect a fuller and richer understanding of the child. Like all aspects of the child's life and functioning, the symptoms of depression are experienced and expressed via age-appropriate cognitions, behaviors, affective tones, motivational forces, social and interrelational patterns, and coping strategies.

The therapeutic model discussed in this chapter integrates the principles of cognitive-behavior theory within a play therapy structure and format. As in adulthood, the negative self-statements and evaluations, distorted and dysfunctional cognitions, and deficits in social-interpersonal skills all correlate with the features and experience of depression. Any therapeutic maneuver to ameliorate the symptoms of depression in children must of necessity be age-appropriate and meet the unique and specific needs of the designated child. The paramount importance and impact of the family dynamics upon the child's situation was also emphasized. Therefore, family intervention was recommended as an invaluable adjunct to play therapy. To produce adaptive changes in the child, those dysfunctional patterns that are embedded in the family system and maintain and exacerbate the child's depressive features must also be radically changed. Play therapy offers a viable modality for effecting constructive changes in depressed children.

References

Abraham, K. (1911). Notes on the psycho-analytical investigation and treatment of manic-depressive insanity and allied conditions. In *Selected Papers on Psycho-Analysis*, pp. 37–156. London: Hogarth.

American Psychiatric Association. (1968). *Diagnostic and Statistical Manual of Mental Disorders*, 2nd ed. Washington, DC: APA.

———— (1980). *Diagnostic and Statistical Manual of Mental Disorders*, 3rd ed. Washington, DC: APA.

———— (1994). *Diagnostic and Statistical Manual of Mental Disorders*, 4th ed. Washington, DC: APA.

Arieti, S. (1962). The psychoanalytic approach to depression. *American Journal of Psychotherapy* 16:397–406.

Arieti, S., and Bemporad, J. (1978). *Severe and Mild Depression*. New York: Basic Books.

Asarnow, J. R., Carlson, G. A., and Guthrie, D. (1987). Coping strategies, self-perceptions, hopelessness, and perceived family environments in depressed and suicidal children. *Journal of Consulting and Clinical Psychology*

55(3):361–366.

Asch, S. S. (1966). Depression: three clinical variations. *Psychoanalytic Study of the Child* 21:150–171. New York: International Universities Press.

Bandura, A. (1977). Self-efficacy: toward a unifying theory of behavior change. *Psychological Review* 84:191–215.

Beck, A. T. (1976). *Cognitive Therapy and the Emotional Disorders.* New York: International Universities Press.

———— (1983). Focus on target symptoms. In *Cognitive Therapy of Depression: New Perspectives*, ed. P. Cryton, pp. 167–208. New York: Raven Press.

Beck, A. T., and Brady, J. P. (1977). The history of depression. *Psychiatric Annals* 7:9–13.

Beck, A. T., Rush, A. J., Shaw, B. F., and Emery, G. (1980). *Cognitive Therapy of Depression.* New York: Guilford.

Bemporad, J. (1978). Management of childhood depression: developmental considerations. *Psychosomatics* 23(3):272–279.

Bemporad, J., and Wilson, A. (1978). A developmental approach to depression in childhood and adolescence. *Journal of the American Academy of Psychoanalysis* 6(3):325–352.

Bibring, E. (1953). The mechanisms of depression. In *Affective Disorders*, ed. P. Greenacre, pp. 13–48. New York: International Universities Press.

Bleuler, E. (1911). *Dementia Praecox or the Group of Schizophrenias.* New York: International Universities Press, 1950.

Bowlby, J. (1969). *Attachment and Loss, vol. I: Attachment.* New York: Basic Books.

Brazelton, T. B. (1992). Depression. In *Touchpoints: Your Child's Emotional and Behavioral Development*, pp. 239–242. Massachusetts: Addison-Wesley.

Carlson, G. A., and Cantwell, D. P. (1979). A survey of depressive symptoms in a child and adolescent psychiatric population: interview data. *Journal of the American Academy of Child Psychiatry* 18:587–599.

———— (1982). Suicidal behavior and depression in children and adolescents. *Journal of the American Academy of Child Psychiatry* 21:361–368.

Centers for Disease Control. (1985). Suicide surveillance report summary, 1970–1980. Washington, DC: U.S. Department of Health and Human Services.

Cohen, F. W. (1971). Mark and the paint brush: how art therapy helped our little boy. In *Therapies for Children: A Handbook of Effective Treatments for Problem Behaviors*, ed. C. E. Schaefer, and H. L. Millman, pp. 68–70. San Francisco: Jossey-Bass, 1977.

Cytryn, L., and McKnew, D. H. (1981). Diagnosis of depression in children: a reassessment. *American Journal of Psychiatry* 137:22–25.

Deutsch, H. (1933). The psychology of manic-depressive states with particular reference to chronic hypomania. In *Neuroses and Character Types*, pp. 203–217. New York: International Universities Press, 1965.

26   The Playing Cure

Dulcan, M. K., and Popper, C. W. (1991). *Concise Guide to Child and Adolescent Psychiatry*. Washington, DC: American Psychiatric Press.

Erikson, E. (1950). *Childhood and Society*. New York: Norton.

———— (1979). Play and cure. In *Therapeutic Use of Child's Play*, ed. C. E. Schaefer, pp. 475–485. New York: Jason Aronson.

Fenichel, O. (1926). Identification. In *The Collected Papers of Otto Fenichel, vol. 1*, pp. 97–112. New York: Norton, 1953.

———— (1941). The ego and the affects. In *The Collected Papers of Otto Fenichel, vol. 1*, pp. 215–227. New York: Norton, 1953.

———— (1945). *The Psychoanalytic Theories of Neuroses*. New York: Norton.

Freud, A. (1965). *Normality and Pathology in Childhood: Assessments of Development*. Madison, CT: International Universities Press.

Freud, S. (1917). Mourning and melancholia. *Standard Edition* 4: 152–170.

Gray, M. (1978). *Neurosis: A Comprehensive and Critical View*. New York: Van Nostrand.

Jacobson, E. (1971). *Depression: Comparative Studies of Normal, Neurotic, and Psychotic Conditions*. New York: International Universities Press.

Jernberg, A., Booth, P., Koller, T., and Allert, A. (1980). *Manual for the Administration and the Clinical Interpretation of the Marschak Interaction Method (MIM)*. Chicago: Theraplay Institute.

Kendall, P. C. (1991). Guiding theory for therapy with children and adolescents. In *Child and Adolescent Therapy: Cognitive-Behavioral Procedures*, pp. 3–22. New York: Guilford.

Kernberg, P. F., and Chazan, S. E. (1991). *Children with Conduct Disorders: A Psychotherapy Manual*. New York: Basic Books.

Kerns, L. L., and Lieberman, A. B. (1993). *Helping Your Depressed Child: A Reassuring Guide to the Causes and Treatments of Childhood and Adolescent Depression*. Rocklin, CA: Prima.

Klein, M. (1935). A contribution to the psychogenesis of manic-depressive states. In *Contributions to Psychoanalysis*, pp. 282–310. London: Hogarth.

Kovacs, M. (1983). *The Children's Depression Inventory: A Self-Rated Depression Scale for School-Aged Youngsters*. Pittsburgh, PA: University of Pittsburgh Press.

Lefkowitz, M. M., and Burton, N. (1978). Childhood depression: a critique of the concept. *Psychology Bulletin* 85(4):716–726.

Lewinsohn, P. M., and Graf, M. (1973). Pleasant activities and depression. *Journal of Consulting and Clinical Psychology* 41:261–268.

Loevinger, J. (1959). *Ego-Development: Conceptions and Theories*. San Francisco: Jossey-Bass.

Lubin, B. (1967). *Manual for the Depression Adjective Check List*. San Diego: Educational and Industrial Testing Service.

Madden, J. R. (1966). Melancholy in medicine and literature: some historical considerations. *British Journal of Medical Psychology* 39:125–136.

Mahler, M. S. (1961). Sadness and grief in childhood. *Psychoanalytic Study of the Child* 48:332-351. New Haven: Yale University Press.

Meichenbaum, D. (1977). *Cognitive Behavior Modification: An Integrated Approach.* New York: Plenum.

Meichenbaum, D., and Goodman, J. (1971). Training impulsive children to talk to themselves: a means of developing self-control. *Journal of American Psychology* 77:115-126.

O'Connor, K. J. (1991). *The Play Therapy Primer: An Integration of Theories and Techniques.* New York: Wiley.

Ostow, M. (1970). *The Psychology of Melancholy.* New York: Harper & Row.

Pfeffer, C. R., Conte, H. R., Plutchik, R., and Jerrett, I. (1979). Suicidal behavior in latency age children. *Journal of the American Academy of Child Psychiatry* 18:679-692.

Puig-Antich, J. (1985). Affective disorders. In *Comprehensive Textbook of Psychiatry,* ed. H. I. Kaplan, and B. J. Saddock, 4th ed., pp. 1850-1861. Baltimore: Williams & Wilkins.

Puig-Antich, J., and Ryan, N. (1986). *Schedule for affective disorders and schizophrenia for school-age children (6-18 years): Kiddie SADS.* Unpublished manuscript. Pittsburgh, PA: Western Psychiatric Institute and Clinic.

Rado, S. (1928). The problem of melancholia. *International Journal of Psycho-Analysis* 9:420-438.

Rie, H. E. (1966). Depression in childhood: a survey of some pertinent contributions. *Journal of the American Academy of Child Psychiatry* 5:653-685.

Schaefer, C. E., ed. (1993). *The Therapeutic Powers of Play.* Northvale, NJ: Jason Aronson.

Schaefer, C. E., and Briesmeister, J. M. (1989). *Handbook of Parent Training: Parents as Co-Therapists for Children's Behavior Problems.* New York: Wiley.

Seligman, M. E. P. (1974). Depression and learned helplessness. In *The Psychology of Depression: Contemporary Theory and Research,* ed. R. J. Friedman, and M. Katz, pp. 109-142. Washington, DC: Winston-Wiley.

Shamoo, T. K., and Patros, P. G. (1990). *Helping Your Child Cope with Depression and Suicidal Thoughts.* New York: Lexington.

Sperling, M. (1959). Equivalents of depression in children. *Journal of the Hillside Hospital* 8:138-148.

Spitz, R. (1946). Anaclitic depression. *Psychoanalytic Study of the Child* 2:313-342. New York: International Universities Press.

Stark, K. (1990). *Childhood Depression: School-Based Intervention.* New York: Guilford.

Stark, K. D., Reynolds, W. M., and Kaslow, N. J. (1987). A comparison of the relative efficacy of self-control therapy and a behavioral problem-solving therapy for depression in children. *Journal of Abnormal Psychology* 15:91-113.

Toolan, J. M. (1981). Depression and suicide in children: an overview. *American*

Journal of Psychotherapy 35(3):311–322.

Waelder, R. (1933). The psychoanalytic theory of play. *Psychoanalytic Quarterly* 2:208–224.

Wenning, K., Nathan, P., and King, S. (1993). Mood disorders in children with oppositional defiant disorder: a pilot study. *American Journal of Orthopsychiatry* 63(2):295–299.

2

Play Therapy for Children with Fears and Phobias

D'Arcy Lyness-Richard

Three-and-a-half-year-old Danny, wearing his favorite Power Ranger paja-
mas, held his father's hand as they began the final part of Danny's new
bedtime routine. Together, they approached the closet in Danny's bedroom.
Danny drew back just a little, as his father opened the closet door and stuck
his head inside.

"Any monsters in here?" the father called into the dark closet. "No
monsters are allowed in here, so if you're in there, get out right now!" Danny's
father checked every corner of the closet. Then he pulled his head out and
concluded, "Nope, not a single monster. You wanna check, Dan?"

The little boy peeked into the closet and called out softly, "Any
monsters? I don't see any monsters. No monsters allowed." He looked at his
father and let out a giggle. "Now look under the bed, Daddy."

Cautiously, father and son peered under the bed, directing their
playfully stern voices past shoes and toys. "Any monsters here? Better not be.
We don't let monsters under here."

The father announced, "All clear. No monsters under here either!"

Danny tiptoed around behind his father. Standing upright, the little
boy assumed his best monster posture and let out a monster roar at his father.
His father wheeled around and opened his mouth in mock surprise.

"Hey, no monsters are allowed in here!" said the father, playing along
with Danny's game.

"It's me, Daddy!" said Danny.

"Oh, Danny! I thought you were a monster!" Laughing, father scooped up his son, placed him in bed, and tucked the covers around him. "Sweet dreams, honey. You're safe and sound. See you in the morning."

Danny, like most children his age, is uneasy about going to sleep alone in his room. He worries about monsters that may be lurking in his closet or under his bed. Sounds and shadows in his quiet, darkened room are transformed by his rich imagination into evidence of the monster's approach. Although part of him knows that there is no such thing as monsters in real life, there is another part of him that is not quite sure. Danny's thoughts and perceptions are influenced by the egocentrism, magical thinking, and limited reality testing that are characteristic of his developmental stage (Piaget 1954, Wadsworth 1989).

It is no wonder that Danny's fear is expressed mainly at bedtime. Bedtime tests his ability to be alone in the dark, separated from his parents to whom he looks for protection. Alone in bed, it is up to Danny to comfort himself, to let go of control, and to give in to sleep. His lingering concerns about whether he is safe all by himself are being expressed concretely as his fear of monsters in the dark. Danny's bedtime routine illustrates his father's playful and supportive way of helping Danny master his concerns. In play, Danny enlists his father's protection as he bravely hunts for monsters, then becomes a monster himself, demonstrating a healthy attempt to master his fear.

Normal Fear in Childhood

Transient preoccupations with such imaginary dangers as monsters, the dark, witches, and other creatures are a normal part of the preschool period. These and other normal fears represent real-life concerns for the child, serve important developmental functions, and pave the way for emotional and cognitive growth (Fraiberg 1959). Erikson (1950) has described the mastery of normal fears as a central task for the child. Engaging in this task allows the child to develop healthy coping mechanisms and other social and emotional resources. The process of exploring and coming to terms with normal fears broadens the child's understanding of the world, and helps to instill a sense of competence to face life's challenges.

In children, as in adults, fear is an emotional and physiologic response to the perception of danger. In a positive light, fear is an adaptive response, promoting safety and in some cases survival. Fear of being burned reminds the child to stay clear of the hot stove. Fear of being abducted or hit by a car motivates the child to use normal caution. Likewise, fears of big dogs, snakes, and strangers help to keep a child safe. Because the child's cognitive skills and life experiences are limited, his perception of danger may be aroused when actual danger is minimal or nonexistent. The child's fear may be aroused by new experiences or by the unknown or unusual. The young child lacks adequate reality testing to distinguish real from imagined danger (Wadsworth 1989), and internal from external experience (Erikson 1950). The child's own inner experiences, such as anger or other strong emotion, may be unsettling or overwhelming and may trigger a fear response. Erikson (1950) differentiates fear from anxiety, noting that fear involves a specific object that may be avoided, while anxiety refers to a more generalized emotional state. Erikson points out that in childhood such a differentiation is not very useful since fear and anxiety often occur simultaneously.

Children's fears are organized around certain developmental themes, and have been discussed by many theorists as arising within the context of particular developmental stages (Erikson 1950, A. Freud 1966, Kagan 1974, Peller 1964, Piaget 1954). Erikson (1950) describes a series of developmental tasks that are explored and resolved during the course of the child's growing experience and maturation. Beginning at birth, the infant's experiences of nurturing and consistent care lead to a perception of the environment as a safe, predictable place. Positive experiences that meet the infant's emotional and physical needs lead to a growing sense of trust. Erikson explained specific fears as representing more generalized social anxieties associated with the developmental concern of a particular stage. For example, the infant's instinctive fear of sudden movement is associated with the emotional concern about the sudden loss of attentive care.

Piaget (1954) described the child's cognitive development, using the term *sensory-motor* to refer to the way in which the infant experiences the world through his senses and explores using his early motor skills. Within this context, fears are related to sensory stimuli that are unfamiliar. The infant fears loud or odd noises, sudden movement, abrupt touch, unfamiliar faces, and large or distorted objects. Kagan (1974) conceptualized anxiety as the individual's reaction to a discrepancy. Anxiety is the infant's response to being confronted with something that does not fit his existing schema. New sensory input may be perceived by the infant as dangerous because it is unknown and is not easily processed or sorted. Further, the infant has limited ability to protect himself from such stimuli. Being unable to move away on his own, the infant may turn away, cry, or cling to a parent.

Lili Peller (1964) and Anna Freud (1966), both psychoanalytic theorists, also placed childhood fears within a normal developmental context. In the psychoanalytic model, childhood is described as a series of sequential phases, each one characterized by particular pleasures and particular apprehensions. Both Peller and Freud noted the child's natural efforts to come to terms with the apprehensions of each stage through play activities.

Specific fears associated with each stage signal the child's struggle with the normal developmental challenges of that stage. Specific fears are concrete manifestations of the child's concerns. They are symbolic for more abstract issues and conflicts the child cannot readily discuss, but is compelled to demonstrate. For example, separation anxiety typically underlies a toddler's fear of the dark. The fear of the dark may be interpreted as symbolic of the toddler's struggle with his central emotional concerns related to separation and autonomy.

Specific fears in childhood, then, are products of the child's developmental stage or task, the emotional concerns or apprehensions that accompany that stage or task, and the child's cognitive ability and imagination. Representing the fear or apprehension of a given stage in such a concrete way serves an important purpose for the child. By creating and externalizing a specific concrete fear, the child is able to begin the process of mastery. Externalizing his fear as a concrete object, the child may then actively consider the problems and solutions, and gain familiarity and understanding. While she learns to accurately interpret the world around her, the child relies on the adult's reassuring instruction and protection.

Because of their relationship to developmental themes, specific fears tend to be rather consistent among children of a given stage (Augustyn 1995, Dixon 1992, Lyness 1993, Schachter and McCauley 1988). Infants respond with fear to sudden movement, loud noises, large or distorted objects, and strangers. Toddlers fear strangers, the dark, and separation from parents. The preschooler's vivid and blossoming imagination, his vulnerability to guilt, and his tendency to use projection result in the creation of elaborate concrete objects of his fear, such as monsters and other scary creatures.

The ability to fantasize about possibilities and to create complex stories further expands the young child's perception of real or imagined dangers. Thus, preschoolers and early school-aged children tend to have "what if . . ." fears. Children in this age group have the cognitive ability to imagine frightening possibilities but lack the real world experience to reassure themselves that the "what if . . ."s rarely happen. These concerns tend to develop as the child ventures out into the world of school and community, leaving behind the safety of parents and the familiarity of home. School-aged children tend to fear injury, thunder and lightning, burglars, kidnappers, and natural disasters.

During adolescence, a more expansive worldview develops and a new vulnerability emerges. Defenses are mobilized to ward off feelings of vulnerability, and adolescents externalize a sense of invulnerability as demonstrated by risk-taking behaviors. The adolescent's underlying apprehensions center around threats to the integrity of the physical or emotional self. Their concerns are often intellectualized and globalized, resulting in specific fears linked to concerns about war or environmental problems. On a more personal level, adolescents tend to fear being physically attacked or being ridiculed.

Since fears are a function of the child's cognitive and emotional development, it should be noted that children with cognitive delays will demonstrate fears consistent with their mental age. Likewise, children with emotional problems or vulnerabilities in a certain area may exhibit regressed fears (Dixon 1992, Lyness 1993).

There are individual differences among children in their tendency toward fearfulness and in the intensity of their fear reactions. Some children are more fearful than others. It is speculated that temperament plays a significant role, and has been noted that shy children tend to be more fearful than children who are more outgoing (Schowalter 1994). Likewise, school phobia is more common among shy children (Schmitt 1995). Social learning is also an important factor in the development of fears (Rutter and Garmezy 1983). It is generally understood that fears can be learned, and often noted that fearful, anxious parents tend to raise fearful, anxious children (Augustyn 1995). Erikson (1950) describes the young child's need for the parental reassurance as he learns to distinguish real from imagined dangers. He noted that if the child perceives the adult's fear then "a panicky sense of vague catastrophe remains as an ever ready potentiality" for the child (p. 408).

Most childhood fears are normal and transitory. Stage-specific fears run their developmental course and gradually subside as the emotional concerns of each stage are resolved. For a child who has adequate emotional support from parents and an age-appropriate repertoire of coping skills, normal fears develop and are mastered gradually without impeding the functioning of the child. They are resolved by the child's playful exploration, the parents' understanding and support, and the child's growing cognitive and emotional skills. The child's healthy and successful attempts to master fears involve the use of emotional defenses, particularly identification, projection, doing and undoing, repetition, and intellectualization (A. Freud 1966). The use of these defenses in the service of mastery of "normal" fears can be observed in the child's play behavior (Lyness 1993).

When Does a "Normal" Fear Become a Symptom?

For some children, specific fears may linger, phobias may develop, or a sense of generalized anxiety may persist. Traumatic experiences cause "normal" fears to take hold and to be more resistant to resolution. Fears related to particular incidents may become generalized. For example, the child who is bitten by a dog may develop a fear of dogs. The fear may become intense, and may lead to the child's avoidance of dogs. In such a case a fear may develop into a phobia.

Fears that were developmentally appropriate when they emerged might persist well beyond a normal duration if the child lacks adequate environmental support or coping skills to accomplish the developmental task associated with the fear. The preschooler's fear of the dark, symbolic of separation fear, is not likely to subside if she experiences repeated abandonment, loss, or neglect. A young child's fear of dogs or monsters, representing underlying concerns about safety from aggression, may persist in an environment where parental aggression is unbridled. Similarly, the child whose parent is impaired, ill, or injured may develop school phobia, demonstrating an ongoing concern about losing the parent. A child who has survived a natural disaster may develop posttraumatic stress disorder. That child may begin to reexperience previously outgrown fears of thunder and lightning, loud noises, the natural environment, or of being alone. The school-aged child with age-appropriate fears of burglars or "bad guys" might not resolve his concerns if he lives in a community where violence prevails. Given the realistic basis for his fear, he might achieve only a partial mastery of his fear. For example, he might rely heavily on the use of identification as a defense. Becoming a gang member or adopting violent, bad-guy behaviors may be the expression of his attempt to master fears of aggression. It is easy to see how this partial resolution, while relieving certain anxiety, will be at the expense of other moral and social developmental tasks. Thus, normal fears can become amplified by troubling situations and may persist, affecting function and developmental progression. A fear that impedes the child's healthy functioning may be considered a symptom of underlying emotional distress and may become the focus of professional intervention.

Phobias are persistent, intense, unrealistic fears that interfere with the child's functioning (American Psychiatric Association 1994). The phobic child may spend inordinate energy avoiding the feared situation or object. She will often recognize that her fear is unrealistic or exaggerated, but continues to be plagued with obsessive thoughts, extreme anxiety, and avoidance behavior. Reassurance typically fails to help the phobic child.

There have been several theories as to the etiology of phobias. Psychoanalytic theory holds that a phobia is a displaced fear (A. Freud 1966). Behavioral explanations have centered on the learned responses through conditioning, and the influence of modeling and social learning (Schowalter 1994). In clinical practice, particular case examples may seem to support one etiology or another. Of the two cases below, the first lends itself to a psychodynamic explanation. The second case illustrates a phobia with a substantial learned component. The case of Judith, presented later in this chapter, reveals multiple etiologic factors that contribute to the development and maintenance of a child's fears and phobic behavior. These cases serve as reminders that the factors specific to each case must be carefully considered in order to plan effective treatment.

Sun Phobia

Nine-year-old Michael's mother had died three months ago, after a long battle with cancer. Michael's father, lost in his grief, had returned to work and had not talked to Michael much about his mother's illness or her death.

Summer came, and Michael had little interest in playing outdoors. His aunt, who cared for him during the day while his father was at work, insisted that he spend time playing outside. Under protest, he did so. One sunny day, Michael's aunt called him to come indoors for lunch. She watched as he crossed the backyard to get to the kitchen door. He ran from one patch of shade on the lawn to another. He was crying by the time he made it to the kitchen door.

"What's wrong, Michael?" his aunt asked.

"I forgot to get my sunscreen on this morning and now I got sun on my skin. Now I will get cancer and die, too!"

Unbeknownst to his family, Michael had developed a phobia of the sun, and had been avoiding it all summer by playing indoors or in the shade, and by protecting himself with magic sunscreen. His phobia could be interpreted as a displacement of his fear of death and loss, coupled with imagined guilt over his mother's illness, and fear of possible punishment for his anger.

Michael was seen by a therapist who helped him to express pain and sadness, loss, guilt, and anger at his mother for getting sick. His father also participated in the treatment, allowing the therapist to facilitate father and son discussions about Michael's mother, her illness and death, and their feelings.

Mother–Daughter Dog Phobia

Six-year-old Jamie's mother brought her to the therapist because of her intense fear of dogs. The fear was so intense that Jamie could not walk to school for fear that she would encounter a dog on her way. Jamie had made a new friend in her first grade class, but could not go to the friend's home once she learned that the friend had a dog. Lately, even stories with dogs, pictures of dogs, and dogs on TV were beginning to upset Jamie.

Jamie's mother confided in the therapist that she, too, had always had an intense fear of dogs. In fact, she still avoided situations where she might see a dog, sometimes at considerable inconvenience. She didn't want Jamie to live with the discomfort she had suffered, and had always told Jamie not to be afraid of dogs.

It is easy to see the learned component of Jamie's fear and how it was modeled by her mother. Despite her words to the contrary, the mother had instilled in Jamie her own belief that dogs are dangerous. The therapy involved behavioral techniques of relaxation training and systematic desensitization for both mother and daughter and was quite successful.

Treatment for Fears and Phobias

It is quite common for troubled children who come to the attention of a therapist to have fears or phobias. In the clinical setting, children may present with symptoms of generalized anxiety disorder, specific phobias, panic attacks, acute stress disorder, posttraumatic stress disorder, or fear-related conditions such as school avoidance, often referred to as school phobia. On the other hand, the child's excessive fear may not be the presenting problem in therapy. Children referred for a wide variety of behavioral and emotional difficulties have fears that need to be addressed in the course of their treatment.

There are several conceptual approaches that are useful in the treatment of fears and phobias. Behavioral counseling techniques are widely recognized for their effectiveness with disorders of anxiety. Underlying the application of behavioral therapy is the assumption that fears and phobias are learned responses that can be unlearned and replaced by other more functional responses. Cognitive-behavioral therapists recognize the importance of the thoughts and beliefs that mediate the stimulus-response patterns (Brems 1993). Cognitive-behavioral interventions center around exploration and modification of the thoughts that accompany the fear-producing stimulus.

Behavioral techniques are largely based on the early work of Jacobson (1938), Wolpe (1958), and Lazarus (1966). Jacobson described a technique known as progressive relaxation in which the patient is coached to systematically tense and then relax muscle groups throughout the body. For example, one might begin by tensing then relaxing the muscles in the toes and feet, then tense and relax the muscles around the ankles, then tense and relax the muscles in the calves of the legs. This process continues until the patient tenses then relaxes all the muscles, usually in a bottom to top order, finally ending with the muscles on the top of the head and scalp. Thus, one progressively relaxes the entire body. Wolpe advanced a concept known as reciprocal inhibition, which is the recognition that two contradictory responses to the same stimuli cannot exist simultaneously. Simply put, it is not possible to experience relaxation and anxiety at the same time.

Applied to the treatment of children, it follows that if a child is relaxed, he cannot at the same time be anxious. Since relaxation is a more rewarding state than anxiety, if a child is taught to relax in response to the anxiety provoking stimulus, then relaxation will gradually replace anxiety as the response to the stimuli. Children can be taught to relax by therapist-coached progressive relaxation or by guided imagery. In progressive relaxation, the child is invited to sit in a comfortable position, close her eyes, and take a few relaxing breaths. While breathing in and out at a comfortable rate, the therapist coaches the child to tense and relax the muscle groups one by one. The use of frequent positive feedback is helpful. Saying "good" after each muscle group is tensed and relaxed is simple and effective. The therapist may suggest that the child feels more and more relaxed with each breath, and that while exhaling the child exhales out all the worries and tensions. The therapist can use tone of voice and cadence of speech to enhance the relaxation process.

"And you can keep on breathing in . . . and out . . . and it feels good . . . how with each breath in . . . you feel a little more relaxed . . . and you can let go . . . of the worries and tension . . . as you breathe out . . . good. Now you can take the muscles of your hands and squeeze them into tight fists, as tight as you can . . . tighter . . . good. Now hold onto that tight fist . . . squeeze . . . one, two, three, and now you can let that hand just relax . . . good . . . just let it relax at your side like a floppy puppet's hand . . . good."

In guided imagery, the child is invited to think of a place he has been or would like to go where he can feel very comfortable and relaxed. The child may then describe the place to the therapist in detail. The therapist may want to know not only what kind of a place it is (tucked into bed, floating on a cloud, sitting in a big easy chair, lying in the grass in the warm sunshine) but also what the child sees when he is in that place, and other sensory details such as feelings and textures, smells and sounds. The therapist then uses these images to guide the child to that place in his imagination while he has his eyes closed.

"And you can close your eyes . . . and you can take some nice, deep . . . breaths . . . in . . . and out . . . and if you like, you can go to your special place . . . where you can feel just as relaxed . . . and cozy . . . as you like. And you have this special place where you can always feel good . . . and safe . . . and everything is okay . . . The pillows on your big chair are soft, and you can cuddle into them . . . just as comfortable as you like. And you can hear the sound of your kitty purring next to you . . . and you can feel her warm furry body . . . And you can smell good smells coming from the kitchen . . . and it feels so good to just be here . . . and be safe . . . in this special place that is just for you."

For treatment of a fear or phobia, progressive relaxation or guided imagery can be coupled with systematic desensitization (Schowalter 1994). Systematic desensitization is a technique designed to diminish and then eliminate a child's fear by gradual exposure to the feared object. Exposure to the feared object is coupled with a more pleasurable or comfortable stimulus (relaxation). In systematic desensitization, the child is asked to develop a list of situations related to the fear. These situations are arranged in order, with the mildly aversive scenes at the bottom of the list, and progressively more anxiety-provoking scenes at the top of the list. The child is taught a relaxation technique. While he is relaxed, the child is asked to visualize the scenes, one at a time, starting with the mildest ones and gradually working up to the more aversive ones. The child is asked to go as high as possible on the list without experiencing anxiety. When he feels anxious, the child is instructed to signal the therapist with a prearranged signal such as lifting a finger. When the child signals that he cannot go further without anxiety, the therapist returns to a less anxiety-provoking scene on the list, allowing the child to regain the state of relaxation. In time and with practice, the child will feel relaxed rather than anxious when faced with the old stimuli. This process may be followed by behavioral rehearsal, which refers to actually rehearsing the situation that has been the cause of fear.

Within a behavioral approach, the therapist assumes a role of helping the child to achieve goals the child sets, or is helped to set, for himself. Contingent positive reinforcement for the child's efforts to achieve goals, such as a sticker chart, is helpful in tracking and underscoring the child's progress. One important aspect of the therapy for a fearful child is helping the child learn to master situations rather than avoid them. Thompson and Rudolph (1983) point out that children have less anxiety about situations if they feel competent. They note that children with separation anxiety, school phobia, or other anxious behaviors tend to be children who are generally preoccupied with worries, dependent on constant reassurances, and lacking a sense of their own ability to master things. Simply by learning how to relax the child can begin to feel successful and competent. He has learned a new skill and has received positive feedback from the therapist about his new accomplishment. Within the therapeutic relationship, such a success serves as a foundation for future joint successes. Behavioral rehearsal can further increase the child's confidence and sense of mastery. Increasing the child's cognitive understanding of a feared situation through discussion about the situation, normalizing some of the reasons for the fear, and discussing and planning ways of handling the situation can promote mastery and therefore reduce anxiety.

Wachtel (1994) emphasizes the importance of teaching the fearful child effective problem-solving skills. She points out that parents tend to offer reassurances or give solutions to the fearful child, but that the fearful child has difficulty making use of such suggestions. Further, children with fears and phobias tend to engage in negative or critical self-talk or other maladaptive underlying beliefs. These elements lead to the child's overgeneralizing from negative experiences and add to the child's distress. Wachtel suggests the therapist ask the child what he could say to himself so that he will be less worried. This technique allows the child to develop a repertoire of positive self-talk. It also shifts the responsibility for handling the anxiety away from the parent, empowering the child to employ his own solution. Such problem-solving skills can be taught in group settings in combination with behavioral interventions such as relaxation training, systematic desensitization, and contingency reinforcement.

Beyond relaxation, systematic desensitization, and behavioral rehearsal, Schowalter (1994) emphasizes the need for reassurance and protection by trusted adults. Parent and therapist can model a safe approach to the phobic object. The practical importance of assessing the extent of the child's realistic need for concern or protection in a feared situation should also be kept in mind.

Turecki (1994) teaches deep breathing, progressive muscle relaxation, and guided imagery to his young patients, then applies systematic desensitization to gradually expose the child to the feared object. He may also use thought substitution and what he calls positive magical thinking, such as suggesting that "magic monster spray" or a brave stuffed animal companion can help a frightened child feel courageous.

Doft (1992) points out that children with phobias often have underlying separation difficulties and intense anger related to loss. Coupling behavioral approaches with psychodynamic techniques such as diaries, drawings, puppets, and other forms of expressive play may help to identify the child's underlying concerns and the causes of anxiety. Psychodynamic and systemic issues will need to be addressed in the therapy for many fearful children (Wachtel 1994).

Thus, the child with fears and phobias will commonly have a variety of therapeutic needs. Specific techniques borrowed from different theoretical models can be utilized to meet the needs of each individual child. For example, a goal to reduce anxiety may be achieved through the behavioral technique of progressive relaxation. Another behavioral technique, behavioral rehearsal, may help the child to actually get into the feared situation and build mastery and confidence. Cognitive techniques like positive self-talk can serve to correct limiting beliefs fearful children have about themselves. The therapist may use a supportive client-centered approach to convey acceptance and positive regard for the child who has experienced many difficulties and failures. Psychodynamic approaches can be used to develop ego skills, to help deal with anxiety, to allow wishes and concerns to be expressed, and to reveal and address dynamic conflicts. A psychoeducational or skill-building approach can be used to help children develop needed competencies to face real-world situations.

Play Therapy for Fearful Children

While children have limited ability to express thoughts and feelings verbally, play is a natural means of communication and self-expression. Erickson (1950, p. 29) wrote, "Children are apt to express in spatial configurations what they cannot or dare not say." Play is the child's natural means of exploration, learning and mastery, and therefore is a natural means to solve problems.

The value of children's play as a diagnostic and therapeutic tool has long been recognized (Erikson 1950, A. Freud 1966, Hellersberg 1964, Klein 1932, Peller 1964, Waelder 1933). "Play is a sign of the child's psychological situation, and can give us leads as to how to intervene properly in childhood conflicts" (Waelder 1933, p. 224).

Anna Freud (1966) used play as a means of putting her young patients at ease. She kept small toys in the therapy room, finding that the opportunity to play provided a comfortable distraction for the child. She observed that inviting a child to play helped to overcome initial resistance to the analyst, enhanced the development of a positive therapeutic relationship, and promoted verbalization in the child. Melanie Klein (1932) underscored the importance of play for understanding the child's wishes, fears, and fantasies. She viewed the child's play as important symbolic communication and interpreted the psychodynamic meaning of children's play in their analytic sessions. Peller (1964) noted that play reveals the child's developmental level, abilities, and capacity for social give and take. Hellersberg (1964) described play activities that correspond to specific developmental abilities.

Erikson (1950) described the unique healing value intrinsic to play. "In play activity the ego finds re-creation and self cure" (p. 209). Play therapy is the specific application of play in the service of treating the psychological problems of the child. Erikson recognized the child's natural tendency to use play in a curative fashion, and the therapist's role as one of facilitating this natural process. Erikson described play therapy as a way in which to "help a child's ego to help itself" (p. 209). Axline (1947) recognized the activity of playing out feelings and ideas as intrinsically therapeutic for the child. She described nondirective or client-centered play therapy in which the therapist's role is to provide a supportive interpersonal atmosphere and opportunities for play, thus facilitating the child's emotional growth.

Play is a flexible medium and can be used in the context of any theoretical framework. Play therapy sessions may have theoretical underpinnings in many different schools of thought (Thompson and Rudolph 1983). In practice, of course, it is the child's specific needs, not the theoretical model, that determine how play can best serve the child. In play therapy, treatment goals are set for a child and play therapy techniques that are aligned with those goals are utilized. There are an infinite number of therapist variables and child-client variables that ensure that play therapy, like any therapy experience, will be unique in each case. The most successful play therapist is one who is flexible in approach and able to utilize techniques that suit the specific needs of the child rather than cling to a specific theoretical orientation or specific technique.

Play therapy sessions can be directive or nondirective, depending on the goal. Play activities may be introduced by the therapist or initiated by the child. The child and the therapist may participate in a play activity together, or the therapist may observe the child's play behavior and offer interpretations to the child. These therapist behaviors may be influenced by the particular theoretical orientation of the therapist. Psychoanalytically oriented child therapists tend to use more observation and interpretation, while behaviorally oriented therapists may participate in a more directive mode with structured activities. A therapist with a client-centered orientation may provide play opportunities that facilitate development of new age-appropriate skills. A skillful clinical child therapist will borrow liberally from all of these models, adjusting her role to fit the needs of the child. With experience in play therapy, the clinician becomes immersed in the unique language and culture of play, which crosses boundaries between schools of therapy, and the application of play in therapy becomes increasingly automatic.

Play therapy is particularly well suited to the treatment of fearful children. Play has its own particular properties that make it a valuable therapeutic vehicle for the treatment of fears. Schaefer (1993) has described fourteen unique therapeutic powers of play that enhance the process of clinical child therapy.

Among them is the mastery of developmental fears. Schaefer (1993), Erikson (1950), Waelder (1933), and Sigmund Freud (1922) have all noted the central role of play in helping the child to master normal developmental fears. It follows that since the child utilizes play spontaneously to overcome normal fears, the same play elements can be utilized in the treatment of fearful and phobic children. Some of the specific curative powers of play that are central to the mastery of fears and phobias will be described and illustrated here.

At the earliest phase of treatment, the therapist can introduce play elements to overcome initial resistance and to diminish the child's normal anxiety about the new situation. Erikson (1964) noted that children cannot resist the temptation to engage in play when the opportunity is presented. The presence of toys in the therapy room evoke in the child the natural desire to play, despite whatever current anxieties the child may have. Even hesitant, fearful children will give in to the temptation to play (Erikson 1964). Schaefer (1993) referred to play's unique powers to *overcome resistance*. Part of the reason for this is that play is purely and *intrinsically pleasurable* (Waelder 1933). The child derives joy from the activity itself. Play replaces other emotions with the *positive emotions* associated with pleasure (Aborn 1993).

Most children come to the therapy room with considerable apprehension and a vague sense that they are being brought to see the therapist because there is something wrong with them. Depending on their beliefs about the reason for therapy, their symptoms, the response of parents and teachers to the symptoms, and the preparation they have received, children may come to the initial visit with feelings of shame, fear, or dread. The nature of the symptom can influence the preconceptions about therapy. For example, children with bed-wetting problems may feel ashamed or embarrassed about their symptom. Children with school failure, or "bad" behavior often have a sense of having been the focal point of parental disappointment or anger and expect the therapist to have negative judgments. Anxious, fearful children may feel frightened of the new situation or of the therapist.

Fearful children will be particularly attentive to the environment and to the person of the therapist. Simple but critical considerations for the initial session include the setup of the therapy room and the therapist's introduction of herself and of the process. The therapist might ask young clients, "What did your mom and dad tell you so far about why they brought you to see me today?" By asking "What did they tell you *so far* . . ." the therapist is allowing that whatever information the child may already have, that there will be more information to come. This allows the therapist to add to the child's understanding without contradicting the parents. Most children will decline to give much of a response to the question, but asking it gives the opportunity to provide a simple and nonjudgmental explanation in order to counter misapprehensions, feelings of shame, or any notion of the therapy as a punitive measure.

Introducing the play materials during the introduction helps overcome resistance. "Would you like to see my playroom? I have some toys you might like to play with. My job is to help children with their worries and anything they're afraid of. Lots of kids come here because they have things they worry about and things that scare them. While we play, I help kids tame the scary things. Maybe you would like me to help you learn how to do that?"

Overcoming Resistance in the Initial Session with Puppet Play

Gloria was a 6-year-old with a history of severe abuse and neglect. Her 3-year-old sister had recently died by drowning in the home, apparently at the hands of their mother. Gloria was placed in foster care while the situation was being investigated. Gloria was believed to be witness to the death of her sister, and had already been subjected to many interviews with social workers, the district attorney, and the police. She was frightened of the police, whom she believed had taken her mother to jail and might take her, too. She was also frightened that her mother would retaliate for Gloria's having "told the truth on her to the judge."

Gloria was brought to therapy by her new foster mother, who was concerned about the traumatic experiences the little girl had faced. She reported symptoms including fearfulness, nightmares, and many episodes of out-of-control behavior. Not surprisingly, Gloria viewed the therapist suspiciously and was hesitant to talk during the initial visit. She sat rigidly in her chair, eyes scanning the room. The therapist offered gentle reassurance and empathy with little response. Gloria eyed the toys, and was invited to play with anything she liked, but she declined. The therapist took a large stuffed dog puppet from the shelf and the puppet initiated a conversation with the therapist.

"Why do you think she doesn't want to play with us, Dr. D'Arcy?" asked the puppet.

"I think maybe Gloria feels a little scared—after all she doesn't know us very well yet, and she's met a lot of new people lately. That's not easy, you know."

"I know. I'm always kind of scared in a new place. Especially if I don't know why I'm there or who the new people are. Can I go over and tell her my name? Maybe she would pet my ears or shake my paw?"

"Why don't you ask her if it's okay?"

"Gloria, can I come over and meet you?" Gloria nodded solemnly. Slowly the therapist moved to sit next to her on the couch. The puppet extended his paw to Gloria. "My name is Ralph. I work here with Dr. D'Arcy. We help children who are scared and worried. This is a safe room and nothing bad will happen to you here. We will take good care of you." Turning to the therapist the puppet asked, "How was that?"

"That was very nice. Thank you. You are helping Gloria feel safe."

"Do you think she would like to scratch my ears? That always makes me feel better. Would you like to, Gloria?"

Slowly the little girl warmed up, tentatively touching the puppet's ears. As the puppet nuzzled her hand, she gave him a more enthusiastic pet, and a shy smile. She glanced at the therapist out of the corner of her eye. Then she lifted the puppet's floppy ear and whispered her concern, "She's not a police lady, is she?"

The puppet exchange allowed Gloria to overcome her initial resistance to the therapist and engage with the therapist through the puppet. A brief playful exchange helped her to voice feelings and concerns to the puppet that she was unable to say directly to the therapist. Play as a therapeutic medium provided familiarity and comfort to this fearful child in the initial session.

The nature of this initial encounter influenced later sessions in which Gloria used a puppet or doll to communicate difficult material to the therapist. Thus, she demonstrated the application of another therapeutic power of play, which Schaefer (1993) describes as play's unique power to *enhance communication* between therapist and child. The child who is guarded or suspicious of adults will relax and talk more freely when play is used as a modality. Play helps the child reveal feelings she may be unable or unwilling to verbalize.

Using Dolls to Communicate Difficult Material to the Therapist

Gloria occasionally brought her own doll, Mary, to therapy sessions. During one visit, Gloria told the therapist that there was a secret Mary would like to tell her. She held Mary to the therapist's ear, and quietly said, "Gloria's real mother used to treat her very mean, and sometimes she hurt her very bad." Thus, a dialogue about Gloria's experiences of abuse was opened between the Mary-doll and the therapist. Eventually, Gloria was able to join in her own voice.

> *Therapist* (to the Mary-doll): That must have hurt Gloria and made her feel very sad inside.
> *Gloria* (animating the Mary-doll): Yes, she feels very bad. Sometimes she was a bad girl, but she didn't want to be bad.
> *Therapist*: I know Gloria doesn't mean to do anything bad. Gloria is a very good girl, Mary. Even if she did a bad thing sometimes. All children do bad things sometimes, but that is just part of learning. Gloria is good all the way to the inside.
> *Mary-doll*: Gloria's mother said she was a very bad girl. Bad to the bone. She hit her on the head and made her stay outside. She wouldn't give her food because she was so bad.

Therapist: It makes me feel very sad to hear that someone treated Gloria that way. But, Mary, I want to make sure you know that it wasn't Gloria's fault.

Mary-doll: She didn't like to be hit.

Therapist: No one likes to be hit. Gloria never deserved to be hit. Hitting is never okay.

Gloria (setting aside the Mary-doll and in her own voice): Right here on my head is where it still hurts from all the hitting. (Gloria lowered her head to show the therapist a spot on top of her head, the way a child typically indicates the location of a "boo-boo" that needs to be soothed. The therapist gently touched the spot.)

Therapist: Oh, sometimes your head still hurts and sometimes your feelings still hurt from all the hitting.

Gloria: Yes. It hurts a lot in my feelings.

While acknowledging the fact that play is intrinsically pleasurable, Sigmund Freud (1961) observed that pleasure alone does not explain why the child plays. He noted that in play the child reproduces situations that were in actuality devoid of pleasure. Waelder (1933) commented on the same phenomenon. He described a child's dentist play, observing that it is often "a highly unpleasurable situation which becomes material or a starting point for a game, played for a time, and then gradually abandoned" (p. 210). Waelder concluded that the experience itself, which may have been too overwhelming, is gradually being assimilated in play. Thus, play began to be conceptualized as a means of working over and reworking of an experience in order to assimilate the associated anxiety.

Freud (1922) recognized play as the child's active attempt to master the experience, noting that "every fresh repetition seems to strengthen this mastery for which the child strives" (p. 13). Waelder (1933) described the significance of repetition in children's play, noting that the child may create the same situation over and over again in order to seek gratification or to achieve mastery of the event. In each playful repetition, the child has the added freedom to change the outcome of the original anxiety-provoking event. Fearful children often use repetition in their play, and take advantage of the unique ability to change the outcome of the original event one or several times. Schaefer (1993) refers to the therapeutic powers of play in the service of *abreaction* and *catharsis*.

Repetition of a Traumatic Theme: Bridge Dream and Swimming Pool Play

Gloria drew a picture of a scary dream she had involving a bridge and some water. In the picture, there were many children sitting and standing on the bridge. Some of the children were falling off into the water below. Gloria continued to add to the picture as she told the story of how the children fell, one by one, into the water. Then they noticed that they were falling off because a witch was shaking the bridge to make them fall. Only some of the children could swim. Some people came by and threw life preservers, but only some of the children could reach them. Some of the children drowned. Gloria drew herself in the water, and continued the story. "Then my foster mom jumped into the water and I climbed on her back and we swam to the shore."

After producing this picture and story, Gloria assembled some play materials and continued the theme. She used a plastic basin as a swimming pool and some small figures to represent people being pushed into the pool by a mean witch. The children cry for help and try to save themselves. Some good mothers help the children out of the water. A good mother calls the police, who come and take the bad witch away to jail. After a while, they send one of the little daughters to jail to check and see if the witch has "turned good" yet. When she is released from jail, she tries to push the little daughter into the pool, and so is returned to jail once again, until she can "get to be good."

Similar swimming pool plays were initiated by Gloria in subsequent sessions. Sometimes figures drowned, and sometimes they were saved. After several variations on this theme, at the conclusion of what was her final swimming pool play, Gloria sighed, "I miss my little sister. I wish she didn't drown."

Gloria had many fears. She was particularly afraid of witches, the dark, and Freddy Krueger and Jason, two scary characters whose particular mode of frightening people is to appear in their nightmares. Gloria had a needle phobia and sleep refusal. She was afraid to sleep, partly because she was afraid of her nightmares, and partly because she was afraid that she might be hurt or killed while sleeping. She often awakened during the night, crying and trembling from a nightmare. Her foster mother had difficulty consoling her at such times. Gloria had great difficulty surrendering to sleep, and preferred to remain vigilant rather than go to sleep. Her need for control generalized into control battles with her foster mother over limits, authority, and basic rules. Neglected in her family of origin, Gloria was used to doing things for herself and not accustomed to parental structure. She was also used to being parental toward her siblings, practiced at making decisions and at finding and preparing food. Fears were among the many issues that needed to be addressed in Gloria's treatment.

Passive to Active: Building a Witch Trap

Gloria told the therapist about feeling afraid to sleep at night for fear of having a nightmare. In a therapy session she was asked to draw a picture about a scary dream. She produced a crayon drawing of Freddy Krueger, complete with bloody claws on his hands and scars on his face. The drawing was so scary that at first Gloria was uncomfortable looking at it. After some discussion of Freddy and examination of the drawing, the therapist offered to keep the drawing of Freddy in the desk drawer of her office. She offered to keep an eye on Freddy, so that Gloria need not worry about him appearing in her dreams. Gloria agreed, and reported no Freddy dreams that week. However, she did report having some scary witch dreams.

The therapist asked her, "What do you think will help keep that witch out of your dreams?"

"I know," Gloria replied, "I will build a witch trap." She drew a picture of herself standing between her foster parents. In front of them stretched a long rope, which was the witch trap.

"I will put my jump rope out in the doorway so that if a witch comes in, she will trip over the rope. My mom and dad will hear her trip, and they will get out of bed and kick her out of our house." She drew a second picture of a small witch being chased away by her foster parents. The foster parents were drawn as large figures pointing the way out the door and shouting, "And stay out!"

In play, the child can assume an active role in a situation that she previously experienced as a passive victim (Schaefer 1993, Waelder 1933). This active, enhanced status is one way for the child to gain control and mastery over the feared object. In play, the child may dominate, tame, or even become the feared object. Anna Freud (1966) described the "ghost-girl" who used the defense mechanism of *identification with the aggressor* to master her fear of ghosts. The girl pretended to be the ghost in order to cross a dark hallway where she feared a ghost was lurking.

Play has a quality of unreality (Waelder 1933), an "as if" quality (Schaefer 1993), which makes it possible to have an abreaction to a traumatic experience. The therapist may help the child to play the experience and have it end differently, or give the child a different role, assisting the child to come to a new assimilation. This unreal, pretend quality allows the child to take on roles that may be normally forbidden (Waelder 1932).

Identification with Forbidden Roles: Bad Doll Mary and Angry Mother

In several play sessions, Gloria was the mother and the doll (Mary) was the bad girl. Gloria initiated the play and took both parts. The therapist observed, then intervened to redirect the play.

Gloria (animating the Mary-doll): I'm hungry.

Gloria (as Mother): You bad girl. You get nothing, you hear me? You are so bad and you get no food!

Mary-doll: Wah! Wah!

Mother (spanking the Mary doll): You stop that crying. You are bad! Bad! Bad!

Therapist: Poor Mary! Mary's crying. Her mother is hitting her and it hurts.

Mother (spanking harder): Bad girl! Bad girl! Bad girl! You shut up and stop that crying.

Therapist (taking Mother's hand gently to stop the hitting): Mother, please stop hitting Mary. You're hurting her. I can't let you do that.

Mother: She needs to be hit. She is a bad bad girl.

Therapist: What did Mary do that was bad?

Mother: She cried.

Therapist: Babies and children cry when they are upset, scared, or hungry. Let's see what can help Mary feel better. (Stepping out of the play and suggesting to Gloria) You play Mary and I will play a mommy and see if I can find out what Mary needs when she is crying.

A variation on this play occurred in another session:

Therapist: Oh, Mary is hungry. She just needs to have something to eat.

Gloria (as Mother): She is greedy.

Therapist: I know Mary. Mary is a good girl. She's hungry and that isn't greedy. (Picks up Mary and holds her) Poor Mary. She feels hurt and upset. She is hungry and all she wants is some good food. Let's fix her some. (To Mary) It's okay, Mary, there's no more hitting.

Gloria initiated play in which she turned the passive experience of verbal and physical abuse into an active one. This time, she played the role of the harsh abusive mother, as well as that of the child. For a while, the therapist observed the play, but made the decision to intervene and redirect the play at a certain point. It was obvious that the harsh treatment was from Gloria's real-life experience, and that Gloria was still clearly identified with the victimized child. Not wanting to condone such abusive treatment, even in play, the therapist chose to limit the abusive behavior and model an alternative.

Since Gloria was sometimes abusive to herself, therapeutic goals included conveying acceptance and caring, and modeling appropriate socialization and empathy skills. Some therapist-guided play sessions were initiated to achieve this goal. The Mary doll and other baby dolls in the therapy room were lovingly fed, bathed, dried, wrapped in blankets. Gloria and the therapist practiced putting baby lotion on the baby dolls, putting them to bed, reading and singing to them, comforting them when they cried, and tucking them into bed. Not surprisingly, Gloria began to "play baby" herself, attempting to fit into a stroller and stating her wish to be pushed by the therapist. The therapist interpreted Gloria's wish to be a baby and how good it felt to be cared for so kindly. Gloria referred to taking care of the babies like a "good mother," and lamented that her "old mother" had been a "very mean mother." Although her wishes could not be altogether gratified, Gloria did enjoy joining the group of baby dolls she had assembled to be read to by the therapist.

Gloria presented to therapy with many problems, including a generalized sense of fearfulness and specific fears that included witches and nightmare monsters. It was easy to see how these fears were related to real-life fears of her abusive mother, and in particular, how the traumatic experience of her sister's drowning death was repeatedly portrayed. Her play and artwork featured themes of witches who tried to drown children and had to be sent to jail in order to become good. A series of traumatic events and real-life dangers had led to the development of her fears. Her therapy addressed her fears by allowing the traumatic events to be expressed symbolically through play and gradually through verbalization. Gloria's play involved repetition of traumatic themes, expression of feared objects through drawing and imagination, assuming an active rather than passive role, and identification with the aggressor. The therapy included the interpretation of symbolic material, allowing opportunities for nondirective play, directing other play, modeling empathy and socialization skills, and providing a safe and nurturing environment.

Many children who present to therapy with problems other than anxiety may also have fears or phobias. Regressive developmental fears may be present because of emotional conflicts or traumas that have hindered mastery. Thus, fears may become the focus of therapeutic intervention at some point during the treatment. Specific aspects of play may be employed to meet the needs of the child. The case of Erick is an example.

Erick: Medical Play for Needle Phobia

Six-year-old Erick's mother was concerned about his difficulty paying attention. He did not listen well at home, or in his kindergarten classroom. He often daydreamed or dawdled rather than attend to the task at hand. He had done rather poorly in kindergarten, had demonstrated only marginal readiness skills, and was about to enter first grade. Erick's mother wondered whether medication would help him pay attention better.

Erick had started to dislike school, and frequently complained of not feeling well in the mornings before school. Often, his mother allowed him to stay home, not being sure whether or not he was really sick. She wanted him to succeed in school, and worried that he was starting off poorly.

Erick's mother reported that he had many other difficulties that concerned her. He was shy and tended to play alone rather than with other children. He didn't like to play outside anymore, ever since the family had moved from their house in the country back to the city neighborhood. The one good thing, Erick's mother said, was that she didn't have to worry about him crossing the street, because he was afraid of being run over in traffic.

Erick's mother thought he seemed more "babyish" than her other children, needing extra closeness with her. He was "scared of almost everything," but especially of the dark. He worried that there were ugly monsters under his bed, and refused to have the lights turned off when he slept. In the pediatrician's office, Erick was terrified of needles, and had needed to be restrained the last time he had bloodwork done. His mother dreaded his upcoming immunization.

The initial interview with Erick and his mother took place in a pediatric setting. Erick was shy and withdrawn. He lowered his head when his mother gently voiced her many concerns about him. It was clear that he had a sense of inadequacy and shame about his problems.

Distancing himself from his mother's words, Eric wandered over to the pediatric equipment mounted on the wall. He pushed the buttons to turn on the otoscope light and began to lift it off its mount. His mother started to scold him not to touch, but the therapist, wanting to give Erick support and to avoid having him lose face further by being reprimanded, offered that he might like to try out the special light, and showed him how to hold it.

A spontaneous medical play activity occurred, with Erick using the light to look in the therapist's ears, then to examine and treat an imaginary injury on her hand. He was offered Band-Aids, alcohol wipes, and a needleless syringe with which he gave the therapist a shot, assuring her that it would hurt a lot. The therapist played the patient role, voicing her fear and pain to her "doctor." Stepping out of the play, the therapist praised Erick for his careful handling of the equipment, and his skillful "shots" and bandaging. He responded with obvious pride.

Practicing with more "needles," Erick made reference to his own needle fears. The therapist offered help with becoming braver for needles, and to teach him a way to get the needles not to hurt so very much, but just to feel like a little pinch. Erick nodded his interest, and he was promised this help when he returned. Thus, Erick and the therapist began their relationship, and the play context for working on Erick's problems was established.

Early in the assessment phase, Erick's school performance problems were investigated. Psychoeducational assessment revealed Eric to be of low average intelligence, with a few scores falling in the mildly mentally retarded range. He was also depressed and felt a sense of inadequacy and failure, and tended to avoid situations he did not know how to master. His weak cognitive skills made it harder for him to master everyday challenges like getting to know his new neighborhood, and he responded to new settings with fear and concern. He had a cautious nature and few good coping skills, which left him bewildered about and frightened of his environment, and preoccupied with danger. Erick's mother tended to overprotect him, partly because she recognized his special needs, and partly because, as she admitted, "I worry a lot about everything."

Placing Erick in the right special educational setting was an early priority, and was easily achieved. Erick had a nurturing teacher who encouraged him and made sure he had success in learning new skills. Quickly he began to enjoy school, and proudly reported his progress to the therapist. With this success as a foundation, Erick's emotional concerns were explored. Helping Erick to overcome some of his fears became the focus of therapy sessions. On most visits, Erick went immediately to the medical equipment and initiated medical play with the therapist.

In an early session, Erick was introduced to the "pinky press," a behavioral technique that was to help him with his needle fear. He was asked to find out which of his arms felt braver and would therefore volunteer to be the arm to get the needle. Quickly making his choice, he seemed to enjoy the notion that one of his arms was so brave. He was then asked to turn his attention to the hand on the opposite arm, which would be used for the "pinky press."

The therapist showed Erick how to press the tip of his pinky finger firmly between the thumb and index finger of the same hand. He was coached to watch the pinky closely, to see if it got paler or pinker. Then Erick was instructed to recite a steady count of 5, while still staring at the pinky and pressing. He was encouraged to press as hard as he could. This technique works, the therapist explained, by putting most of the "ouch" from the needle arm into the pinky. She suggested that only a little pinch would be felt where the needle was. As long as the pinky could take it, the therapist told him, the arm could, too.

Erick practiced several times, then when he was ready, the therapist asked his permission to give the needle arm a small pinch (simulating a needle) to see how it felt.

"I can hardly feel it. It doesn't hurt," said Erick. "Pinch harder," he insisted.

Erick was praised for his success at learning the pinky press so well. He was reminded that he could use this next time the nurse had to give him a needle, and it would work just as well for him. Practicing the pinky press became a small segment of several subsequent sessions, working up to a practice in which the nurse came into the room and uncapped a "practice needle" while Erick did his pinky press. These segments usually followed some medical play in which Erick was the doctor.

Finally came the real test. The immunization visit was scheduled in pediatric clinic. The therapist was present to coach him, and Erick proudly told the nurse he could take the needle from his mother's lap. Erick uttered brief dismay when he caught a glimpse of the "real" needle being uncapped, but quickly recovered when he was reminded that the nurse would watch the needle and he needed to watch the pinky.

"Pinky ready? Press. Press one, press two, press three, press four . . ." The nurse announced "all done" before Erick counted to five. He accepted congratulations all around and was so obviously surprised and excited by his newfound success that he asked the nurse to give him another needle (she declined).

The play context was established in Erick's first session. The spontaneous medical play was initiated by Erick himself, and provided an opportunity for *abreaction*, and a shift from *passive to active*, two key therapeutic elements of play (Schaefer 1993). By starting from a nondirective position, the therapist could be responsive to the content Erick introduced. In play, he had indicated one of his ongoing concerns—needle phobia—and his generalized fear of even painless pediatric procedures. These medical fears became the focus of a therapeutic intervention that was therapist-initiated and structured. The pinky press is a behavioral technique that incorporates systematic desensitization and behavioral rehearsal, as well as allows a shift to activity from passivity. Erick's active tasks were to select the arm, look at the pinky, observe it for color change, and count to five while pressing the pinky.

Erick's play therapy sessions, by circumstance, took place in a modified pediatric examination room. This turned out to be an added benefit. He had the opportunity to have more relaxed, more positive, and more masterful experiences in a place that had been the source of considerable anxiety in the past. The pinky press technique incorporated Erick's ability to use fantasy (the magic power of the pinky press to transfer the ouch away from the arm getting the needle) and allowed him to distance himself from both the arm and the pinky as he considered them as independent of himself as he wondered, for example, which arm felt braver.

In Erick's case, a variety of therapeutic goals were established. The most immediate problem of school placement was handled first. Erick's special educational needs were apparent, and failure to address them in the proper setting had already been an ongoing source of failure to Erick. Providing Erick with a way he could "learn" how to cope with the needle carried the added message that Erick could indeed learn well. His sense of pride and autonomy was enhanced accomplishing such a feat of bravery. This set the tone for sessions to follow and soon Erick presented to the therapist yet another "scary thing" he wanted to master.

Erick and the Bloody Monsters

Most of Erick's sessions took place with his mother present in the room. Again, this was influenced by the pediatric office setting in which the therapist was working, and parents were accustomed in this setting to being present for the pediatric visit. This situation has the added benefit of involving the parent in the child's treatment and modeling approaches they may use at home.

Most of Erick's sessions began with a brief conversation between Erick's mother and the therapist about Erick's progress. While this was going on, Erick was invited to play nearby with whatever toys or art materials he liked. After a few minutes, the therapist focused attention on him, sometimes joining him in play, sometimes making observations about his play.

In one session, Erick made a crayon drawing of "scary, ugly, bloody monsters." These, he told the therapist, were what lived beneath his bed. Having the light on kept the monsters under there, he explained, because "they only come out in the dark."

After some verbal exchange about the monsters, the therapist wondered aloud what monsters were scared of. She suggested that perhaps the scary ugly bloody monsters were afraid of the light, just like some children were afraid of the dark. The thought of the monsters being afraid made Erick laugh gleefully. The therapist suggested Erick draw another picture, this time showing what monsters looked like when they were scared, which he happily did. He drew his bed with the monsters under it.

He showed his drawing to the therapist and to his mother. "Now they are small. I made them very small," he said. "Stay under there, you chicken-'fraidy-cats!" He taunted them.

"How would you like to have some more magic power over those monsters?" the therapist asked. Erick was invited to close his eyes was guided to his imaginary safe, brave place. He was asked to pretend he was holding a magic flashlight. He was led through a brief guided fantasy during which it was suggested to him that while he held the magic light, the monsters couldn't hurt him. He smiled, his eyes still closed. He was invited to pretend he was taking the light into his room, and to try shining it under the bed at the monsters.

"They are trying to hide," he reported, "but I am shining them. Now they are running away . . . they are all gone. Ha!" Erick made several more crayon drawings, making the monsters small and himself big, and giving them scary faces and scared faces.

At one point, Erick's mother related a story that shed light on the development of his medical fears, and possibly explained the specific nature of Erick's bedtime fears. When he was 4 years old he fell and cut his chin, requiring stitches. "He had blood all over him," reported his mother. "His face, his hands, his clothes. He was a bloody mess." A team of nurses and doctors had tried unsuccessfully to hold him down for the stitches. Finally, he needed to be strapped to a board to be held still. She seemed a little ashamed of his behavior. "He was always afraid after that," said his mother sadly. "No wonder he was scared," remarked the therapist, trying to legitimize his fear. "Getting stitches can be scary, especially when you are just a little boy." Erick showed his scar to the therapist who complimented its rugged appearance and commented on his bravery for going through such a scary thing as getting stitches. "And now he is much bigger and has gotten so very brave."

In the next session, the therapist introduced some hospital playthings, including a toy ambulance, gurneys, and some cloth dolls. Erick was thrilled with the new additions to the play materials and spontaneously took on the various roles of ambulance driver, patient, and doctor, and assigning his mother and the therapist roles as well. They talked about stitches, and the therapist explained how special thread is used to sew up a cut to let it heal until it is all better again. Erick practiced stitching up the cloth patient with embroidery thread and a needle, and applying special medicine so the doll wouldn't feel the hurt. These play activities allowed Erick to gain mastery over an earlier traumatic experience. His play involved repetition, changing the outcome, passive to active, and identification as he played different roles and gradually assimilated the anxiety associated with his early medical trauma.

Judith: Phobia of the Dark

Eleven-year-old Judith had a phobia of the dark, and couldn't tolerate being in her room alone at night without all the lights on. Each evening before dark, she closed the curtains in every room of the house so she couldn't see that it was dark outside. Her preoccupation with the darkness interfered with her ability to concentrate on her homework in the evenings. She dreaded bedtime, and watched the clock anxiously as it approached. She begged for someone to stay in the room with her as she slept, or to be allowed to sleep in the living room while the adults were awake. Judith was having difficulty concentrating in school, and was preoccupied during the day with worry about having to sleep in her own room that night. No amount of reassurance helped Judith overcome her fear.

Though Judith had always been afraid of the dark, the intensity of her fear and her phobic behaviors had recently escalated. History revealed that Judith had slept in the same bed with her mother from birth until she was 11 years old. Judith's mother suffered from "nervous problems." Judith's father had abandoned the family some years earlier. Judith's mother had kept her close, concerned about the dangers posed by the world outside of their safe cocoon. Judith had developed very little independence.

Recently, Judith and her mother had moved into the home of Judith's adult sister. Judith's sister felt that Judith had been overprotected by their mother, recognized the mother's mental health problems, and hoped through the new living arrangements to provide an opportunity to foster Judith's independence. Judith and her mother now for the first time had separate rooms. Her sister had allowed Judith to choose furnishings and paint for her own room, hoping to make it something Judith would enjoy. She became very concerned when she realized the extent of Judith's fears of being alone, her phobia of the dark, her excessive worry, and difficulty concentrating in school.

In Judith's case it was easy to see that there was a significant separation problem underlying her phobia. Judith's phobic behaviors also resulted in the secondary gain of extra adult attention and concern. Further, Judith's mother had modeled fearfulness during her early years, contributing a significant learned component to her phobia. Being a temperamentally shy child, Judith was prone to an intensified fear response.

Therefore, in addition to behavioral techniques aimed at unlearning phobic responses, the dynamic conflicts, affects, and temperament factors needed to be addressed in Judith's therapy. Judith's treatment combined behavioral, cognitive, psychodynamic, and supportive play therapy techniques.

Judith: Treatment for Darkness Phobia

Judith presented as a rather shy and timid girl who maintained a cautious distance from the therapist. Some initial play sessions served a diagnostic purpose as well as helped to create a working alliance with Judith. In the first play session, Judith chose to play with the dollhouse and a family of dolls that she moved around in a rather rigid and constricted fashion. Eventually, the therapist joined in the play by taking the part of a doll neighbor and initiating play activity in which the dolls introduced themselves, made friendly overtures, and enjoyed some shared activities. Judith demonstrated the ability to be somewhat more responsive and playful. She also showed a clear preference for someone else to take the lead, showing her what was permitted and expected.

In the second session, Judith was offered art materials and produced two crayon drawings of "two best friends" with tears rolling down their cheeks who had moved "far away from each other."

These initial sessions provided information about Judith's shy temperament, her tendency to be passive and dependent, her rigid style, avoidance of interaction, and her difficulty playing freely. Her drawings revealed the separation theme, and perhaps referred to the fact that she and her mother, who had previously shared a bed, now had separate rooms.

The next several play sessions were aimed at helping Judith to begin to form a relationship with the therapist. The therapist provided play and art materials and maintained a nondirective position, offering assistance and a supportive, attentive presence. The therapist commented positively on Judith's abilities and conveyed interest in Judith's play. Judith was slow to warm up to the therapist, but slowly developed a positive responsiveness. She became increasingly verbal, made more eye contact, smiled occasionally, and enlisted the therapist's participation in play activities.

Judith knew that the reason she was brought to therapy was because she was scared of the dark and scared to sleep in her own room. She admitted that she was sometimes scared walking home from school, and preferred to be picked up by her sister. She admitted to being angry about the new sleeping arrangements. Her feelings were acknowledged and legitimized.

The therapist asked Judith if she knew what it meant to feel relaxed, which was then defined with Judith as "comfortable and safe, the opposite of scared, and a feeling that everything is okay." The therapist offered to help Judith be able to have relaxed feelings more than scared feelings, saying that it would take practice, but the therapist was sure that with time Judith would be able to feel relaxed whenever she wanted to. Judith was taught progressive relaxation. This was practiced for ten minutes of every session.

The therapist introduced a behavioral rehearsal game in which she and Judith used the therapy room to practice going into a dark room. The game began with going to the doorway (with hallway lights on), turning out the lights, and looking into the darkened therapy room. Gradually, they ventured into the therapy room in the darkness, pretending it was a cave, a basement, a haunted house, a jungle. They made magic necklaces as special protection to wear into the dark, and held hands as they entered together. They made shadows on the wall with their hands and with puppets. Judith practiced her bravery by closing the door, which made the room darker still. These activities served to build confidence and comfort. Judith initiated a game of "hide-and-seek" in the darkened room in which she would hide and the therapist would look for her. When the therapist approached, Judith would jump out of her hiding place and "scare" the therapist. Thus, Judith demonstrated the use of identification with the "scary thing" as a way of mastery over her fears. The progressive relaxation was eventually practiced in the darkened therapy room.

Another issue in Judith's treatment was her lack of age-appropriate skills and confidence. She had little autonomy, was very dependent, and certainly doubted her own abilities to protect, comfort, or do for herself. This contributed to her fearfulness. Judith's dependent attitude angered her sister who "refused to baby her anymore." Judith's sister complained that Judith did little to help around the home, and that even her two smaller cousins did more household chores. Judith had no experience with helping around the house, had always maintained her dependent stance, often demanding that things be done for her, and whining when she was given a task by her sister. Sometimes, Judith agreed to help with the dishes, but instead dawdled in the soapy water and didn't accomplish the task. These kinds of passive-aggressive gestures on Judith's part indicated her anger. She was furious about being abandoned by her father, and about not being nurtured or protected adequately by her mother. The therapist also speculated that Judith's dawdling in the soapy water had a soothing and comforting effect on her.

The therapist decided to introduce water play to the sessions. A dishpan, some small plastic toys and dishes, sponges, and warm soapy water were provided. After some initial reluctance, Judith began to play in the water with growing enthusiasm. She clearly enjoyed pouring water from cups onto her hands and arms and swishing her hands around gently to produce bubbles. The therapist commented on how nice and relaxing it feels to play in the water, and Judith nodded. She engaged the therapist's participation in the play, and enlisted her help often to hold a vessel while she poured into it. "It's nice to have someone to be with, someone who can help you when you need or want them to," commented the therapist.

Judith asked for water play during several subsequent sessions. The therapist continued to provide help, attention, and support. Gradually, she encouraged Judith to help as well by filling the dishpan and by helping with the cleanup. With acknowledgment and praise for these helpful behaviors, Judith began to initiate them on her own, and carried them out proudly, together with the therapist. Judith washed and put away all the dishes and toys, rinsed bubbles out of the sink, and wiped the countertop with a paper towel. Judith's autonomy and age-appropriate behaviors were reinforced by the therapist's praise. Judith was given more responsibility while the therapist continued to provide nurturing play materials, support, acknowledgment, and attentive help.

Eventually, and after discussion with Judith's sister, the therapist presented Judith with a proposal. "Your sister Ellen tells me that she sure could use some extra help at home, especially at mealtime. I told her how helpful you can be, and how we have been washing all the toys every week and cleaning up. She had not known about that grown-up part of you before.

"So I have been thinking of something, and I want to tell you my idea. I know that you like to have Ellen read to you at night, but lots of times she can't because she is still too busy with all the kitchen jobs. You are good at washing, good at cooking some things, good at putting things where they go. Your little cousins are too small to do all the things you can do. So I wonder how it would be if you were to be in charge of some of the mealtime jobs while Ellen is doing others. You can help Ellen like you help me with our cleanup. That would be such a big help to Ellen, and she would have more time to read with you after because of your help. What do you think?"

Judith indicated her interest with a nod and a shy but unmistakably proud smile. Together, they drafted a list of small jobs that Judith would like to do. These included washing the dishes, setting the table for dinner, and pouring the milk. In exchange, Judith would have special one-on-one time during which Ellen would read to her. Thus, Judith gained nurturing time, gave up regressive and passive behaviors, and added age-appropriate behaviors of helping at home.

Instituting this new pattern at home proved to be helpful providing a foundation that was necessary before Judith's phobia could be dealt with directly. It was apparent that underlying issues having to do with nurturing and security needs kept the phobia in place. Judith needed to be reassured that she was protected and nurtured in her family and in the world. She needed to have ways of satisfying her own need to be soothed and comforted. She needed to exercise some age-appropriate skills and to develop some autonomy, confidence, and pride. She needed her family to provide nurturing care while gently insisting on her age-appropriate participation.

Once these elements were more securely in place, Judith's phobia could be addressed more directly. Judith's progressive relaxation had been continuously practiced in weekly therapy sessions for several months. Guided imagery was also used to help Judith relax. Judith's favorite imagery involved relaxing play with warm soapy water, feeling safe and relaxed, with someone there to play with her, help her, and make sure that everything is okay. Systematic desensitization was used to help Judith prepare for being in her room alone. A sticker chart was used as contingent reinforcement for nights she was able to sleep in the room alone, then for nights she was able to have the lights turned off. Judith was given a tape of her favorite guided imagery to use at bedtime, and was eventually successful at putting herself to sleep.

The therapy continued after Judith's darkness phobia had been addressed. Play therapy sessions allowed her to express issues related to separation, loss, abandonment, and to continue to develop healthy skills to cope with anxiety. In recognition of Judith's vulnerability to separation, the therapy was terminated gradually with provisions for "checkups" after weekly sessions were discontinued.

Summary

Play is the child's natural means of exploring and mastering normal fears and anxieties. The child "plays out" his fears spontaneously as he experiences the demands of developmental phases and the apprehensions associated with normal development. Play has unique properties that make it the ideal tool for the child to use. These include the properties of fantasy, catharsis, abreaction, and role play.

In play, the child may begin to master normal anxiety by externalizing it and transforming it into a concrete specific "pretend" object. Thus, the child uses his imagination to represent the fear, and then can identify with the object of his fear by pretending to be the scary creature himself. In play, he can take an active role in banishing or taming the feared object. Traumatic events that cause anxiety can be represented, acted out, and repeated in playful scenarios the child creates. These plays can be embellished, changed, and repeated until the anxiety is assimilated. In play the child can assume another role or create a different ending to a real-life event. He can move from being a passive victim of his anxiety to an active master of his fear.

Play therapy is the application of the special properties of play in the service of healing the child's psychological problems. Because one of the central functions of play is to help the child master anxiety, play therapy is particularly well suited to the treatment of the child with fears and phobias. Many children who come to the attention of a therapist have fears or phobias as a presenting symptom. Children who are referred for therapy with other primary problems may have fears or phobias that need to be addressed during the treatment.

Play therapy techniques may be designed to suit the child's therapeutic needs, regardless of the theoretical orientation of the therapist. Play therapy techniques may be based on behavioral, psychodynamic, or client-centered approaches, and techniques may be liberally mixed within the therapy of a given child. An eclectic approach allows the skillful play therapist to borrow and adapt techniques that facilitate the child's use of the specific curative properties of play, and to adjust her therapeutic role to fit the needs of the child.

References

Aborn, A. (1993). Play and positive emotion. In *The Therapeutic Powers of Play*, ed. C. E. Schaefer, pp. 291–307. Northvale, NJ: Jason Aronson.

American Psychiatric Association (1994). *Diagnostic and Statistical Manual of Mental Disorders*, 4th ed. Washington, DC: American Psychiatric Association.

Augustyn, M. (1995). Fears. In *Behavioral and Developmental Pediatrics: A Handbook for Primary Care*, ed. S. Parker, and B. Zuckerman, pp. 140–142. Boston: Little, Brown.

Axline, V. (1947). *Play Therapy*. Cambridge, MA: Houghton Mifflin.

Brems, C. (1993). *A Comprehensive Guide to Child Psychotherapy*. Boston: Allyn & Bacon.

Dixon, S. D. (1992). Two and one-half to three years: emergence of magic. In *Encounters with Children: Pediatric Behavior and Development*, 2nd ed., pp. 265–275. St. Louis: Basic Books.

Doft, N. (1992). *When Your Child Needs Help: A Parent's Guide to Therapy for Children*. New York: Harmony.

Erikson, E. H. (1950). *Childhood and society*. New York: Norton.

——— (1964). The initial situation and its alternatives. In *Child Psychotherapy*, ed. M. R. Haworth, pp. 106–110. New York: Basic Books.

Fraiberg, S. (1959). *The Magic Years*. New York: Scribner.

Freud, A. (1966). *The Ego and the Mechanisms of Defense*. New York: International Universities Press.

Freud, S. (1961). *Beyond the Pleasure Principle*. New York: Norton.

Hellersberg, E. F. (1964). Child's growth in play therapy. In *Child Psychotherapy*, ed. M. R. Haworth, pp. 168–176. New York: Basic Books.

Jacobson, E. (1938). *Progressive Relaxation*. Chicago: University of Chicago Press.

Kagan, J. (1974). Discrepancy, temperament, and infant distress. In *The Origins of Fear*, ed M. Lewis and L. Rosenblum. New York: Wiley.

Klein, M. (1932). *The Psycho-Analysis of Children*. London: Hogarth.

Lazarus, A. (1966). Behavioral rehearsal vs. non-directive therapy vs. advice in effecting behavior change. *Behavior Research and Therapy* 4:209–212.

Lyness, D. (1993). Mastery of childhood fears. In *The Therapeutic Powers of Play*, ed. C. E. Schaefer, pp. 309–322. Northvale, NJ: Jason Aronson.

Peller, L. E. (1964). Libidinal development as reflected in play. In *Child Psychotherapy*, ed. M. R. Hayworth, pp. 176–184. New York: Basic Books.

Piaget, J. (1954). *The Construction of Reality in the Child*. New York: Basic Books.

Rutter, M., and Garmezy, N. (1983). Developmental psychopathology. In *Handbook of Child Psychology*, 4th ed., ed. P. Mussen, pp. 775–911. New York: Wiley.

Schachter, R., and McCauley, C. (1988). *When Your Child is Afraid*. New York: Simon & Schuster.

Schaefer, C. E. (1993). What is play and why is it therapeutic? In *The Therapeutic Powers of Play*, pp. 1–15. Northvale, NJ: Jason Aronson.

Schmitt, B. D. (1995). School avoidance. In *Behavioral and Developmental Pediatrics: A Handbook for Primary Care*, ed. S. Parker, and B. Zuckerman, pp. 251–255. Boston: Little, Brown.

Schowalter, J. E. (1994). Fears and phobias. *Pediatrics in Review* 15(10):384–388.

Thompson, C. L., and Rudolph, L. B. (1983). *Counseling Children*. Monterey, CA: Brooks/Cole.

Turecki, S. (1994). *The Emotional Problems of Normal Children: How Parents Can Understand and Help*. New York: Bantam.

Wachtel, E. F. (1994). *Treating Troubled Children and Their Families*. New York: Guilford.

Wadsworth, B. J. (1989). *Piaget's Theory of Cognitive and Affective Development*, 4th ed. New York: Longman.

Waelder, R. (1933). Psychoanalytic theory of play. *Psychoanalytic Quarterly* 2:208–224.

Wolpe, J. (1958). *Psychotherapy by Reciprocal Inhibition*. Stanford, CA: Stanford University Press.

3

Play and Perfectionism: Putting Fun Back into Families

Risë VanFleet

Background

"My daughter is a perfectionist!" "My son never gives up until he gets it 'just right'." These were phrases that parents used to say with pride. Perfectionism was a characteristic to be proud of. Describing children as perfectionistic implied that they worked hard, did their best, persevered when faced with obstacles, excelled at their activities, and showed promise of successful accomplishments in the future. Many adults who describe themselves as perfectionistic would also attribute their successes and high levels of achievement to that characteristic. Aiming for perfection may serve as a motivational force for some: "If I didn't set high standards for myself, I probably wouldn't do as well."

As with most personality or behavioral characteristics, however, perfectionism has a down side as well. Children and adults who are perfectionistic can be anxious, rigid, afraid of making decisions or taking risks, obsessive or compulsive, and they may experience difficulties in their work and social relationships. This chapter examines these negative features of perfectionism and how play therapy can help reduce them.

In the past decade, researchers, clinicians, and authors of parenting and self-help books have begun to identify perfectionistic-like traits in children and adults as potentially problematic (Ackerman 1989, Burns 1989, Fields 1991, Freeman and DeWolf 1989, Mallinger and DeWyze 1992; Rapoport 1989, Smith 1990). While perfectionism in itself is not considered a psychological disorder, it can lead to maladaptive behaviors and relationships, and it has been linked with obsessive-compulsive disorder (Rapoport 1989) and depression (Burns 1980, Persons 1989).

"Practice Makes Perfect"

This phrase, heard by many in their formative years, suggests perfection as a worthy goal. While a single phrase does not create a perfectionist, some people believe they should try to be perfect in all that they do. In addition, they believe that if they try to do things perfectly, they will be rewarded for their efforts (Burns 1989). Perfectionists typically set unrealistically high standards for themselves and others, and they then measure performance and even self-worth against those standards. When the standard is unachievable (i.e., perfection), they are in essence setting themselves up for constant failure and disappointment. Setting high standards and striving for excellence can lead to noteworthy accomplishments and satisfaction for people, but aiming for a perfection that is never attainable can yield the opposite results: immobilization and discouragement.

While all people need to feel a sense of control in their lives, perfectionists often feel this need in the extreme. They can place enormous pressure on themselves with their unrealistic expectations. This can result in a variety of maladaptive patterns such as procrastination, rigidity, attempts to control others, drivenness, an inability to relax, self-deprecating thoughts, avoidance of decision making, difficulty adapting to change, fear of intimacy, social inhibitions, demandingness, lack of spontaneity or humor, and avoidance of risk-taking behaviors (Burns 1989, Mallinger and DeWyze 1992, Smith 1990).

Perfectionism is not necessarily an all-or-nothing phenomenon. While some people may be perfectionistic in most of the things they do, others may be perfectionistic in some pursuits and not in others. Burns (1989) has suggested different types of perfectionism that can lead to unhappiness: appearance perfectionism, emotional perfectionism, identity perfectionism, moralistic perfectionism, performance perfectionism, relationship perfectionism, and sexual perfectionism.

Perfectionistic Children

Clinicians in recent years have noted an increase in children referred to therapy for perfectionism-related problems (VanFleet 1992a, 1993a). Examples include a 6-year-old girl who refused to leave her home and would throw tantrums if her knee socks were not lined up to exactly the same place on both legs, a 6-year-old boy who, although capable of writing full sentences, would only scribble in his school workbooks, a 4-year-old girl who would not play pin-the-tail-on-the-donkey at her birthday party "because I might not get it right," and a 9-year-old boy who would forgo playing with his friends to study for hours every night after receiving the "upsetting" grade of 95. Perfectionistic children do not meet the diagnostic criteria for obsessive-compulsive behavior, but their perfectionistic anxieties or behaviors interfere with their daily functioning in some way.

Perfectionism also has the potential to disrupt children's psychosocial development. The process of learning involves venturing into the unknown. Children who are afraid to make mistakes or to take risks may limit their learning. Children who do not stray from the familiar to explore their world are not likely to live up to their potential. Perfectionistic children may also have a reduced ability to adapt to change. Children who try to exert excessive control over other children or in their social interactions may have difficulty developing lasting friendships.

Because perfectionism has not been recognized as a potential problem for children's psychosocial development until recently, information about it is based largely on clinical observations rather than research. Very little information is available about treatment options as well. It is possible that traditional treatment approaches have paralleled those used with childhood obsessive-compulsive disorder, relying on behavior therapies and parenting skills training (Rapoport 1989). This area is ripe for study.

Sources of Childhood Perfectionism

Children may develop perfectionistic tendencies—both adaptive and maladaptive—from many different sources.

Unrealistic Expectations of Parents

Parents may inadvertently develop unrealistic expectations of their children. If they are unfamiliar with basic child development information, they may draw inaccurate conclusions about their children when they discuss and compare them with other family members and friends. Their own high hopes for the best for their children may also result in extraordinary expectations. Parents may believe that their children's development reflects their adequacy as parents, and consequently they may push their children to be "perfect." Parents may convey these high expectations directly or quite subtly. When children ask adults to stop praising them so much, they may be communicating that the praise conveys further expectations of high performance. Reinforcement has become another pressure to be perfect.

Unrealistic Expectations of Teachers

Teachers as well may place unrealistic demands on children. Unfortunately, it is not unusual to hear children complain that a teacher has compared them to a sibling or to another family member: "Why can't you work as hard as your brother?"

Highly Structured Lifestyles

Sometimes a family's lifestyle can convey unreasonable expectations. Elkind (1981, 1984, 1987, 1994) has detailed the developmental perils of hurrying children's development. As families enroll their children in numerous sports programs, music and dance lessons, foreign language classes, and fast-track academic programs, children have less time to play and to be just kids. It should be noted that many of these activities are valuable for children to learn new skills and experience new things; it is the excessive degree to which parents involve children in such activities that can be harmful. When children are scheduled for structured activities nearly every evening of the week after preschool or school, their time for their own natural play and exploration is seriously diminished. Parents are usually well intentioned—they want their children to have all the opportunities other children have. But the longer-term results may be children who feel pressured to be perfect or always needing to prove themselves.

Perfectionistic Parents

Children may develop perfectionistic tendencies when they have parents who are perfectionists themselves. The parents provide models of perfectionistic attitudes and behaviors.

Family Addiction Problems

When children grow up in addictive households, they may strive to be perfect as a way to adjust to the family's situation or to compensate for their own perceived inadequacies (Ackerman 1989, Smith 1990).

Conflictual or Broken Homes

Children who live in families with much conflict or other dysfunctional patterns as well as children of divorce may react in ways similar to children from addicted families. Perfectionism may be a means of coping with the family distress or of trying to "make it better." For example, it is common for children to blame themselves for their parents' divorce. They may try to behave "extra good" in the hopes that it will bring their parents together again.

Commercial Advertising

Television and magazine ads for children's products such as clothing or toys are often aimed at the children themselves. Some ads even for very young children appeal to children's needs to fit in with other children or to "look cool." This may contribute to children's attitudes that one must behave in narrowly prescribed ways in order to be accepted. Advertisements that appeal to parents' needs to have the best for their child, such as designer clothing or the latest sophisticated toys, can sometimes be reflected in parents' behaviors and expectations. Parents who spend much time and money on their children's clothing and who frequently praise their children for looking good might be contributing to the development of appearance perfectionism.

Play Therapy for Perfectionistic Children

Elkind (1981) has described play as an "antidote to hurrying." Play therapy can be beneficial to perfectionistic children in a variety of ways. The rationale for using play therapy with perfectionistic children is described below, followed by descriptions of the therapeutic powers of play that appear to affect these children.

The Case for Play Therapy

Perfectionistic children can sometimes appear to be quite serious. That may be true of their parents or other family members, too. Other perfectionistic children who ordinarily display the full range of emotions, including lightheartedness and joy, may become more intense under circumstances in which they feel they must be perfect. At those times, they may take themselves quite seriously and be hard on themselves if they don't live up to their own or others' expectations. Parents, teachers, or friends may tell them to "lighten up."

Play therapy offers these children a relief-valve for the stress they feel as well as an opportunity to be themselves without external pressures. By using the natural therapeutic qualities of play, therapists can help perfectionistic children modify their excessive needs for control, achievement, or conformity to unrealistic standards. In many ways, true play is the antithesis of perfectionism. If children can play, they may be able to counteract the negative aspects of their perfectionism. Specific ways in which play can benefit perfectionistic children follow.

Therapeutic Powers of Play

Several therapeutic powers of play seem relevant to perfectionistic children and their families. These are described briefly below.

Overcoming Resistance

Perfectionistic children can resist forms of therapy that appear to place even more pressure on them to conform to adult standards. Like perfectionistic adults, they may find it difficult to be in therapy at all if they view therapy as a reminder that they are not perfect. (Perfect people wouldn't have problems, and even if they did, they'd be able to handle them on their own.) Play therapy does not place further demands on children, nor does it require them to talk about their problems. Play is natural for children, and its use as a therapeutic modality can help the therapist build rapport with the child.

> A 9-year-old girl had been very resistant to a prior course of therapy that had encouraged her to talk about her problems. Her initial therapist referred her for play therapy after several unproductive sessions. Initially the girl appeared skeptical about the play sessions, but she was drawn to the blackboard. Before long she was writing on the board and playing school. After two sessions of solitary school play, she asked the therapist to become her student. This initial interaction led to positive therapy outcomes.

Communication

Perfectionistic children may use play to communicate the anxieties and stresses they feel. When children express these feelings and have them accepted and understood by a therapist, they are likely to feel relieved. This may be particularly true if the parents are involved in the actual play, as in filial therapy, and begin to understand their children's reactions better and consequently modify some of their expectations.

Competence

If they use perfection as the yardstick against which they measure themselves, children may feel inadequate and incompetent. They may feel as though they can never live up to others' or their own expectations. Play therapy can assist these children to progress at their own rate and to try new things in a nonthreatening and nonjudgmental environment. This permits them to develop skills or ideas in ways that can enhance their self-esteem.

> A 7-year-old boy had a history of giving up easily when attempting new or difficult tasks. During play therapy, he took great interest in the dart guns, but he had trouble pulling back the levers to shoot them. He quickly moved on to other things. Over the course of three sessions, he returned to try shooting the dart guns more and more frequently. The therapist did not intervene because the boy had not asked for help. Finally he was successful at

shooting the gun, and he renewed his efforts to play with the guns. This pattern repeated itself with other toys and tasks in the playroom. He eventually tried more challenging activities.

Creative Thinking

Perfectionistic children sometimes spend so much time trying to "do it right" according to someone else's standards that they fail to consider new or unique solutions to problems. They often avoid risk taking for fear it will lead to failure. Play therapy provides an opportunity for these children to experiment with new ideas or behaviors in an accepting climate. Play does not require the child to get it right because there is no right way to play. With the pressure to succeed or to avoid mistakes removed, children are free to use their creativity to solve problems or to express themselves.

Catharsis

Perfectionistic children may be quite reserved in their expression of feelings, especially ones that they perceive to be negative. Sometimes these children have been praised for being so grown up or tough because they don't cry or display anger. Sometimes they feel they must be strong and show no emotion to protect their families, which are undergoing difficult times. Play therapy offers a release valve for feelings that children have held inside.

An 8-year-old boy whose mother was undergoing intensive treatment for cancer tried hard to help his father with household chores, took responsibility for keeping his younger siblings busy, and seemed generally contented. Whenever his parents raised the topic of his mother's cancer treatment, he quickly changed the subject, saying he knew all about it already. Family members, teachers, and medical personnel praised him for being "such a brave boy for his mother." During play therapy, he eventually played extensively with the doctor's kit. He played the role of menacing doctors who did "mean" things to their patients. The doctor characters pinched and dropped their patients (usually, the puppets), refused to let them eat, and even stabbed them with the rubber knife. After several sessions of this, he verbally began to discuss his fears about his mother's illness and whether or not she would ever get better.

Relationship Enhancement

Stinnett and DeFrain (1985) found that one of the key characteristics of strong families was that they took part in fun or playful activities together. Using play therapy within the family context, as filial therapy does, provides families with the skills to be more playful with each other. This can strengthen parent–child relationships and the family as a whole. This can be beneficial for perfectionistic families who may tend to be serious and task-oriented at the expense of fun. Play and humor serve an important bonding function (Metcalf and Felible 1992).

> The adoptive parents of a 5-year-old boy expressed concern that he did not seem to show many signs of affection for them. Filial play sessions in which each parent held special play times with the boy helped them feel more connected. The parents learned that they had been too "adult" in their interactions and were pleased at the delight their son showed when they played with him.

Perspective

Perfectionistic children and adults tend to take themselves quite seriously. Metcalf and Felible (1992) have suggested the use of humor to help adults realize they are not the center of the universe. Play can do the same for children. When playing, children tend to focus on their play activity rather than on themselves. Furthermore, play therapy helps children learn to accept themselves as they are rather than as they should be. In these ways, play helps children keep a more balanced perspective on themselves.

> A perfectionistic 4-year-old girl was referred for play therapy because she became extremely upset whenever she made a "mistake," such as coloring outside the lines or spilling something. During her first play session she spilled a few drops of water and tearfully told the therapist, "I'm sorry! I'm sorry! I messed up your whole playroom!" After several play sessions during which the therapist was accepting of the child's feelings as well as of the water spills, the girl began intensive water play, pouring the water from container to container nearly the entire session. After three such sessions, the child began pouring from different heights, deliberately spilling and splashing in the water. The therapist reflected the fun the girl was having. The girl laughed and commented, "Don't worry. It's only water and it dries right up. Next time I'm going to make Play-Doh soup!" Shortly thereafter, her parents reported that her tendency to become upset with herself had diminished considerably.

Play Therapy Approaches for Perfectionistic Children and Families

For the reasons cited above, play therapy can be a very beneficial approach to help perfectionistic children and families. The subsections that follow describe a variety of play therapy approaches that have been applied successfully with this population. In addition to the play interventions, the use of parent education/ training and cognitive therapy as supports for play therapy are described.

Child-Centered Play Therapy

Child-centered play therapy (CCPT) can work very well for perfectionistic children because it is designed to accept children as they are and to avoid placing external expectations on them. Child-centered play therapy (Axline 1969, Landreth 1991) provides a nondirective playroom environment in which the children have a great deal of choice and control over the play. CCPT therapists create a warm, accepting atmosphere to help children feel comfortable in expressing a wide range of feelings and ideas through their play. Therapists have faith in children's ability to solve many of their own problems if given a nurturing environment, so they allow the children to lead the activities in the playroom: children select the toys to use and how they wish to play with them. Child-centered play therapists use empathic listening skills to help the children feel accepted just as they are. Therapists typically work with one child at a time in order to give their undivided attention. This type of play therapy is most applicable to children between the ages of 3 and 12.

The goals of CCPT are to help children express themselves without fear of rejection, to facilitate their development of a sense of independence and mastery, to strengthen their self-esteem and self-confidence, and to help them develop feelings of security within safe, clear boundaries. These goals parallel the needs of perfectionistic children closely.

Child-centered play therapists must be skilled in the application of four primary skills: structuring, empathic listening, child-centered imaginary play, and limit setting. Structuring involves establishing the overall guidelines for the play session. Empathic listening is used to convey to the child acceptance and understanding of the child's feelings. Child-centered imaginary play involves the therapist playing out various imaginary roles as directed or suggested by the child. Limit setting involves informing the child of the few necessary play session rules and enforcing consequences if the child breaks them. All of these skills are used in accordance with the humanistic, nondirective principles of play therapy described by Axline (1969).

The behavior of perfectionistic children in child-centered play therapy can vary widely. It is common for their initial play to reflect concern for the "rules" of this new environment or attempts to win the therapist's approval. They may be uncomfortable when they perceive that they've done something wrong, for example, spilling the water or not picking up the toys at the end of the session (not required in CCPT). Because these children often are focused on trying to meet others' expectations, they may become anxious with the ambiguity of the play sessions. They may also show signs of anxiety when the therapist fails to provide them with the evaluative feedback – positive or negative – to which they are accustomed. By empathically listening to their feelings, child-centered play therapists eventually help perfectionistic children realize that it's acceptable for them to have positive feelings about themselves in lieu of external validation. For example, a therapist who responds, "You're proud of the drawing you made" when the child holds up some artwork is giving the message that it's okay to be proud, regardless of the therapist's opinion.

Play themes of perfectionistic children often reflect orderliness, cleanliness, sequencing of toys or objects, and inclusion (such as the need to use all of the doll family members, all of the blocks, all of the puppets, etc.).

A 6-year-old boy spent many of his initial play sessions organizing the playroom, tidily setting up the dollhouse, or carefully arranging toys as items for sale in his "store." He carefully established the rules of the store and houserules for the doll family, and then played accordingly. He also became very upset when the play session was over and he had not put the toys away. After several sessions he began making Play-Doh creations that became increasingly messy. Eventually he began adding water to make "goop." Because he had previously been very upset whenever he would accidentally spill things in the playroom or at home, his ability to tolerate some messiness could be viewed as a sign of progress. Shortly after his "goop"-making began, his parents reported that he seemed more relaxed at home, especially when things didn't go as he expected.

Probably the most prominent play theme of perfectionistic children is control. This is expressed in countless ways. They may take on parent or teacher roles and boss the therapist (as child or student) to do their bidding. They may place unreasonable demands on the characters in their imaginary play. Their need for control is often seen in their need to win at various playroom activities. Perfectionistic children who fear failure often set situations up that ensure their victory. For example, a child may create a special card game to play with the therapist in which he/she develops rules that favor the child alone.

A 10-year-old girl enjoyed playing a ring-toss game with the therapist. She would stand within two feet of the post to ensure that all of her rings landed properly, yet she required the therapist to stand over 10 feet away. She laughed whenever the therapist missed and commented, "I'm better than you are. You're lousy at this game!" As she appeared to gain confidence in her ring-tossing skills, she used more equal conditions: they both tossed from the same distance away. She eventually improved in her ability to risk failure.

Aggressive themes are also common among perfectionistic children. They may express anger and frustration when activities or tasks they choose in the playroom don't work out as they had hoped. Perfectionistic children may express anxious, depressed, or timid feelings in their play as well. A child-centered play therapist who attends to and accepts all of these feelings in children can help the children accept themselves.

Filial Therapy

Perfectionism in children rarely occurs in isolation. It usually has been influenced by family dynamics, or it can affect the family's relationships. While parents' expectations can give rise to perfectionistic behavior in children, the child's rigidity, anxiety, or other behavioral features can be frustrating for the rest of the family.

Because of the potential two-way interaction between childhood perfectionism and family relationships, a preferred mode of treatment is filial therapy. Filial therapy effectively incorporates play therapy into family therapy. In this case, the parents conduct child-centered play sessions with their own children, thereby removing the need for the child to develop a whole new relationship with a therapist (except in complex cases in which play therapy with a therapist might be offered as well as filial therapy). Like play therapy, it is appropriate for use with children between the ages of 3 and 12. Modifications can be used with other children.

Filial therapy has been described in detail elsewhere (Guerney 1983, VanFleet 1992b, 1994a,b). Filial therapy involves parents as the primary change agents for their own children. Filial therapists train and then supervise parents as they conduct child-centered play sessions with their own children. They also help the parents deal with their own concerns and teach them a variety of parenting skills. Filial therapy is a nonthreatening approach that helps the children, the parents, and the family members' relationships with each other. It is applicable to a wide range of emotional, social, and behavioral adjustment problems in children and families. Its psychoeducational thrust makes it useful as a family enhancement or prevention method as well.

Filial therapy seems ideally tailored to the needs of perfectionistic children and their families. First, it involves both the child and the parents in play sessions and increases their awareness of the importance of play for healthy psychosocial development. Second, it provides a nonthreatening atmosphere in which families can "try on" new ways of relating, ways that are more sensitive and less demanding of each other. Third, its psychoeducational nature makes it more "acceptable" to perfectionistic families who might view therapy as a sign of their own imperfection but who value learning new skills and concepts. Fourth, it provides parents with first-hand understanding of the pressures their perfectionistic children might be feeling. As parents begin to understand the meaning of their children's play, they sometimes begin to see the role they play in establishing unrealistically high standards for their children or in modeling perfectionistic behavior. Fifth, after a period of training and supervised play sessions with their own children, parents learn how to move the play sessions to the home setting and to continue them as part of their family development. They also learn how to use the skills and concepts used in the play sessions in broader life contexts. In this way, filial therapy empowers families to make changes for themselves, not only while they are in therapy but also in the future.

The sequence of filial therapy starts with a training period for the parents. The therapist teaches them the four primary skills used in child-centered play sessions: structuring, empathic listening, child-centered imaginary play, and limit setting. This typically takes two to four sessions. The parents then hold weekly 30-minute play sessions with their children, on an alternating one-on-one basis, under the therapist's supervision. The therapist initially focuses on the parents' skill development, providing encouragement and reinforcement as well as suggestions for improvement. As parents become more proficient in the conduct of the play sessions, usually after four or five sessions, the therapist shifts the focus from skill development to understanding what the children are expressing through their play. Filial therapists help parents learn to recognize play themes and what they are likely to mean to the children. It is usually at this stage of therapy that parents' understanding of their children's feelings and needs increases, and parents begin to see how they affect their children. As parents become motivated to modify their own behavior, the therapist works with them to make the desired changes, all the time modeling the same understanding, acceptance, and patience that they expect the parents to show to their children. When parents have developed sufficient competence and confidence in conducting and understanding the filial play sessions, the therapist assists them in transferring the play sessions to the home setting. The therapist continues to monitor progress through meetings with the parents on a weekly or biweekly basis. During this phase of therapy, the therapist continues to discuss family dynamics with the parents, helps them use the play session skills in other areas and times of their lives, and teaches them additional parenting skills.

Filial therapy is particularly useful with perfectionistic children because the acceptance and understanding the children receive in the playroom are coming directly from the parents. This can directly counteract some of the nonaccepting, judging, or pressuring messages parents may have given to the children earlier. Furthermore, as parents develop their empathic listening skills, they are often better able to see their children's viewpoints and feelings, and this can help parents modify aspects of their own behavior that might contribute to the negative aspects of their children's perfectionism.

The play sessions usually trigger important issues for the parents and filial therapist to discuss. When parents are involved as partners in therapy, as they are in filial therapy, they are usually eager to discuss what they are learning about their children and themselves. Filial therapy tends to reduce family resistance, making it easier for parents to raise deeper concerns, such as their own perfectionistic traits or self-perceived imperfections, and to look for feedback and assistance from the therapist.

After having four filial play sessions with her perfectionistic 5-year-old daughter, one mother commented in the post–play session discussion that she was a perfectionist herself. She could see much of herself in her daughter's rigid, non–risk-taking play, and she feared that her daughter would become as anxious and depressed as she felt much of the time. Further discussion revealed that the mother put a great deal of pressure on herself to be the perfect mother, the perfect wife, the perfect housekeeper, the perfect attorney (her profession), the perfect Brownie leader, the perfect church member, and the perfect "neighborhood mom," not to mention the perfect filial therapy client! She said she had always been unable to tell anyone how inadequate she felt until she realized through her filial play sessions with her daughter that her drive for perfection may be damaging to both her daughter and her. She then agreed to a brief course of individual therapy to help her modify some of her own perfectionistic attitudes and behaviors.

Filial therapy can be modified for adolescent children. For older children, parents can substitute "special times" for the child-centered play sessions. Special times are usually one on one and child centered as well. Parents permit their children to select activities within reasonable and financial constraints in which they participate together. Parents then try to remain as empathic and accepting of the child as possible. Special times can include board games, an after-dinner discussion about a topic of the child's choosing, going to the park, listening to music together, or going out to eat. This process can contribute to greater understanding between the parent and the adolescent and help the child feel more accepted for who he/she is.

Cognitive Therapy

Cognitive therapy, as originally developed, is not a form of play therapy, but it can help with the drawbacks of perfectionism and can support more playful, lighthearted attitudes. Knell (1994) has gone a step further by developing cognitive-behavioral play therapy.

Cognitive therapy is based upon the premise that people's thoughts, beliefs, and interpretations (cognitions) are the primary determinants of their emotional reactions. Based upon the work of Aaron Beck, Burns (1980, 1989) has described ten forms of distorted cognitions which lead to exaggerated or unnecessary negative reactions. Some of these are typical of perfectionistic children and adults:

All-or-nothing thinking: This occurs when people see things as black or white, without flexibility. Perfectionists might think something like, "I made one mistake. That means I'm a failure."

Magnification and minimization: Magnification involves blowing the situation out of proportion or exaggerating its importance, while minimization involves discounting the situation's importance or value. Perfectionists tend to magnify their faults and minimize their positive qualities or behaviors.

Should statements: People tell themselves they ought to be doing things a particular way, trying to motivate themselves by saying, "I should do this. I shouldn't do that." People also use "should" statements in reference to others: "He shouldn't be doing that." Basically, "should" statements involve people's beliefs that their expectations or hopes should be met. Perfectionists tend to use many "shoulds" with themselves and others. Many of their high expectations are revealed in their "should" statements: "My son should do as well in school as I did." "I should have been firmer with the kids when they were little so they'd be more responsible now."

Personalization and blame: People hold themselves personally responsible for outcomes that aren't completely under their control. Perfectionists may blame themselves and others when situations do not work perfectly as planned.

Perfectionists may engage in any of the forms of distorted thinking, but those listed seem to predominate. Cognitive therapists help people recognize the distortions in their own thinking and then learn ways of modifying their thought patterns so they can be less enslaved by them. This approach is a direct method for tackling the cognitions that cause and maintain the negative, less functional aspects of perfectionism. Cognitive therapy works well with perfectionistic adolescents, parents, and other adults. Furthermore, perfectionistic parents who learn to modify their own distorted thoughts and statements can provide more adaptive role models for their younger children.

Parents who worry when their children are not perfect and who blame themselves for their children's idiosyncrasies can learn to focus on their children's uniqueness and expect their children to be different, rather than holding onto the mistaken belief that their children must be like all others in order to be normal. A perfectionistic adolescent who continually chastises herself for saying something stupid to her friends can learn to accept and think about the things she does well while accepting occasional social stumbles as part of being human.

Burns (1980, 1989) has detailed a number of approaches using cognitive restructuring that can be helpful to perfectionists. Cognitive therapy can work well with filial therapy or with parent education because it can be provided in a similar psychoeducational format and can help people cope with the anxieties that are created as they take more risks or try to be more playful.

Knell's (1994) work on cognitive-behavioral play therapy is applicable to younger children. Play activities, verbal communication, and nonverbal communication are used to help children modify their "self-talk," beliefs, emotions, and behaviors. For example, toys might be used to model positive coping self-statements for the child. As applied to perfectionism, the therapist might use a puppet or doll to demonstrate that it's okay to do something imperfectly. For example, the puppet might draw a picture, make a mistake, and then say aloud to itself, "That's okay. The rest of the picture still looks very nice. Maybe I can turn this extra line into something interesting."

In summary, cognitive therapy and cognitive-behavioral play therapy can be used alone or can be very useful adjuncts to other types of play therapy and filial therapy for perfectionistic children and their (sometimes perfectionistic) families.

Other Family Interventions

There are a number of other approaches and ideas that can be used with perfectionistic children and their families.

Family Storytelling

For some families, storytelling can offer a nonthreatening way to learn about each other while reducing unrealistically high expectations. Parents can use stories to model more lighthearted, less perfectionistic methods for coping with life's stresses. VanFleet (1993b) has outlined ways clinicians can work with families to help them develop their own storytelling processes and skills.

Practice Being Imperfect

Therapists can help parents find ways to help their children practice being imperfect as a way to help them see that imperfection need not be devastating.

A perfectionistic 5-year-old girl had received a great deal of praise from her parents and grandparents for her ability to "color within the lines." She began to color in her coloring books so meticulously that it took her several hours of work to complete one picture. She did not seem to enjoy it as much as she had previously, and she often cried when she colored outside the lines. Using a therapist's suggestion, her parents helped take some pressure off the girl by suggesting she deliberately color outside the lines in a couple of spots. This permitted the child to continue coloring without the pressure of making a "perfect drawing." This intervention helped her enjoy coloring again.

Careful Use of Reinforcement

It is important for parents to realize how their use of reinforcement might be contributing to the pressure on their perfectionistic child. Clinicians can help parents learn to provide praise and recognition not only for achievement and final outcomes, but for the effort they apply regardless of final outcome. Parents may also need to provide more validation for the child's just *being*, that is, their specialness and uniqueness, with less emphasis on the things the child *does* or *achieves*.

Realistic Expectations

If parents do not have a solid background in child development, they may have developed unrealistic expectations of their children at different ages. Therapists can provide training and guidance for parents in helping them form realistic expectations of their children, based on the children's ages and abilities. Parenting skills training in general can be helpful to families of perfectionistic children.

Careful Use of Language

In perfectionistic families, the word *perfect* is used frequently. As someone achieves a goal or masters a task, they might say, "That's perfect." The "P-word" might be used in giving praise as well: "You look perfect tonight!" Excessive use of the word should be avoided. To reduce the negative impact of perfectionism, families might place more emphasis on excellence or doing one's best than on the ever-unattainable "perfection." Trying to change their language on an everyday basis can feel overwhelming or unnecessarily nit-picky to some parents, and the therapist may need to use caution and sensitivity when discussing this issue.

Family Fun Night

Families who discover that their members' perfectionism has stemmed from or resulted in a serious atmosphere at home can implement a family fun night on a regular basis. This consists of involving the entire family in an interactive, relatively noncompetitive, entertaining or lighthearted activity. The primary purpose should be to have fun together. Competitive activities should be selected only if everyone in the family is able to participate in them with humor and without a strong need to win. Therapists can help families select appropriate activities and then discuss the results.

Limit Setting

When children become compulsive about their schoolwork or other activities, parents may need to set limits in order to help the children learn to balance the different parts of their lives.

The parents of the 9-year-old boy who neglected his friendships in order to study excessively to improve his grade of 95 established a time limit on his studying because he did not seem able to do so. Initially, he responded with anxiety and anger, but he eventually became more efficient in his studying and reestablished his friendships in the neighborhood.

Humor Development

Metcalf and Felible (1992) view humor as a set of developed psychological and physiological skills. Therapists can seek innovative ways to help families re-kindle or develop their humor and playfulness. It is important in so doing to remember that humor may be quite different for different families and individuals. While perfectionistic children and adults may need a nudge to become more lighthearted or to access their sense of humor, they are not likely to respond well to efforts to "force" humor or play on them. Part of the therapeutic task is to find the play or humor intervention that matches the family's situation and its members' personalities.

Case Illustration

To protect client privacy, this case study is a composite of several different families. The problems, family dynamics, and interventions realistically illustrate the application of filial therapy to perfectionistic children and their families, however.

Debbie was a 7-year-old girl whose parents had divorced one year prior to referral. She was an only child. Her father had been transferred to a job across the country so she had had little contact with him since her parents' divorce. She lived with her mother. Her second-grade teacher had suggested counseling to her mother because Debbie was refusing to complete schoolwork. Debbie had told her teacher that she didn't want to make any mistakes, and she knew she was going to. Debbie, who had been in an advanced reading class, had also asked the teacher if she could return to the intermediate reading class even though she was doing quite well with the advanced material. Debbie had received A's when she was in the intermediate group and was receiving B+'s in the advanced group.

Debbie's mother, Louise, reported that Debbie had always had trouble adjusting to change and the divorce had been difficult for her. Louise said

Debbie had always been a "really good girl" and had tried to please those around her. A full developmental and social history revealed a number of perfectionistic behavior patterns. Louise said she considered both herself and Debbie to be perfectionists. Louise agreed to try filial therapy.

The parent training phase of therapy was unremarkable. Louise was eager to learn and use the play session skills. She was ready to begin play sessions with Debbie after two training sessions.

Early Therapy

During the initial play sessions with her mother, Louise explored the playroom somewhat, but played mostly with the dollhouse, which reminded her of her own dollhouse at home. She looked around the playroom from time to time, but rarely left the dollhouse area. This continued for three play sessions. Louise was able to use the listening skill well, but had difficulty refraining from suggesting activities for Debbie. On several occasions, she suggested that Debbie play with other toys. No limit setting was required, and Debbie did not involve Louise in her imaginary play.

After these early sessions, the therapist discussed with Louise her use of the skills. Louise indicated it was very difficult for her to refrain from suggesting play activities. "Debbie seemed afraid to check out the other toys, and I really wanted her to know it was okay if she did." Louise also said this was quite typical of their interactions in any new situation: "I always have to pave the way for Debbie. She doesn't take the initiative, and I worry that she'll end up being a follower rather than a leader." The therapist empathically listened to Louise's concerns and then explained that Louise may unintentionally be giving Debbie the message that Debbie wasn't competent to do these things for herself. Louise had not thought of her behavior in that context before. She began to see how the play sessions might help Debbie to make more decisions on her own.

During the fourth and fifth sessions, Debbie selected other toys to play with. She enjoyed playing with the kitchen set, although she became visibly upset when she spilled some water on the floor. She tentatively punched the bop bag a couple of times during the fourth session, and then looked quickly to see her mother's reaction. In each of these cases, Louise was very accepting and empathic. The therapist praised Louise for her use of the skills.

As Louise began to feel confident conducting the play sessions, the therapist began discussing more of Debbie's play themes with her. Louise had no trouble seeing how Debbie seemed to want her (Louise's) approval for nearly everything she did in the playroom. Louise found it difficult at first to avoid praising Debbie, but eventually learned to reflect Debbie's feelings with non-evaluative, accepting comments such as, "You're really proud of your drawing. You really want me to like it, too." Debbie seemed disconcerted by these reactions at first but eventually decreased the frequency with which she sought her mother's validation.

By the sixth session, Debbie began playing more vigorously with the bop bag. She punched it and tossed it around the room for nearly half the session. Although Debbie was initially uncertain about using the bop bag, Louise's accepting reflections helped her realize it was fine to play with it. The rest of the session, she played cards with Louise, always arranging to beat her mother. She ended the session with "52-card pickup" in which Louise had to pick up all the cards three times. Debbie giggled as she ordered her mother to keep picking up the cards.

Louise expressed some concern about Debbie's aggressiveness after this session. She admitted that she wanted Debbie to be less timid but that she didn't want her to become a bully, either. This led to an insightful discussion of Louise's own discomfort with anger and aggression. The therapist helped her see that this play was not unusual and that Debbie seemed to be taking more control of the play sessions, a possible sign that she was using them to please herself and to work on her own issues.

Home Play Sessions

It was at this point that Louise and the therapist jointly decided it was time to transfer the filial play sessions to the home setting. Louise was conducting the play sessions very well and seemed to be able to handle the variety of things that came up. After the therapist discussed how to transfer the sessions, Louise began holding them with Debbie weekly at home. Louise then met with the therapist on a biweekly basis to discuss the most recent two play sessions.

Debbie's play during the home sessions continued to reflect control themes. During the eighth through tenth sessions, she played the part of a mother who bossed her daughter around all the time. Debbie asked Louise to play the daughter. She also played the part of a teacher who never seemed satisfied with her student's (Louise's) work. Initially, Louise was quite worried that Debbie perceived her as a bossy, unloving mother. The therapist helped Louise see that this play was not necessarily a direct reflection of how Debbie saw things but that it did seem to indicate that she was expressing an awareness that adults place many demands on children. During her next meeting with the therapist, Louise admitted that she had not realized how many expectations she had heaped on Debbie. She had monitored her own behavior during the intervening weeks and had begun to recognize subtle messages she had given to Debbie about performing well, pleasing people, not expressing anger, and so on.

It was at this time that the teacher reported to Louise that Debbie was doing better in school. She was trying the work again, and she didn't seem to become as upset if she made mistakes. Louise used what she had learned through the play sessions to discuss with Debbie how mistakes were a good way to learn things and that it was fine to make them sometimes.

Late Therapy

Debbie continued to make progress. She continued to enjoy play with control themes, and she also began to take more risks in the playroom. She created games that she sometimes lost or that were actual challenges for her. The therapist worked with Louise during this time to expand her use of the play session skills to other aspects of their lives. Louise began using the empathic listening skill when Debbie expressed frustrations about school, her teacher, keeping up with her classmates, etc. Louise commented, "In the past I always just tried to reassure her that she would do fine. I never realized how seriously she was taking everything. Now I think I really hear her, and I can help take some of the pressure off her. I think this has helped me to loosen up and not put so much pressure on myself, too."

When the presenting problems seemed to have resolved, the therapist began to discuss a phased-out discharge with Louise. Louise planned to continue the play sessions indefinitely at home because they both were enjoying them. Louise had also begun to play more with Debbie outside of the play sessions. Debbie appeared to be much more relaxed during the final play session, which the therapist observed prior to discharge. She was in command of the play sessions and showed none of the initial uncertainty. She freely selected the toys she wanted and did not hesitate to tell Louise how she wanted to play. This observation seemed to confirm the reports of Debbie's progress in school and at home.

Debbie and Louise completed therapy after holding eighteen filial play sessions (sixteen therapy sessions). Louise reported that they were still doing fine at a nine-month telephone follow-up with the therapist.

Conclusion

Perfectionism usually has been seen as a positive characteristic. Perfectionistic people often attribute their successes to their high standards, ambitious goals, and other perfectionistic qualities. Perfectionism can have its drawbacks, however, including anxiety, immobilization, rigidity, and interpersonal relationship difficulties. Clinicians and child development experts have reported more frequent instances where perfectionistic attitudes and behaviors in children have been related to adjustment problems. These children can be quite serious, anxious, depressed, inflexible, compulsive, and fearful of risk taking and potential mistakes. Their need to "always be right" or "always to win" can interfere with their learning or social relationships.

Play can help counteract the drawbacks to perfectionism, helping children to accept themselves as they are and to develop in their own unique ways. Play therapy can be particularly useful in helping children overcome adjustment problems or in preventing more serious difficulties arising from their perfectionistic characteristics. Filial therapy, which combines play therapy and family therapy, can effectively address the family dynamics that can be related to childhood perfectionism. Other methods that help families play, laugh, and have fun together can help provide a balance that contributes to the family's psychosocial well-being.

This chapter has described some of the salient issues in clinical and preventive work with perfectionistic children and their families. The study of perfectionism is in its infancy. Current information and ideas are based largely on clinical observations. Research is needed on the sources of perfectionism in children as well as its adaptive and maladaptive dimensions. Play therapy seems to offer the beneficial effect of moderating the negative aspects of perfectionism in children and in families, but research is needed in this area as well.

References

Ackerman, R. J. (1989). *Perfect Daughters: Adult Daughters of Alcoholics.* Deerfield Beach, FL: Health Communications.

Axline, V. M. (1969). *Play Therapy* (rev. ed.). New York: Ballantine.

Burns, D. D. (1980). *Feeling Good: The New Mood Therapy.* New York: New American Library.

———— (1989). *The Feeling Good Handbook.* New York: Plume (Penguin).

Elkind, D. (1981). *The Hurried Child: Growing Up Too Fast Too Soon.* Reading, MA: Addison-Wesley.

———— (1984). *All Grown Up and No Place to Go: Teenagers in Crisis.* Reading, MA: Addison-Wesley.

———— (1987). *Miseducation: Preschoolers at Risk.* New York: Knopf.

———— (1994). *Ties That Stress: The New Family Imbalance.* Cambridge, MA: Harvard University Press.

Fields, D. (1991). *Too Old Too Soon: Protecting Your Child from Instant Adulthood.* Eugene, OR: Harvest House.

Freeman, A., and DeWolf, R. (1989). *Woulda, Coulda, Shoulda: Overcoming Regrets, Mistakes, and Missed Opportunities.* New York: Silver Arrow Books.

Guerney, L. F. (1983). Introduction to filial therapy: training parents as therapists. In *Innovations in Clinical Practice: A Source Book,* vol. 2, ed. P. A. Keller, and L. G. Ritt, pp. 26–39. Sarasota, FL: Professional Research Exchange.

Knell, S. M. (1994). Cognitive-behavioral play therapy. In *Handbook of Play Therapy: Advances and Innovations,* vol. 2, ed. K. O'Connor, and C. Schaefer, pp. 111–142. New York: Wiley.

Landreth, G. L. (1991). *Play Therapy: The Art of the Relationship*. Muncie, IN: Accelerated Development.

Mallinger, A. E., and DeWyze, J. (1992). *Too Perfect: When Being in Control Gets Out of Control*. New York: Fawcett Columbine.

Metcalf, C. W., and Felible, R. (1992). *Lighten Up*. Reading, MA: Addison-Wesley.

Persons, J. (1989). *Cognitive Therapy in Practice: A Case Formulation Approach*. New York: Norton.

Rapoport, J. L. (1989). *The Boy Who Couldn't Stop Washing: The Experience and Treatment of Obsessive-Compulsive Disorder*. New York: Plume (Penguin).

Smith, A. W. (1990). *Overcoming Perfectionism: The Key to a Balanced Recovery*. Deerfield Beach, FL: Health Communications.

Stinnett, N., and DeFrain, J. (1985). *Secrets of Strong Families*. New York: Berkley.

VanFleet, R. (1992a). *Play and perfectionism: Helping anxious children and parents*. Presentation at the annual convention of the Pennsylvania Psychological Association, Pittsburgh, PA, June.

———— (1992b). Using filial therapy to strengthen families with clinically ill children. In *Innovations in Clinical Practice: A Source Book*, ed. L. Vande-Creek, S. Knapp, and T. L. Jackson, vol. 11, pp. 87–97. Sarasota, FL: Professional Resource Press.

———— (1993a). *Play and perfectionism: Helping anxious children, parents, and corporate executives*. Presentation at the annual International Play Therapy Conference, Atlanta, GA, October.

———— (1993b). Strengthening families with storytelling. In *Innovations in Clinical Practice: A Source Book*, vol. 12, ed. L. VandeCreek, S. Knapp, and T. L. Jackson, pp. 147–154. Sarasota, FL: Professional Resource Press.

———— (1994a). Filial therapy for adoptive children and parents. In *Handbook of Play Therapy: Advances and Innovations*, vol. 2, ed. K. O'Connor, and C. Schaefer, pp. 371–385. New York: Wiley.

———— (1994b). *Filial Therapy: Strengthening Parent–Child Relationships through Play*. Sarasota, FL: Professional Resource Press.

4

Play Therapy for Selective Mutism

Jo Ann L. Cook

Selective mutism is a relatively rare disorder. The primary behavioral feature is the lack of speech in selected social situations where speech is expected. This is frequently apparent in settings such as school, although the child is typically capable of communicating verbally in certain other situations and/or with specific individuals. The child with elective mutism elects to be silent in the company of others or selects to speak only with particular individuals. This phenomenon was described as early as 1877 by Kussmal (cited in Wright et al. 1994) as aphasis voluntaria and was followed by fourteen European authors prior to Tramer's (1934) coining the term *elective mutism*. This classification has recently been changed to the term *selective mutism* with the publication of the American Psychiatric Association's (1994) *Diagnostic and Statistical Manual of Mental Disorders, DSM-IV*. The change in terminology from elective to selective mutism indicates that this condition is no longer viewed as primarily controlled by the child alone.

Tramer (1934) had related the case of a boy who displayed speech at home consistent with age expectations and yet refused to speak with his teacher. Elective mute children were described as anxious, sensitive, and unusually shy in the presence of strangers. This presentation may be contrasted with behavior at home, where the child generally speaks with the family but may behave in a negative, immature, and aggressive manner (Laybourne 1979, Pustrom and Speers 1964, Wright 1968). The combination of predisposition to shyness followed by trauma during the period of speech development or later has been reported (Parker et al. 1960). Lesser-Katz (1986) described children with selective mutism as having been normal prior to entry to a school experience at age 3 and having experienced no severe trauma. Others have suggested viewing selective mutism as a delay in skills development of very reticent children in the social use of language (Van Kleck and Street 1982).

Numerous authors describe the mother/child relationship as overenmeshed, with the mother overprotecting and overindulging the child as a factor perpetuating the problem (Browne et al. 1963, Hayden 1980, Parker et al. 1960, Wergeland 1979, Wilkins 1985, Wright 1968). Other investigators have written about family shyness, parental history of shyness or increased anxiety levels in the parents (Hayden 1980, Kolvin and Fundudis 1981, Parker et al. 1960, Wergeland 1979, Wright 1968). Selective mutism, then, begins in early childhood and may not be readily apparent until school entry when the child refuses to speak to teachers, classmates, and other strangers (Cunningham et al. 1983, Kolvin and Fundudis 1981, Labbe and Williamson 1984). The child's early experiences at school are frequently noted for unwillingness to enter the classroom independently and showing little or no interest in participation in the classroom activities (Parker et al. 1960). Given that the problem frequently presents in the classroom, the selective mute child is at significant social/emotional and educational risk.

Background of the Disorder

Elective mutism was classified as a mental disorder by the World Health Organization in the ninth revision of *International Classification of Diseases*, ICD-9-CM (Commission on Professional and Hospital Activities 1978). Classification was subsumed under the domain Disturbance of Emotions Specific to Childhood and Adolescence as one of the disorders of "sensitivity, shyness, and social withdrawal." The *DSM-III* (American Psychiatric Association 1980) included the diagnosis under the general category of Other Disorders of Infancy, Childhood, or Adolescence. The revised *DSM-III-R* (American Psychiatric Association 1987) identified the essential diagnostic feature as a "persistent refusal to talk in one or more major social situations" (p. 88). This replaced the previous edition's (*DSM-III*) requirements of inhibition of speech in "nearly all social situations" and "not due to another mental or physical disorder." The other criterion was that the child have the ability to comprehend spoken language and to speak. The *DSM-IV* (American Psychiatric Association 1994) changed the term to *selective mutism* and increased the diagnostic criteria to five:

A.   Consistent failure to speak in specific social situations (in which there is an expectation for speaking, e.g., at school) despite speaking in other situations.
B.   The disturbance interferes with educational or occupational achievement or with social communication.

C. The duration of the disturbance is at least 1 month (not limited to the first month of school).
D. The failure to speak is not due to a lack of knowledge of, or comfort with, the spoken language required in a social situation.
E. The disturbance is not better accounted for by a Communication Disorder (e.g., Stuttering) and does not occur exclusively during the course of a Pervasive Developmental Disorder, Schizophrenia, or other Psychotic Disorder.

[American Psychiatric Association 1994, p. 115]

There has been some controversy regarding the diagnosis in regard to whether selective mutism should be considered a separate identification as a form of emotional disturbance or viewed as one of a broader group of emotional disorders. There is advocacy for a perspective on selective mutism as a variant of social phobia (Black and Uhde 1992, Crumley 1990, 1993, Golwyn and Weinstock 1990). Shreeve (1991) likened selective mutism to stranger anxiety during early emotional development, a view shared by Lesser-Katz (1988), who described a group of selective mute children in a Head Start program in which the majority were withdrawn, compliant, and seemingly "frozen" around strangers, similar to the infant stranger anxiety stage. This reaction was viewed as an avoidance response in situations where they were unable to cope. A subgroup in that study were described with oppositional behavior. Kurth and Schweigert (1972) found aggressive behavior in a study of twenty-nine selective mute children.

While several subtypes of elective mutism have been suggested relative to personality features (Friedman and Karagan 1973, Hayden 1980), Hooper and Linz (1992) have consolidated the primary personality features presented in the literature as children with anxious depressed features and children with manipulative-oppositional features. They also suggest the possibility of a third type with mixed features and suggest subdivisions in conceptualizing individual treatment planning by specific presentation. In addition, differences with respect to presentation of speech by degree has led to their proposal that speech be viewed on a "continuum of silence," from failure to speak in given social situations to reluctant speech (Blake and Moss 1967, Hooper and Linz 1992). Children who demonstrate reluctant speech do not speak spontaneously but may respond to questions. Viewed as a less severe form of selective mutism (Louden 1987), it requires different treatment, and has a better prognosis (Louden 1987, Mace and West 1986, Morin et al. 1982). Many children exhibit transient mutism on entry to school with a high incidence in the immigrant population (Bradley and Sloman 1975, Brown and Lloyd 1975). However, the diagnosis of selective mutism is reserved for those whose comprehension of the new language is sufficient but continue to refuse to speak (American Psychiatric Association 1994).

Description of the Disorder

Selective mutism occurs with an incidence of 0.3 to 0.8 per 1,000 (Brown and Lloyd 1975, Fundudis et al. 1979, Parker et al. 1960). However, Hesselman (1983) relates that there may be as many as 7.2 in 1,000 5-year-olds who do not speak during the initial months of school. The prevalence decreases with age (Wright et al. 1985) due to the number of diagnosed children who begin to speak, with a significant decrease reported after 5 to 10 months of school (Brown and Lloyd 1975, Kolvin and Fundudis 1981, Wright et al. 1985). Therefore, persistent elective mutism is a rarer disorder (Reed 1963). However, with identification by strict criteria during preschool, spontaneous remission is rare and poor prognosis may result if notable improvement does not occur before the age of 10 (Kolvin and Fundudis 1981).

Hayden (1980) surveyed a total of 122 selective mute children and concluded that in the rare cases of spontaneous remission, the child had later stopped speaking again. The disorder is possibly underreported and may occur more frequently than had previously been assessed (Hesselman 1983, Shvarztman et al. 1990). This may be due to the greater attention that is focused on children with disruptive behavior in the classroom rather than on children whose behavior is primarily a problem to the children themselves (Lesser-Katz 1986). Unfortunately, mutism is frequently accepted in preschool children and inadvertently reinforced (Colligan et al. 1977, Dmitriev and Hawkins 1974). Children labeled as nonspeaking by classmates may reduce their own personal expectation of speaking in school.

Onset of selective mutism is noted during the early years of life in 80 percent of this population, while abrupt presentation occurs with school entry in 12 to 20 percent (Kolvin and Fundudis 1981, Wright 1968). Typical emergence is described as an insidious emergence of silence during the early years (Kolvin and Fundudis 1981, Wright 1968). The age of onset in cases reported in the literature ranges from 3.7 to 14 years (Wilkins 1985) with typical onset being prior to or during the preschool years at a mean age of 3.6 years (Wright 1968). Most referrals for intervention occur between the ages of 5 and 10 (Halpern et al. 1971, Hayden 1980, Kolvin and Fundudis 1981, Parker et al. 1960, Wright 1968, Wright et al. 1985). Some cases have been reported with onset not occurring until, or mutism lasting into, adolescence (Kaplan and Escoll 1973, Wassing 1973). Wilkins (1985) reported a duration of mutism ranging from 7 months to 9 years with a mean of 5.1 years, while Wergeland (1979) reported cases in which the symptoms remained from 2 to 12 years. Sex ratios have been reported as higher with girls (Hayden 1980, Kolvin and Fundudis 1981, Wergeland 1979, Wilkins 1985, Wright 1968) although Brown and Lloyd (1975) reported a higher incidence in boys and Hesselman (1983) found no support for prevalence by sex. In general, incidence ranges from equal by sex ratio to more frequent in girls (Krohn et al. 1992). Obsessive-compulsive behaviors have been cited in some cases (Laybourne 1979, Pustrom and Speers 1964). No evidence of neurologic disorder or brain damage has been characteristic (Louden 1987).

Some studies have been limited to children within the normal IQ range (Parker et al. 1960, Wergeland 1979), while others have reported a wide range of intellectual functioning (Hayden 1980) from subnormal to superior (Wright 1968). Friedman and Karagan (1973) found IQ scores within the range of 56 to 97 with a mean of 83. Due to subjects' nonverbal presentation, intelligence is sometimes reported only by performance scores similar to those of deaf children. Wright (1968) reported that ten of his twenty-four cases had been retained because teachers were not able to assess their progress.

Selective mutism was viewed as an intractable condition with report of only ten of a sample of twenty-four children evidencing improvement on follow-up (Kolvin and Fundudis 1981). Improvement in prognosis was associated with early intervention when the treatment resulted in improvement in speech behavior (Hayden 1980, Wright et al. 1985). Unfortunately, intervention during the preschool years has been rare, as the child's reluctance to speak to strangers is often viewed as normal shyness. Formal recognition may not occur until entry to school, when the child's presentation is observed in relation to the increased expectation for speech in the classroom. Researchers following selective mutes long term relate that they continued to exhibit problems initiating social interactions (Furst 1989, Hesselman 1983). In view of the reported resistance to treatment, advocates have recommended that identification and treatment occur earlier (Hesselman 1983, Shvarztman et al. 1990, Wright 1968, Wright et al. 1985).

There is increasing evidence that family as well as child factors should be addressed in comprehensive treatment planning (Atoynatan 1986, Lesser-Katz 1986, Lindblad-Goldberg 1986, Louden 1987, Meyers 1984). Information regarding family communication patterns, history, and adjustment of the child following entry to school can help identify time of onset. Brown and Lloyd (1975) found twice the number of mute siblings when compared with a group of matched controls.

A number of factors have been reported in the literature as predisposing characteristics of selective mute children and their families. Selective family characteristics have included shy parents and siblings, family patterns of non-speaking (Brown and Lloyd 1975, Lindblad-Goldberg 1986, Meyers 1984, Parker et al. 1960), familial psychopathology including a symbiotic mother/child relationship (Bakwin and Bakwin 1972, Hesselman 1983, Kolvin and Fundudis 1981, Lindblad-Goldberg 1986, Meijer 1979, Parker et al. 1960, Wright 1968), and bilingual families (Bradley and Sloman 1975, Cline and Kysel 1987, Meyers 1984, Rosenbaum and Kellman 1973, Sluzki 1983). Child characteristics have included traumatic physical or social events including entry to school (Parker et al. 1960, Wright et al. 1985), speech problems, slow speech development (Kolvin and Fundudis 1981, Wright 1985), emotional and physical immaturity (Hesselman 1983, Kolvin and Fundudis 1981), timidity, shyness, social withdrawal (Kolvin and Fundudis 1981, Meijer 1979, Salfield et al. 1950), behavior problems, enuresis, encopresis (Eldar et al. 1985, Hooper and Linz 1992, Kaplan and Sadock 1981, Kolvin and Fundudis 1981, Lindblad-Goldberg 1986, Wergeland 1979), and overdependence on mother, early separation, or insecure attachment (Halpern et al. 1971, Kayden 1980, Parker et al. 1960, Pustrom and Speers 1964, Wright et al. 1985).

Wilkins (1985) compared twenty-four diagnosed selective mutes with the same number of matched controls previously diagnosed with emotional disorders. One-third of the selective mutes, but none of the controls, had a history of delayed speech or articulation problems. All of the selective mutes lived in two-parent families but half of the families in both groups were cited as having marital discord. Mute children were more frequently described as "anxious, depressed, and manipulative" and had mothers who were overprotective. The numbers of shy children were similar in both groups. Differences between groups were statistically significant and supportive of selective mutism as a separate condition distinguishable from other emotional disorders. Kolvin and Fundudis (1981) compared selective mute children with children with speech disorders and normal controls, and reported that 50 percent of the mute children had speech abnormality or immaturity and had spoken notably later. A range of speech/language impairment has been reported from 28 to 50 percent (Kolvin and Fundudis 1981, Wilkins 1985, Wright 1968).

In summary, the condition of selective mutism is a chronic disorder viewed as historically resistant to treatment (Kolvin and Fundudis 1981, Kupietz and Schwartz 1982, Labbe and Williamson 1984, Lazarus et al. 1983, Reed 1963, Sanok and Ascione 1979). Identification by strict criteria has shown that spontaneous remission is highly unlikely (Hayden 1980). Improved outcome is associated with early intervention and could prevent the development of secondary problems such as academic concerns and progressive social and emotional isolation (Krolian 1988). Thus, a review of traditional strategies and outcomes becomes important in identifying interventions with demonstrated effectiveness.

Traditional Treatment Strategies

Varying levels of success and failure have been reported in the treatment of selective mutism. The literature includes reviews of clinical studies that are primarily single case studies or studies of small numbers of cases (Friedman and Karagan 1973, Kratochwill et al. 1979, Labbe and Williamson 1984, Reed 1963, Wright 1968, Wright et al. 1994). The majority of treatment strategies have been behavioral and psychodynamic (Wright et al. 1994). Behavioral interventions have been shown to be successful in treating selective mutism, while reports regarding traditional psychotherapy, psychoanalysis, and hypnosis were discouraging (Browne et al. 1963, Lazarus et al. 1983, Wergeland 1979). Other treatments have included family therapy (Krohn et al. 1992), speech therapy (Krolian 1988, Wright et al. 1985), psychopharmacologic treatment (Black and Uhde 1992, Golwyn and Weinstock 1990), and play therapy (Atlas 1993, Sluckin et al. 1991) including behavioral application (Barlow et al. 1986) and group play therapy (Barlow et al. 1986, Bozigar and Hansen 1984, Lesser-Katz 1988, Roe 1993).

Some interventions concurrently involved family members (Atoynatan 1986, Barlow et al. 1986), while others involved professionals and children in the child's school (Richburg and Cobia 1994, Roe 1993). There are reports of simultaneous interventions in several environments in which the child had presented muteness (Lachenmeyer and Gibbs 1985) as well as clinic settings (Reid et al. 1967) and hospital treatment (Krohn et al. 1992, Krolian 1988, Wassing 1973). Wergeland (1979) related a positive therapeutic effect in seemingly resistant cases resulting from changing the child's environment alone. Bozigar and Hansen (1984) attributed improvements in four subjects to group therapy, although the children had also been transferred to different schools following group intervention as part of the treatment.

Superficial interventions such as advice, suggestions, and admonitions have been ineffective in obtaining speech from selective mutes, as was traditional psychotherapy (Elson et al. 1965, Mora et al. 1962). Eleven cases reported by Wergeland (1979) and ten by Browne and colleagues (1963) were described as having poor outcome following long and difficult treatment with traditional psychotherapy. Counterproductivity of inpatient treatment has been expressed (Heil et al. 1985, Mitchell 1985, Murray 1983, Wergeland 1979). Successful interveners have advocated early diagnosis and intervention (Hayden 1980, Hesselman 1983, Kurth and Schweigert 1972, Sluckin 1977, Wright et al. 1985) and generalization to other environments including school (Hesselman 1983, Sanok and Ascione 1979, Watson and Kramer 1992).

Overall, behavioral programs have demonstrated the most consistent success in decreasing the symptoms of selective mutism (Cunningham et al. 1983, Kratochwill 1981, Labbe and Williamson 1984, Rees 1986, Williamson and Donald 1977). Reed (1963) proposed the view of elective mutism as a learned pattern of behavior that was represented by two types. One type was described as immature and manipulative with muteness maintained by social reinforcement, such as attention from parents and teachers. The second type was reported as anxious and tense, with muteness applied as an avoidance mechanism. Critics had expressed concerns that behavioral interventions confined to symptom treatment frequently produced prompted versus spontaneous speech (Conrad et al. 1974), and resulted in difficulties with generalization (Kehle et al. 1990). However, they were more effective and less lengthy than psychodynamic approaches (Kratochwill et al. 1979, Lazarus et al. 1983, Wright et al. 1985). Also, reports of success in the literature were persuasive in view of the chronicity of the problem and potential consequent problems in social isolation and education.

Behavioral studies limited to provision of positive reinforcement for vocalizations in specific settings frequently resulted in limited or no success (Griffith et al. 1975). Researchers have increasingly agreed that a combination of procedures was needed to produce observable changes in speech patterns of selective mutes (Sanok and Ascione 1979, Wulbert et al. 1973). Success has been reported with various behavioral interventions including contingency management programs, shaping (reinforcing successive approximations to speech such as lip movement and whispering), escape avoidance procedures (expressing an expectation for speech and not allowing a child to leave until speech is produced), and stimulus fading (gradually increasing the number of people and environments in which verbalization is rewarded) (Carr and Afnan 1989, Cunningham et al. 1983, Labbe and Williamson 1984). Most efforts focused on contingency management rewarding verbal behaviors and extinguishing non-verbal responses (Labbe and Williamson 1984). Procedures such as stimulus fading are employed to generalize the speech to different situations (Cunningham et al. 1983, Labbe and Williamson 1984, Richards and Hansen 1978). Reinforcement sampling, allowing the child to play with a reinforcer that will later be earned through speaking, has successfully been employed (Austed et al. 1980, Williamson and Donald 1977). The use of audiotape (Albert-Stewart 1986) and videotape self-modeling (Holmbeck and Lavigne 1992, Kehle et al. 1990, Pigott and Gonzales 1987) representing the child performing the desired behavior, has been shown to result in acquisition of appropriate speech that generalized to new settings and persons with short-term treatment. Single-subject multimethod, multisetting designs have also been described (Labbe and Williamson 1984, Lachenmeyer and Gibbs 1985, Watson and Kramer 1992). Behavioral interventions have been successfully applied directly in the classroom environment (Bauermeister and Jemail 1975, Calhoun and Koenig 1973, Piersel and Kratochwill 1981).

Wright (1968) reported high treatment success rates with twenty-four children, of "heterogeneous" grouping, although they all had a history of refusing to talk in school. Intervention was based on the Hawthorne Center approach, which employed use of behavior procedures, including escape avoidance and family and school involvement. This resulted in findings of 79 percent excellent to good and 21 percent fair to poor outcomes. A recent effectiveness study of the Hawthorne Center approach was cited as resulting in high rates of success with eighty-five percent demonstrating excellent and others falling in the fair range of outcome (Krohn et al. 1992). Kolvin and Fundudis (1981) reported that 46 percent of subjects in behavioral treatment approaches continued to show improvement at 5 and 10 years posttreatment. Sluckin and colleagues (1991) followed twenty-five selective mute children from two to ten years postreferral. They reported findings of improved status in children treated with "behavioral play therapy" for shaping speech and stimulus fading with reinforce-ment for generalization as compared with standard school-based remedial programs. A further finding was association of poor prognosis with current or past mental illness in the family. Recommendations included attention to selective mute children in families with mental illness as notably at risk and warranting early intensive treatment, preferably with family involvement.

Most authors indicated the importance of combining family involvement with other approaches due to associated findings with family factors. Meyers (1984), in a review of the available family therapy literature, concluded that elective mutist's families and family dynamics were involved in the symptoma-tology, which expresses a family conflict. Positive outcome was described with family therapy (Carr and Afnan 1989, Furst 1989, Meyers 1984). Improvement in the child was reported in cases in which the mother and child received individual therapy including a case in which the mother only was seen and the child showed parallel improvement (Meyers 1984). Parker and colleagues (1960) described a treatment combination of individual and family therapy with school consultation and reported success with twenty-seven children who all spoke within two years. Lindblad-Goldberg (1986) combined family and play therapy with stimulus fading in the school setting with successful outcomes.

Pharmacological treatment of selective mutism is reported in limited cases in the literature. Reference was made to the nearly universal characteristic of social anxiety with selective mutes. Authors viewed selective mutism as a variant of social phobia and described previous successful pharmacological treatment of social phobia (Black and Uhde 1992, Golwyn and Weinstock 1990). Golwyn and Weinstock (1990) described a 7-year-old girl with a two-year history of mutism treated successfully with phenelzine resulting in increased spontaneous speech that generalized to teachers and peers. Prior to treatment she had been mute, ridiculed by peers, and considered for placement in an emotionally handicapped class. Intellectual ability was above average and blood chemistries and thyroid tests were normal. Her mother had a history of alcohol abuse and her father was treated for panic disorder with phenelzine.

Black and Uhde (1992) reported their treatment of a 12-year-old girl with elective mutism. She began to initiate speech in the classroom and converse spontaneously with peers and adults four weeks after receiving fluoxetine with gains maintained at seven-month follow-up. Family history was notable for parental shyness. The child had a history of separation anxiety until age 5 and social avoidance that increased with age, and she was diagnosed with mild/moderate social anxiety during the treatment phase. Intellectual abilities were in the bright normal range but she had few friends, limited social activities, and was teased and ridiculed by peers. Authors reported dramatic improvements in these two subjects with pharmacological treatment following long-standing sympto-matology and failure to respond to previous nonpharmacological interventions. Conclusions were that the fluoxetine or phenelzine should be considered in similar long-standing cases when they present with significant impairment and other forms of intervention have proven unsuccessful.

Play therapy has also been reported as effective in the treatment of selective mutism. Individual play therapy with a 5- and with a 6-year-old girl resulted in generalization to speech in the school setting (Weininger 1987). Similar results were generated through child play therapy and parent consultation (Parker et al. 1960) and in parent/child play therapy and family therapy (Atlas 1993). Group play therapy was successful in improving speech and social behavior in the classroom (Bozigar and Hansen 1984), and sibling group play therapy (Barlow et al. 1986) also generalized within a two- to nine-month span. Preschoolers with selective mutism have also been shown to benefit from group play interventions as reported by Roe (1993), while Wright and colleagues (1985) reported preschoolers showed positive outcomes with short-term intervention in a six-week diagnostic nursery.

Rationale for Play Therapy

The therapist who begins treatment of a selectively mute child with an initial expectation of speech is likely to experience the mute child's silence as an inevitable insult to one's self-esteem (Ruzicka and Sackin 1974). Exclusive requirements for verbalization from these children become self-defeating in attempts to establish a therapeutic relationship (Barlow et al. 1986) and follow a history of failure in eliciting speech by numerous important adults in the children's lives. Fortunately, play therapy with a seasoned therapist allows for a variety of presentations and does not rely on verbal expression for communication. To the contrary, the use of play as a medium for therapy incorporates the unique qualities of childhood in which play is the child's natural form of communication (Chethik 1989). Such an open stance allows acceptance of silence or actions as communication in themselves and prepares for the dissolution of the barrier of muteness, which has allowed the child to resist other adults as well as children in the past. With the development of an alliance through play, the therapist can move the play through the levels in which interventions can be accomplished.

The typical child with selective mutism and characteristic resistance and anxiety can be addressed in play therapy, which recognizes that the young child's affective world is simultaneously developed and expressed through the active and partially verbal form of play (Sandler et al. 1980). Chethik (1989) discusses differences between adult and child therapy: "The major divergence is the form of communication. The language of the child is more concrete and the dialogue between child and therapist is often in action and behavior, the language of play" (p. 65). According to Anthony (1986), children talk more freely, more spontaneously, and are less defensive through the language of play, regarding it as a special realm removed from the stresses and demands of daily

life. Chethik encourages child therapists to take advantage of play as a specialized form of communication bridging primitive behavior and verbalization by
making the office a "playground" so the child's world can be projected and
therapeutic interventions can occur.

Since play therapy is a medium that views the child's communication at
multiple levels, it allows the child to enter a specialized child-focused experience
in which communicative expressions and interactions are typically expected and
accepted in a variety of forms. Because the child's main problem does not lie in
a lack of language per se but in its application with different people and different
settings, there is ample opportunity to provide the child with a variety of
developmentally appropriate play experiences to build upon their initial level
of functioning. Following the establishment of a foundation of initial acceptance
of interaction via nonverbal communications and play actions, the play therapist just as easily accepts the child's speech, which will follow. This allows the
child to develop self-confidence and the ability to communicate appropriately by
verbal as well as nonverbal means and to combine these rather than to use them
exclusively as he had in the past. Mace and West (1986), in their analysis of
demand conditions associated with reluctant speech in children, suggested play
as a natural comparison, which actually promotes speech in children. Play is
described as a natural situation in which there is freedom from speech demand,
and adult and peer attention are easily accessible. The play therapy approach
contrasts with interventions designed to produce speech on demand. It allows
development of social communication through play, a typical method by which
children interrelate through materials, increasing proximity, joint focus, and
shared experiences during the preschool years (Partin 1932).

Generalization of the new behaviors frequently occurs spontaneously with
other people and in other settings such as the classroom (Barlow et al. 1986,
Parker et al. 1960, Roe 1993, Shreeve 1991) just as these behaviors had emerged
spontaneously within the play therapy sessions. The child's initiations as well as
responses in demand situations and an increasing repertoire of play skills with
peers are also frequently reported by parents and teachers during the therapist's
consultations with them. Verbalizations may also likely be reported by other
adults and children without solicitation given that such occurrences are often
the first observations of spontaneous speech by the child in such settings
following months or even years of silence. Generalization of new ways of
behaving and communicating can also be enabled in other dyadic as well as in
closed and fluid group settings, which can co-occur with individual therapy
work, or the group may represent a primary mode of treatment. The opportunity of the play therapist to further serve in developmental facilitation to other
environments encourages the supportive socialization of the child in settings of
previous withdrawal and silence. The child's innate interest in playing is an
avenue that can easily be further incorporated by the teacher and/or parent
with invitations for peers or siblings as play partners and role models. General-

ization strategies allow the child to continue to develop the self-confidence to communicate ideas and feelings in an age-appropriate manner in all environments including school socialization and educational experiences.

Therapeutic Powers of Play

The advantages of using play therapy for selective mutism can be illustrated by reference to specific curative powers of play proposed by Schaefer (1993). Schaefer posited fourteen factors from which the therapeutic benefits of play therapy derive. Although these benefits are generally viewed as co-occurring during the therapeutic process, they can be discussed separately to permit a clearer representation of the application. The primary therapeutic powers of engagement and treatment involve communication for the expansion of the child's verbal and nonverbal repertoire, overcoming resistance toward development of a collaborative alliance, competency for experience of mastery in play and communicative experiences and growth in self-esteem, and positive emotion to enable expression of a full range of emotions in social interaction including adaptive management of anxiety. Although this discussion will be limited to these four therapeutic factors, it is conceivable that other factors might be added based on the unfolding of the individual case. For example, many mute children have experienced trauma, and abreaction would be employed to assist in their emotional expression of the traumatic experience and mastery and assimilation of the event. Many other mute children require assistance to master developmental fears given their high-frequency identification with anxiety and maladaptive coping abilities. Others with parent/child relationship issues could be best addressed through attachment formation. Role play, game play, and creative thinking would further enhance the selective mute child's social perspective, social interaction, and problem-solving abilities and prognosis for social inclusion. These factors would find generous application in individual as well as group settings.

Communication

Communication issues bring the selective mute child into therapy. These issues, if confined to verbal expression by another approach, could easily revolve around the child's response set of mutism and withdrawal. Fortunately, play therapy views the expression of the child in play as a full expression of the self in childhood. Play is as valuable as verbal expression for communication and even more so in assessing and intervening in the emotional realm (Landreth 1993). As children play out emotions they can become aware, through the therapist's interactions and reflections, of the emotional content associated with their restrictions in affect, behavior, and speech. The opportunity to express a wider range of affects and behaviors evolves as they determine control of their varied emotional levels and become less constricted in their behavior. This allows increased self-awareness and development of a range of degrees of self-control and self-expression.

Choices in materials, play themes, and actions lend content, which, combined with the reflection of accompanying affect, provide the child with information about himself and his experience in vivo. There is no need to await verbal communication, for the child and therapist are in constant ongoing communication through the play. The level of communication may remain within the play metaphor or be drawn to the level of the child's involvement and personal content. Careful bridging is required, however, to avoid confrontational material that could hinder the communicative growth. The level of overt and direct communication from the child may initially be subtle or may be responded to as if intended and be rewarded with more consistent responsiveness. Movement, postures, and gestures provide entrée for responsive communication through mirroring the pace and level at which the child initiates communication as well as providing alternatives in expression for the child to emulate. Offering the child too much verbiage or too quick a pace can result in a break in the rhythm to which the child has become accustomed and comfortable. The pace and responsiveness will vary from child to child and can be viewed in comparison to their historical patterns of speech, fully expressed possibly only at home, and never expressed in other social environments.

The initial vocalizations of the child may evolve through a variety of means such as noisemaking, repetitive sounds, humming, whispers, or verbalizations ranging from monosyllables or phrases to complete thoughts. However, as this phenomenon emerges it becomes only one part of the communicative content incorporated in the ongoing total communication of playing out oneself in the here and now. Over time, the full pattern of communication becomes an envelope within which the child and therapist are increasingly mutually involved in synchrony. The ongoing play also continues to provide content that may be communicated jointly by action and reaction, emotion and emotional response, and comment and reply. The integration of play, thought, emotion, and expression encourages evolution of a more fully experiencing and expressive child characterized by active involvement and open communication. The child can communicate easily with the now-familiar adult therapist and with unfamiliar adults and with peers in a variety of forms and in age-expected situations. Providing a direct communicative transition through other dyads or through groups may or may not be necessary. It should, however, incorporate an initial level of transition that allows the child to maintain self-confidence. Generalization through work with the teacher and parents and other children in the therapy has also been accomplished successfully by this author and other writers (Bozigar and Hansen 1984, Roe 1993).

Overcoming Resistance

Many children are anxious and silent during the initial session of therapy. However, the experience in initial engagement of a selective mute child follows months or years of selective silence and passive resistance likely accompanied by anxiety and withdrawal. Any personal techniques proven fruitful with previous children initially presented as shy, quiet, or withdrawn will certainly meet with a lack of or very limited success with a child who has had a long succession of experiences in selecting a mute response. However, the clarity with which the muteness presents demonstrates the child's limited repertoire of responses for coping with new situations and adults. This is also true for the inhibitions they experience in the environments they regularly attend with other children who are actively and verbally engaged in playing and learning. Bow (1993) stresses the initial importance of having the parents inform the child about the referral. Bow also suggests further steps to overcome resistance such as the factors of the therapist's personality, establishment of the relationship, initial contact, and combining play and therapy.

The engagement of the selectively mute child requires a therapist's communication and the presence of acceptance, support, and extreme patience as the child has not likely been drawn in effectively by an adult stranger in an unfamiliar setting. To the contrary, this is just the type of situation in which the child expresses his disorder. He will also enter this relationship with previous expectations and patterns of behavior. The constant availability, approach through a child-oriented environment and medium, and open communication regarding the purpose and expectations of the play work form a clear and open channel that will eventually be rewarded with an alliance. The development of a therapeutic relationship with the selective mute child has to be successful where countless others have failed to elicit cooperative responses. Therefore, the important traits of patience and keen observation for gradual trends will be well served as they are attributes required and frequently rewarded in child play therapy.

The interrelationship of play and therapy, cemented with the personality and role of the therapist, can yield a significant benefit toward overcoming resistance. The play environment itself and the experience of an accepting adult play partner are likely to be a strict departure from the surrounds in which the mute child has met other adult strangers in the past. The familiar and safe activities allow the child to choose and maintain a comfortable activity and working/playing distance (Chethik 1989) and to assume an active or passive role of his choice. This is going to be unlike previous forced choice or forced speech situations that have frequently been unsuccessful with these children. Previous limitations by active and verbal involvement or passive nonverbal resistance become end points in a broad continuum. The child finds himself in a unique environment where he can find acceptance and reward in being himself and, with decreased resistance, align himself with the therapist in discovering many other ways to act, feel, and express himself.

Competence

The child with selective mutism, now in school and already perceived with questionable social and academic competence, is likely to be infrequently expected to speak or assumed not to know the response requested by the teacher. Classmates inform newcomers to the classroom that this child "can't talk." Peer relationships that develop are often dependent ones with other children speaking for the child, and expectations are reflected to him that he never will speak. Teasing by peers will ensue with increasing age and has likely already begun from his siblings. Countless opportunities to engage in desired or special activities have been lost due to an inability to make verbal requests or to respond verbally. Other opportunities that might be tempting and pleasurable are forgone to avoid the potential of having to meet new people. The feeling of being "frozen" or wanting to run away continues to emerge in new situations and with new people. There is no realization of how to request assistance in these new situations or even to verbally express to the teacher the need to go to the bathroom or describe conditions of illness, pain, or mistreatment by other children. Behavioral problems at home are frequent. Parents and teachers are exhausted with the child's continued cloak of silence, which returns daily as the child approaches the school. Coping by passive avoidance or silence has become an increasingly difficult and unrewarding way of life. The child, however, knows no alternatives within his repertoire as he has likely been experiencing an insidious onset of shyness and determination not to communicate verbally from the earliest years of life (Kolvin and Fundudis 1981, Wright 1968).

The opportunity to play and grow in competence with a supportive adult in therapy can allow the selective mute child a second chance to experience and internalize some measure of control and mastery in his life. His long-term experience and framework of approaching life full of anxiety and fears have resulted in a motivation toward avoidance and rigid passivity rather than involvement and persistence to mastery. Play can provide the invaluable link for the child to generate and develop new skills and a sense of accomplishment and control in his world. With proceedings continually and specifically focused on the results of his own efforts, the process allows for differentiation of previous rigid patterns of noninvolvement and withdrawal to full involvement only in specified situations and with specified people.

The ongoing experience in problem solving through play allows the child to internalize an approach to resolution of difficult situations with less rigid patterns and more adaptive responses. Through a close matching of skills to challenge, the child can gain competencies while enjoying the process (Csiks-zentmihalyi 1989, 1990). Play and the development of competencies are interrelated. According to Kirschenblatt-Gimblett (1979), "The idea is that there is a kind of play-competence spiral: learning leads to more sophisticated play, and play provides a kind of mastery that leads to more learning, which leads to more sophisticated play, and so forth" (p. 23). However, the mere provision of play materials and a play environment will no more encourage the social/verbal competencies or play interactions of a mute child than having been on the playground or in the company of age-appropriate peers. Such models have long been available and the child continues to be limited in social/verbal play interactions and competencies. It is, rather, the mediated quality in the play that allows the child to transcend his previous rigid boundaries. The adult serves as a developmental facilitator or "filter" between the child and the environment to encourage, focus, extend, and reflect on the child's achievements as they occur (Yawkey 1982). This interaction encourages the transmission of intellectual and emotional resources and the development of the child's social, emotional, and cognitive competencies.

Vygotsky (1978) describes a construct termed "ZPD, the zone of proximal development" (p. 86). This construct represents the distance between the child's actual independent developmental problem-solving skills and his developmental ability with mediation. This perspective has been supported in the idea that social pretend play (Miller and Garvey 1984) and language skills (Sachs 1980) are derived through social interaction with the child and a play partner. The length and complexity of play episodes have been shown to increase through mediation by a teacher as compared with peer play episodes (Bruner 1980). According to Bruner (1984) the mediator provides a scaffold or framework including the provision of a stimulating environment, assisting the child to make choices, and reflecting on the child's achievements and mastery. This enables the child to reflect and verbalize his own competence. This process, from external action of play to internalized symbolic levels, provides a basis for guiding future actions. Thus, play mediated by adults can yield the most complex levels of play and language as well as sustained involvement.

The child self-selects the elements of content of his or her life to play through to mastery, thus avoiding the negative feelings associated with the real-life event. Erikson (1950) posited that young children could improve their coping abilities for feared real-life situations through playing out fear-related mastery themes. Such mastery-oriented play has been shown to result in subsequent reduction of anxiety in the feared situation with children as young as preschoolers (Erickson 1958, Parks 1988). It has also been effective in engendering the social self-confidence of selective mute children to independently and spontaneously speak in school for the first time (Barlow et al. 1986, Parker et al. 1960, Roe 1993, Shreeve 1991).

Positive Emotion

According to Schaefer (1993), the beneficial outcome of positive emotion in play therapy is an ego boost. This is derived through the experience of fun and enjoyment in play, which is restorative from emotions of anxiety and negative expectations. The child with selective mutism has frequently gone through the motions of playing and relating outside the home but has often been denied the positive emotions that could accompany and encourage further risks in those directions.

The entrée to the therapeutic relationship through play and the playful dimension involved encourage the experience and expression of positive emotion. Discussion of competence has previously alluded to the gradual assimilation and relief in the realm of anxiety through mastery play. This gradual change is also accompanied by the potential for alternative pleasurable experiences to replace those previously anxiety evoking. This would be highly beneficial to selective mute children who are frequently socially withdrawn or avoidant and experience extreme anxiety when there is a requirement to interact with strangers (Black and Uhde 1992, Golwyn and Weinstock 1990, Lesser-Katz 1988, Shreeve 1991). A significant benefit of play therapy for selective mute children would then come from their experience of enjoyment and freedom in child-oriented, self-chosen activities to counteract the anxiety and self-restriction experienced in the past. This would encourage the desire to reexperience pleasurable activities with other children and adults with an expectation of a positive outcome rather than the previously evoked fear and avoidance. The benefits to the child will experientially develop in areas of competencies and increased self-esteem, social communication, enhanced relationships, and the alleviation of anxiety. However, the engagement of the child and his motive for risking change lies in large measure in the positive emotions and experiences he internalizes in the sessions and the expectation that they will recur.

The referral source(s), likely the school and/or parents, probably hold expectation for successful intervention with the occurrence of generalized speech alone. They may not be aware of the child's holistic experience in attempting to deal with the unfamiliar world of unfamiliar people that confronts him by multiples with increasing age. It would then become incumbent upon the therapist to encourage the broader view of success for the child himself as intra- as well as interpersonal. Not only would success be assessed if he would speak when adults deem it required or appropriate for him to do so, but also that the emotional transition can be accomplished in service to the child. There is evidence that these improvements move in parallel to the improvements in speech (Kolvin and Fundudis 1981). It might begin with an appreciation of the emotional issues of anxiety and/or anger as well as the frustration with the outward nonverbal behavior that drove the search for treatment. A full circle can then be accomplished allowing the child to develop the ability to enjoy playing and communicating so he moves forward with the skills and positive orientation that he lacked at the onset to meet future challenges of childhood.

Approach

A suggested approach used with success in nine previous cases, and partial success with one child withdrawn prematurely to enter speech therapy, has utilized centrally and foremost individual client-centered child play therapy with an adjunct parent and teacher consultation model. As always, the path of this type of work varies with the needs of the child. Experience has borne out in these cases that the children lead in the manner and direction of their priority need for the process. Many of these children expressed their changed perceptions through metaphorical stories with puppets or play figures:

> "There was a fish who always swam under the water. He learned how to swim to the top and peep out and then to leap out and look around and now he is a flying fish."

> "A white mouse was always hiding. Then it learned how to play pranks on people and hide and laugh. These are two girls. They are bored. They will go to the beach. One girl is going to put her head in the sand but she is just playing."

> "This is a turtle who took 100 years to come out of its shell. It finally got some glasses and came out and looked around and said, 'It sure has taken me a long time to get here.' "

The metaphorical transformations were also accompanied by physical movements to a new place or a higher ground indicative of a shift or change in perspective. Careful observation of their thematic content with emotional resolutions and conceptual clarifications has moved in tandem with increased expressive skills and use of speech in the individual sessions. In turn, this has led to gradually generalizing self-confidence and speech in their various environments as well as in new settings and with new people.

When children initially also exhibited separation anxiety, one of the parents would be included in the play session and phased out, generally in the first session but sometimes requiring several sessions. During the course of the work, various techniques have been used or made available including puppetry, use of telephones and tape recorders, photography, and structured game play. Variations in settings or conditions have been introduced at times including working in different areas of the clinic setting, having visits outside or in the park, playing at school in various areas within which the child's school day would occur, bringing a friend or siblings into the session, and participating in small groups or fluid groups.

Initial assessments were conducted through parent and teacher interviews, child observations, direct or indirect evaluations of the child, and behavioral checklists. Understanding the parent/child relationship is part of this process, and modifying problems in the relationship may need to be a part of the treatment plan. Likewise, some essentials are assessing the teacher/child relationship and developing positive strategies for addressing the child in the classroom. Information regarding previous interventions and their degree of success or failure is also important. Ongoing assessments were conducted through the progress in the play sessions, parent and teacher reports, and observations in the school settings at intervals. Interestingly, all but one case self-generalized to the school setting with spontaneous as well as demand speech and varying degrees of social initiation.

Follow-up at periods of one to five years posttreatment has indicated that the children seen in individual play therapy continue to speak in school, in new situations, to generalize their play skills, and to make new friends. Several rarely initiated verbally in the full group classroom but would respond when the teacher called on them and would speak spontaneously in small groups within the class. The length of therapy ranged from four months to 1½ years. All of the children had normal to above normal intelligence and three had diagnosed speech and language disorders. They ranged in age from 3½ to 9 years with 50 percent preschoolers, 30 percent kindergartners, and 20 percent in elementary school. Only one child required repeated school visits and classroom interventions to generalize verbal skills to that setting. The child who withdrew prematurely had followed a speech therapy model and moved from selective mutism to reluctant speech.

The parent and teacher work also varied based on the needs and progress of the child. Recommendations included play materials based on the child's interests and skills with which to encourage play and socialization, dyadic play with the addition of a play partner and progression to a fluid group, and outings that would result in immediate rewards for speech such as requesting a free cookie at the bakery or ordering in a fast-food restaurant. Some parents or teachers have also required consultation in behavioral and/or anxiety management for assisting the child at home or at school.

The work with the children requires patience and a total focus on the observably gradual although individually monumental changes in their patterns. The support and involvement of the parents and teachers require follow-up, encouragement, and provision of suggestions they can implement that are likely to result in some observable measure of success. By the time the children are referred for professional help, they have usually been mute for months or years and teachers and parents have implemented numerous strategies in attempts to elicit speech from them. However, parents and teachers will inevitably expect a global and rapid cure when the referral is finally made. Their active involvement has multiple benefits. They provide support for the child's encouragement of effort. Ongoing work outside the session serves to generalize and strengthen the child's skills and increase self-confidence. It also serves to prevent repetition of previous unsuccessful efforts in frustration to elicit speech with threats, punishments, and admonishments, which can result in setbacks to the change process that has been set in motion.

Case Illustration

Reason for Referral and Background

Roth was referred by his parents at age 3 years, 9 months on the recommendation of his preschool and a psychologist friend of the family. Although the child had not spoken in school for over a year, the referral was prompted when the teacher observed another child standing on his hand and, although he was in obvious pain, Roth uttered no sound. Prior to this year, he had spoken to a few classmates individually but even that speech ceased after December break and never returned. He frequently returned home with his lunch unopened because he did not ask for assistance. He refrained from asking to go to the bathroom resulting in an accident and other near accidents. The other children, aware of his silence, picked on him and blamed him for problems in the classroom, aware that he would not express denial or blame others.

Socialization and play skills were immature. Play with peers consisted primarily of playing "chase" games without verbalization although he would sometimes emit a squeal, chase, and wait for them to reverse roles. At group activities, such as birthday parties, he remained on the periphery. He was physical and pushy regarding his space and materials with peers and at home with his younger sister.

Behavior at home was described as frequently oppositional. He overreacted when disciplined. He was further described as perfectionistic and compulsive with behavior patterns that were fixed and rigid. He spoke with parents and his sibling but did not speak when adults or other children came into the home. He did not speak on the telephone even to grandparents. When the family went out in public, he asked his parents to speak for him.

Medical and Developmental History

Prenatal, birth, and developmental histories were unremarkable excepting temperamental shyness and selective mutism. Parents had first noted his social withdrawal at a child's birthday party when he was 2. When he saw all the children and adults in the group, he put his head down and became silent. After this observation, the parents began to notice he would put his face in his hands and lie down when spoken to by unfamiliar persons. Similar patterns of shyness and withdrawal continued into preschool where he was sometimes verbal with a few peers and then mute for over a year prior to referral.

Psychosocial

Roth was the older of two children. Father was a physician. Mother completed two years of college. Father volunteered a history of being "morbidly shy," which continued into adulthood. He viewed his personal life as a "highly predictable life pattern, not a social animal." He continued to experience discomfort in groups of people. Mother had been academically and socially successful in school and described herself as talkative. She viewed part of her role as making the social contacts for the family. The younger child, a daughter, age 2½, rarely spoke in preschool, although she had been highly verbal at home prior to entry. Parents described Roth as exhibiting a variety of interests at home including games, books, educational computer games, and sports activities. No incidence of trauma, major illness, or separation from parents was identified.

Assessment

Procedures used included parent interview and referral history, the Behavioral Style Questionnaire (McDevitt and Carey 1975), the Child Behavior Checklist (Achenbach 1988), the Developmental Profile-II (Alpern et al. 1984), developmental checklists, play and behavioral observations, and school observation and teacher interview.

Results

Parent ratings on the child temperament questionnaire were notably elevated for withdrawal, consistent with the Achenbach checklist on which withdrawal was above the 98th percentile. Parent report on the Developmental Profile-II represented development within normal limits on physical, self-help, social, academic, and communication domains. Unobtrusive language sample and observations of preschool skills indicated language within normal limits and weaknesses in fine motor coordination. Observations at school revealed an attentive child whose behavior in the larger group was withdrawn with head dropped and fingers in his mouth or pulling at his lip. During small group activities, he seemed less preoccupied and somewhat more spontaneous and involved. He was nonverbal.

Initial Stage

During the initial stage efforts were directed toward providing opportunities for interaction through play including verbal and nonverbal communication.

Resistance was met by mirroring and following the child's lead and pace, level of communication, and interests. Increasing opportunities were provided within which the child could respond and initiate in the individual work, and these were further encouraged outside the sessions through the parents and teachers. Emotional content was attended to and labeled, with particular attention to and joining in of positive affects while offering or modeling age-appropriate alternatives for coping. The child's competencies in range of play skills increased as did communication, which moved from avoidance to noisemaking and whispering, including some initial verbal requests for assistance.

Therapy

During the initial stages of therapy, Roth was verbal with his mother in the waiting room but he became immediately silent when the therapist entered the room. His affect with mother was positive and his speech was spontaneous and age appropriate. His initial level of play was categorization, with lining up of like toy vehicles. There was some noisemaking but no speech. As his work progressed, he began to introduce people into the vehicles and to whisper to himself. Occasionally, he would laugh aloud. His affect began to brighten when he showed off by performing tricks with toys. Increasing complexity began to emerge in his play. He turned his back when there was any discussion of the purpose of his work but obviously listened intently as his movements ceased. Following one such discussion, he introduced the toy school bus filled with children en route to a school. Then he placed all the children standing on top of their desks with the teacher on the roof of the building, which he viewed as quite comical. When one child fell from his perch, he placed him in a toy wheelchair. Then he initiated a telephone call to the therapist and related his first spoken message, a three-sentence request for help from the fallen child.

Consultation

During this period, Roth's teacher was quite frustrated as he continued to be totally nonverbal at school. A plan was determined for her to observe which child or children he exhibited interest in so that she could place them together with more frequency. Mother would be encouraged to invite these children home to play. Parents were telling metaphorical stories to Roth at home, "Russ Stories," regarding a resilient child who overcame his fears. He asked for them repeatedly and they were told frequently. His first public speech was reported when he attended a birthday party and spoke to his parents aloud in the presence of the group. Their primary complaints at this time were behavioral and strategies were developed to reward compliance at home. They had begun to invite more playmates to the home and to reward the child for risk taking, "being 4 years old." They were also differentially attending to age-appropriate rather than regressive speech. Roth was beginning to talk on the telephone, although he was using infantile speech.

Middle Stage

During the middle stage, communication through play had increased to enable a working through of the child's issues, which were replaced by his own emerging focus on competency. Following previous experiences in playing out, labeling, and coping with emotional content, he became intense and spontaneous in playing out a full range of emotions including positive emotion with frequent laughter. Communication now included a variety of vocalizations, noisemaking, gestures, and play with increased use of speech in his normal voice and all used appropriately to context. He was exhibiting increased ability to control his actions and voice and use them purposefully including participation in play and game activities with peers through corrective developmental experiences being offered in play therapy as well as by his parents and teacher. Risk taking was encouraged by reinforcing trying "something new" and "being 4."

Therapy

Roth continued to exhibit increasing animation and intense affect ranging from loud laughter to aggression in the sessions. He also continued to communicate by the telephone announcing himself by "Hello" and then saying a few sentences in his normal voice. He began to speak in the waiting room in a normal tone having progressed from silence to whispering when the therapist entered the room.

He began to incorporate in his play a hospital as well as the school and school bus. He filled the school bus with children and moved it toward the school building accompanied by a variety of vocalizations including humming, motor sounds, laughing, and periodic speech. He continued to place the teacher atop the school and the students on top of their desks. From this representation emerged a powerful and destructive boy figure who flew around wildly in a helicopter and destroyed the entire school area. An angry policeman followed and knocked the teacher down, after which all the children were able to fly away. There also emerged a playhouse near the school area where figures lived and interacted verbally and playfully. There was increasing and bolder use of his voice with the emergence of the powerful boy figure.

During successive play with the above content, all the child figures became more powerful by mounting one anothers' shoulders when they were in the school building. Later, there was destruction of the entire scene by the child, himself, portrayed as a playful giant. Over time, the teacher was reintroduced in a whimsical manner leaping to the roof accompanied by the child figures as they all slid playfully down the chimney together. The variations in his speech continued to increase to include different vocalizations or voices for different characters. He introduced the effect of being trapped with children locked in lockers but able to escape independently and fly around the room.

The play was becoming less forceful and destructive. One day the wrecking of the school took a new resolution with the children each individually transported to a new place, the playhouse where interaction included speech. Each was given an individual place to sit in the new house. The policeman was trapped in the locker while all the children escaped to the new place in safety. Roth continued to initiate telephone calls and speak in his normal voice. Sometimes he would respond through the figure of Oscar the Grouch who would peep out, then close the lid on his garbage can to indicate he did not want to talk, while other times he would be appropriately conversant. After the session in which the children were safely transported to a new place, he began to express an interest in structured games and in bringing his friend to the sessions. He was able to play appropriately in dyads and groups of up to four children and maintain appropriate use of speech.

Consultation

During this period, parents had been inviting children to the home to play. Roth was interacting well in these dyads and learning to play board games. He was beginning to engage in dramatic play and perform "shows" with his friends. He had been talking to his swimming teacher. Parents planned to add his sister to the swimming lessons and gradually incorporate other children. The summer camp counselor reported that Roth had verbally expressed his dislike of another child's interference with his project. When he spoke, the children yelled and clapped. The counselor was going to encourage children to approach him singly in play more frequently and to provide more opportunities for him to respond verbally. By this time, he would ask for a cookie at the bakery and order in fast-food restaurants. The teacher was providing the parents with songs and recitations used in the classroom to practice at home. She was also incorporating the games he enjoyed at home and in the play therapy sessions in the classroom.

Final Stage

The final stage focused on generalization and preparation for termination of direct services. Increased efforts were directed in enabling communication, self-confidence, and competence in all his environments including preparation for a new school. This included consultation with the current and new school and simulations with Roth to prepare for participation with his class on stage in a school program and for being interviewed and evaluated at a new school. Use of audiotape enabled simulations as well as self-modeling. His abilities continued to generalize through the help of his parents and teacher and his increased self-confidence and skills.

Therapy

Roth continued to evidence an interest and enjoyment in playing board games. He expressed his preferences for favorites as well as trying "something new" each session. During a visit to the school, the therapist and teacher worked two fluid play groups with Roth laughing aloud. This was the first time the teacher had heard his voice. The frequency of loud and spontaneous laughter and sense of humor became more obvious in the playroom and at school. Children informed the teacher, "If you make Roth laugh, he'll talk to you." Roth began to closely observe and model the social behavior of his friends. In individual sessions, he introduced a series of puppet shows in which characters were all initially aggressive and noisy. He was the "boy" who introduced the "scary show" and he had the idea that the story should be saved on audiotape. The puppet shows evolved not only through the transformation of aggressive animals, whose negative qualities were changed by magical characters, but also through Roth's announcements at the beginning of the shows about the anger and fear the characters would display as well as his means of control of their emotional changes. He described the changes as moving from "scary" to "funny" puppet shows. "There is the turtle who was too afraid. He heard a noise and went inside. It sounded like a scary thing. He didn't know what it was. The other puppet told him to sing. The turtle will always go in the shell when I talk to him and come out when I tell him not to be scared."

The series of puppet shows continued to be taped and Roth took them home and listened to them and played them for his parents. During this period, Roth was involved in a school play and sang with his group on stage but stopped whenever his teachers looked at him. In the session following the school program he expressed his plan for a longer story, "a singing talking puppet show for both sides on the tape." He announced each character and had them step up to the recorder and speak at his cue. During the following session, he announced a new character, "the flying boy puppet." He pulled back the curtains of the puppet stage to reveal that he, himself, would play the new role on the stage and that the story should comprise two tapes, front and back, and be played in his class. With this began an exchange of tapes with the teacher in which the classroom activities of the day would be provided for use as speech background in the play sessions and she would be involved with the puppet show tapes. The continued puppet show stories also incorporated new casts of characters including the Tin Man from *The Wizard of Oz* who was perched atop the puppet stage. "The Tin Man is resting on top of the stage. He will speak when they find him. He is not ready to talk but when they see him he starts to talk." Following this puppetry, Roth moved out of the playroom to visit and play games in the adjoining kitchen area. In this setting, he was appropriately verbal during visits in which he chose to play board games. Preparation for termination was begun and visits included playing outside, in the park, at his school, and within various other settings where his speech continued to generalize.

Consultation

By this time, Roth had begun to speak to his teacher on the telephone and was increasingly reported to speak with peers in school. The school program in which he sang with his class appeared to have been a breakthrough for him with his peers. He was speaking with company in the home and also in the carpool. He had begun to answer questions from strangers and talk on the telephone in his full voice. He had been to a new school and was individually tested and accepted for kindergarten with no observations of any atypical behavior or reluctant speech. This marked less than one year from the initial session during which he had been seen for weekly half-hour visits.

Roth is currently in kindergarten and speaks in the classroom group. He has verbally participated in several school programs including singing and dancing with his class. He has friends at school and invites them to play afterward. His parents continue to have close involvement with the school and the speech/language coordinator who consults with the teacher on increasing his initiation skills in the classroom.

Conclusion

Information is available to assist with the early identification and treatment of selective mute children including factors that present the highest risk and indicate the need for family work. Children whose early treatment results in speech have the best prognosis and can circumvent secondary factors of social, emotional, and educational problems. Roe (1993) attributes successful outcome in therapy to early identification, treatment, and generalization "early in their school lives before patterns of behavior and relating had become too firmly set" (p. 139). We need not repeat the previous long waiting periods to see if children will "grow out of it." When a child is severely withdrawn and not interacting with others after the initial period in school, urgent attention is required (Tough 1976). The young child in the case study represents a typical age at presentation. He now enjoys social and educational experiences and successes to help balance the disappointments and failures that will also come. He has a voice with which to share all of these and the means for playing them out as well. He does not have to wait and suffer in silence. Neither should the others.

References

Achenbach, T. (1988). *Child Behavior Checklist for Ages 2–3*. Burlington, VT: University of Vermont.

Albert-Stewart, P. (1986). Positive reinforcement in short-term treatment of an elective mute child: a case study. *Psychological Reports* 58:571–576.

Alpern, G., Boll, T., and Shearer, M. (1984). *Developmental Profile-II*. Los Angeles, CA: Western Psychological Services.

American Psychiatric Association. (1980). *Diagnostic and Statistical Manual of Mental Disorders*, 3rd ed. Washington, DC: APA.

American Psychiatric Association. (1987). *Diagnostic and Statistical Manual of Mental Disorders*, 3rd ed., rev. Washington, DC: APA.

American Psychiatric Association. (1994). *Diagnostic and Statistical Manual of Mental Disorders*, 4th ed. Washington, DC: APA.

Anthony, E. (1986). The contribution of child psychoanalysis. *Psychoanalytic Study of the Child* 41:61–87. New Haven, CT: Yale University Press.

Atlas, J. (1993). Symbol use in a case of elective mutism. *Perceptual and Motor Skills* 76:1079–1082.

Atoynatan, T. (1986). Elective mutism: involvement of the mother in the treatment of the child. *Child Psychiatry and Human Development* 17(1):15–27.

Austed, L., Sininger, R., and Stricken, A. (1980). Successful treatment of a case of elective mutism. *Behavioral Therapist* 3(1):18–19.

Axline, V. (1969). *Play Therapy*, rev. ed. New York: Ballantine.

Bakwin, H., and Bakwin, R. (1972). *Behavior Disorders in Children*. Philadelphia: W. B. Saunders.

Barlow, K., Strother, J., and Landreth, G. (1986). Sibling group play therapy: an effective alternative with an elective mute child. *School Counselor* 34(1):44–50.

Bauermeister, J., and Jemail, J. (1975). Modification of "elective mutism" in the classroom setting: a case study. *Behavior Therapy* 6:245–250.

Black, M., and Uhde, T. (1992). Elective mutism as a variant of social phobia. *Journal of the American Academy of Child and Adolescent Psychiatry* 31:711–718.

Blake, P., and Moss, T. (1967). The development of socialization skills in an electively mute child. *Behavior Research and Therapy* 5:349–356.

Bow, J. (1993). Overcoming resistance. In *The Therapeutic Powers of Play*, ed. C. Schaefer, pp. 17–40. Northvale, NJ: Jason Aronson.

Bozigar, J., and Hansen, R. (1984). Group treatment of elective mute children. *Social Work* 29:478–480.

Bradley, S., and Sloman, L. (1975). Elective mutism in immigrant families. *Journal of the American Academy of Child Psychiatry* 14:510–514.

Brown, J., and Lloyd, H. (1975). A controlled study of children not speaking at school. *Journal of the Association of Workers with Maladjusted Children* 3:49–63.

Browne, E., Wilson, V., and Laybourne, P. (1963). Diagnosis and treatment of elective mutism in children. *Journal of the American Academy of Child Psychiatry* 2:605–617.

Bruner, J. (1980). *Under Five in Britain*. Ypsilanti, MI: High/Scope Press.

———— (1984). *Child's Talk*. New York: Norton.

Calhoun, J., and Koenig, R. (1973). Classroom modification of elective mutism. *Behavior Therapy* 4:700–702.

Carr, A., and Afnan, S. (1989). Concurrent individual and family therapy in a case of elective mutism. *Journal of Family Therapy* 11:29–44.

Chethik, M. (1989). *Techniques of Child Therapy: Psychodynamic Strategies*. New York: Guilford.

Cline, T., and Kysel, F. (1987). Children who refuse to speak. *Children and Society* 4:327–334.

Colligan, R. W., Colligan, R. C., and Dillard, M. (1977). Contingency management in the classroom treatment of long-term elective mutism: a case report. *Journal of School Psychology* 15:9–17.

Commission on Professional and Hospital Activities. (1978). *International Classification of Diseases (9th rev.)—Clinical Modification*. Ann Arbor, MI: Author.

Conrad, R., Delk, J., and Williams, C. (1974). Use of stimulus fading procedures in the treatment of situation specific mutism: a case study. *Journal of Behavior Therapy and Experimental Psychiatry* 5:99–100.

Crumley, F. (1990). The masquerade of mutism. *Journal of the American Academy of Child and Adolescent Psychiatry* 29:318–319.

———— (1993). Is elective mutism a social phobia? *Journal of the American Academy of Child and Adolescent Psychiatry* 32:1081–1982.

Csikszentmihalyi, M. (1989). Optimal experience in work and leisure. *Journal of Personality and Social Psychology* 56:815–822.

———— (1990). *Flow: The Psychology of Optimal Experience*. New York: Harper and Row.

Cunningham, L., Cataldo, M., Mallion, C., and Keyes, J. (1983). A review of controlled single-case evaluations of behavioral approach to the management of elective mutism. *Child and Family Behavior Therapy* 5:25–49.

Dmitriev, V., and Hawkins, J. (1974). Susie never used to say a word. *Teaching Exceptional Children* 6:68–76.

Eldar, S., Bleich, A., Apter, A., and Tyano, S. (1985). Elective mutism: an atypical antecedent of schizophrenia. *Journal of Adolescence* 8:289–292.

Elson, A., Pearson, C., Jones, D., and Schumacher, E. (1965). Follow-up study of childhood elective mutism. *Archives of General Psychiatry* 13:182–187.

Erickson, F. (1958). Play interview for four-year-old hospitalized children. *Monographs of the Society for Research in Child Development* 23 (serial no.

69).

Erikson, E. (1950). *Childhood and Society.* New York: Norton.

Friedman, R., and Karagan, N. (1973). Characteristics and management of elective mutism in children. *Psychology in the Schools* 10:249–254.

Fundudis, J., Kolvin, I., and Garside, R. (1979). *Speech Retarded or Deaf Children: Their Psychological Development.* London: Academic Press.

Furst, A. (1989). Elective mutism: report of a case study successfully treated by a family doctor. *Israel Journal of Psychiatry and Related Sciences* 26:96–102.

Golwyn, D., and Weinstock, R. (1990). Phenelzine treatment of elective mutism: a case report. *Journal of Clinical Psychiatry* 51:384–385.

Griffith, E., Schnelle, J., McNees, M., et al. (1975). Elective mutism in a first grader: the remediation of a complex behavioral problem. *Journal of Abnormal Child Psychology* 3:127–234.

Halpern, W., Hammond, J., and Cohen, R. (1971). A therapeutic approach to speech phobia: elective mutism re-examined. *Journal of the American Academy of Child Psychiatry* 10:94–107.

Hayden, T. (1980). Classification of elective mutism. *Journal of the American Academy of Child Psychiatry* 19:118–133.

Heil, M., Kunze-Turmann, M., Fegert, J., and Meitinger, H. (1985). Home treatment. *Zeitschrift fur kinder-und Jugend-psychiatrie* 6:163–176.

Hesselman, S. (1983). Elective mutism in children: 1877–1981. *Acta Paedopsychiatrica: International Journal of Child and Adolescent Psychiatry* 49:297–310.

Holmbeck, G., and Lavigne, J. (1992). Combining self-modeling and stimulus fading in the treatment of an electively mute child. *Psychotherapy* 29:661–667.

Hooper, S., and Linz, T. (1992). Elective mutism. In *Child Psychopathology: Diagnostic Criteria and Clinical Assessment,* ed. S. Hooper, G. Hind, and R. Mattison, pp. 409–459. Hillsdale, NJ: Lawrence Erlbaum.

Kaplan, H., and Sadock, B. (1981). *Modern Synopsis of Comprehensive Textbook of Psychiatry.* Baltimore: Williams and Wilkins.

Kaplan, S. L., and Escoll, P. (1973). Treatment of two silent adolescent girls. *Journal of the American Academy of Child Psychiatry* 12:59–71.

Kehle, T., Owen, S., and Cressy, E. (1990). The use of self-modeling of an intervention in school psychology: a case study of an elective mute. *School Psychology Review* 19:115–121.

Kirschenblatt-Gimblett, B. (1979). What is good play? In *Learning Through Play,* ed. P. Chance, pp. 218–224. New York: Gardner.

Kolvin, I., and Fundudis, T. (1981). Elective mute children: psychological development and background factors. *Journal of Child Psychology and Psychiatry* 22:219–232.

Kratochwill, T. (1981). *Selective Mutism: Implications for Treatment and Research.* Hillsdale, NJ: Lawrence Erlbaum.

Kratochwill, T., Bordy, G., and Pearsel, W. (1979). Elective mutism in children. In *Advances in Clinical Child Psychology*, ed. B. Lahey and A. Kazden, pp. 193–240. New York: Plenum.

Krohn, D., Weckstein, S., and Wright, H. (1992). A study of the effectiveness of a specific treatment for elective mutism. *Journal of the American Academy of Child and Adolescent Psychiatry* 31:711–718.

Krolian, E. (1988). Speech is silver, but silence is golden: day hospital treatment of two electively mute children. *Clinical Social Work Journal* 16:355–377.

Kupietz, S., and Schwartz, I. (1982). Elective mutism: evaluation and behavioral treatment of three cases. *New York State Journal of Medicine* 82:1073–1076.

Kurth, E., and Schweigert, K. (1972). Causes and courses of mutism in children. *Psychiatrie, Neurologie, und Medizinische Psychologie* 24:741–749.

Labbe, E., and Williamson, D. (1984). Behavioral treatment of elective mutism: a review of the literature. *Clinical Psychology Review* 4:273–293.

Lachenmeyer, J., and Gibbs, M. (1985). The social-psychological functions of reward in the treatment of a case of elective mutism. *Journal of Social and Clinical Psychology* 3:466–473.

Landreth, G. (1993). Self-expressive communication. In *The Therapeutic Powers of Play*, ed. C. Schaefer, pp. 41–63. Northvale, NJ: Jason Aronson.

Laybourne, P. (1979). Elective mutism. In *Basic Handbook of Child Psychiatry*, vol. 2, ed. J. Noshpitz. New York: Basic Books.

Lazarus, P., Gavilo, H., and Moore, J. (1983). The treatment of elective mutism in children within the school setting: two case studies. *School Psychology Review* 12:467–472.

Lesser-Katz, M. (1986). Stranger reaction and elective mutism in young children. *American Journal of Orthopsychiatry* 56:458–469.

———— (1988). The treatment of elective mutism as stranger anxiety. *Psychotherapy* 25:305–313.

Lindblad-Goldberg, M. (1986). Elective mutism in families with young children. *Family Therapy Collections* 18:31–42.

Louden, D. (1987). Elective mutism: case study of a disorder of childhood. *Journal of the National Medical Association* 79:1043–1048.

Mace, F., and West, B. (1986). Analyzing of demand conditions associated with reluctant speech. *Journal of Behavior Therapy and Experimental Psychiatry* 17:285–294.

McDevitt, S., and Carey, W. (1975). *Behavioral Style Questionnaire*. Phoenix, AZ: Manuscript Copy.

Meijer, A. (1979). Elective mutism in children. *Israel Annals of Psychiatry and Related Disciplines* 17:93–100.

Meyers, S. (1984). Elective mutism in children: a family system approach. *American Journal of Family Therapy* 12:39–45.

Miller, P., and Garvey, C. (1984). Mother–baby role play. In *Symbolic Play*, ed. I. Bretherton, pp. 101–130. New York: Academic Press.

Mitchell, J. (1985). Long standing elective mutism. *College of Speech Therapists Bulletin* 395:1.

Mora, F., Devault, S., and Schopler, E. (1962). Dynamics and psychotherapy of identical twins with elective mutism. *Journal of Child Psychology and Psychiatry* 3:41–52.

Morin, C., Ladovceur, R., and Cloutier, R. (1982). Reinforcement procedure in the treatment of reluctant speech. *Journal of Behavior Therapy and Experimental Psychiatry* 13:145–147.

Murray, D. (1983). A stubborn silence. *Nursing Mirror*, November, pp. 38–42.

Parker, E., Olsen, T., and Throckmorton, M. (1960). Social casework with elementary school children who do not talk in school. *Social Work* 5:64–70.

Parks, J. (1988). Play and anxiety reduction in fearful preschool children. *Dissertation Abstracts International* 50(10-B):4780.

Partin, M. (1932). Social participation among preschool children. *Journal of Abnormal and Social Psychology* 27:243–269.

Piersel, W., and Kratochwill, T. (1981). A teacher-implemented contingency management package to assess and treat selective mutism. *Behavioral Assessment* 3:371–382.

Pigott, H., and Gonzales, F. (1987). Efficacy of videotape self-modeling in treating an electively mute child. *Journal of Clinical Child Psychology* 16:106–110.

Pustrom, E., and Speers, R. (1964). Elective mutism in children. *The Journal of the American Academy of Child Psychiatry* 3:287–297.

Reed, F. (1963). Elective mutism in children: a re-appraisal. *Journal of Child Psychology and Psychiatry* 4:99–107.

Rees, J. (1986). A case of elective mutism in a five year old girl. *Behavioral Approaches with Children* 10:7–12.

Reid, J., Hawkins, N., Keutzer, C., et al. (1967). A marathon behavior modification of a selectively mute child. *Journal of Child Psychology and Psychiatry* 8:27–30.

Richards, C., and Hansen, M. (1978). A further demonstration of the efficacy of stimulus fading treatment of elective mutism. *Journal of Behavior Therapy and Experimental Psychiatry* 9:57–60.

Richburg, M., and Cobia, D. (1994). Using behavioral techniques to treat elective mutism: a case study. *Elementary School Guidance and Counseling* 28:214–220.

Roe, V. (1993). An interactive therapy group. *Child Language Teaching and Therapy* 9:133–140.

Rosenbaum, E., and Kellman, M. (1973). Treatment of a selectively mute third-grade child. *Journal of School Psychology* 11:26–29.

Ruzicka, B., and Sackin, H. (1974). Elective mutism: the impact of the patient's silent approach upon the therapist. *Journal of the American Academy of*

Child Psychiatry 13:551–560.

Sachs, J. (1980). The role of adult-child play in language development. In *Children's Play*, ed. K. Rubin, pp. 33–48. San Francisco: Jossey-Bass.

Salfield, D., Lond, B., and Dusseldorf, M. (1950). Observations of elective mutism in children. *Journal of Mental Science* 96:1024–1032.

Sandler, J., Kennedy, H., and Tyson, P. (1980). *The Technique of Child Psychoanalysis*. Cambridge, MA: Harvard University Press.

Sanok, R., and Ascione, F. (1979). Behavioral intervention for childhood elective mutism. *Child Behavior Therapy* 1:46–49.

Schaefer, C., ed. (1993). *The Therapeutic Powers of Play*. Northvale, NJ: Jason Aronson.

Shreeve, D. (1991). Elective mutism origins in stranger anxiety and selective attention. *Bulletin of the Menninger Clinic* 55:491–505.

Shvarztman, P., Hornshtein, I., Klein, E., et al. (1990). Elective mutism in family practice. *Journal of Family Practice* 31:319–320.

Sluckin, A. (1977). Children who do not talk at school. *Child Care Health and Development* 3:69–79.

Sluckin, A., Foreman, N., and Herbert, M. (1991). Behavioural treatment programs and selectivity of speaking at follow-up in a sample of 25 selective mutes. *Australian Psychologist* 26:132–137.

Sluzki, C. E. (1983). The sounds of silence: two cases of elective mutism in bilingual families. *Family Therapy Collections* 6:68–77.

Tough, J. (1976). *Listening to Children Talking*. London: Ward Lock Educational.

Tramer, M. (1934). Elektiver mutismus bei kindern. *Zeitschrift fur Kinderpsychiatrie* 1:30–35.

Van Kleck, A., and Street, R. (1982). Does reticence mean just talking less? Qualitative differences in the language of talkative and reticent preschoolers. *Journal of Psychology Research* 2:609–629.

Vygotsky, L. (1978). *Mind in Society: The Development of Higher Mental Processes*. Cambridge, MA: Harvard University Press.

Wassing, H. (1973). A case of prolonged mutism in an adolescent boy: on the nature and condition and its residential treatment. *Acta Paedopsychiatrica: International Journal of Child and Adolescent Psychiatry* 40:53–96.

Watson, T., and Kramer, J. (1992). Multi-method behavioral treatment of long-term selective mutism. *Psychology in the Schools* 29:359–366.

Weininger, O. (1987). Electively mute children: a therapeutic approach. *Journal of the Melanie Klein Society* 5:25–42.

Wergeland, H. (1979). Elective mutism. *Acta Psychiatrica Scandinavica* 59:218–228.

Wilkins, R. (1985). A comparison of elective mutism and emotional disorders in children. *British Journal of Psychiatry* 146:198–203.

Williamson, D., and Donald, G. (1977). The treatment of reluctant speech using contingency management procedures. *Journal of Behavior Therapy and Experimental Psychiatry* 8:155–156.

Wood, D. (1980). *Teaching the Young Child: Some Relations Between Social Interaction, Language, and Thought.* New York: Norton.

Wright, H. (1968). A clinical study of children who refuse to talk in school. *Journal of the American Academy of Child Psychiatry* 7:603–617.

Wright, H., Holmes, G., Cuccaro, M., and Leonhardt, T. (1994). A guided bibliography of the selective mutism literature. *Psychological Reports* 74:995–1007.

Wright, H., Miller, M., Cook, M., and Littman, J. (1985). Early identification and intervention with children who refuse to speak. *Journal of the American Academy of Child Psychiatry* 24:739–746.

Wulbert, M., Nyman, B., and Snow, D. (1973). The efficacy of stimulus fading and contingency management in the treatment of elective mutism: a case study. *Journal of Applied Behavior Analysis* 6:435–441.

Yawkey, T. (1982). Effect of parents' play routines on imaginative play in their developmentally delayed preschoolers. *Topics in Early Childhood Special Education* 2:66–75.

Part II

STRESS REACTIONS

5

Play Therapy for Children from Divorced and Separated Families

Donna M. Cangelosi

Background

In 1992 the divorce rate in this country was one and one half times greater than it had been in 1972 and nearly three times greater than it had been in 1962. Consequently, the number of children affected by broken marriages has increased dramatically. While statistics vary depending on geographic location, it is estimated that one-third of all school-age children will experience parental divorce before they reach the age of 18.

Divorce sets in motion a series of changes in the entire family's living arrangement. For children, who, of course, are not involved in the decision to divorce, these changes can be extremely confusing. Children are unable to comprehend the complexities of divorce and attempt to use their limited resources to make sense of it. Longitudinal research suggests that regardless of the age of the child, his/her reaction to parental divorce begins precisely at the point when one parent physically leaves the home (Hetherington et al. 1978, Wallerstein and Blakeslee 1989, Wallerstein and Kelly 1972, 1980). As such, a distinction between the legal date of divorce and the actual breakup of the family unit is crucial in understanding the child's response to the divorce.

Description of Children from Divorced Families

Every child interprets the meaning of his/her parents' breakup. Factors such as age, gender, developmental issues, cognitive ability, ethnic and cultural background, self concept, prior experience with loss or abandonment, temperament, quality of relationships with parents, familiarity with divorce, available support system, and the actual divorce itself play a role in the child's perceptions of the family breakup. While each of these influences is extremely important, most researchers have described the effects of parental divorce based on age-related developmental differences that exist among preschoolers (ages 3 to 5), early (6 to 8), and later (9 to 12) school-age children, and adolescents. This chapter addresses the effects of divorce on children prior to adolescence and the value of play therapy for addressing their needs.

Preschoolers

Preschoolers faced with parental divorce commonly demonstrate increased levels of anxiety, sadness, neediness, guilt, irritability, and apathy. They show less initiative and a decreased sense of happy and task-involved affect than do preschoolers from intact homes. Common behavioral symptoms include whining, clinging, attention seeking, separation anxiety, sleep disorders, and cognitive confusion. Regressive behaviors such as soiling, thumbsucking, and bedwetting as well as pseudomature behaviors have also been noted. The latter is particularly true among preschool girls. Among boys, increases in fantasy, aggression, and oppositional behaviors are commonly observed (Hetherington et al. 1978, 1979, McDermott 1970, Wallerstein and Kelly 1972, 1980). Bewilderment over the loss of father and anxiety about losing mother has been repeatedly noted among preschoolers following parental divorce. In one study (Wallerstein and Kelly 1972) preschoolers expressed a desperate longing for their father and feared that he would replace them with a new child. They frequently expressed self-blame and took full responsibility for their father's departure. Many pinpointed a specific incident that had caused the father to leave. Wallerstein and Kelly found such self-accusations to be highly resistive to educational interventions and noted that many of these children suffer from low self-esteem and feelings of helplessness and confusion.

Follow-up studies of preschoolers six years after their parents' divorce have suggested that while boys tend to adapt a stable pattern of externalizing, impulsive, and antisocial behaviors, girls tend to respond with internalizing behaviors such as withdrawal, depression, and anxiety (Hetherington et al. 1985). Such patterns commonly lead to more prompt clinical interventions for boys because of the disruptive nature of their symptoms.

The School-Age Child

It has been suggested that the trauma of parental divorce can cause the school-age child to become preoccupied with family issues at a time in the developmental process when focus should be on external endeavors such as academic achievement and peer relationships (Guidubaldi et. al. 1983, Wallerstein and Blakeslee 1989, Wallerstein and Kelly 1976a,b). Wallerstein and Kelly noted that early latency children (ages 6 to 8) tend to display overt signs of grief following the family crisis, while older latency children (9 to 12) are able to employ defense mechanisms to modulate the pain associated with parental divorce.

Early latency children tend to be preoccupied with issues of loss and separation and evidence profound grief reactions similar to those experienced by children following the death of a parent. These children commonly express a longing for the departed parent, which in most cases, is the father. It has been reported that such longings are not related to any particular qualities of the antecedent father–child relationship. To the contrary, neglectful and/or abusive fathers are frequently missed as intensely as fathers who maintain positive relationships with their children. Early latency youngsters tend to retain their loyalty to both parents, in spite of the vast psychic costs. A wish for parents to reunite is very common among this age group. Girls in particular tend to hold tight to the fantasy of a faithful, caring father who will someday return (Wallerstein and Kelly 1972, 1976a,b).

Late latency and preadolescent youngsters frequently present with strong feelings of anger as well as identity confusion resulting from changes in the parent–child relationships. Many of these youngsters demonstrate a pervasive sense of loneliness and isolation often stemming from the realization that they were powerless in preventing the family breakup. Wallerstein and Kelly (1972, 1976b, 1980) have noted that many late latency children feel that they are "on their own." Still others deliberately isolate themselves from both parents in order to escape from "choosing sides." Late latency youngsters experience intense conflicting loyalties that often result in acute anxiety and somatic symptomatology. In contrast to early latency youngsters, late latency children tend to form an alliance with one parent, usually the custodial parent, which is aimed at actively rejecting the noncustodial parent. They often express embarrassment and shame about the family breakup.

Follow-up studies of school-age children reveal long-standing issues related to the longing for the noncustodial parent, confusion about the causes of the divorce, a strong desire for reconciliation and profound loyalty conflicts (Bonkowski et al. 1985, Hess and Camara 1979, Wallerstein and Kelly 1976a,b, 1980). The distress of school-age youngsters manifests itself, on a long-term basis, as anger, delinquency, poor school performance, moodiness, temper tantrums, behavioral problems, psychosomatic complaints, hypomania, and identity conflicts. A very high incidence of depression, anxiety, low self-esteem, problems with peer relations, and a precocious thrust into adolescence have also been reported (Wallerstein and Blakeslee 1989, Wallerstein and Kelly 1980).

Long-Term Adjustment to Parental Divorce

Wallerstein and Kelly (1980) note that parental divorce, in and of itself, is not as important a determinant of the child's long-term psychological adjustment as is the chain of events that is set in motion by the initial separation. They proposed that the assimilation of divorce-related changes is a process that continues to unfold throughout the development of the child. Regardless of the child's age, adjustment to parental divorce is intricately linked to six factors: the extent to which parents resolve and let go of conflicts and anger, the custodial parent's parenting skills, the extent to which the noncustodial parent maintains a consistent visiting pattern and helps the child to overcome feelings of rejection, the range of personality assets and deficits of the child prior to the divorce, the quality and quantity of support systems available to the child and family, and the extent to which the child overcomes anger, resentments, and depression.

Traditional Treatment Strategies

A variety of therapeutic techniques and modalities have been used to assist children from divorced and separated families. Psychotherapy groups designed specifically for preschool, latency, and preadolescent children have become increasingly popular since the mid-1970s. Most of these groups are school-based, time-limited (six to twelve weeks), and involve several major goals: clarifying and validating divorce-related feelings, experiencing that peers share similar feelings and thoughts, gaining a realistic picture of the divorce situation, and improving communication, self-esteem, and coping skills (Farmer and Galaris 1993, Hammond 1981).

Many psychotherapy groups are structured and typically incorporate creative activities such as role play, art work, movement exercises, phototherapy, music, games, film strips, writing projects, workbooks, diaries, and direct instruction. Structured activities are believed to serve as nonthreatening stimuli that promote conversation among group members (Hammond 1981). In contrast, less structured groups for children of divorce and separation commonly operate under the premise that children will project their internal concerns onto neutral stimuli and that this process will help them to work through divorce-related issues. Such groups commonly use toys, play, and other manipulative materials.

Gendler (1986) demonstrated that given puppets, peers, and a minimal amount of structure and direction, children from divorced and separated families will work cooperatively to create dramas that powerfully and poignantly convey their deepest concerns and fantasies.

Experiences and feelings too painful to talk about, as well as parts of themselves long hidden and unexpressed, came pouring out through the adventures and mishaps of make-believe creatures extending from the end of their arms. Production of the plays allowed these youngsters, so buffeted by events in their families, to become chroniclers of their past experiences and feelings, and for a few moments at least, authors of their life scripts. [p 52].

Some of the modifications in structured and nonstructured therapy groups that have been described in the literature have included groups with children of heterogeneous ages (Farmer and Galaris 1993); conducting concurrent parents' groups (Farmer and Galaris 1993); involving parents as cotherapists (Cebollero et al. 1987); and involving siblings in group therapy (Cebollero et al. 1987). Farmer and Galaris (1993) note that in general, there has been a movement in recent years to involve parents and family members in the group process.

Gardner (1993), who has worked primarily with children on an individual basis, has noted that parental involvement is very important when dealing with divorce-related issues. He believes that children of divorce are most likely to be effectively helped with their adjustment difficulties when the therapist works closely with the parents. Gardner advocates inviting parents to sit in on their child's therapy sessions so that they can gain a better understanding of the child's needs and help to address them between sessions.

Campbell (1992) also believes that effective treatment for children of divorce requires parental involvement. Drawing on research which shows that children's adjustment to parental divorce is related to (1) the quality of their parents' postdivorce relationship and (2) the quality of their relationship with both parents following the divorce, Campbell contends that therapists must work directly with both parents. He recommends the use of structural and strategic family therapy techniques aimed at reducing the frequency and intensity of conflict between parents and helping parents to understand how important it is that their child maintain a positive relationship with both of them. It is believed that achieving these goals with parents helps to alleviate the child's loyalty conflicts, which are presumed to be the major underlying cause of children's psychological distress following parental divorce.

Many books have been written to assist parents with various aspects of divorce. Gardner (1977) and Wallerstein and Kelly (1980) were among the first mental health professionals to write books focused on helping parents to anticipate and deal with the problems that could arise in children following divorce. Since that time, a plethora of books, workshops, newsletters, and organizations such as Parents Without Partners have been formed to educate and support divorced individuals so that they can effectively parent their children.

Educational books have also been written for children. Gardner's (1970) *The Boys and Girls Book about Divorce*, serves as a guide to help children anticipate and cope with divorce-related changes, issues, and feelings. Illustrated books for younger readers, such as *Dinosaurs Divorce* (Brown and Brown 1986), use a similar factual approach and address the reader directly. In contrast, illustrated books such as *At Daddy's on Saturdays* (Girard and Friedman 1987) address the child indirectly vis-à-vis a story about a child who is experiencing a problem related to parental divorce. This use of stories, commonly known as bibliotherapy, works on the premise that through identification with the main character the reader is able to experience and express feelings about his/her own situation. This, in turn, leads to insight, integration, and improved coping. Early (1993) notes that a disadvantage of bibliotherapy is that children in treatment are often too vulnerable and defensive about their feelings and internal pain and may find the issues conveyed in stories overly confrontational and "too close to home."

The *Divorce Workbook* by Ives and colleagues (1985) provides a partial solution to this problem. This interactive book provides definitions, commentaries from other children, and room for young readers to write or draw their own responses to divorce-related issues. Designed as a tool for parents, teachers, and counselors, this workbook was developed to help children actively express, explore, and understand feelings about divorce. The authors advocate allowing children to move through the workbook at a pace that is comfortable for them, selecting activities to meet the needs of individual children, and using the book as an adjunct to individual or group counseling.

Rationale for Play Therapy

Children have difficulty verbally expressing feelings, thoughts, and concerns. This difficulty is compounded in children of divorce, who often experience a profound sense of fear, anger, guilt, helplessness, and loneliness. These youngsters expend a great deal of psychic energy warding off their painful feelings. Thus, directly raising issues related to divorce conflicts with the child's need to protect him/herself and often increases the child's anxiety and level of resistance (Early 1993).

Play therapy provides a vehicle for communication that is nonthreatening, nonintrusive, and sensitive to the developmental needs of children. It allows traumatic material to emerge in a disguised form that is manageable, safe, and intrinsically pleasing for children. Play therapy serves as a bridge to the child's inner world. It provides therapists with a tool for communicating empathy and intervening in a manner that is attuned to the child's symbolic language and emotional needs. Robinson (1991) writes: "In the act of play, a child may discover a connective bridge between his isolation and the therapist's empathic understanding" (p. 221).

Therapeutic Powers of Play Involved

The therapeutic powers of play involved in treating any individual child will vary depending on his/her emotional and developmental needs, personality, current life situation, and presenting problems. Each of these factors must be carefully considered when treating children from divorced families. In addition, it is important to consider the time frame of the divorce experience. For example, children who enter treatment before or immediately following the breakup of their family tend to have very different needs than youngsters who have had some time to adjust to divorce-related changes. Table 5–1 shows the most common difficulties and presenting problems of children from divorced and separated families.

Because children of divorce present with such a wide variety of presenting problems and needs, the therapeutic powers of play that may be useful in treatment can vary. The powers of play that are of use in treating these youngsters can include overcoming resistance, communication, mastery, creative thinking, catharsis, abreaction, role play, fantasy, metaphoric thinking, attachment formation, relationship enhancement, enjoyment, and game play. As noted by Schaefer (1993), these powers overlap. However, in the interest of clarity, they will be discussed separately.

Overcoming Resistance

> *There is little that gives children greater pleasure*
> *than when a grown-up lets himself down to their level,*
> *renounces his oppressive superiority and plays*
> *with them as an equal.*
> *Sigmund Freud*

Effective clinical work with any population requires that the therapist find a way to make treatment safe for the client. Children from divorced and

Table 5–1
Most Common Difficulties and Presenting Problems

Denial of the family breakup
Bravado/repressed feelings about the shock
Guilt (frequently caused by self-blame)
Acting out of anger
Internalization of anger, depression, or anxiety
Regression (especially in younger children)
Precocious behavior
Withdrawal/isolation from family and friends
Excessive worry
Separation anxiety
Fear that custodial parent will die or leave
Overdependence on custodial parent/clinginess
Anger and blame toward one or both parent
No outlet for anger and fear (causes sleep disorders, insecurity, psychosomatic complaints)

separated families generally do not find it safe to discuss feelings openly due to confusion, loyalty conflicts, and a sense that "something is wrong" with the way they feel. Like all children, these youngsters do not have the capacity to put words to feeling states. Segal (1984) notes that their inability to discuss feelings prolongs the grieving process. As such, he recommends the use of therapeutic techniques that rely on symbolic communication.

Play is the child's natural way of communicating and is not only safe but has been repeatedly found to provide therapists with a "window to the child's world" (Landreth and Perry in Schaefer and Kaduson 1994, p. 47). There is no better way to establish a therapeutic alliance with children than to meet them on their terms, and play is the most natural way of doing this.

Communication

> *Play affords direct access to a child's*
> *unconscious. Play for the child is like*
> *free association for the adult.*
> Melanie Klein

Play provides children from divorced and separated families with a vehicle to express and play out both conscious and unconscious material. This provides clinicians with a diagnostic understanding of the inner world of the child. The child's perceptions, emotions, and thought processes are revealed via play themes. Natural observations of preschoolers following parental divorce have revealed play themes that revolve around aimless searching and attempting to "fit" objects together. The play of school-aged children has revealed themes of emptiness, deprivation, anger toward the mother from driving the father away, and an insatiable hunger (Wallerstein and Kelly 1972). These observations highlight the power of play not only for understanding children but for assisting them in working through the troubling feelings associated with parental divorce.

Mastery

> *Play puts the child into an active*
> *position and converts felt deprivation*
> *into felt relief.*
> A. J. Solnit

Play allows children who have been traumatized by parental divorce to transform this event, which was experienced passively, into one in which s/he is active and more powerful. This play process allows children to gradually assimilate unpleasant experiences at a pace that is comfortable and within the child's control. This in, turn, promotes mastery and a sense of well-being.

Creative Thinking

> *In play we can find the roots of our adult*
> *capacities to think creatively and flexibly, to*
> *innovate, adapt, change.*
> Ashley Montague

Play helps children develop creative ways to cope with the pain and confusing changes associated with parental divorce. Making up "play" solutions and solving the problems of make-believe characters allows children to think in new ways and develop their problem-solving skills. Using play, therapists can convey options to children through the use of displacement. For instance, in play therapy, it is not the child who needs to talk to others, but the doll. Such interventions allow children to think in new ways about their own situations and helps them to find alternative solutions to problems.

Catharsis

> *Through the manipulation of toys, the child can show*
> *more adequately than through words how he feels*
> *about himself and the significant persons*
> *and events in his life.*
> Haim Ginott

Play serves a cathartic function for children of divorce by providing them with an opportunity to discharge feelings of anger, grief, anxiety, and self-blame. This therapeutic power is most useful when it leads to improved insight. It is advisable that play therapists use catharsis with discretion as it can overwhelm the fragile ego of some children who have experienced loss and trauma.

Abreaction

> *We can be sure that all happenings, pleasant or*
> *unpleasant, in the child's life, will have*
> *repercussions on her dolls.*
> Jean Piaget

Abreaction allows children to relive stressful events and the emotions associated with them. Children who experience abrupt parental separation and other traumas frequently engage in play that repetitiously centers on the upsetting event. It is this repetition that allows children to express and work through overwhelming affective states and to gradually assimilate and master these emotions. The play therapist can assist children of divorce by setting up play situations that enable them to reexperience an event or a relationship in the safety of the therapy room where the outcome can be more positive (Schaefer 1993). The play therapist can anticipate problems and help the child to prepare for them vis-à-vis play dialogues. This can help the child to develop skills needed for anticipating and preventing problems. Likewise, the play therapist can steer play themes so that the child can become aware of options and more positive outcomes can ultimately take place.

Role Play

> Play gives children the opportunity to search for
> and experiment with alternative solutions
> to their problems.
> Jerome Singer

Role play experiences provide a safe vehicle for children of divorce to try out new behaviors, rehearse new roles, and prepare for upcoming events such as a visit with an estranged parent, the first day at a new school, or a day at court. Having the opportunity to role play and "become" another family member can help children of divorce better understand the experiences of other family members. This can bring about increased empathy, an improved understanding of the complexities of the divorce, and decreased loneliness.

Fantasy

> In the safe disguise of play, the child can balance
> power, reward himself with fabulous riches,
> vanquish those who do not do his bidding,
> and devour his enemies.
> Beverly James

In the world of fantasy, children do not have to be small, powerless, and at the mercy of adults. Children of divorce, who are largely helpless regarding the changes in their families in real life, benefit from play therapy, which gives them the opportunity to create a world of their choosing. This aspect of play provides these youngsters a much needed sense of control and helps them to compensate for feelings of powerlessness that are frequently experienced in real life.

Metaphoric Thinking

> Children are natural mythologists. They beg to
> be told tales and love not only to invent but to enact
> falsehoods.
> George Santayana

Working within the metaphor of play or make believe allows therapists the opportunity to convey therapeutic messages to children from divorced and separated families. Sources of conflict, fear, hostility, and affective states as well as adaptive solutions to problems can be communicated vis-à-vis stories, fantasy play, and drawings. Early (1993) notes that stories unite troubled children with the experience of others. By identifying with symbolic characters in stories, children from divorced families can work through difficulties and find solutions to problems. Gendler (1986) found that puppet play can also serve as powerful metaphors for these youngsters. She provided the following "divorce ceremony," which was created by a group of third graders as an example.

(The couple marches in to the sound of taps)
Judge: John, do you take this woman to be your awful divorced wife?
John: I do.
Judge: Mary, do you take this man to be your awful divorced husband?
Mary: I do.
Judge: I now pronounce you divorced man and wife. You may hit the bride!
(The couple hits each other while the children cry.) [p. 51]

Attachment Formation and Relationship Enhancement

> Playing is a form of relating and begins
> very early when parents start cuddling, tickling
> and playing with their infants.
> Theodore Isaac Rubin

Children from divorced and separated families often present with a sense of being lonely and lost between two shores. In such cases one of the most important treatment goals is for the therapist to join the child and help him/her form a bridge between the separate worlds of his/her parents. Developing a play dialogue with the child decreases the child's loneliness and instills a sense of hope that s/he can feel connected and understood. Robinson (1991) writes:

Through play, the therapist actively attunes to the child's symbolic language. This creates a new and reparative form of "object relationship" in which the adult moves caringly into the child's world. The empathic interaction experienced by the child within the play resonates with the early developmental need for parental attunement and synchrony. Staying within the child's fantasy and using the metaphors offered by the child therapeutically create the sense of attunement. Therapeutic attunement kindles hope, an essential element for the beginning of therapy. [p. 221]

Establishing a trusting relationship with the therapist allows the child to disengage from parental conflict and is a necessary prerequisite for the establishment of a therapeutic alliance. The latter provides a sense of safety, which is necessary for the child to work through feelings of loss, anger, and self-blame and begin to achieve trust and realistic hope in interpersonal relationships.

Enjoyment

> *Imaginative play can make for a happy childhood.*
> Jerome Singer

Hetherington and colleagues (1979) observed differences in the play behavior of preschoolers from intact homes versus those from divorced and separated families. Youngsters from intact homes engaged in "imaginative play," which was social, dramatic, and cooperative. In contrast, children of divorce engaged in less social play and more solitary and functional activities. The play behavior of the divorce group was more constricted, narrower in focus, shorter in duration, and resulted in more unoccupied and onlooker behaviors.

This study demonstrates that the experience of parental divorce can overburden young children and interfere with their developmental need to engage in carefree imaginative play. Play, in and of itself, can be therapeutic to these children by providing them with a sense of happiness and well-being and an antidote to the stresses of their real-life situation.

Game Play

> *The manner in which a child approaches a game,*
> *his choice and the importance he places on it,*
> *indicate his attitude and relationship to his environment*
> *and how he's related to his fellow man.*
> Alfred Adler

Gardner was among the first mental health professionals to introduce a therapeutic board game for children, which he called the "Thinking, Feeling, Doing" game. Gardner used this game for assisting children from divorced families who needed some structure and prompting to discuss their thoughts and feelings. Over the years a wide variety of board games have been designed specifically for children dealing with thoughts, feelings, and changes related to various aspects of divorce. Traditional board games such as chess and checkers have been adapted to help these youngsters work through divorce-related issues and develop improved coping skills. One such game entitled "Feeling Checkers" provides children with an opportunity to discuss feelings, which are written on the bottom of game pieces, each time the opponent is jumped.

Approach

A psychodynamic approach for treating children from divorced and separated families will be described throughout the remainder of this chapter. This approach is based on the tenets of ego psychology and recent research that has outlined the needs and challenges of children from divorced and separated families. The underlying theory of ego psychology is that we all possess a greater or lesser ability to mediate internal processes, environmental demands, and conflicts that arise between these two forces. Working from an ego psychology perspective provides play therapists with an understanding of ego processes that work effectively as well as those that are undeveloped, lacking, or in need of support. This paradigm is particularly applicable to children who are adjusting to parental divorce and separation because it stresses adaptation, improved functioning, and getting the child back on track. Anna Freud (1965) noted that the primary goal of child therapy is to remove obstacles that impede the child's development and to strengthen the child's ego resources so that improved functioning can take place and the "task of development" can be completed.

Description of Psychodynamic Play Therapy

Anna Freud saw play as a behavior that is mediated by the ego to deal with conflicts stemming from both intrapsychic and environmental demands. She held that play provides a great deal of information regarding the inner world of children, but warned that this information is incomplete and must be supplemented with data about the child's developmental history and environment. As such, parental involvement is necessary not only in the assessment phase but throughout treatment. Following is a description of the psychodynamic assessment process, treatment planning, and some general guidelines for conducting play therapy with children from divorced and separated families.

Psychodynamic Assessment

Psychodynamic play therapy for children of divorce and separation begins with a thorough diagnostic assessment of the child. The first step is to meet with both parents, either together or separately, to gather information regarding the child's difficulties, current functioning, relationships, reactions to the family breakup, and developmental history. These interviews can also provide the therapist with an opportunity to gain an understanding of the history, parenting styles, and pre- and postdivorce experiences of the child's parents. The therapist can form a working alliance with parents during this process by listening to them in an unbiased, caring manner.

Parent interviews provide the therapist with an understanding of the child's external world following the family breakup. Conducting a play assessment with the child provides complementary information regarding the child's inner world and emotional concerns. The play assessment is done by interacting with the child and observing his/her spontaneous play; the psychodynamically oriented therapist gathers information regarding the child's concerns, conflicts, mechanisms for coping and resolving conflict, defenses, perceptions, interpersonal style, and overall level of development. This information is assessed in the context of the child's current and past experiences and developmental history. Recommendations and a treatment plan are based on this information.

It is helpful to set up a feedback session with the child's parents to discuss findings and the recommended treatment plan, to educate them about therapy, to elicit their involvement in the therapeutic process, and to discuss confidentiality issues. The therapist can remain on neutral ground with both parents by implementing a "no secrets" policy with them. Such a policy asserts that any information that is shared with the therapist, by either parent, is available to the child and to the other parent. In contrast, communication between the child and therapist is best kept confidential except in dangerous situations.

Treatment Planning

According to Wallerstein (1983) children of divorce must master six interrelated, hierarchical coping tasks that take place in addition to the routine developmental tasks faced by all children. The first three are acknowledging the reality of the marital rupture, disengaging from parental conflict, and pursuing customary activities within one year of the initial separation. It is only after these three tasks are accomplished that the child can progress to subsequent challenges, which are mastered over a period of many years. These involve resolving feelings related to the partial or total loss of a parent from the family unit, working through feelings of anger and self-blame, and accepting the permanence of parental divorce. Finally, during adolescence, or perhaps at entry to young adulthood, the child of divorce is faced with the challenge of achieving realistic hope regarding intimate heterosexual relationships.

I find it helpful to use this list of psychological tasks as a guide for assessing where the child is in terms of his/her adjustment to the family breakup, and for determining those powers of play that can help to meet the child's needs. Table 5-2 lists these psychological tasks and the therapeutic factors of play that contribute to mastery of each. It is noteworthy that although achieving realistic hope is a challenge that is mastered during adolescence, preliminary work in this area can be done vis-à-vis play therapy.

Conducting Treatment

The basic premise of psychodynamic play therapy is that following the child's lead will provide the therapist with valuable information regarding the child's

Table 5-2
Psychological Tasks and Corresponding Therapeutic Factors

I.   Acknowledging the reality of the marital rupture:

overcoming resistance*	mastery*
catharsis	abreaction
game play	metaphoric thinking*

II. Disengaging from parental conflict and distress, and resuming customary pursuits:

overcoming resistance	mastery
creative thinking	fantasy
attachment formation	relationship enhancement
metaphoric thinking	enjoyment

III. Resolving loss and
IV. Resolving anger and self-blame:

overcoming resistance	mastery
communication	creative thinking
fantasy	role play
catharsis	abreaction
attachment formation	relationship enhancement
metaphoric thinking	game play

V.   Accepting the permanence of the divorce:

overcoming resistance	mastery
communication	role play
abreaction	catharsis
fantasy	metaphoric thinking
game play	

VI. Achieving realistic hope regarding relationships:

overcoming resistance	mastery
role play	creative thinking
attachment formation	relationship enhancement
metaphoric thinking	

*Overcoming resistance is a necessary prerequisite for each task.
Metaphoric thinking and mastery are involved in overcoming each task.

inner world. The child is encouraged to play spontaneously and the therapist "joins" the child by engaging in a play dialogue. This is done by encouraging the child to guide the therapist regarding what s/he should say, be, or do. The child writes the script, and the therapist serves as the actor utilizing the metaphor of play. By demonstrating enthusiasm and involvement in the child's play, the therapist establishes him/herself as someone who is emotionally accessible and attuned to the child's needs. This sets the stage for the therapeutic relationship and allows the therapist to gradually insert interventions aimed at replacing maladaptive defenses, symptoms, thoughts, and behaviors with age-appropriate coping skills.

The primary goal of psychodynamic treatment is to make the child's conflicts, concerns and disappointments apparent so that they can be resolved. This is done gradually, first by pointing out conscious thoughts and behaviors, and later by addressing more threatening feelings and defenses. The therapist uses four sequential interventions to do this: confrontation, clarification, interpretation, and working through. Confrontation and clarification deal with conscious behaviors and are precursors to interpretation.

Confrontation involves pointing out a play theme or observable behavior to bring it to the child's awareness. *Clarification* takes this a step further and involves asking questions to increase the child's awareness of feelings that are related to the behavior or play theme. *Interpretation*, which deals with unconscious processes, is an explanation that the therapist provides to help the child understand the meaning of the behavior or play theme. This is first done by interpreting vis-à-vis indirect means such as metaphors that manifest in the child's play. Later, when the child's insight is heightened, more direct interpretations are made by the play therapist. This progression of interpretations provides insight and enables the child to work through areas of conflict or concern. The process of *working through* allows the child to view the conflictual situation in a realistic manner and results in a decreased need for defensiveness (Glenn 1992). The therapist helps the child adapt healthier, more age-appropriate coping skills.

Working within the paradigm of ego psychology, the therapist functions as an educator when information is needed to enhance the child's understanding of his/her feelings, thoughts, or family situation. With children from divorced and separated families it is important for the therapist to validate and normalize the child's feelings and concerns by sharing what is known about divorce. For example, if a child's play reveals issues of separation anxiety related to mother, the therapist might point out that "the doll" is worried that something will happen to Mom now that Dad has moved away. In addition, a helpful intervention would be to highlight that "many children" also feel this way when their father moves away.

Play Therapy Techniques

A variety of play therapy techniques can be used when treating children from divorced and separated families. The therapeutic powers involved in drawing and art techniques, symbolic play techniques, role play techniques, and therapeutic board games will be discussed. A description of exercises useful for working with children of divorce will also be provided.

Drawing and art techniques can be used for assessment purposes, for overcoming resistance, communicating, promoting fantasy, metaphoric teaching, and relationship enhancement. The "squiggle game" developed by Winnicott (1971) is a projective tool that is helpful for developing a dialogue with children. The therapist draws a squiggle and asks the child to turn it into something. The child then draws another squiggle and the therapist turns it into an object, person, or scene that can foster communication regarding divorce-related issues. This activity is fun and is frequently used as an icebreaker for resistant or timid children. The "Before and After Series" (Cangelosi 1994) involves asking the child to draw one picture of his/her family before the divorce and another picture of the family after the divorce. This exercise can promote a discussion of changes, losses and adaptations that are brought about by parental divorce. The "Wished-for Family Technique" (Cangelosi 1994) involves asking the child to draw (1) a picture of his/her whole family and (2) a picture of his/her "Wished-for Family." Inclusions, exclusions, and the physical placement of family members can provide the therapist with valuable diagnostic information and a vehicle for discussing the child's relationships.

The use of toy materials such as dolls, puppets, masks, and telephones promote symbolic play that provides children with an opportunity for communication, catharsis, abreaction, fantasy, learning through metaphor, and mastery. Kuhli (1993) described the use of two houses in treating children with separation issues. This technique is particularly helpful during the early stages of divorce when children are coming to terms with the fact that their parents will be living in separate homes. The availability of two houses in the playroom provides the child with an opportunity to work through confusion and gain a realistic understanding of where his/her place will be in each home. Toy soldiers can be used to help children work through trauma associated with parental conflict and confusion related to "taking sides" and loyalty conflicts. In addition, using telephones or puppets can provide the therapist with an opportunity to interview children and insert information vis-à-vis the metaphor of pretend play.

Storytelling activities provide children of divorce with a vehicle for communication, creative thinking, metaphoric learning, and mastery. Gardner's mutual storytelling technique, which involves asking the child to make up a story and tell the moral of the story, gives the therapist an understanding of the child's concerns and thought processes. The therapist responds to themes of the story by retelling it with a new, more adaptive ending pertinent to the child's situation. Early (1993) finds it less threatening to read complex tales that are seemingly removed from the child's conscious experience. Afterward, the therapist engages the child in a dialogue regarding the message of the story. This is done verbally or by asking the child to draw a picture about the story. The child's associations will reveal his/her own concerns, feelings, and thought processes. This information is used to confront therapeutic issues, clarify emotional reactions, or interpret the meaning of the child's associations as is deemed appropriate. Early has found a number of classic stories particularly helpful when working with children from divorced and separated families. For example, she notes that "Cinderella" and "Hansel and Gretel" will pull for themes of loneliness, loss of family security and altered family relations; "The Ugly Duckling" will uncover feelings related to abandonment and rejection; and "The Emperor's New Clothes" will elicit feelings about the fallability of formerly trusted authority figures.

Role playing can also be used as a vehicle for metaphoric teaching and to promote creative thinking, communication, and mastery. However, this technique also provides for catharsis and abreaction as it allows children to reexperience conflictual situations. Levenson and Herman (1993) note that role playing can provide the child with an opportunity to undo feelings of helplessness via reversal of roles or identities. They write, "Although it is a verbal technique and requires some sophistication in language use and comprehension, it taps the stream of consciousness and underlying conflictual material by allowing the child to use repetition as a tool toward mastery over an event that stimulated unresolved issues or conflicts" (p. 230).

Therapeutic board games are particularly helpful when working with latency and preadolescent children who have difficulty expressing feelings. Board games tend to be perceived as nonthreatening and can be used to overcome resistance; promote communication of consious and unconscious material; and foster creative thinking, attachment formation, socialization, enjoyment, and mastery of divorce-related issues.

Case Illustration

Lisa was 7½ years old when she was brought for treatment by her mother and father. Her parents, who had separated one month earlier, reported that Lisa had become increasingly timid, fearful, "depressed looking," and "emotionally closed," since their breakup. In addition, Lisa had stated on several occasions that she wished she had never been born.

The separation had been an amicable one. As such, the parent interviews were conducted with both parents together. Lisa, the older of two children, was described as an "extremely sensitive, insecure child." Her parents believed that Lisa was blaming herself for the breakup despite their numerous attempts to explain that the separation had nothing to do with her.

The reason for the referral was entirely related to Lisa's emotional state as she was not demonstrating any behavioral problems. To the contrary, Lisa was an "A" student and had good relationships with peers and family members alike. There was a price to this, as Lisa was the kind of child who put a tremendous amount of pressure on herself to achieve good grades. In addition, she frequently did not express her needs in order to avoid conflict with others. Lisa reportedly worried a lot and lacked self-confidence in all areas. Since her parents' breakup she had become fearful and clingy with her father, who had left the home and was staying with his parents. Lisa's parents felt that she had a poor self concept despite their attempts to praise her talents and neutralize her harsh standards. Interestingly, her mother identified with many of Lisa's difficulties and said that she had struggled with a lack of confidence, worrying, and self-blame throughout her life.

During the play assessment, Lisa presented as a very appealing, soft-spoken child who was excessively cautious, polite, and timid. During our first session, she spontaneously drew a picture of a park that included a tree, swing set, bicycle, sun, and several big birds. The picture was drawn on a large sheet of paper. Nonetheless, Lisa selectively limited herself to a very small section toward the top of the paper, which caused the scene to appear as if it were floating. Upon completing the picture, Lisa colored everything very neatly and then proceeded to demonstrate how dark and "blue" her world was by coloring over the entire picture with a dark blue crayon. This was done in a very controlled, meticulous manner and resulted in a park scene that was overshadowed by blueness.

Lisa ironically described the picture as "happy" when in actuality it was anything but happy. It was constricted, ungrounded, and uncheerful, lacking apples on the apple tree, people on the swings, and sunlight. The scene appeared dark, abandoned, and desolate. However, on the positive side, it did include a healthy tree and clearly demonstrated that behind the darkness was a well-equipped park that was not only functional, but had the potential for growth and fun! This drawing seemed to be an autobiographical representation of Lisa. While depression was dulling her world, and her sense of self was ungrounded, her ego seemed to be quite healthy. Politeness and constricted affect were adapted as defenses to keep uncomfortable and threatening feelings in check and to prevent conflict in interpersonal relationships.

Play therapy one time per week and supplemental parent counseling were recommended to address Lisa's difficulties. The short-term treatment goals for Lisa were:

1. to provide a safe arena for Lisa to attain a better understanding and acceptance of her parents' separation;
2. to lessen self-blame and related depression by
   • providing a vehicle for Lisa to express (rather than stuff) feelings related to sadness and loss as well as blame, anger, and other uncomfortable feelings
   • helping Lisa find ways to effectively and comfortably express both positive and negative feelings and needs to others;
3. to promote communication and closeness between Lisa and her parents to help her overcome feelings of loss, abandonment, fearfulness, and separation anxiety;

4. to promote Lisa's involvement in age appropriate, fun activities so that she could begin to disengage from parental conflict and develop improved self-esteem.   ·

The long-term goals for Lisa would be to help her work through feelings of loss, abandonment, anger, and self-blame; to integrate anger and other uncomfortable emotions; to address Lisa's harsh standards and help her to set more realistic goals for herself; to help Lisa accept whatever decisions her parents came to regarding their marriage; and to aid in her developing realistic hope, confidence, and expectations in interpersonal relationships.

During the initial phase of treatment, Lisa used several sessions to draw a floor plan of her house on a poster-sized piece of paper. She became increasingly involved in this project and was motivated to include every detail. This seemed to be Lisa's way of holding on to the way things were before Dad had left the home. When Lisa completed the drawing she chose four dolls who would live in it; a mother, father, blonde daughter (Lisa was the only member of her family with blonde hair), and a baby. The mother doll was placed in a chair that was in the far corner of the kitchen, while the rest of the family was placed in the living room clear across the house. Anger toward Mom and a wish to take care of Dad was noted in this session. The daughter took on the role of caregiver to the hungry dad who did not know how to cook. When asked about this, Lisa explained that it was "the mom's fault that the dad was hungry." This play theme and issues related to being "better than Mom" repeated in various forms in the weeks that followed. During this time, counseling sessions with Lisa's parents were used to explore ways to help Lisa see that the decision to separate was made by both parents.

Approximately six weeks into the treatment, Lisa's father informed me that he was going to be moving out of his parents' house and into an apartment. It was recommended that Lisa and her sister be brought to the new apartment before the move-in date to prepare them for the change, to show them where they will be sleeping during their visits, and to provide an opportunity to discuss their questions and concerns. Lisa's father did this and, in the session that followed, Lisa played with the dollhouse. She made up a story about a mom throwing a dad out of the house. The children proceeded to tell the mother that they "hate her for making Daddy go away." This was done with more emotion than I had ever noticed in Lisa. She was significantly less constricted during this session and for the first time was in touch with feelings toward her own mother.

In the weeks that followed Lisa became overtly angry toward her mother. This was manifested in what her mother described as a "chronically annoyed tone of voice and impatient attitude." Parent counseling was used to support Lisa's mother, who was sophisticated enough to see that this shift was an indication of progress. She responded very intuitively to Lisa's anger and understood it as Lisa's first open admission that she had some feelings about the separation. During this period, Lisa's parents worked together to remind Lisa that the decision to separate was a mutual one whenever this was appropriate.

During this phase of the treatment, Lisa demonstrated increased amounts of anxiety about leaving her father whenever their visits were coming to an end. He reported that Lisa talked in a regressed fashion during these separations. During one of her play therapy sessions Lisa made up a story about a father doll who was smoking a cigarette in the living room while watching television. The daughter doll, who was sitting next to him, ran upstairs and started to cry because she was "worried" that Dad would die from cancer. This session was used to address "the doll's" anxiety about losing her father, her feeling that she must take care of him, and the daughter's feelings about the smoke that was making her cough. During this session, Lisa was able to express that she "hated the smell of cigarette smoke" and that it was "annoying" when her father smoked when she and her sister were in the room. Lisa noted that "he never did this when he lived with Mom." Lisa communicated these feelings in a spontaneous, comfortable manner. A shift was occurring in her defensive structure, which made it possible for her to express "annoyed" feelings toward a loved one rather than stuffing or ignoring these emotions.

It became increasingly apparent that the therapist had become a safe person for Lisa to talk with. In one session while playing the squiggle game, Lisa drew a ghost and proceeded to describe a dream she had had about a ghost who was haunting her house. Lisa started to cry as she continued to describe the dream, which was replete with themes of death and loss—themes that paralleled Lisa's recent experience. The father who had once lived at home with Lisa was, in fact, becoming more and more of a "ghost" as time went by and the separation became final. Lisa was using her therapy sessions to work through, understand, and master the reality of her parents' breakup and to figure out a new way of relating to her parents separately.

In the weeks that followed, a metamorphosis occurred. Lisa seemed to actively seek out opportunities to discuss her feelings and experiences. She developed an interest in the "Feeling Checkers" board game and chose to play it nearly every week. She used this game to discuss a wide range of emotions, sad ones about missing her father, happy ones about spending time alone with Mom, and excited ones about field trips at school. By the fifth month of treatment, Lisa talked more and more about peers, school, and age-appropriate concerns. She expressed a desire to come for therapy every other week because she wanted to spend time with her friends after school. Due to the fact that she had made so much progress and was not showing any signs of depression, this was a welcomed request. It indicated that Lisa was feeling better about her parents' breakup; was capable of expressing her feelings and needs; was pursuing healthy, age-appropriate activities; and was secure enough in the therapeutic relationship to begin to let go.

Lisa continued treatment on a twice-a-month basis for three more months. During this time she discussed changes in her relationships with her parents, differences in her parents' rules and homes in general, and frustrations related to family and peer relationships. Lisa used her last two sessions to make a coat of armor on which she drew three things that could help her when problems arose. She drew a picture of her talking to her mother, a picture of her talking to her father, and a picture of her playing kickball with two girlfriends. These pictures were drastically different from the park scene that Lisa drew during our first session. They were not dark or "blue"; they involved reaching out to others; and ironically, they reflected that "playing" can be helpful.

Before leaving her last session Lisa asked if she could bring home the floor plan that she had drawn during the initial phase of treatment. This snapshot of the home that Lisa had lost when her parents separated symbolized security and something that was known. The future, in contrast, was still unknown. However, the fact that Lisa was leaving with a coat of armor made it clear that she was back on track and better equipped to understand and cope with the changes and adjustments that were forthcoming. She learned that she could reach out to her parents and friends, and on some level understood that play would provide both an antidote and a solution to problems and stressors.

Conclusion

Wallerstein and Kelly (1980) used the metaphor of Dorothy losing her home via a tornado to illustrate the devastating loss of physical and psychological stability that children experience when their parents separate. Parental divorce leaves children vulnerable and overwhelmed by mixed and often conflicting emotions. Children lack the cognitive capacity to understand the complexities of parental divorce and typically cannot verbalize their concerns, feelings, and thoughts.

Longitudinal studies indicate that parental divorce burdens children with worries and responsibilities, brings about a decrease in spontaneous, imaginative play, and causes these youngsters to grow up too quickly. Play therapy is a particularly useful modality of treatment with these youngsters. It provides an opportunity for fun and for symbolic expression, which meet the interests and developmental needs of children. Simultaneously, play therapy provides a nonthreatening vehicle for communication, abreaction, understanding, and mastery of the emotions and challenges that are brought about by parental divorce.

A recent study (Friedman et al. 1995) indicates that parental divorce is associated with a shorter life span due to the extent of stress that it precipitates. Play is an antidote for stress. When it is used as a therapeutic modality, play serves to restore the carefree spirit of childhood, which is so frequently lost in the midst of parental divorce.

References

Bonkowski, S. E., Boomhower, S. J., and Bequette, S. Q. (1985). What you don't know can hurt you: unexpressed fears and feelings of children from divorcing families. *Journal of Divorce* 9:33–45.

Brown, L. K., and Brown, M. (1986). *Dinosaurs Divorce: A Guide for Changing Families.* Boston: Little, Brown.

Campbell, T. W. (1992). Psychotherapy with children of divorce: the pitfalls of triangulated relationships. *Psychotherapy* 29:646–652.

Cangelosi, D. M. (1994). *Play as a medium for assessing and treating children from divorced and separated families.* Paper presented at the Ninth Annual Summer Play Therapy Training Institute. Secaucus, NJ, August.

Cebollero, A. M., Cruise, K., and Stollak, G. (1987). The long-term effects of divorce: mothers and children in concurrent support groups. *Journal of Divorce* 10:219–228.

Early, B. P. (1993). The healing magic of myth: allegorical tales and the treatment of children of divorce. *Child and Adolescent Social Work Journal* 10:97–106.

Farmer, S., and Galaris, D. (1993). Support groups for children of divorce. *American Journal of Family Therapy* 21:40–50.

Freud, A. (1965). *Normality and Pathology in Childhood: Assessment of Development.* Madison, CT: International Universities Press.

Friedman, H. S., Tucker, J. S., Schwartz, J. E., et al. (1995). Psychosocial and behavioral predictors of longevity. *American Psychologist* 50:69–78.

Gardner, R. A. (1970). *The Boys and Girls Book about Divorce.* New York: Jason Aronson.

———— (1977). *The Parents Book about Divorce.* New York: Jason Aronson.

———— (1993). *Psychotherapy with Children.* Northvale, NJ: Jason Aronson.

Gendler, M. (1986). Group puppetry with school-age children: rationale, procedure and therapeutic implications. *The Arts in Psychotherapy* 13:45–52.

Girard, L. W., and Friedman, J. (1987). *At Daddy's on Saturdays.* Morton Grove, IL: Albert Whitman.

Glenn, J. (1992). *Child Analysis and Therapy.* Northvale, NJ: Jason Aronson.

Guidubaldi, J., Cleminshaw, H. K., Perry, J. D., and McLaughlin, C. S. (1983). The impact of parental divorce on children: a report of the nationwide NASP Study. *School Psychology Review* 12:300–323.

Hammond, J. M. (1981). *Group Counseling for Children of Divorce: A Guide for the Elementary School.* Ann Arbor, MI: Cranbrook.

Hess, R. D., and Camara, K. A. (1979). Post-divorce family relationships as mediating factors in the consequences of divorce for children. *Journal of Social Issues* 35:79–96.

Hetherington, E. M., Cox, M., and Cox, R. (1978). The aftermath of divorce. In *Mother/Child, Father/Child Relationships,* ed. J. H. Stevens and M. Mathews, pp. 149–176. Washington DC: National Association for the Education of Young Children.

———— (1979). Play and social interaction in children following divorce. *Journal of Social Issues* 35:26–47.

———— (1985). Long-term effects of divorce and remarriage on the adjustment of children. *Journal of the American Academy of Child Psychiatry*

24(5):518–530.

Ives, S. B., Fassler, D., and Lash, M. (1992). *The Divorce Workbook: A Guide for Kids and Families.* Burlington, VT: Waterfront.

Kuhli, L. (1993). The use of two houses in play therapy. In *Play Therapy Techniques,* ed. C. E. Schaefer, and D. M. Cangelosi, pp. 63–68. Northvale, NJ: Jason Aronson.

Levenson, R. L., and Herman, J. (1993). Role playing. In *Play Therapy Techniques,* ed. C. E. Schaefer, and D. M. Cangelosi, pp. 225–236. Northvale, NJ: Jason Aronson.

McDermott, J. P. (1970). Divorce and its psychiatric sequelae in children. *Archives of General Psychiatry* 23:421–427.

Robinson, H. (1991). Visitation with divorced father provokes reemergence of unresolved family conflicts: case of Charlie, age 10. In *Play Therapy with Children in Crisis,* ed. N. Boyd-Webb, pp. 217–236. New York: Guilford.

Schaefer, C. E., ed. (1993). *The Therapeutic Powers of Play.* Northvale, NJ: Jason Aronson.

Schaefer, C., and Kaduson, H., eds. (1994). *The Quotable Play Therapist.* Northvale, NJ: Jason Aronson.

Segal, R. M. (1984). Helping children express grief through symbolic communication. *Social Casework* 65:590–599.

Wallerstein, J. S. (1983). Children of divorce: the psychological tasks of the child. *American Journal of Orthopsychiatry* 53:230–243.

Wallerstein, J. S., and Blakeslee, S. (1989). *Second Chances: Men, Women, and Children a Decade After Divorce.* New York: Ticknor & Fields.

Wallerstein, J. S., and Kelly, J. B. (1972). The effects of parental divorce: experiences of the preschool child. *American Academy of Child Psychiatry* 14:600–616.

———— (1976a). The effects of parental divorce: experiences of the child in early latency. *American Journal of Orthopsychiatry* 46:47–56.

———— (1976b). The effects of parental divorce: experiences of the child in later latency. *American Journal of Orthopsychiatry* 46:256–269.

———— (1980). *Surviving the Break Up.* New York: Basic Books.

Winnicott, D. W. (1971). *Therapeutic Consultations in Child Psychiatry.* New York: Basic Books.

6

Rubble, Disruption, and Tears: Helping Young Survivors of Natural Disaster

Janine S. Shelby

In each life, there are moments that leave an imprint in the mind and heart and spirit, moments that transcend lesser times and enable a person to stretch beyond what he has known, into a new realm of discovery.

Clark Moustakas

Nothing remained standing against the dusky sky, except for the child. Neither a tree, nor a house, nor a pet had been spared, and the girl had seen the destruction of them all. She stood perfectly still, staring wide-eyed at the wreckage that had once been her world. Tall for her seven years, the girl's vertical figure rose conspicuously from the flattened land, exaggerating the sense of implausibility in the already unfathomable day. In horror and shock, she stood—as the land seemed to lie—mourning her losses and counting her words.

I approached the girl slowly, unsure how to help her accommodate to this strange reality. When I knelt beside her, the girl's paralysis surrendered to words. "This is the end of the world," she said with certainty, and repeated, "This is the end of the world." Soon afterward, we watched the sun set across the devastated land, ending the third day after Hurricane Andrew's siege on the only world she had ever known.

Throughout the ages, countless children have experienced "the end of the world." Inevitably, other children will stand, in horror and shock, against the backdrop of future tragedies. Too often, other child therapists will watch the setting sun as I did on that day, desperately lacking preparation and training to help the youngest survivors.

Natural disaster is an expense of living within the motion of a dynamic universe; it is an inevitable part of the cosmos. Yet, most people regard disastrous events as aberrations that will not befall them. This tendency to downplay the likelihood of catastrophe is so entrenched that when calamities do occur, usual beliefs of imperturbability are shattered (Janoff-Bulman 1992). These assumptions of safety, predictability, and meaning (i.e., people cause bad things to happen) must be modified in the face of unsafety, uncertainty, and random destruction.

As survivors grapple with the devastation that surrounds them, profound levels of stress may ensue. If the stress is not successfully negotiated, survivors will enter a state of crisis, characterized by extreme levels of cognitive and behavioral disorganization. If this period is not dealt with effectively, the consequences can be long-lasting.

In spite of the inevitability of disaster, most clinicians do not read about disaster crisis intervention until they face catastrophe in their own communities. Therapists—often with little or no background in disaster mental health—are drawn by community necessity into the realm of emergency crisis intervention. Local therapists are often called upon to become "instant experts" following disaster. Those with expertise in high-risk populations, such as children and older people, may be in demand. Child therapists, in particular, are called upon to identify and assist children at risk, and to disseminate information to media and other professionals.

This chapter can help prepare play therapists to work with the youngest survivors of future disasters. It describes how children use play to move from crisis to confidence as they learn to manage their distress. My conclusions are drawn, in part, on the work of the first generation (Pynoos and Eth 1985) of child disaster researchers, who compiled a wealth of anecdotal evidence to guide child therapists. I also owe a great deal to the hundreds of children who have trusted me with their hurricane, earthquake, fire, and flood stories. In the sections that follow, I will share my experiences as a disaster mental health provider and researcher, highlighting the lessons that the children themselves have taught me about how they need to heal.

Historical Overview

Natural disasters have occurred since the beginning of time, leaving physical effects that were documented—and sometimes even mythologized—in historical literature and art. Whereas material damage from natural disaster has been met with awe regarding the strength of nature, psychological damage has historically been met with indifference and denial. Psychological damage has often been considered a sign of personal weakness rather than evidence of nature's strength.

Although posttraumatic reactions have been documented for several hundred years, formal recognition of these responses as a psychiatric diagnosis has been relatively recent. Trimble (1985) recounted disaster-related responses described in historical documents from the seventeenth, eighteenth, and nineteenth centuries. However, it was only in the last century, through wartime experiences and through the development of employee's compensation insurance (which provided financial and legal incentive to attend to the responses of disaster survivors), that scientific interest arose in this area.

Throughout the study of posttraumatic stress, advancements in theory and research have been heavily influenced by the experiences of veterans of war. Symptoms observed among combat veterans were put forth as criteria for Post-Traumatic Stress Disorder (PTSD) in the *DSM-III* of 1980. Although this marked an overdue first step in acknowledging posttraumatic effects on survivors of trauma, this diagnosis focused on adult experiences. The distinct and special symptoms of children were ignored in this manual.

The *DSM-III-R* expanded the previous *DSM-III* PTSD criteria to include a few symptoms thought to be the child corollaries of the adult PTSD experience (e.g., the adult criterion of "recurrent and intrusive distressing recollections of the event" with the added note that children may exhibit "repetitive play in which themes . . . of the trauma are expressed" (American Psychiatric Association 1987, p. 424). However, many symptoms known to occur in children remained absent from the PTSD criteria in this revised edition, such as increased dependency, decreased bladder and bowel control, and loss of confidence in parental abilities to provide for children.

The *DSM-III-R* specified that the duration of the disturbance must last at least one month. This criterion left many child therapists questioning the diagnosis of children who exhibited PTSD-like responses prior to the one month marker. While one month may not be a lengthy amount of time for an adult, a month's duration is a significant proportion of a young child's life. A month in the life of a 3-year-old is proportionately equal to a year in the life of a 36-year-old, or two years in the life of a 72-year-old. Consider the absurdity of criteria that would require older adults to display trauma-related symptoms for two years before meeting criteria for PTSD. Yet, the PTSD criteria assume no temporal relativity for children. As a result, young children may not meet the diagnostic criteria until they suffer from what would be considered among adults to be chronic – and more severe – PTSD.

The *DSM-IV* advances the diagnosis of children with PTSD and related disorders (Table 6–1), although the criteria continue to underappreciate children's distinct experience. A new category – acute stress disorder (ASD) – has been added to classify persons who demonstrate PTSD-like responses prior to the one-month marker. The criteria for PTSD also include more corollary symptoms in children, although many posttraumatic symptoms commonly found in children remain absent.

The notes included in the *DSM-IV* point out children's disorganization and agitation, reliance upon play, nonspecific frightening content in dreams,

Table 6-1
Summary of *DSM-IV* PTSD and ASD Criteria

Posttraumatic Stress Disorder

A. The person experienced an event that was perceived as significantly threatening and the person's reaction involved fear, helplessness, or horror (disorganization or agitation in children)

B. The event is persistently recalled through memories (repetitive play may occur in children), dreams (frightening dreams without disaster-specific content in children), a sense of reliving the experience (reenactment in children), distress over stimuli related to the event, physiological reactivity in response to stimuli related to the event

C. Avoidance of associated stimuli

D. Increased arousal

E. Duration of symptoms in Criteria B, C, and D longer than one month

F. Significant distress or impairment is present

Acute Stress Disorder

A. The person experienced an event that was perceived as significantly threatening and the person's reaction involved fear, helplessness, or horror (disorganization or agitation in children)

B. Dissociative symptoms are present such as lack of emotional responsivity, a daze-like response, derealization, depersonalization, or amnesia

C. Persistent recalling through memories, dreams, a sense of reliving the experience, distress over stimuli related to the event

D. Avoidance of related stimuli

E. Anxiety or increased arousal

F. Significant distress or impairment is present

G. Duration of at least 2 days and no more than 4 weeks within the traumatic event

H. Not due to substance use, a medical condition, or psychosis

and tendency to behaviorally (rather than cognitively) reexperience the event. Although many other symptoms typical of young survivors are not included in the *DSM-IV*, the notes that are included provide a more developmentally sensitive basis on which to evaluate children's posttraumatic reactions than was true in previous editions.

Whereas many of the criteria in the PTSD category contain notes for children, the Acute Stress Disorder (ASD) classification does not. Therefore, for example, a child who engages in repetitive play does not meet the ASD criterion of intrusive reexperiencing of the traumatic event. This lack of sensitivity to developmental differences will probably result in the underdiagnosis of children suffering from ASD.

The disproportionately small amount of attention given to child survivors is summarized by Peterson and colleagues (1991) as follows: "While the vast majority of writing on PTSD has been about soldiers, it may be that children are the foremost victims of PTSD" (p. 65). As other authors have cautioned (Garmezy 1986, Webb 1991), diagnostic labels common in adult diagnoses simply may not be appropriate for children. In short, the world of psychiatric diagnosis recognizes *children's* profound—and sometimes distinct—responses to traumatic events only sluggishly.

Recognizing Children's Postdisaster Responses

The PTSD criteria are limited in documenting children's posttraumatic respons-es. The ASD diagnosis completely overlooks characteristic symptoms of chil-dren's posttraumatic response. Therefore, it is important for clinicians to recog-nize children's posttraumatic symptoms beyond those listed in the *DSM-IV*.

The following symptoms have been noted among children across many disasters. Children may show regressive behaviors such as clinging, loss of toilet training skills, and increased dependency. Sleep disturbances such as insomnia may occur. Non–disaster-specific fears as well as fears that are disaster specific may increase. For example, many children describe fears of film villains such as Freddy Krueger, monsters, and other fictional characters. Younger children may be more fearful of animals and noises that are not obviously related to the disaster. In one study following Hurricane Andrew, parents reported equal levels of disaster-specific fear and non–disaster-specific fear in their children (Shelby 1994b).

The Crisis State and Children in Crisis

Veteran observers of child disaster survivors have noted that some children develop PTSD, ASD, and other posttraumatic symptoms while other children do not. What is the underlying process that leaves some children resilient and others in crisis?

In every organism, stress is an adaptive mechanism for returning the state of equilibrium. However, prolonged stress takes a physiological, psychological, and physical toll on people.

Stress occurs when a precipitating event changes the homeostatic balance. If this precipitator is judged by someone to be negative (see also Lazarus and Folkman 1984 for a discussion of the importance of appraisal of the precipitating event), the person tries a familiar coping strategy to alleviate distressing feelings. If the response is successful in reducing the subjectively experienced distress, the desired equilibrium state returns. If the response is unsuccessful, another strategy is employed. As each successive coping attempt is met with failure, tension rises. The person eventually enters a state of crisis if resources do not exist or are not employed to reduce distress. Crisis is, therefore, an extreme and acute variant of stress, characterized by severe cognitive and behavioral disor-ganization.

This state is so extreme as to be incompatible in the long-term with human existence. That is, no one can remain in the crisis state for very long. The crisis state is widely believed to endure no longer than about six weeks, consistent with Lindemann's (1944) observations. In optimal circumstances, the crisis state may lead to positive growth—that is beyond precrisis functioning (Baldwin 1979). This is not to say, however, that adaptive resolution invariably occurs. Maladaptive coping responses may leave the person at less effective functioning levels than the precrisis status. Nevertheless, the crisis period is recognized as critical to subsequent recovery.

Following disaster, the experience of profound loss is felt by both children and adults, but children face special issues. Van Ornum and Mordock (1983) suggest that children in a crisis state may actually suffer more intensely, because their sense of self is not as deeply embedded as adults' sense of self. Given that children have fewer established patterns of coping, the ensuing chaos they experience may be particularly profound. (See Figure 6–1.)

Paradoxically, disaster mental health work with children is particularly rewarding because of children's propensity to develop skills during this period that go beyond their precrisis levels of functioning. Intervention with children usually involves giving them words and strategies with which they then interpret

Figure 6–1. "The earthquake really caused a lot of damage."

and frame the disaster. Intervention also includes expanding their coping repertoire, which leads to positive growth along with recovery.

Crisis Intervention with Children

Traditional Treatment Strategies

For many years, it was believed that children were resilient enough to withstand virtually any traumatic event. It was believed that children's reactions to trauma were transient and short-lived, minimal at worst. Early treatment strategies were thus geared toward adults. Interventions were directed toward alleviating the distress of adults, who were expected to pass along psychological benefits to their children.

Although studies continue to suggest that there is a positive association between parental responses and children's level of distress, it is clear that children also show posttraumatic reactions independent of their parents. This highlights the need for direct intervention with children.

Core Therapeutic Issues

When I approached the 7-year-old girl after Hurricane Andrew, I wondered what I could possibly do in my brief time with her, given the absolute devastation of her world. I had not yet learned the techniques that I will describe below. However, the writings of play therapy pioneers offered wisdom that directed my intervention with her. These critical elements of intervention with children transcend the circumstances surrounding the child's distress.

"Remaining with" the child in crisis is critical. Moustakas (1966) portrays his experiences with a boy facing death: "I remained with Jimmy, as one person with another, facing a crisis in life. I remained with his perceptions, with his feelings. As far as it is humanly possible for one person to be in the center of the world of another, I was there, offering myself, my skills, and my strength" (p. 11). Traumatized children need to be heard in the presence of another who is not afraid to grieve with them. They need someone to accept their suffering in its cruel entirety.

Winnicott (1971) highlights the importance of play as therapeutic work: "Where playing is not possible then the work done by the therapist is directed towards bringing the patient from a state of not being able to play into a state of being able to play" (p. 38).

Below, I will suggest specific strategies for "playing with" young survivors of disaster.

Crisis Intervention Play Therapy

From an empirical standpoint, crisis interventions for children are not well understood (Vernberg and Vogel 1994). I present below a number of intervention strategies that I have found useful. I describe these interventions within a descriptive model of children's posttraumatic recovery processes. Although not empirically derived, this framework nevertheless provides an assessment tool for clinicians as they evaluate children's recovery processes. It also guides play therapists as they select appropriate intervention strategies. Before turning to these specific strategies, I will discuss the underlying issues of play therapy, catharsis, abreaction, and mastery.

The Value of Play

Historically, the value of verbalizing the traumatic incident has been recognized (Baldwin 1979), but children's limited verbal capacities make the traumatic experience difficult to convey verbally.

The natural mode of communication for children is play (Axline 1947, Landreth 1991, Levy 1939, Lowenfeld 1939, Moustakas 1966, Schaefer 1993, Winnicott 1971). Children's coping attempts are thus reflected in their need to "play-it-out" rather than "talk-it-out" (Axline 1947, Van Ornum and Mordock 1983). However, play is not only useful as a means of expressing distress. Erikson (1964) viewed play as the child's vehicle for achieving a sense of mastery over traumatic events.

The recurrence of disaster themes in children's play is a noted symptom of child disaster survivors. However, the fact that these themes occur in children's play also constitutes a rich tactic for crisis intervention.

The Role of Catharsis

In the treatment of child survivors of natural disaster, the prevailing therapeutic view has been that expression of feelings, or catharsis, is a key element in recovery. Catharsis has been defined as "the arousal and discharge of strong emotions (positive and negative) for therapeutic relief" (Schaefer 1993, p. 8). This venting has been presented as a means of keeping anxiety at a tolerable level, thus preventing acute disorientation (Klingman 1987).

However, the concept of catharsis has always been a complex and controversial one, and many theorists believe that catharsis, in the form of expression of feelings, is not fully adequate to influence the person unless there is also a mental reorganization of one sort or another (e.g., Blatner 1985, Murray 1985, Nichols and Efran 1985). Some clinicians believe that the elements of affective release in catharsis should be followed by a stage in which the therapist helps the child assimilate the meaning of the feelings (Schaefer 1993).

Some have argued that a posttraumatic reorganizational process occurs inherently. Veteran researchers of children and disaster postulate that this cognitive reorganization occurs as children attempt to make sense of the calamity that befell them. Thus, the therapeutic intervention may foster more adaptive posttraumatic construals of the disaster.

The Role of Abreaction

Therapeutic reexperiencing of traumatic events has historically been viewed as a standard approach to treatment. This sort of reexperiencing, or abreaction, has been defined as "the reliving of past stressful events and the emotions associated with them" (Schaefer 1993, p. 8). By reexperiencing the traumatic event in the presence of a supportive listener, it is believed that the distressing event loses its potency.

Pynoos and Nader (1988) warn that children need to do more than reexperience; they need to replenish their reduced sense of mastery and control following the disaster. Likewise, Galante and Foa (1986, p. 362) noted that the children they studied "seemed to need an opportunity to master the earthquake experience as well as discharge feelings."

There is little research addressing the question of whether catharsis or abreaction is sufficient for change. However, some preliminary research points to the importance of reassimilating the traumatic event in a way that leaves the survivor with a personal sense of competence. In a project I conducted following Hurricane Andrew, I compared two treatment approaches. In one intervention, therapists used a therapeutic coloring book with children, which encouraged them to express their feelings about the disaster. In the second intervention, therapists used the same coloring books, but added an activity (described below) which was designed to promote a sense of mastery over the feared event. Children self-reported significantly more benefit from the intervention involving the mastery-oriented technique (Shelby 1994b).

A Framework for Play Interventions

The descriptive model I present below is based on the premise that play is the preferred treatment approach for children. The interventions I suggest draw on the therapeutic principles of catharsis and abreaction, although I also highlight children's need to master their fears.

This descriptive framework is drawn from disaster relief work logs of children's psychological issues and of my intervention strategies (Shelby 1994a). In both individual and group interventions, children seemed to raise similar types of issues. Gradually, I became aware that these phases seemed to occur in a more or less predictable pattern (Table 6–2).

This pattern occurred more or less sequentially, with considerable overlap

Table 6-2
Seven Principles in Children's Adaptation to Natural Disasters

1. Safety and security
2. Catharsis, abreaction, and empowerment
3. Reducing distortions
4. Restoring power to adults
5. Mourning and ritualism
6. Returning hope and putting the disaster in a broader context
7. Termination

among phases two, three, and four. I describe these phases in the following sections.

Safety and Security.   In the immediate aftermath of disaster, children are concerned with physical safety and emotional security. Children need to reestablish some sense of security within themselves, in their parents, and in the world. Parents may need help in providing for their children's physical and emotional needs.

Implementing the principle. In this first stage, reassurance and information are the focus of treatment. Children should be helped to develop a safety plan. First, ask the child to select active, self-protective procedures when threatened by disaster-related stimuli (e.g., "Get under the table in the hall when I feel an aftershock" or "Go to higher ground when the flood water gets too close"). Second, the children develop a plan for eliciting help from others such as parents, teachers, or Red Cross workers. Children should be allowed to choose the person or persons whom they ask for help, as some children lose faith in their parents' ability to help them.

In a well-structured crisis intervention program, the children rehearse their safety plans through disaster drills, and then reconvene with the interventionist, who reassures them that now they know what to do. This intervention strategy is similar to those proposed by others (Ayalon 1983, Pynoos and Eth 1986). Pynoos and Eth suggest that the therapist attend to the child's inner plan of action—the fantasy about what would remedy the situation—whereas Ayalon's focus is more tangible, mapping alternatives for future encounters with danger.

In disaster relief shelters, designate a place for children to play. The play area provides children the opportunity to express their feelings within a therapeutic and developmentally sensitive context. For parents, the play space offers respite from caregiving responsibilities, and creates a central station for educating parents about children's postdisaster needs.

Too much disorganization is overwhelming for children in crisis. Encourage children to express the chaos in their world in a restricted zone, such as a sand tray or in a designated area of the room. Remind them that the play space is a safe place where things work by rules. It is important for children to experience the play area and classrooms—which for them are microcosms of the rest of the world—as manageable, organized, comfortable, and secure.

Parents may need education, support, and guidance as they make postdisaster living arrangements. Parents may also need to be encouraged to provide appropriate reassurance to their children (e.g., encourage parents to say that they will do everything they can to keep their children safe).

Catharsis, Abreaction, and Mastery. When they are less preoccupied with safety concerns, children are then in a position to begin processing their trauma. The goals of this phase are to facilitate children's expression of their experience, including reenactment, and to foster a sense of empowerment over the feared event. The latter process, obtaining a sense of mastery, has been described both empirically and anecdotally as critically important to subsequent recovery (Benedek 1985, Frederick 1985, Shelby 1994b, Shelby and Tredinnick 1995).

I present a disproportionately large number of strategies in this section for two reasons. First, I believe that the bulk of the therapeutic work occurs within this phase. Through expression, reliving, and reassimilating the traumatic event and by developing feelings of mastery over their fears, children's fundamental sense of agency is restored. Second, intervention strategies reported by other authors have tended to focus on these issues, which suggests that many clinicians also view this phase as critical to subsequent recovery.

Fundamentals of retelling. Young disaster survivors need to include disaster-related details in their "disaster stories." Yet, many clinicians are unsure what to ask children about their disaster experience. Thorough interviews—whether through play or more verbal methods—facilitate children's expression of the disaster experience as they remember and define it. The child's subjective disaster experience is framed by his or her answers to the questions "Who?" "What?" "Where?" "How?" "When?" and "Why?" In the following section, I offer suggestions to facilitate therapists' understanding of the child's subjectively experienced disaster.

Who was present during the disaster? Did anyone leave following the disaster (parents sometimes leave children with extended family or friends so the parents can focus on damage repairs)?

What damage occurred from the child's perspective? What were the child's sensory experiences during the disaster (sight, sound, smell, taste, touch)? What chain of events ensued following the first knowledge of the disaster? Include all events from "When did you first know there was going to be a hurricane?" or "When did feel the earthquake?" through the current situation of the child during the interview.

Clinicians usually know objectively when the disaster occurred. However, children may have associations (see also Terr 1991 for a discussion of omens) related to events that occurred simultaneously (e.g., if the earthquake happened at nap time, the child may relate sleeping to the disaster).

Where, specifically, was the child during the disaster? Where does the child believe the disaster occurred (e.g., in a localized area or widespread)?

How and why did the catastrophe happen? Explore the child's attributions and causal myths.

Typically children end their stories at the most traumatic moment (e.g., "And then my mom was screaming and the walls fell down. The end."). Press them to continue their stories, to describe events up to the present.

Implementing catharsis and abreaction. Although some children may verbalize their experience, most children prefer less verbal methods of describing their disaster stories. The following strategies help children complete the task of retelling:

- A dollhouse with family figures helps children demonstrate the disaster experience.
- Puppets are helpful as children reenact the disaster and express their feelings.
- Therapeutic coloring books encourage children to express their experiences. These books usually supply factual information about the disaster and provide children the opportunity to color or draw their own experiences and feelings.
- Free drawing provides an easy means of catharsis. Pynoos and Eth (1986) note that a reference to the traumatic event inevitably appears in children's drawings when interventions are conducted soon after the traumatic event.
- Speaking into the microphone of a children's tape recorder is appealing to many school-aged children as a means for verbalizing their experiences.
- Showing video tapes of disaster-related footage encourages children to express their disaster stories verbally or through drawing (Galante and Foa 1986). Reading stories or playing audio tapes of other children describing their postdisaster coping experiences may also facilitate expression of personal disaster stories (Galante and Foa 1986). Caution is in order when using this intervention, however, as some children may feel increased distress from viewing the disaster on film or from hearing the trauma of other children.

Implementing mastery. Following the expression of the traumatic event, I believe that children need to feel a sense of mastery over the feared stimulus. However, it might be argued to the contrary that instilling a sense of empowerment over the feared event is unrealistic. Consistent with developmental literature, however (Bjorkland and Green 1992), I argue that children naturally overestimate their abilities and their sense of control of the world. Part of returning children to predisaster functioning levels, then, implies helping children restore overestimations of their abilities. Several techniques can be used to restore a sense of empowerment in the children.

In Pynoos and Eth's (1986) 90-minute posttraumatic interview with children, children are encouraged to draw pictures and then to tell stories about their drawings. Following the child's description of the drawing, the clinician points out the inevitable reference to the traumatic event that appears in the drawing or in the child's description. The child is then asked to recount central aspects of the traumatic experience (including the central violent action, all of the child's sensory experiences, and the worst moment).

Pynoos and Eth follow this expression-based portion of their interview with a segment characterized by themes of punishment and retaliation. In this phase, the child is encouraged to fully express "revenge fantasies," which are regarded as a key element in the intervention. Adapting this technique for use with disaster survivors, the child might be asked, "What would you like to see happen to the earthquake (storm, tornado)?" After the children have described their fantasies, Pynoos and Eth recommend turning children back to reality by commenting to the child that it feels good to do something now when there was nothing that you could do then.

Other experiential methods of acting out revenge fantasies can be used to help children regain a sense of control. What I have termed the "experiential mastery technique" (EMT) is one such approach. Children draw pictures of the disaster and then tell what the disaster did to them and to their homes. Reticent children are prompted by interventionists who speak to the drawings as follows: "Hey, you hurricane, I don't like you because you bothered my friend. We don't like you because you . . ." (the therapist pauses and waits for the child to provide an answer). Children may respond to the drawing or to the therapist, who then speaks to the drawing on behalf of the child. Following this description, the children are instructed to say anything they want to the drawing and then to do anything they want to it (such as scribble over it, rip it up, or throw it away).

On the eighth day following Hurricane Andrew, a 3-year-old Cuban-American boy was brought for crisis intervention in a disaster relief center by his mother. She reported that he had been fearful and clinging since the day of the storm. The child was instructed to draw a picture of the hurricane, and he told it several times "usted es muy malo" ("you are very bad"). The interventionist then told him that now he could do whatever he wanted to do to the hurricane he had drawn. He smiled and promptly wadded up the picture and ran across the building to throw it away. He repeated the exercise several times, with increasingly positive affect. He finally announced that he was finished and smiled brightly. His mother, who believed a miracle had taken place, said that this was the first time he had smiled or left her side since before the disaster.

The same exercise was repeated with a 6-year-old girl following the North-ridge earthquake. This child drew the earthquake carefully, documenting much of the damage that had been incurred in her home. When encouraged to do whatever she wanted to the earthquake, she asked for envelopes. She carefully folded her drawing, sealed the envelope, and then taped the envelope "just to be sure." "Now, I can decide if that bad earthquake ever gets out of there," she proclaimed, "and I'm gonna keep it in my room in a box so that it won't ever get away."

Another experiential technique was developed by Laura Orenstein, a Red Cross Mental Health worker, after the Northridge Earthquake of 1994. Called the "aftershock dance," it provides a symbolic method for reducing children's aversion to the recurring aftershocks and to further their sense of empowerment. The children stand in a circle holding hands as the therapist calls out "after-shock." The therapist and children then squirm and dance until the therapist says "Stop. It's over." The children are instructed to "freeze" when they hear the word "stop." Each child, in turn, calls out the commands as the rest of the group responds by dancing and freezing. Following this activity, aftershocks are discussed more realistically and appropriate safety precautions are reviewed.

Large cardboard boxes provide a rich medium through which children can abreact and master their trauma (Shelby 1994a). The boxes are used to represent the buildings involved in the disaster (e.g., houses or schools). Instruct the children to leave the boxes in their compressed, two-dimensional state as they line up in rows that represent streets.

The reenactment occurs as follows: children pretend to carry out the activities that occurred prior to the disaster (e.g., sleeping or going to school); they simulate the disaster (e.g., banging their boxes on the floor to reenact an earthquake or turning in circles to emulate the motion of a tornado); then they flop down on their boxes to represent the damaged buildings. With the children lying on the floor, the therapist asks if anyone has ideas about what the children can do to build the neighborhood again. Invariably the children yell, "Let's stand up and open the boxes!" and "Build it back again!" Cheering the children on, the therapist asks back, "So you're telling me that you believe you can build it back again?" The children shout affirmations. Pressing the point, the therapist can build excitement by cheering and asking, "Who can build the neighbor-hoods?" as the children burst with anticipation. Finally, the children are instructed to open their boxes and rebuild their neighborhoods. Exuding a sense of empowerment and resolve, the children may decorate their "new buildings" with paints, crayons, or markers.

A variation of this "box therapy" can be applied to children who will relocate because of the disaster. Lead the children in a victory march across the shelter, classroom, or office to a "new neighborhood," where the children then decorate their boxes with paint, glitter, stickers, and streamers. When at the new location, emphasize that any place at all can feel like home, and that working to make things look nice helps it to feel like a good home.

Three weeks after Northern California rivers flooded homes near Pajaro, California, one young survivor fearfully waited in an American Red Cross Shelter. Her parents reported that she refused to reenter the family's flood-damaged home, she showed a marked decrease in her appetite, and she seemed generally listless.

During a group intervention at the shelter, 4-year-old Angelica reluctantly accepted a box and watched cautiously as the other children lined their boxes in rows. She nodded affirmatively as the interventionist recounted how the rain made the river rise and how the children felt scared. To simulate the water, the interventionists rolled spools of blue yarn across the children and their boxes. The interventionists then tossed dark colored felt, to represent mud, which stuck to the children and to their "houses." After the children had thoroughly entangled themselves in the yarn and distributed the "mud" among each other, we called a stop to the action. "Look at this terrible mess," exclaimed the interventionist. "Does anyone have any ideas about what we can do to make things better?" "Clean it up," said one girl.

We WiLL Recover

Figure 6–2

"Call FEMA [Federal Emergency Management Agency]," said an older boy. "Fix our houses and I will help my brother," called out a protective sibling. It was not as easy for Angelica to see a solution to the damaged world she knew. She announced decidedly, "Nothing. We can do nothing. And I am never going into my house again."

The other children began the process of disentangling themselves and shoving the debris into a pile. They organized themselves and worked handily together. Without moving, Angelica watched them. When the interventionist gave the command to color the houses and open them, Angelica did not climb into her box as the other children did. Yet, she began to paint her box with bright colors. One by one, the children proudly announced that their houses were ready. Angelica steadily drew. The older children began a victory march with their boxes into the gymnasium where their families were sheltered. Angelica worked on. The other interventionists and I did not interrupt her work, as we could see the intensity of all her doubt and fear portrayed in her careful painting. The single most important task of her world in that moment was to create a livable "house" out of her cardboard box.

At last she stood up, although she continued to inspect her box. Then, she looked cautiously around the room for the remnants of the imaginary rain and mud. "All gone?" she asked. "All gone except for that little piece," I answered, pointing to a small felt strip near her "house." I hoped she would accept the chance to "clean up the neighborhood" as her peers had done. "Oh, that," she said. "That's nothing." Without stopping, she ran to pick up the felt, threw it in the trash, climbed into her house, and began to parade back to her family. As she left she sang, "It's a long way back to Mexico," which is the chant that children playing hide and seek call out to the seeker. It is a chant that only the fearless children dare to deliver.

Angelica returned to her real house the next day, cardboard box in tow. Her parents reported that Angelica entered the house without incident, and "helped clean all day."

We can provide older children the opportunity to express and master their traumatic experience through poetry or essays.

The media may provide opportunities for some older children to master their trauma by developing a sense of self as a sort of expert. This form of intervention is not appropriate for all children and should be considered with caution. For some children, however, this intervention can have striking benefits. Having the opportunity to share their experience with their communities through print or television is a powerful form of catharsis. Upon seeing themselves, their art, or their poetry in print or on television, many children take pride in their newfound role as "experts" who now know how to survive disaster. They learn that their words or images are powerful and important, which is quite a contrast to the helplessness and unimportance that pervade many trauma survivors' self-perceptions. The attention they receive through the media is perceived by them as acknowledgment of their special status.

Reducing Distortion. The phase just described attempted to arm children with feelings of mastery over the feared stimulus. With a restored sense of empowerment, children can concentrate on the corrective information provided in the third phase, which is aimed at altering their mistaken beliefs.

Children have many misconceptions about the disaster. The portions of adult conversations and newscasts that they hear lead children to develop their own causal myths of the disaster. In contrast to debriefing models proposed for adults (cf. Mitchell and Everly 1994), I observed that prepubescent children tend to respond best by ventilating emotions before dealing with their thoughts. This idea is consistent with developmental literature indicating that children gradually mature from emotion-based behavior to more cognitively based response styles. Children accommodate information and express their thoughts about disaster most thoroughly when interventions have first helped them *feel* better — as opposed to *thinking* differently. The shift in feelings comes during the empowerment phase. The change in thoughts occurs later on in the recovery process.

Implementing the principle. Here is a list of activities from which children can be taught about the disaster, both to educate them and to correct their misconceptions.

- Build a model of the earth, and demonstrate the geological process of the natural disaster. Repeat explicit statements that people do not cause natural disasters.
- To reduce children's sense of pervasive disaster, show a large map of the United States or a globe to the children. Show children the affected area but ask them to notice all of the other areas where people did not experience the disaster. Then, ask children to find out where their parents or grandparents have lived. When they return with the information, have children color those areas of the map or globe. This reminds children that disasters do not affect the whole country or the entire world.
- Invite television meteorologists to visit groups of children to provide instruction and to answer disaster-related questions.
- After children have been given factual information, they can write letters or prepare a handbook for other children who might experience a similar disaster. Send these books and letters to other classrooms, or store them for shipping to another community following a future disaster. Teachers, parents, or therapists can use the children's descriptions as a measure of the children's levels of understanding and distortion. Some children may need additional information to reduce their causal myths and distortions.

Restoring Power to Adults. For most children, moving out of the crisis state involves reestablishing some sense of faith in their parents' ability to care for them and in adults' ability to organize the world. Following Hurricane Andrew, I observed:

> After the initial stress of the storm, many children found their parents unable to provide them with the necessities of living that had previously been furnished automatically. Many children experienced their parents screaming, crying, and being out of control, as never before. Some children were forced into parent-like roles by events of the storm. For example, children sometimes held walls and doors against the force of the wind, while their parents were frozen in shock. The loss of confidence in their parents' ability to control events in the world left children feeling vulnerable to the cruelties and dangers of life, when previously they were buffered by parental assurances of protection. [Shelby and Tredinnick 1995, pp. 393–394]

Implementing the principle. Here is a list of strategies for strengthening children's confidence in adults.

- Hold an informal "parent appreciation" ceremony. Explain to children what actions parents have taken to provide for the family (e.g., returned to the home to clean up, or applied for governmental assistance). Have children present their parents with certificates of appreciation for all that the parents have done since the disaster.
- Ask children to color pictures of their parents, and then to describe their parents to group members or therapists. Following this discussion, ask each child to describe the things that his or her parents did during or following the earthquake to help. (Be careful not to suggest that parents succeeded in keeping the children safe during the disaster, as some children suffer injuries in disasters or are abandoned by parents.)
- To strengthen awareness of adult rebuilding efforts, invite adults involved in community relief efforts to speak about their roles. Invite representatives from fire and police departments, construction workers, Red Cross personnel, building inspectors, and anyone willing to answer children's questions and to remind the children that rebuilding is under way.
- Help children act out the role of adults as the children pretend to rebuild their devastated communities. Provide appropriate toy tools, uniforms, and materials to encourage children to sustain their role play. Be sure to provide pretend telephones or play walkie-talkies so that children can problem solve and call on each other to perform the necessary postdisaster building tasks.

This activity goes beyond enhancing children's sense of mastery. Through their reliance on peers, they develop a deep sense of community.

Figure 6–3. "Good things will come from bad when people work together."

- Have children act out the role of parents teaching children to survive a similar disaster (Galante and Foa 1986).

On a broader level, parents' sense of responsibility and empowerment may also need to be enhanced. Here I will suggest interventions focused on parents' postdisaster needs in both shelter and school settings.

Shelters. Particularly in shelter settings, where parents have few responsibilities and little decision-making power, it is important to provide parents with whatever opportunities exist to regain responsibility for their children. The following suggestions may be useful in these settings:

- Close shelter play areas during mealtimes. Allow parents sole responsibility for obtaining all meals and snacks for their children (rather than having a staff member bring food to the children). This allows children to see their parents as providers.
- Offer excess toy donations to parents rather than handing them out to the children. Parents may select items for their children and then present their children with the toys.
- At the end of each day, after the play area is closed to children, invite parents into the play space to choose one book or toy to enjoy with their children at bedtime.
- Plan family activities such as picnics, Boy Scout sing-alongs, movies, and other entertainment. Announce the activities to the parents, who can then surprise their children.

Schools. Following disaster, many parents may have questions about their own or their children's posttraumatic symptoms. School-based outreach programs provide an effective forum to disseminate information and quell rumors. The following suggestions may be useful in these settings:

- Designate and educate a professional to serve as a consultant to parents about postdisaster adjustment. Many parents simply need to hear that the reactions they are observing are normal and these reactions will probably decrease over time.
- Send information to every parent describing common symptoms, referral sources for help with persistent problems, and contact information for consultations.
- Plan a school meeting, separating children from adults, giving parents an opportunity to ventilate their concerns with each other. Provide consultation and educational materials to parents. A therapeutic group may be simultaneously scheduled for the children.

Mourning and Ritualism. With the flourish of activity that characterizes most communities during the recovery effort, it is easy to overlook the need to grieve. The children with whom I have worked following several natural disasters have taught me that they need to process their losses, particularly their dead or missing pets and their stuffed animals or dolls. Having acquired a sense of safety, mastery, understanding, and restored faith in adults, children are then ready to deal with their grief.

Implementing the principle. These strategies enhance the therapeutic process of mourning:

- Hold a memorial for pets or stuffed animals. Ask children to bring drawings or memorabilia to a special area of the shelter play space or classroom. Ask the child to say the name of the pet or stuffed animal and to describe what a good companion it was.
- A minister might volunteer to hold a brief nondenominational eulogy, recognizing the importance of these special friends.
- Encourage children to construct a special book or collage about their pet or stuffed animal. Remind them that this is theirs to keep, and that they can always remember how special their animals were to them.

Returning Hope and Putting the Disaster in a Broader Context. By this stage, children have spent a great deal of time focusing on the disaster. It is important to help them put the disaster in perspective. That is, they need to recognize the disaster as one event in life, rather than allowing it to obscure all of the previous events in their lives. The following interventions are useful to achieve this end:

- Have the children construct "life books." These books include pages in which the children draw various personal "portraits," such as pictures of themselves when they were babies, a drawing of their families, and drawings of their favorite toys. They can list their friends, and complete questionnaires about their favorite TV show, game, food, and vacations or outings. On one page, the children can draw themselves before and after the disaster. For children involved in therapeutic groups, one page might also be devoted to drawing the group, the classroom, or life in the shelter, with space for the children to collect autographs from each other, teachers, or staff.
- Joyner (1991) suggests a cognitive play technique that is useful with older children and adolescents. Explain to the child that sometimes, in the aftermath of disaster, all the stressors are like tape recorders sending bad messages about who we are. Help the child make new "good tapes" by asking the child to self-report four special qualities. Then, instruct the child

to "imagine a tape recorder is in your head . . . playing these four messages" several times a day.
- Conduct guided imagery sessions. These experiences are designed to help the children use their ability to imagine positive outcomes to buffer them from the inevitable hardships they face in a disaster-devastated community.

The guided imagery that I suggest is as follows: Have the children imagine what things will look like when "our world is new again." Children can imagine what their new or reconstructed rooms will look like, what their new or rebuilt homes will look like, and streets and neighborhoods. For school-aged children, we continue by turning the focus of the imagery inward.

Children may want to close their eyes during the imagery. I ask them to feel the air move in and out of their bodies. I ask them to notice the way they breathe, how the air is cool when they breathe in and warm when they breathe out. "Now," I say, "imagine that a little light is within you – it is a small light but it is very powerful. At first, your light is small, and you can only barely see your newly built home. Then your light grows larger. Bigger and bigger until you can see your new home. Your light grows larger still. Brighter and brighter it becomes until you can see your new house, your street, and your neighborhood. Everything is strong and newly built. You can see anything you want to see, and the whole world is new again. [Pause as children imagine their worlds.] This light is the part of yourself that wants so much for the rebuilt world to come back again. It feels excited about the day when things will be new again. Nothing can take this light away from you. This special light is yours to keep and you can use it any time you want, to imagine the world when things are new again."

With preschool children, a "magic wand" game is useful to achieve a similar goal. The interventionist says that this wand will help the children imagine the whole world new again. One by one, the children hold the wand, say a magic word, and then imagine what the world will look like, their homes, their rooms, their toys, when everything is built again. Each child describes or draws what is imagined before passing the wand to another child.

Termination. The impact of disaster-related losses may leave some children hypersensitive to feelings of abandonment and loss. Many children in crisis bond to their therapists. The play therapist becomes part of the indelibly etched disaster memory, essential to the healing child as an introject of strength and hope. Therefore, it is important to provide children a sense of closure in their disaster work.

If children have worked through the disaster-related issues described in the previous phases, their coping repertoire is considerably expanded. For many children this means that they successfully resolved their crises. This is not to say that all posttraumatic responses disappear completely; some children continue to show mild or moderate stress reactions. Global functioning, however, approximates or extends beyond predisaster levels of functioning for most children. For children who need a psychotherapy referral, these interventions facilitate the child's ability to participate in and benefit from future psychotherapy. Nevertheless, termination can be difficult.

Implementing the principle. The following termination activities are suggested:

- Some children need concrete representations of the intervention area or classroom, and of the interventionists (or teacher). Give an instant camera photograph or a stuffed animal from the intervention play area to the children to help them retain the sense of safety and empowerment they felt during the earlier interventions.
- Reaffirm children's strengths. Pynoos and Eth (1986) point out the importance of reminding young survivors how courageous they are. They also suggest that the clinician respectfully thank the child for sharing his or her experiences with the interviewer.
- Planting flowers or trees may not be possible in some postdisaster settings, but it is a powerful way to commemorate the overall disaster experience and sense of growth. Give each child a plastic or paper cup that is personalized by the children with paint or markers. Then, fill each cup halfway with unfertilized soil. Tell the children that before the disaster they were like the regular dirt, but now they are like rich soil that can help things grow. Next, add fertilizer to the children's cups while reminding each child to think of how he or she is stronger now. Finally, have each child pour the contents of the cup into the area around the newly planted tree or flowers. Ritualistically, tell each child "You have something that will help all living things grow strong and beautiful." Children can keep their cups to remind them of their ability to make "new life."
- Sitting in a circle, have the children stare at each other's faces to memorize them. The children might choose to hold hands. Ask the children to close their eyes to see if they can envision their friends and counselors/teachers. After each child responds affirmatively, say, "As long as you can see me and your friends when you close your eyes, you will always have us in your heart."
- Children outline their hands on construction paper and then trace the hand of a friend or therapist on the same sheet of paper. These drawings are concrete representations of the security, growth, and integration achieved during the therapeutic process. Many children pack these memoirs away with their most precious items.

A Final Consideration

In this chapter, I presented disaster-focused interventions for young survivors of catastrophe. However, for some children the natural disaster is the least traumatic experience in a pervasively frightening world.

Temporary living arrangements with relatives or in shelters may mean that other adults observe parent–child interactions quite intensely. In some cases, issues of child abuse and neglect may surface. The crisis interventionist must preeminently serve as advocate for the child, making child abuse reports as mandated. For some children, the most important postdisaster crisis intervention involves reporting ongoing abuse.

In other cases, the source of children's distress may involve the disaster, but not in the expected way. For example, some children are deeply upset by the loss of friendships due to moving, or by the emotional reactions of their parents. The therapist must be attentive to each child's unique experience, and tailor intervention approaches to meet the child's greatest need. That is, intervention strategies should be child-centered rather than disaster-centered.

Conclusion

The memory of a natural disaster is counted among the most frightening moments of many people's lives. The senselessness of random destruction plays on survivors' sense of safety, well-being, and immortality. Cataclysmic forces remind survivors of how utterly powerless they are. Particularly for children who have fewer established patterns of coping, the affects of disaster can be particularly profound.

Considering the enormous physical devastation wrought by natural disaster, it is hard to conceive how the psychological experience of children – who may be the most vulnerable survivors – has been so widely overlooked. This tendency persists in theory, diagnosis, and treatment of children with posttraumatic responses.

The foremost of victims, the least diagnosable, and the least studied in therapy outcome research, the children of disaster are in the weakest of all positions to demand treatment for their posttraumatic issues. Yet, I have seen firsthand that early intervention with young survivors and their parents play a pivotal role in subsequent recovery.

The child in crisis is lost in the divide between the terror left by the disaster and the predisaster sense of well-being, between fear and awe, between powerlessness and self-sufficiency. The playing cure exists in the place where that which *cannot* be forgotten meets the replenishing parts of self that *can* be remembered or grown.

As my time with the 7-year-old survivor of Hurricane Andrew drew to a close, she wrote a good-bye letter to me. In it, she simplistically defined the essence of her psychological experience with me. I have often used her words to guide my role as an interventionist, and to gauge other survivors' therapeutic progress. She scrawled the misshapen letters that read "You the care. You the hope. I is the strong. I servive."

References

American Psychiatric Association. (1980). *Diagnostic and Statistical Manual of Mental Disorders*, 3rd ed. Washington, DC: APA.

_____ (1987). *Diagnostic and Statistical Manual of Mental Disorders*, 3rd ed., rev. Washington, DC: APA.

_____ (1994). *Diagnostic and Statistical Manual of Mental Disorders*, 4th ed. Washington, DC: APA.

Axline, V. M. (1947). *Play Therapy: The Inner Dynamics of Childhood*. Boston: Houghton Mifflin.

Ayalon, O. (1983). Coping with terrorism. In *Stress Reduction and Prevention*, ed. D. Meichenbaum, and M. Jaremko, pp. 407–429. New York: Plenum.

Baldwin, B. A. (1979). Crisis intervention: an overview of theory and practice. *Counseling Psychologist* 8:43–52.

Benedek, E. P. (1985). Children and psychic trauma: a brief review of contemporary thinking. In *Post-Traumatic Stress Disorder in Children*, ed. S. Eth, and R. S. Pynoos, pp. 1–16. Washington, DC: American Psychiatric Press.

Bjorkland, D. F., and Green, B. L. (1992). The adaptive nature of cognitive immaturity. *American Psychologist* 47:46–54.

Blatner, A. (1985). The dynamics of catharsis. *Journal of Group Psychotherapy, Psychodrama, and Sociometry* 37:157–166.

Erikson, E. (1964). Toys and reasons. In *Child Psychotherapy*, ed. M. R. Haworth, pp. 3–11. New York: Basic Books.

Frederick, C. J. (1985). Children traumatized by catastrophic situations. In *Post-Traumatic Stress Disorder in Children*, ed. S. Eth, and R. S. Pynoos, pp. 73–99. Washington, DC: American Psychiatric Press.

Galante, R., and Foa, D. (1986). An epidemiological study of psychic trauma and treatment effectiveness for children after a natural disaster. *Journal of the American Academy of Child Psychiatry* 25:357–363.

Garmezy, N. (1986). Children under severe stress: critique and commentary. *Journal of the American Academy of Child Psychiatry* 25:384–392.

Janoff-Bulman, R. (1992). *Shattered Assumptions: Toward a New Psychology of Trauma*. New York: Free Press.

Joyner, C. D. (1991). Individual, group, and family crisis counseling following a hurricane: case of Heather, age 9. In *Play Therapy with Children in Crisis*, ed. N. B. Webb, pp. 396–415. New York: Guilford.

Klingman, A. (1987). A school based emergency crisis intervention in a mass school disaster. *Professional Psychology: Research and Practice* 18:604–612.

Landreth, G. L. (1991). *Play Therapy: The Art of the Relationship.* Muncie, IN: Accelerated Development.

Lazarus, R. S., and Folkman, S. (1984). *Stress, Appraisal, and Coping.* New York: Springer.

Levy, D. M. (1939). Release therapy. *American Journal of Orthopsychiatry* 9:713–736.

Lindemann, E. (1944). Symptomatology and management of acute grief. *American Journal of Psychiatry* 101:141–148.

Lowenfeld, M. (1939). The world pictures of children. *British Journal of Medical Psychology* 18:65–101.

Mitchell, J. T., and Everly, G. S. (1994). *Critical Incident Stress Debriefing: The Basic Course Workbook.* Ellicott City, MD: International Critical Incident Stress Foundation.

Moustakas, C. (1966). The dying self within the living self. In *The Child's Discovery of Himself,* pp. 8–27. New York: Ballantine.

Murray, E. J. (1985). Coping and anger. In *Stress and Coping,* ed. T. M. Field, P. M. McCabe, and N. Schneiderman, pp. 243–261. Hillsdale, NJ: Lawrence Erlbaum.

Nichols, M. P., and Efran, J. S. (1985). Catharsis in psychotherapy: a new perspective. *Psychotherapy* 22:46–58.

Peterson, K. C., Prout, M. F., and Schwarz, R. A. (1991). *Post-Traumatic Stress Disorder: A Clinician's Guide.* New York: Plenum.

Pynoos, R., and Eth, S. (1985). Introduction to the progress in psychiatry series. In *Post-Traumatic Stress Disorder in Children,* ed. S. Eth, and R. S. Pynoos, pp. ix–xvi. Washington, DC: American Psychiatric Press.

———— (1986). Witness to violence: the child interview. *Journal of the Academy of Child Psychiatry* 25:306–319.

Pynoos, R., and Nader, K. (1988). Children who witness the sexual assaults of their mothers. *Journal of the American Academy of Child and Adolescent Psychiatry* 27:567–572.

Schaefer, C. (1993). *The Therapeutic Powers of Play.* Northvale, NJ: Jason Aronson.

Shelby, J. S. (1994a). Psychological intervention with children in disaster relief shelters. *The Quarterly* 17:14–18.

———— (1994b). *Crisis intervention with children following Hurricane Andrew: a comparison of two treatment approaches.* Unpublished doctoral dissertation, University of Miami.

Shelby, J. S., and Tredinnick, M. G. (1995). Crisis intervention with children following natural disaster: lessons from Hurricane Andrew. *Journal of Counseling and Development* 73:491–497.

Terr, L. (1991). Childhood traumas: an outline and overview. *American Journal of Psychiatry* 148:10–20.

Trimble, M. R. (1985). Post-traumatic stress disorder: history of a concept. In *Trauma and Its Wake: Vol. 1. The Study and Treatment of Post-Traumatic*

Stress Disorder, vol. 1, ed. C. R. Figley, pp. 5–14. New York: Brunner/ Mazel.

Van Ornum, W., and Mordock, J. B. (1983). *Crisis Counseling with Children and Adolescents.* New York: Continuum.

Vernberg, E. M., and Vogel, J. M. (1994). Interventions with children after disasters. *Journal of Clinical Child Psychology* 22:485–498.

Webb, N. B. (1991). Assessment of the child in crisis. In *Play Therapy with Children in Crisis*, ed. N. B. Webb, pp. 3–25. New York: Guilford.

Winnicott, D. W. (1971). *Playing and Reality.* New York: Tavistock/Routledge.

7

Play Therapy with Sexually Abused Children

Pamela E. Hall

Background

The treatment of sexually abused children is a relatively new frontier in the clinical field because previous beliefs about abuse often dismissed the legitimacy of such accounts by children. The reported number of cases of sexually abused children has dramatically increased in the past two decades. In 1978 the incidence of reported abuse cases was 1.87 per 10,000 children. By 1984 it had climbed to 15.88 per 10,000 nationally and the rate has increased since then (American Bar Association 1988). This is due in large part to recent mandatory reporting laws and the corresponding increase in reported cases. There have also been massive public education efforts, teaching both parents and children what constitutes abuse and stressing that professional guidance is often required to cease abusive tendencies.

Statistics on the extent of the problem of sexual abuse of children are difficult to obtain. Reports from child protective agencies seem to be the best estimates; however, they do not include cases that are investigated and dismissed or cases that are never reported. Also statistics vary depending on the type of sexual abuse, such as fondling, intercourse, and so forth (Haugaard and Reppucci 1988). Studies have estimated that as high as 20 percent of the female population may have had an experience of sexual abuse at some point in their lives (Russell 1986).

The study of dissociative disorders shows that while 100 percent of the cases of dissociative identity disorder (DID), formerly multiple personality disorder, begin in early childhood, fewer than 8 percent of cases are properly diagnosed (Kluft 1985b). Hornstein and Putnam (1992) report that the average child with DID has previously received an average of 2.7 incorrect diagnoses. Thus, young children have not been provided the treatment they need. Child therapists are encouraged to assess for dissociation and address the dissociative experiences of traumatized children in their play therapy approach when appropriate. The proper diagnosis of a dissociative disorder can be most helpful in confirming the integrity of a child's allegations of sexual abuse. It has now been estimated that in documented and researched cases of dissociative disorder there is a positive history for sexual abuse in 97 percent of the cases (Putnam et al. 1986).

Many stressful problems in modern society are the likely reasons for an increase in child sexual abuse, including parental drug/alcohol abuse, divorce, casual sexual encounters that lead to strangers in the home, overworked parents, and socioeconomic factors. The specific causal factors of sexual abuse of young children remain unclear. Most theories point to a parental background of similar abuse repeated on the child, thus creating a cycle of abuse.

Research data on both the prevalence and etiology of sexual abuse toward young children is limited. There are many factors that contribute to this paucity of attention to the sexual abuse issue, especially regarding early school-age children. Some of these are political in nature, while others are financial or professional. Also, sexual abuse of young children is a complex phenomenon. Professionals who seek to help these children must be sensitive to these issues.

Due to problems of verification and the lack of physical evidence, children frequently do not receive protection from the perpetrators of their sexual abuse. Also, early school-aged children have a limited capacity to describe sexual abuse or verbally express the fear and intimidation that dominate their psyches. Older children also feel humiliation and shame.

In the absence of a well-organized verbal account of abuse, physical evidence becomes the only tangible method by which a protective response can be elicited from the authorities. The sexual abuse of young children, however, is often nonviolent and playful, and does not involve penetration, so there is no physical evidence. There may be no bruises, lacerations, or burns on the body, either internally or externally. The lack of evidence makes the child's allegations of sexual abuse highly suspect.

It is essential for clinicians to recognize that young sexually abused children are often reporting a crime for which they cannot provide any proof. There is only the child's limited account of the incident and subsequent emotional reaction. The reaction can be observed and carefully documented by the professionals who are treating the child. This is a crucial role of the therapist.

The mandatory reporting laws regarding sexual abuse have been somewhat successful in creating pressure on responsible members of society, including mental health professionals, to take seriously reports of the abuse of children. In a study conducted by psychologists at the University of South Carolina, "more than one-third of 295 clinical, counseling and school psychologists surveyed admitted that they had seen children whom they suspected to be abused, but did not report their suspicions to the child protective services" (APA 1989). Professionals often cite poor handling of cases by child protective services and fear of ethical violations and malpractice claims as reasons for not reporting abuse.

Clinicians should be aware that *the first treatment for sexual abuse is to stop the abuse!* This is a necessary and indispensable prerequisite for effective psychological treatment. Therapists of early school-aged children can employ therapeutic play as a· powerful tool in their work with the sexually abused child. Young children have a limited capacity to verbally express their pain; however, through the healing power of play these traumatized children can be given an opportunity to express and work through the various conflicts and fears they developed as a result of the abuse. It is the play experience that is the essence of healing as the child begins to relate an account of abuse and survival.

Description of Sexually Abused Children

Sexually abused children do not have a certain look on their face. There are no specific indications that signal the professional that a child is being sexually abused. Thus, the clinician must be sensitive and open to the child's reports of abuse. Disclosures about abuse usually begin in a subtle manner and focus initially on the least extreme forms of abuse the child has endured. As trust develops with the therapist, more detailed information may be revealed. Children must overcome immense intimidation and personal shame in order to report sexual abuse. All claims should be regarded seriously and investigated fully.

One additional complication occurs when child abuse is discounted and the child is left with no protection. These children are driven to private, internal solutions in an effort to escape the abuse. They may develop an internal world into which they retreat for comfort and solace. This coping strategy often develops into a dissociative disorder, the most extreme form being dissociative identity disorder. Many sexually abused children manifest a host of other mental health difficulties or behavioral problems.

Sexually abused children usually enter into therapy with a wide variety of presenting problems. Their symptoms can mimic those of a learning disability, such as poor attention and concentration and declining school performance. They may have difficulty retaining information and appear anxious or withdrawn in the classroom. Children with a dissociative disorder as a result of extreme and repeated abuse often fluctuate dramatically in their school performance, from excellent to deficient performance in an episodic manner. Another symptom picture is the oppositional child with temper outbursts and/or inappropriate sexual behavior toward other children. Still other youngsters may present as compliant and clingy, manifesting regressive behaviors previously outgrown, such as bed-wetting, whining, stranger anxiety, and fearfulness.

Because sexual abuse is often repetitive and chronic, many of the routine posttraumatic indicators may be hidden or have already progressed into a more chronic form. In such cases, children may become somewhat adapted to the abuse and evidence more entrenched personality types or behavioral disturbances.

At present, despite increased awareness about abuse issues, there still remains no diagnosis or recognized child sexual abuse syndrome in the *Diagnostic and Statistical Manual of Mental Disorders (DSM-IV)* (APA 1994). There is a section on "Problems Related to Abuse or Neglect," but there are no established, recognized criteria set forth as the standard symptoms of a sexually abused child. Many cases are diagnosed as posttraumatic stress disorder (PTSD) in an effort to recognize the life-threatening nature of the abuse experience and the traumatic response of the child. In extreme cases, children may be diagnosed with dissociative identity disorder (DID) because they may have developed an entire personality system as a defense against ongoing, inescapable abuse.

Additional posttraumatic symptoms that children may describe include recurrent dreams of the abusive event(s), repetitive intrusive images and thoughts of the event, and reliving of the event as if it were occurring in the present (flashbacks). There may be intense psychological or physiological reactivity in the child when he/she is exposed to external or internal cues that resemble or are symbolic of the sexual abuse. In the therapy room, the clinician will often note that many children make strenuous efforts to avoid any conversation or feelings regarding the sexual abuse. They may wish to avoid any activities, people, and places that remind them of the abuse incidents. When questioned about abuse, many children will demonstrate a difficulty or inability to recall important aspects of the sexual trauma. Their accounts may often seem confused or inconsistent. While this can be a great difficulty for the legal system in their efforts to prosecute, it does not necessarily prove that a child's reports of sexual abuse are false. Confusion and difficulty with full recall are common, natural reactions to trauma, as in the posttraumatic stress disorder syndrome.

Children may be diagnosed as depressed if they display such posttraumatic symptoms as detachment from friends and family, or a noticeable loss of interest in their usual play activities. Sometimes sexually abused children may relate a fantasy of being dead or of aggressively overpowering others in an effort to regain their lost sense of personal empowerment. These children may feel unable to experience a sense of being loving toward siblings, friends, and others. Children may also have difficulty sleeping and experience night terrors and outbursts of anger. They may be hypervigilant or become easily startled.

The myriad symptoms require the clinician to be attuned to each individual child's report of abuse. Each sexually abused child will have his or her own particular combination of abuse-related symptomatology. The therapist must be familiar with all the possible symptoms of an abused child and must treat each case individually. The determination of sexual abuse must be made as the information is provided by the child, without leading questions or pressure to reveal suspected abuse. An experienced therapist may suspect abuse far sooner than a child is able to reveal it. In such cases care must be taken to be sure that the information regarding possible abuse comes from the child.

Traditional Treatment Strategies

Traditional treatment strategies with sexually abused children include a stepwise progression from initial assessment to longer-term treatment efforts focused on the sexual abuse experience. Individual talk therapy focuses initially on building rapport with the child and establishing an alliance of trust. Eventually, there is a revelation of the abuse experience. The next phase requires the therapist to address the pain such abuse has caused and to accompany the child through such existential questions as "Why me?" and "How could someone do this to me?" It is impossible to answer such questions. The therapist must provide support through this critical phase of therapy. The ending phase of treatment brings forth a renewed sense of self and personal strength. The questions cease and the ambiguity of the reasons for the abuse is better tolerated. Responsibility for the abuse is placed onto the perpetrator, which then generates a newfound sense of freedom and self-worth.

Strand (1991) describes six phases of treatment with the sexually abused child: (1) conducting a developmental assessment, (2) taking a sexual abuse history, (3) establishing ego-enhancing strengths for the child, (4) assisting the trauma to surface and assessing the impact of the trauma, (5) working through the trauma, and (6) gaining resolution of the trauma. While these phases of treatment appear to be distinct, children will generally vacillate back and forth through several phases of treatment, manifesting the corresponding needs in each phase. There is very little description in the literature of the "working through" phase of treatment, which has been described as the longest phase (Strand 1991).

Traditional treatment strategies have assumed that there is a point of resolution of the trauma (Herman 1992). For children, it is when the child can discuss the events of the abuse without significant emotional distress. A certain distance and objectivity does develop for the child who has been abused, given good treatment and appropriate supports; however, it may not be accurate to conclude that the child ever fully resolves the trauma. Traumatic events in one's life usually change an individual in significant ways forever. For the sexually abused child, these ways are far-reaching. It may be that the child's disclosures lead to a breakup of the family system with corresponding changes in socioeconomic level. A child may never see an abusive parent again or may be required by the court to see that parent in a terrifying, unsupervised visitation setting on a regular basis for many years because there was insufficient evidence to verify the child's account of abuse. The child will live with these consequences of reporting abuse for the rest of his or her life, and the changes caused by the abuse present difficult challenges at each new developmental stage.

Art Therapy

Art therapy is a useful modality in the treatment of the sexually abused child. It has proven to be a cathartic as well as a powerful projective technique in revealing a child's innermost thoughts and concerns. Children benefit from reviewing their art productions throughout treatment. Art can be used as a compelling visual illustration of a child's past traumatic experiences. Art may be the only medium through which some particularly traumatized children can express themselves emotionally. The common threat sexually abused children hear is "Do not ever tell" about the abuse. For many children, this means there is danger in verbalizing the experience of abuse. Art therapy, being nonverbal, can ease this burden and fear. When working with children with dissociative disorders, various alters may excel in artistic ability. These personalities often emerge to take on the role of revealing through art renditions the aspects of the abuse that are too difficult to verbalize to the therapist (Cohen and Cox 1995).

Family Therapy

Family therapy can be extremely powerful in the treatment of the sexually abused child; however, there are numerous circumstances that must first be carefully evaluated. If a parent is the perpetrator of the abuse, a careful determination must be made as to whether he/she accepts responsibility for the abuse. It is also important that the perpetrator be in individual therapy. The single most common and grievous error made by therapists and social agencies is to compel the sexually abused child to be in family therapy with a parent who denies the abuse. If a parent does admit the abuse, it can be most healing for the child and adult involved to confront the abusive behavior and work it through together. The child can obtain validation and an apology, and develop hope that the future can be different once the parent has received proper treatment. If such recognition on the part of the adult does not occur, however, there is no chance for such resolution. The child will feel his or her account of the abuse has been ignored, which is a devastating assault on his or her perception of reality.

In circumstances in which the abuser is someone outside of the home and immediate family, it is most desirable to enlist family support for the child. Children need to see their parents as their protectors. When children are abused, often by trusted caregivers, their trust in their parents' ability to care for them is threatened. Family sessions can help reestablish a feeling of trust, security, and validation between the parents and the child.

Group Therapy

Group therapy of the sexually abused child is less commonly used, although there is evidence that it has been quite helpful for adults. Abuse cases involving children engender so much legal activity, such as court procedures, repeated examinations, testimony, and so on, that group therapy may feel like an impersonal chaotic experience. Group treatment with children who have been sexually abused is most beneficial when there is no further court involvement, and after individual therapy has successfully concluded or is in the final stages. The focus of sexual abuse groups for children should be on specific issues rather than open-ended, and the topics addressed should emphasize empowerment and resolution rather than recounting incidents or details of abuse. The rationale for such groups is to allow the child to break the secrecy attached to the abuse and to provide opportunities to develop trust and experience empathy (Courtois 1988).

Play Therapy

Burgess (1987) discusses the concept of *traumatic encapsulation*, in which feelings regarding sexual abuse are defended against and the child is left essentially unable to express his or her feelings openly. Play therapy is an effective remedy to this blockage because it liberates the child to begin to emote freely without the need to translate emotion into verbal expression. Play themes naturally and spontaneously emerge in a cascading display of emotional reactions to the abuse. Simultaneously, the play experience generates a feeling of relief and mastery, which is essential to the ultimate well-being of the child.

Rationale for Play Therapy

The sexual abuse of children often involves secrecy, which stifles the child's expression of all the emotions resulting from the trauma. Normal developmental pathways are blocked, which can then cause a wide variety of psychological problems. Most approaches to the treatment of sexual abuse suggest that the individual reexperience the trauma in a therapeutic context by describing the events that occurred and then experience the accepting, nurturing responses of the therapist. Conflicts are clarified and self-blame is relieved.

In revealing and reexperiencing the trauma in a therapeutic context, it is not the reliving of the abuse per se that heals but rather the therapist's assisting the child to actively identify, question, examine, and dispel any destructive messages communicated during the abuse. These messages are usually related to the child's lack of self-worth and absence of personal power. The abuser's disrespect for the child's body makes the child feel deserving of the abuse and obligated to subordinate him/herself to the needs of another. These messages must be processed in therapy at a child's level of comprehension. Play, being a child's natural way of communicating, provides a valuable tool by which to examine and resolve these destructive messages.

Play activity is young children's primary mode of emotional expression. The early work of talented child therapists like Melanie Klein (1976) established that play is the major way of tapping into the unconscious fantasies, dreams, fears, and anxieties of young children. Play therapy is the most valuable technique to employ with sexually abused children because the atmosphere of play allows a young school-aged child to feel at ease quickly. Sexual abuse is an overwhelming, anxiety-provoking issue for the young child. Play techniques can be interspersed with discussions about abuse to help titrate the anxiety that is elicited in exploring the issue of abuse with the child. In addition, much information about the child's reactions to the abuse can be gleaned from allowing play themes to emerge in the context of therapy.

Children who have been sexually abused typically present with play themes of good and bad, submissive and dominant confrontations, overpowering "bad guys," and highly sexualized themes between boys and girls or mommies and daddies. In all these themes the child is attempting to sort out and make sense of the various confusing images and interactions that have taken place during the incidents of sexual abuse. Play becomes an open road to the innermost part of the child's mind. It is through play that the intricacies of the child's pain can be tapped and identified. For the child, these anxieties and concerns are expressed and released in the context of therapeutic play. This release is usually an empowering and validating experience for the child.

While employing the "playing cure" the therapist has an opportunity to observe and monitor the progress of the child's conflicts in vivid and descriptive play themes. For many children traditional talk therapy on such a frightening and humiliating subject as sexual abuse is very difficult to do. They become flooded with anxiety and are unable to talk in depth about the trauma. In play therapy the child can work through the trauma in an indirect fashion, which will create less anxiety for the child. All the stages of healing and resolution can be seen in the child's play. For example, messages about the child's lack of personal power are counteracted in play themes of physical power, personal strength, and victory over intruders or threatening images. As the therapist affirms the play themes, he/she also affirms a new message to the child—that it is okay to heal, to feel one's personal power, and to assert that power when feeling threatened by others. In addition, playful therapeutic exercises and projects can be done to reinstate healthy attitudes about one's private parts and about how to resist someone who touches them in inappropriate ways.

Therapeutic Powers of Play

Schaefer (1993) describes fourteen therapeutic powers of play, all of which are significant in the treatment of the sexually abused child. The initial power, overcoming resistance, is especially important in dealing with the sexually abused child. Although this is often perceived as a beginning task in therapy, for the sexually abused child establishing a working alliance is an ongoing trust issue. These children have been confronted with the pain and reality of adult betrayal. The therapist is faced with the task of counteracting these experiences.

The second therapeutic power of play, communication, takes place within the play therapy experience. Young children who have been sexually abused need to be assisted to verbalize their pain and overcome the fear of telling what has happened to them. Many of these children have been threatened that something terrible will happen to them or their family if they tell about the sexual abuse. The therapist's task is to find a way that the child can communicate his or her conscious and unconscious reactions about the abuse. Puppets and anatomically correct dolls help many sexually abused children express through actions and play themes what they cannot say in words. Because a sexually abused child is told by the perpetrator not to tell anyone, the experience has a hypnotic effect on the child; the trauma incident becomes an experience of focused attention not unlike a trance induction. The abuser's authoritative instructions not to tell have a strong influence on the child. The use of indirect play methods, therefore, can be very effective in bypassing the anxiety the child feels about telling. An abuser may also tell the child that what is happening is not real but only the child's imagination. The child may then suffer from tremendous self-doubt about his or her perceptions.

The therapist must ascertain the child's level of knowledge about sexual issues and body parts and then record the child's accounts of abuse in the child's own language.

The third power of play Schaefer discusses, mastery, is an essential aspect of working with children who have been sexually abused. These children must gain mastery in order to build a much needed sense of self-esteem. Children who have been sexually abused find themselves in a position of total powerlessness. This is often seen in the quality of their play in early stages of therapy. Play behavior is usually frenetic and chaotic when talking about abuse. This quality of the play communicates the child's overwhelming anxiety, feelings of powerlessness, and lack of mastery. As the therapist assists the child to gradually contain and structure their play themes into masterful accomplished stories, a model of empowerment is communicated to the child. The idea of hope and restoration of personal power is communicated, and through these messages the child begins to regain self-esteem. In addition to mastery over internal conflict, sexually abused children will experiment with their level of physical competence and strength. Because sexual abuse involves the physical domination of one person over another, the therapist should often give the child opportunities to display his or her strength and physical prowess. The therapist should validate the child's physical strengths and encourage the child to explore the outer limits of his or her physical powers. The child may boast about his or her physical abilities to the therapist, who should respond with support, admiration, and affirmation. The therapist may also encourage parents to involve the child in various physical activities with peers.

The fourth therapeutic power involved in play is creative thinking. Schaefer writes that the beneficial outcome of play regarding creative thinking leads to a child's increased ability to derive innovative solutions to problems. The strengthening of these problem-solving skills is extremely important when working with early school-aged children who have been sexually abused. Through the play activity they can be encouraged to design their own ways of protecting themselves from future assaults. They can learn methods to identify their problems and fears and then generate ways to solve them. Through finding solutions, sexually abused children can regain a sense of personal power and mastery. They learn that they can figure out ways to protect themselves. In addition to focusing on themes of self-protection, creative thinking tasks in play can facilitate verbal empowerment. Children can find new ways to verbally express their dislike of and resistance to being abused. Thus, they learn effective, verbal, assertive problem-solving skills.

The fifth and sixth therapeutic powers of play, catharsis and abreaction, deal mainly with the issue of processing emotionally laden material. For the sexually abused child, the therapist offers a safe environment in which the child can experience the emotional release that catharsis can provide. In the same way, the therapist assists the child to metabolize the past trauma through repetitive abreaction experiences. The abreactions that occur within the context of play therapy are often repetitive and initially disorganized and incomplete. As therapy progresses, more information is usually revealed; however, young children rarely present with a fully developed, chronologically well-organized, abreaction presentation. They may move back and forth between actual events that occurred during abusive incidents and fantasy material of efforts toward mastery. This occurs as the psyche attempts to help mediate the child's anxiety while in the midst of an abreaction experience. The therapist must carefully take time with the child to review the play product and determine from the child's report what parts are factual and what parts are fantasies. Much catharsis also occurs within the context of play themes that seem unrelated to the sexual abuse experience. Play therapy is the most useful technique in allowing the sexually abused child freedom to express all sorts of unconscious conflicts about good and bad, dominance and submission.

The seventh therapeutic power of play, role play, emerges as children pretend in a context of interactive dramas. Through experimentation with role reversal, sexually abused children assume a power position over other characters who may be trying to dominate them. Frequently, the therapist will end up playing the role of the "bad guy" and allowing the child to dominate the "bad guy" figure. Role play also helps children develop a sense of empathy.

What is most important for the sexually abused child is restoring a sense of personal power. The therapist can gear role play experiences to focus on family roles, parental roles, and sibling roles, and on the conflicts the child may have with each of these. For example, the sexually abused child will be in conflict not only about a loving parental figure that may have abused him or her, but also about the parent who failed to provide protection from the sexual abuse. The therapist may also use role play to assist the child in understanding the roles of the judges, lawyers, and child protection workers involved in the court procedure, if one is pending. Such role play experiences can help the child to begin to organize what he or she wishes to communicate about what happened. In long-term play therapy, sexually abused children can develop fantasy characters that can be effectively used to process unconscious conflicts regarding feelings of anger, grief, anxiety, rage, and betrayal.

The eighth therapeutic power of play, fantasy, can bring escape and relief from unmet needs. For these children, fantasies often center around fulfilling unmet needs such as the need for protection, for personal empowerment, and for finding unconditional, nonsexualized love.

The ninth therapeutic power, metaphoric teaching, can be employed with the sexually abused child through fantasy and role play sessions. Children can create powerful characters and develop insight through the indirect use of metaphor, guided by the therapist. Themes of freedom, personal integrity, and victory over being dominated should be emphasized.

Sexually abused children struggle with the conflict between the normal idealization of their parents as perfect adult role models and the contradictory information that these same adults have hurt them or failed to protect them. Metaphoric teaching through play may assist children in resolving their broken idealistic views of their parents. Therapists can address these children's conflicts and help them to gain the insight necessary to develop a more realistic view of their parents as individuals with their own conflicts and problems. For the young school-aged child this is a gradual task that will proceed as the child matures.

The tenth therapeutic power, attachment formation, results in the child's ability to feel a sense of attachment to the therapist, which reproduces a positive parallel of the parent–child relationship. In working with the sexually abused child this issue is particularly emotionally charged. One technique developed by Jernberg (1979) is called Theraplay. This approach provides the child with pleasurable sensorimotor experiences similar to those usually experienced by an infant interacting with a parent. These include interactions such as tickling, carrying piggyback, and other forms of physical exchange between the therapist and the child. While this approach can be valuable in helping to foster attachment, the therapist must be extremely careful in utilizing such interactions with young children who have been sexually abused. These patients may have a fear of being touched, and it is important that physical boundaries between the therapist and child remain clear. One alternative recommendation would be to encourage the nonabusive parent(s) to perform some of these early therapeutic touch interventions at home or in sessions as an adjunct to the treatment process. This would give a nonabusive parent an opportunity to repeat earlier experiences with the child that would allow the child a period of regression and then restabilization by experiencing what early "good touching" with a trusted adult should feel like.

Sexually abused children may attempt to touch the therapist in inappropriate ways. This is an excellent opportunity to directly address concepts of good and bad touching. Conversely, sexually abused children may be extremely fearful of touch and then gradually become more able to touch or interact in appropriate ways with the therapist. This can be regarded as a sign of significant therapeutic progress. The therapist must continue to maintain clear boundaries and encourage the child to talk openly and freely about touching.

The eleventh therapeutic power of play, relationship enhancement, is the most essential aspect of play therapy treatment with the sexually abused child. Self-esteem, self-actualization, and the ability to be close to others are fostered through the therapeutic relationship. This is both a quality experience in the here and now and a corrective emotional experience for the child's past boundary violations. The child should feel respected, cherished, valued, and nurtured in this interchange. Self-actualization is fostered by enabling the child to feel successful in appropriate, nonabusive and nonexploitive interactions with others. The child can also experience a sense of closeness to others without fear and without the need for vigilant self-protection.

The therapy experience should have strong impact on the child throughout his or her life. Sexual abuse affects one's lifelong relationships with others and with one's environment. The therapist can have impact on these relationships. If a child's ability to relate to other people is restored, he/she will then be able to go out into the world and fashion new healthy positive relationships by which to be nurtured and valued. This is the greatest gift the therapeutic relationship can give to the child who has been sexually abused.

The twelfth therapeutic power of play therapy, positive emotion or enjoyment, is the most soothing element for the sexually abused child. Often the therapy room is one of the few places, if not the only place, the child can escape the pressures of a chaotic family and misdirected parental expectations. For the sexually abused child especially, the therapy playroom is a refuge of peacefulness and orderliness from an often overwhelming, overstimulating, emotionally charged family environment. In families of lower socioeconomic status, this chaos in which the child lives is often quite overt, including multiple caregivers, drug and alcohol abusers, dangerous neighborhoods, lack of privacy, and very limited financial resources. The sexually abused child from higher socioeconomic levels is still confronted with family chaos, although it is more covert, such as custody battles that drag on for years, arguments over the available financial resources, and change of schools because of higher mobility, relocations, and split-custody arrangements.

Fashioning a play therapy experience that is cathartic, validating, and empowering but also soothing and fun is of great value to the child. The play therapy serves as a stress antidote as well as a source of encouragement and hope for the future. Thus, discussions of stressful material regarding abuse issues are balanced by positive experiential play. But the session should always begin and end with positive play.

The thirteenth therapeutic power of play, mastering of developmental fears, fosters a sense of growth and development for the sexually abused child. Schaefer (1993) refers to a technique designed by Wolpe (1958) called systematic desensitization, which has been used effectively to treat such conditions as anxiety, phobias, and fear responses. Schaefer applies Wolpe's concepts of anxiety reduction to the play experience. Therapists can expose children to a fear stimulus while they are in the comfortable, positive surroundings of the playroom, thereby neutralizing the fear response previously associated with that fear stimulus. Schaefer recounts the deconditioning of a child from fear of the dark through such desensitization experiences.

The sexually abused child may have numerous anxiety-provoking stimuli that require deconditioning interventions. If these are not addressed, these same regressed fears will often carry over into adulthood and become more entrenched and difficult to ameliorate. Adult patients may engage in many years of psychotherapy for a phobia or anxiety-related response that is connected to early childhood trauma that has been repressed. Treatment for such fear responses in the early school-age years can have positive impact on the child's problems and can resolve these fear responses for life. These fears may include fear of being alone; fear of the dark; fear that yelling or arguments will lead to physical violence; fear that expressing feelings may lead to drastic consequences; fear of sleeping, if abuse occurred at night; fear of taking baths, if abuse occurred in the bathroom; fear of wearing certain types of clothing that the child may believe caused him or her to be abused; and fear of being without certain articles of clothing, if the abuse occurred when the child was not wearing a particular garment, such as sleeping without underwear. Some of these fears may be addressed in a desensitization fashion, while others will simply need to be talked about or played out in fantasy play.

The fourteenth and final therapeutic power of play is ego strengthening and the development of social skills. Children's interest in games usually begins around age 5 or 6, so games are an excellent way for the therapist to begin to establish rapport. They provide an excellent segue into discussion about rules in our society and what happens to people who break them. Rules of normal social behavior and appropriate parental treatment of children can also be addressed through the medium of playing with games. Physical games are also quite useful in helping to develop a child's physical prowess while promoting well-balanced attitudes toward one's play partners. Supervised group game-play experiences with the sexually abused child may help to correct inappropriate interactions with peers, particularly reenactments of violation of personal space and boundaries.

Schaefer's therapeutic powers are interwoven during the therapeutic play and should be an integral part of the treatment framework. A therapist employing this approach with the sexually abused child addresses all the major issues involved in the treatment process.

Approach

Description

Therapy with the sexually abused child must address both the short- and long-term needs of the child. Short-term needs center around play themes of fear about initial disclosure and its effects on the child and the rest of the family unit if the abuser is a family member. Interventions that focus on feelings of safety and protection are crucial. Schaefer's (1993) therapeutic powers of communication and attachment are central play themes, as are encouraging creative thinking and problem-solving skills. Relationship enhancement also begins with the client's disclosure to a therapist, because that is when the issue of trust arises. A child must trust a therapist in order to reveal information about sexual abuse; thus, it is at this point that an attachment formation is established and relationship enhancement therapy work can commence.

Long-term needs center primarily around ego strengthening and healing from the abuse. Several of Schaefer's (1993) therapeutic powers of play are mobilized in the extended work with sexually abused children. The specific configuration of techniques used and therapeutic powers focused on vary depending on the intensity of the child's internal conflicts. The therapist's flexibility and responsiveness to the child's needs are essential. For example, a child struggling with fear of disclosure cannot be rushed into revealing aspects of abuse. The therapist may feel pressure to learn the details, but passing on such pressure to the child could be devastating. For example, a child with any fear reaction, such as fear of the dark, may be able to accept behavioral deconditioning interventions in later phases of therapy; however, a "lights-on" policy in the bedroom at night may be necessary in earlier stages of the therapeutic work. This same patient stance is essential when working with the sexually abused child.

Kluft (1991) discusses a "rule of thirds" in his work with sexually abused patients. This approach also works well in child play sessions. The first third of the play session should be to establish connection with the child and affirm an atmosphere of safety. The middle third of the play session should be used to address issues of trauma. The last third of the session should be dedicated to reestablishing a positive sense of self-esteem, providing closure, and refocusing on the enjoyment of play so that the child leaves the session with a sense of stress relief and with a feeling of invigoration.

A treatment plan should respond directly to each child's particular needs. There are various play techniques, including symbolic play, play with natural media (sand, water, food, etc.), drawing and artistic craft works, storytelling, role playing, imagery, board games, and even high-tech computer games, which can be incorporated into an individualized treatment plan to meet the child's psychological needs (Schaefer and Cangelosi 1993). This individualized approach to play therapy will communicate to the sexually abused child that his/her needs are being heeded and respected, and the child will feel honored and valued. This is the most powerful message a therapist can impart to a child who has endured such tremendous psychological pain at such an early age. This approach reestablishes a sense of personal value and self-worth in the child.

Techniques

The initial phase of contact often requires some form of assessment regarding the allegations of abuse. This is critical in determining the range and type of services needed by the child. The format of the initial assessment is often dictated by the circumstances of the referral.

Assessment strategies with the sexually abused child often include the use of anatomically correct dolls. Therapists also use these dolls during treatment. Other tools that are appropriate and can be helpful are books, tapes, and stories about abused children. However, they can also become an encumbrance in cases with heavy court involvement, since there is no standard by which to present such material to the child. For example, it is not uncommon for the presentation of anatomically correct dolls to be viewed as leading a child to discuss sexual abuse. Proper accepted practices and protocols should be followed when working with the dolls as a method of assessment or to encourage disclosure (Goodman and Bottoms 1993). The extent of court involvement must be ascertained by the therapist, which will then help to determine what materials are best to use.

A systematic assessment of dissociative symptoms in the sexually abused child is essential to ensure adequate and effective treatment planning. The assessment of dissociation will also identify serious complications such as a dissociative identity disorder early in treatment. Assessment can help to determine the extent of the trauma endured by the child as well as the treatment plan required. Children who manifest definite dissociative symptoms are most likely to have been repeatedly and severely abused/traumatized to the extent that they needed to maximize the use of dissociative defense capabilities. Such children require specialized treatment that addresses the various aspects of self ("alters") they have created to help them cope with conflicting emotional needs and reactions. The task is to integrate these competing aspects of self into one fully functioning self. Specific treatment for dissociative features is a new approach; it is essential once an accurate diagnosis of dissociative disorder is established.

Conducting an Assessment

The therapist begins an assessment for dissociative disorder in children by asking a series of questions. Early school-aged children are able to describe their dissociative symptoms if they are asked modifications of the questions in the Structured Clinical Interview for DSM-IV: Dissociative Disorders Revised (SCID-D-R, Steinberg 1994b), which is an assessment tool that comprehensively evaluates the severity of five core posttraumatic and dissociative symptoms: (1) amnesia, (2) depersonalization, (3) derealization, (4) identity confusion, and (5) identity alteration (Steinberg 1994a). Researchers have reported good-to-excellent reliability and validity of the SCID-D in assessing trauma and sexual abuse survivors (Boon and Draijer 1991, Goff et al. 1992).

Since the SCID-D is the most reliable assessment tool to date in evaluating the effects of trauma (Steinberg et al. 1993), the child therapist can simply modify the SCID-D questions for the comprehension level of the younger child. The SCID-D is a semi-structured interview tool. Therefore, modification of the questions will not affect the validity of the results as long as the child is questioned about all five core symptoms of dissociation. Young children are capable of providing eloquent examples of their dissociative experiences and the effect on their personal lives. For example, when asked about amnesia one child said, "Oh yes, that's when I have fast days." Further inquiry revealed that he would leave for school in the morning and the next thing he knew, he was playing outside with friends after school without remembering how he got home.

Children often describe depersonalization experiences such as floating above their bed at night or escaping through the ceiling of their room to another dimension. They will describe derealization experiences such as feeling isolated from friends. One child said, "Well, first I'm playing with my friends and then it's like I don't even know them anymore. . . . A couple of times I couldn't remember my best friend's name and he looked very weird to me, so I got scared." Early school-aged children will usually describe identity confusion and identity alteration very openly once they are asked about it.

Identity confusion is the subjective feeling of an internal war between dissociated aspects of self, while identity alteration is the outward behavioral manifestation of acting like a different personality (Steinberg 1995). Young children will reveal the "alters" within them easily because they are often unaware that this is not normal. They are displaying a natural phenomenon: the use of the defense of dissociation. It feels normal and comfortable as a means to mediate intense emotional impulses and stimuli. While the intense reliance on a dissociative defense mechanism is not normal per se, it is an adaptive mode of coping with the intense traumas of the past in the present. The older the child, the more he/she will be sensitized to the difference between him- or herself and other children. As this awareness grows, children begin to conceal the inner world they have created to survive their personal trauma. Therapists who treat sexually abused children must become familiar with the symptoms of dissociation. Early detection of dissociative symptoms is essential to solid treatment planning and the effective resolution of the internal conflicts originating from sexual abuse.

Children with dissociative disorders who are not diagnosed early often show poor academic performance despite their bright intellectual capacities. The first case reports on the use of the SCID-D in adolescents (Steinberg and Steinberg 1995) reveal that misdiagnosis in early childhood can lead to years of misguided efforts by therapists and teachers. The accurate diagnosis of a dissociative disorder is, therefore, critical to effectively treat the sexually abused child. Recovery from a dissociative disorder requires that the child receive treatment (including play therapy) specifically focused on the symptoms of dissociation.

Treatment Considerations

Children who come to treatment with the presenting issue of sexual abuse have numerous urgent needs. The foremost of these needs is for protection from continued abuse. The therapist must play a central role in attempting to protect the child through appropriate professional channels. This may include making a report to the child protection agency and staying involved with the investigation process to ensure the child receives comprehensive services.

The next essential step in treatment is to establish with the child the proper boundaries of the therapy relationship. Children should be allowed to ask any questions they wish regarding the role of the therapist. Confidentiality is a difficult issue when dealing with sexual abuse. While early school-aged children are accustomed to their parents knowing all their personal information, there still may be times when they express a desperate need for confidentiality. They may ask their therapist not to tell one or the other parent about the disclosures of abuse. When a child expresses these concerns it is particularly significant because the child's fears usually are of being further punished for revealing the abuse or being left unprotected in an abusive situation.

The safety concerns of the child may be a genuine and terrifying issue. The request for confidentiality is actually a request for protection. The therapist

188 The Playing Cure

needs to think ahead about his/her actions and how they will ultimately affect the child. The therapist could take an action that is consistent with proper treatment guidelines and still in some way hurt the child. For example, in general practice the therapist interviews both parents when sexual abuse is disclosed by a child. There may be times, however, when interviewing a parent suspected of abuse may engender danger for the child. The parent may openly deny such allegations. After the interview session, the child must then go home with the parent, and the child is left unprotected. If a therapist decides to interview a parent suspected of abuse, he/she must first be sure there are adequate safety supports for that child before any questioning about abuse can proceed. This task is more wisely left in the hands of the proper legal authorities.

Children involved in court proceedings may have many questions about them. In such cases, the therapist must proceed with the awareness of eventual court involvement. Treatment approaches usually include the necessary court preparation of the child in an effort to desensitize the child to the intimidating atmosphere of the courtroom setting. This is a difficult task because preparation efforts may later be viewed in the court context as a therapist's leading or programming a child to give certain responses. In an effort to make a child feel more comfortable in the court setting, the therapist may review information the child had previously revealed in early treatment sessions. It is often months or even years before the child must appear in court.

As children begin to heal from the abusive incidents, they may forget certain details of the trauma they had originally reported in therapy. They may rely on what they had confided to the therapist months or years ago as if this were a piece of their memory base.

Clinicians working with children who have been abused must take careful notes after sessions, specifically focusing on the child's verbalizations and behaviors, not just on their professional opinions. These notes are most useful when they are illustrated with quotes from the child, because children have their own unique way of expressing their pain in a poignant manner.

Recently, new efforts have been made to ease the anxiety for children giving testimony (Haugaard and Reppucci 1988). These efforts include allowing them to testify behind a screen or on closed-circuit television. Thus the child does not face the alleged perpetrator. However, there still are long time delays from the moment of the child's initial report of abuse to the court hearing. Therapists are left with the task of psychologically preparing the child for the court experience, which goes against the natural tendency in healing to move forward and not dwell on the abuse. Sexually abused children long to "be like other kids." The play therapy process helps reestablish such feelings of normalcy in the child. It is unfortunate that this urge for normalcy is in direct contradiction to the task the court demands of the child, which is to recount the abuse in detail. In preparing the child for court, the therapist must be cautious not to compromise the child's sense of well-being and mental health.

All children, even very young children, should be permitted to express their desires regarding their future interactions with a perpetrator parent. This is essential in satisfying the emotional and safety needs of children who have been victimized. They must be included in the court procedures carefully interviewed, and their desires must be considered.

Case Illustration

Anne, a 6-year-old, first came to therapy after nearly a year of court involvement. There had been a successful decision on the part of the court to not permit her to have visits with her father, who was the alleged abuser. This decision was based on the feelings of the child. Anne, an intelligent, verbal child, was quite definite in her decision not to see her father because he would not admit that the abuse occurred or apologize to her for his behavior.

Presenting problems with this child included pervasive difficulties sleeping, nightmares, and aggressive interactions with peers at school and at home. She was unable to attend to classroom activities, and begged daily to go to the school nurse claiming a wide array of physical complaints, the most frequent of which was a chronic stomachache. Anne's grades were poor and inconsistent with her teacher's estimations of her intellectual potential.

The initial phase of therapy focused on establishing rapport and subsequent trust. There was no need to gain information about the specifics of the abuse because court involvement was already resolved. In such a case, it is best to allow ample time before broaching the issue of abuse. This allows the therapist to assess the child's level of ego strength and to help shore up defenses for later work when the abuse will be addressed. Unstructured fantasy play was the intervention of choice during this initial phase because it helped to reveal Anne's methods for coping with anxiety. Her play was initially quite disorganized and she would slip into trancelike states in which she would howl like a wolf or act out other animal-type roles.

The initial work revealed that Anne was flooded with anxiety and searching for efforts at mastery. She presented one play theme of being a schoolteacher. The therapist then guided this theme into more structured masterful play sessions centered around themes of control and personal power. Soon Anne was able to direct the therapist in the role as the "student." This indicated that Anne was developing and internalizing a sense of personal power and control. Additional play themes developed in which Anne became quite dominant and bossy as the teacher. She began to chastise the imaginary students and the therapist, indicating a need for release from anger and fears of domination. Anne was moving closer to the sexual abuse. At this point no specific discussion was pursued; however, Anne was provided opportunities to indirectly express her anger and fantasies of domination with a series of puppets and other play figures. Sand play was also used to help Anne project some of her more angry feelings at inanimate objects rather than at the therapist directly, because it was apparent that Anne was becoming attached to the therapist and needed her to be her partner in the work to come. Assisting Anne in directing her needs for dominance onto play figures helped to indirectly communicate that there was no risk of losing or alienating the therapist she had come to trust. Next, Anne raised numerous repetitive themes of conflict and struggle between family figures. Initially, these struggles were chaotic and disorganized. Over time her battles became more focused, and family members began to use verbal confrontation rather than physical violence as a solution to their dilemmas. This particular phase of treatment lasted approximately six months.

The next phase of therapy involved Anne regressing to test out the strength of the therapeutic relationship. She would attempt to hang on the therapist and made numerous comments about the therapist's appearance such as hair color, eyeglasses, height, weight, and clothes. Role play was used to help Anne express such curiosity in more socially appropriate ways. During this phase it became clear that Anne was also preoccupied with not becoming fat, even at her young age. This concern heralded possible risk factors for a future eating disorder. Artwork was employed to assist Anne in gaining a better self-image and positive attitude toward her body.

Anne would build fortresses out of materials in the playroom. She would then crawl into the fort and play a variety of hide-and-seek themes. This was interpreted as testing the constancy of the therapist to be there and reassure her of the stability of the therapeutic relationship. These more regressed infantile games were of great delight to Anne and appeared to successfully establish a feeling of trust, in that she then began to reveal bits and pieces of her sexual abuse experience. She spoke about her visits with her father in his room at her paternal grandmother's house. She expressed confusion, anger, and feelings of abandonment because the abuse allegedly occurred while her grandmother was at home downstairs. These revelations of sexual abuse were interspersed with alternating play efforts and board games coordinated by the therapist to keep a sense of structure available to Anne. This provided an anchor of safe tasks she could return to when the anxiety became too great, a useful technique in working with sexually abused children. It enables them to titrate the emotionally charged material a little at a time while still feeling a sense of control.

Anne's gradual disclosure of the sexual abuse experiences led her into a period of confusion and then anger at her father for his actions. Techniques shifted in this phase away from structured play. Anatomically correct dolls were presented for Anne to express her feelings and provide further details of the abuse. The dolls were responded to with ambivalent feelings of excitement about playing with those "special dolls" and feeling overwhelmed at times to the extent that she would hide the dolls, throw them around in disgust, or lock them away. During this time, communication was an active therapeutic factor in the play. Anne was experiencing the safety of the therapeutic environment where she could express openly all her feelings without fear of repercussions or further abuse. She had also learned that no one knew of her disclosures and that her beloved family members were not injured in any way despite her father's threats. Eventually the play with these dolls became more organized and less sexualized. New play themes of cooperation and mutual respect emerged. These were good opportunities to use role play again to model healthy interpersonal interactions of an appropriately assertive nature.

Anne had manifested some moderate symptoms of dissociation during the phase of initial assessment. Throughout the therapy these dissociative features were addressed whenever they arose. Her imaginary companions each represented a different intense emotion that Anne had difficulty expressing without tremendous anxiety. Interventions with play figures in a sand tray and a variety of structured play experiences were the primary modalities in which the therapist could convey to Anne the values of integrating all emotions into a full sense of self. Children with dissociative features will readily discuss their conflicting sides. They are much more willing than adults to surrender these defenses if they are provided a safe environment and alternative resources through which to express their emotional pain. Kluft (1985a) has described rather rapid treatment of dissociative symptoms in young children due to the fact that their defense system is not entrenched.

At some point during the treatment of all young sexually abused children the issue of assertiveness must be thoroughly addressed. The most effective way of accomplishing this is via the role play method. In addition, during the anger phase, structured play therapy (Hambridge 1993) was introduced to assist with the release of intense emotion. Balloon bursting was used on a few occasions to give Anne a feeling of release mixed with joy and excitement.

There are three behavioral strategies that directly teach young school-aged children to master self-protection. These strategies were reviewed with Anne to give her a newfound sense of empowerment and foster a sense of mastery in protecting herself from future hurtful situations. The three general strategies given to children are (1) to say "no" emphatically, (2) to attempt to get away from the dangerous situation, and (3) to report the occurrence to an adult they can trust (Conte 1991). Anne was able to practice these strategies with the therapist. She felt a sense of mastery and increased self-confidence.

During this period of healing, Anne began to focus on her budding physical strengths. She would cartwheel her way in and out of the therapy room, and demonstrate splits and cheers and various dance gestures she practiced with a friend at home. Interventions from the therapist focused on ego enhancement at this point. Her physical strength was admired and encouraged. Her supportive custodial parent was directed to enroll her in sports activities of her choice and allow her ample time to play outside. The goal here was to orient Anne toward applying what had been experienced in therapy regarding relationship enhancement to her sphere of peer relations.

Upon termination Anne appeared to be well within the normal limits of a latency-aged child. Her focus was externally directed on friends and school activities. She was demonstrating significant improvement in being able to sleep undisturbed throughout the night. She was generally less fearful, more assertive, and expressed a sense of healthy self-esteem. Treatment was terminated at this time with the direction to the parent that future developmental strides may create a resurgence of issues that may cause anxiety or need to be addressed in therapy at a future time. For the present time, it was determined to be most important for Anne to view herself as a healthy, normal child, "just like all the other kids." This is precisely what she verbalized as her wish when she first entered therapy. It is what she said she felt like when she left therapy.

Conclusion

This chapter described the detailed and intricate interplay required when working with early school-aged children who have been sexually abused. The therapist is privileged to witness the dynamic human spirit in a process of renewal. Therapeutic interventions must address the main psychological needs of the child. It is recommended that a comprehensive initial assessment be conducted including a screening for possible dissociative disorder symptoms. The SCID-D method is the most extensively researched clinical tool to assess these traumatized children.

Treatment with the sexually abused child is a serious, long-term, and multifaceted endeavor. Brief therapy cannot address depth issues. The therapist must respect the child's healing process and allow it to unfold naturally. The therapy process can prove to be a mutually enriching experience for both the child and the therapist, but the therapist is the navigator of the child's progress.

Play therapy is a curative method by which to address the traumatized child. Issues of sexual abuse are often difficult for a young child to verbalize, but through the healing modality of play the child can reveal and resolve complex conflicts and intense feelings. Play can help focus children more clearly and reduce the increased anxiety usually found in abused children. The natural aspects of play make therapy less threatening and can encourage the child to be more open, less guarded, and more spontaneous. Play replenishes in the child the feelings of joy and hope that are often threatened as a result of abusive experiences.

The decision to use play therapy techniques and employ Schaefer's therapeutic factors of play will ensure that the major issues regarding the processing of trauma are addressed. Play therapy allows children to deal with intensely painful material in an indirect manner so as not to decrease their present functioning or require them to continually recall and discuss abusive experiences. The thrust of all play interventions is industrious, positive, and ego-enhancing, which powerfully propels the child forward to new stages of growth and personal empowerment.

Resolution of the issue of sexual abuse is lifelong, although dysfunctional reactions and anxieties can be remedied via periods of therapeutic contact throughout various developmental stages. Detecting sexual abuse in the early school-aged child is an important service professionals can provide. The most effective treatment for sexual abuse above all else is to stop the abuse. Once this task is accomplished, the healing process will begin as the child reclaims his or her indomitable spirit.

References

American Bar Association. (1988). *Sexual Abuse Allegations in Custody and Visitation Cases*. Washington, DC: American Bar Association.

American Psychiatric Association. (1994). *Diagnostic and Statistical Manual of Mental Disorders*, 4th ed. Washington, DC: American Psychiatric Association.

American Psychological Association. (Fall 1989). Clinicians don't always tell of suspected abuse. *APA Monitor*. Washington, DC: American Psychological Association Press.

Boon, S., and Draijer, N. (1991). Diagnosing dissociative disorders in The Netherlands: a pilot study with the Structured Clinical Interview for DSM-III-R Dissociative Disorders. *American Journal of Psychiatry* 148:458–462.

Burgess, A. (1987). Child molesting: assessing impact in multiple victims (part 1). *Archives of Psychiatric Nursing* 1:33–39.

Cohen, B. M., and Cox, C. T. (1995). *Telling Without Talking: Art as a Window into Multiple Personality*. New York: Norton.

Conte, J. (1991). Overview of child sexual abuse. In *Review of Psychiatry*, ed. A. Tasman, and M. Goldfinger, pp. 283–307. Washington, DC: American Psychiatric Press.

Courtois, C. (1988). *Healing the Incest Wound: Adult Survivors in Therapy*. New York: Norton.

Goff, D. C., Olin, J. A., Jenike, M. A., et al. (1992). Dissociative symptoms in patients with obsessive-compulsive disorder. *Journal of Nervous and Mental Disease* 180:332–337.

Goodman, G. S., and Bottoms, B. L. (1993). *Child Victims, Child Witnesses: Understanding and Improving Testimony*. New York: Guilford.

Hambridge, G. (1993). Structured play therapy. In *Play Therapy Techniques*, ed. C. E. Schaefer, and D. M. Cangelosi, pp. 45–61. Northvale, NJ: Jason Aronson.

Haugaard, J. J., and Reppucci, N. D. (1988). *The Sexual Abuse of Children: A Comprehensive Guide to Current Knowledge and Intervention Strategies*. San Francisco: Jossey-Bass.

Herman, J. L. (1992). *Trauma and Recovery*. Basic Books.

Hornstein, N. L., and Putnam, F. W. (1992). Clinical phenomenology of child and adolescent dissociative disorders. *Journal of the American Academy of Child and Adolescent Psychiatry* 31(6):1077–1085.

Jernberg, A. M. (1979). Theraplay technique. In *The Therapeutic Use of Child's Play*, ed. C. E. Schaefer, pp. 345–349. New York: Jason Aronson.

Klein, M. (1976). The psychoanalytic play technique. In *The Therapeutic Use of Child's Play*, ed. C. E. Schaefer, pp. 125–140. New York: Jason Aronson.

Kluft, R. P. (1985a). Childhood multiple personality disorder: predictors, clinical findings and treatment results. In *Childhood Antecedents of Multiple Personality*, ed. R. P. Kluft, p. 168–196. Washington, DC: American Psychiatric Press.

——— (1985b). The natural history of multiple personality disorders. In *Childhood Antecedents of Multiple Personality*, ed. R. P. Kluft, pp. 197–238. Washington, DC: American Psychiatric Press.

——— (1991). Multiple personality disorders. In *Review of Psychiatry*, vol. 10, ed. A. Tasman, and S. Goldfinger, pp. 161–188. Washington, DC: American Psychiatric Press.

Putnam, F. W., Guroff, J., Silberman, E., et al. (1986). The clinical phenomenology of multiple personality disorder: 100 recent cases. *Journal of Clinical Psychiatry* 47:285–293.

Russell, D. E. H. (1986). *The Secret Trauma: Incest in the Lives of Girls and Women.* New York: Basic Books.

Schaefer, C. E. (1993). What is play and why is it therapeutic? In *The Therapeutic Powers of Play*, pp. 1–15. Northvale, NJ: Jason Aronson.

Schaefer, C. E., and Cangelosi, D. M. (1993). *Play Therapy Techniques*. Northvale, NJ: Jason Aronson.

Steinberg, A., and Steinberg, M. (1995). Using the SCID-D to assess dissociative identity disorder in adolescents: three case studies. *Bulletin of the Menninger Clinic* 59(2):221–231.

Steinberg, M. (1994a). *Interviewer's Guide to the Structured Clinical Interview for DSM-IV: Dissociative Disorders-Revised (SCID-D-R)*. Washington, DC: American Psychiatric Press.

——— (1994b). *Structured Clinical Interview for DSM-IV Dissociative Disorders: Revised (SCID-D-R)*. Washington, DC: American Psychiatric Press.

——— (1995). *Handbook for the Assessment of Dissociation: A Clinical Guide.* Washington, DC: American Psychiatric Press.

Steinberg, M., Cicchetti, D., Buchanan, J., et al. (1993). Clinical assessment of dissociative symptoms and disorders: the Structured Clinical Interview for DSM-IV: Dissociative Disorders (SCID-D). *Dissociation* 6(1):3–15.

Strand, V. (1991). Victim of sexual abuse. In *Play Therapy with Children in Crisis: A Casebook for Practitioners*, ed. N. B. Webb, pp. 69–91. New York/London: Guilford.

Wolpe, J. (1958). *Psychotherapy by Reciprocal Inhibition*. Stanford, CA: Stanford University Press.

Part III

EXTERNALIZERS

8

Play Therapy for Children with Attention-Deficit Hyperactivity Disorder

Heidi Gerard Kaduson

One of the most common childhood disorders, attention-deficit hyperactivity disorder (ADHD), is frequently seen in clinical practice. Characterized by persistent and excessive problems with self-control, it runs a gamut of behaviors such as inattentiveness, impulsivity, and restlessness. Poor school performance and inadequate interpersonal relationships are often by-products of a nervous system with excessive, unharnessed energy.

The diagnostic criteria of the *DSM-IV* (APA 1994) lists developmentally inappropriate attention difficulties, impulsivity, and overactivity as the core features of ADHD. The distinguishing difference between ADHD children and others is the intensity, the persistency, and the patterning of these symptoms (Wender 1987). Existing in between 3 and 5 percent of school-age children, the male-to-female ratios range from 4:1 to 9:1, depending on the setting (i.e., general population or clinic) (APA 1994).

This chapter discusses identifying, understanding, and remediating ADHD through a multimodal approach. Inherent in this approach is play therapy.

Common Characteristics

There are five common characteristics of ADHD (Barkley 1990) in children. The first, attention or vigilance, is a multidimensional construct that refers to problems with alertness, arousal, selectivity, sustained attention, distractibility, or span of attention (Hale and Lewis 1979). ADHD children get bored very fast.

Because they have difficulty keeping themselves involved, they may look distractible. Douglas (1983) suggests that ADHD children have their greatest difficulties with sustaining attention to tasks or vigilance. This is sometimes apparent in free-play settings, as evidenced by a short duration of attention to each toy and frequent shifts in play across various toys (Barkley and Ullman 1975, Zentall 1985).

The second characteristic, impulsivity, is also a multidimensional construct (Milich and Kramer 1985) and produces poor delay of gratification. ADHD youngsters cannot wait for anything. They need it now! Clinically, ADHD children are often noted to respond quickly to situations without waiting for instructions to be completed. They lack an adequate appreciation of what is required in the setting. One child defined it as feeling like falling: "You know it is happening, but you cannot stop it." These children fail to consider the possible negative consequences of situations or behaviors, and seem to engage in frequent, unnecessary risk taking. ADHD children take chances on a dare, especially from a peer. They are always the ones who are caught. An example would be one child daring an entire group to pull the school fire alarm for fifty dollars. The ADHD child will immediately run to pull the alarm, while the other children consider the consequences of suspension, the fact that the boy may not have fifty dollars to give to them, and so on.

When ADHD children want something that is under another's control and they must wait, they often badger excessively during the waiting interval. One mother admitted that she no longer tells her ADHD child about plans for the future, because from the moment she reveals they are going on vacation in three months, the child will constantly ask about it and want to leave immediately.

Third, ADHD children present with excessive levels of activity for their age. Motor activity, such as running or always being on on the go; vocal activity, such as making animal noises, humming constantly, and yelling loudly; and restlessness, fidgeting, and generally unnecessary gross bodily movements are commonplace (Stewart et al. 1966). These movements often seem purposeless. When ADHD children work independently in class, they are prone to leave their seats and move about the room without permission. They appear restless, move their hands while working, swing their legs, and play with things unrelated to their work. In addition, Barkley and colleagues (1983) note that direct observations of ADHD children's social interactions generally demonstrate excessive speech and commentary. Often, children with ADHD carry on their own conversations with neither interest nor regard for whether others comment or join in.

The fourth characteristic is what Barkley (1990) refers to as deficient rule-governed behavior. Behavior regulation by the anticipation of consequences may be fundamentally lacking in children with ADHD (Barkley 1990). These children seem to have a great deal of difficulty complying with parental and teacher commands. Some researchers hypothesize that ADHD children have higher-than-normal thresholds for arousal by stimulation. As environmental stimulation decreases, hyperactivity and inattention increase as a means of compensating for this reduction. This purportedly maintains an optimal level of central nervous system arousal (Zentall 1985). It is clear that ADHD children have trouble with self-control and problem solving. Rule-governed behavior, important for training control of impulsive responses and delaying gratification, is difficult for them. Barkley, at a CH.A.D.D. (Children and Adults with Attention-Deficit Disorders) conference in 1993, presented the view that ADHD consists of developmental deficiencies in the regulation and maintenance of behavior by rules and consequences.

Fifth, ADHD children, with increased performance variability, may earn A's and F's in the same subject at different testing times. Douglas (1972) noted this problem in observations of ADHD children performing reaction-time tasks or serial problem solving, and many others have reported on it since. ADHD children seem to have larger standard deviations of performance on multitrial tasks. They also appear to be underachievers in school. Many times these children are labeled as lazy or not doing their best, and this obviously affects self-esteem.

Components

Creating a composite picture of the effects of ADHD can help in gaining an understanding of the life and personality style of these children.

Behavioral Manifestations

Attention

First and foremost, ADHD children have a short attention span, approximately one-third that of their agemates (Barkley 1990). While this is considered a stable phenomenon, in fact it is not (Copeland and Love 1991). Both attention and inattention are quite variable and dependent on internal and external factors. For example, a child may have no problem attending to Nintendo or television, but may ignore or "tune out" the teacher and/or parents. On the other hand, s/he may be attentive to a teacher who is especially absorbing.

While everyone's ability to attend is dependent on motivating factors, again it is a matter of degree. Inattention and inability to concentrate characterize virtually every child with ADHD. Reported as short attention span, daydreaming, inability to focus or listen to explanations, following directions, and staying on task, all are major problems. Even in the smallest task, snags can occur. Parents generally report that "S/he doesn't listen." This inattentiveness is present in daily activities as well.

Distractibility is a characteristic that contributes to inattentiveness and usually goes hand in hand with it. By definition, it is a tendency to become sidetracked by stimuli that are not relevant to the task at hand. Distractions can be both internal, such as thoughts and/or fantasies, or external, such as noise in the room or cars passing. ADHD children are easily distracted by extraneous noises. They seem to have all the stimulation of the world bombarding them at once. It is difficult for them to ascertain what are relevant stimuli and what are not. In a playroom, for example, these children may hear noises that no one else has heard. They continue doing what they are doing, but will ask: "What was that?"

When parents and teachers do not understand the problems inherent to ADHD they can be unsympathetic and punitive in their responses. Many, in fact, view their children as having selective attention deficit for school and homework. They are understandably confused when they see them attending for long periods of time to activities they enjoy. In many cases, it is the motivation that is different, not necessarily the task.

Concentration difficulties become most obvious under conditions of familiarity, boredom, repetition, and fatigue. When interest or motivation is strong, they can concentrate quite well. The body may, in fact, secrete additional hormones that stimulate increased neurotransmitter release in the brain, thus improving the regulation of attention centers (Copeland and Love 1991).

Children with ADHD are equally if not more frustrated by their attention deficits as are their parents and teachers. Every child wants mastery, success, and achievement. ADHD children expend extraordinary effort to achieve what their nonafflicted peers do.

Hyperactivity

Typically, the behavior that is the most easily recognized in ADHD children is hyperactivity. Its signs include (1) restlessness and fidgeting; (2) diminished need for sleep; (3) excessive talking; (4) unusual amounts of running, jumping, or climbing; (5) difficulty listening; (6) motor restlessness during sleep (kicking covers off, moving constantly); and (7) difficulty staying seated at meals or in class. These children are constantly moving about the room or on the go. As infants they may seem very restless. After putting them to sleep in one part of the crib, they end up at the opposite end, even before they have started crawling. Some have feeding and sleeping problems. Many parents complain that their children haven't slept through the night in years. They also tend to leave their cribs early by climbing out. As toddlers, they seem to run before walking. Mothers and fathers become exhausted as these children's energy level is significantly higher than anyone can handle. Meals are usually a problem because they are constantly trying to move out of their high chair or seat, fidgeting with eating utensils, moving feet and banging against the table, rocking back and forth, and the like. Parents report that mealtime is a major chore, and no one eats well.

In school, hyperactivity presents itself in similar ways: fidgeting, drumming fingers, shuffling feet, tapping pencils, and appearing to be in constant motion. ADHD children have difficulty sitting still, talk nonstop, and they are very loud and disruptive. Their hyperactive behavior may cast them in the role of class clown, as things happen to them because of their constant movement. These children are driven from within, and little external structure or control makes a significant difference.

The ADHD child is not always hyperactive. In certain situations, s/he appears very calm and focused. When the child receives one-on-one attention from an adult, or when doing something s/he really enjoys, little movement is seen. This leads adults to the conclusion that, because the child is calm some of the time, s/he is intentionally defiant and willful when, in fact, s/he is not.

In general, research findings indicate that hyperactive children are not more active than the random population in all settings. The more restrictive the environment and the more concentration needed, the more likely differences in activity level will be found. This is especially true in restlessness and off-task behavior. In unusual or unfamiliar settings, they often behave very much like other children. One mother reported that she feels she could control her daughter's activity level by renting a stranger every day.

Impulsivity

A classic problem of ADHD, impulsivity leads to the most negative attention. Research has shown that this core symptom or behavior is the most enduring and serious in adolescence and adulthood (Weiss and Hechtmann 1986).

Signs of impulsivity include (1) excitability, (2) low frustration tolerance, (3) acting before thinking, (4) disorganization, (5) poor planning ability, (6) excessively shifting from one activity to another, (7) difficulty in group situations that require patience and taking turns, (8) being constantly in trouble for deeds of omission as well as deeds of commission, and (9) frequently interrupting.

The abilities to think before acting, to tolerate delay, and to consider consequences of one's actions constitute the ingredients of impulse control and are important elements for success in life. By age 6, most children have gradually learned to delay gratification. ADHD children, however, do not. They get upset easily, have very low frustration tolerance, and express such feelings. ADHD children may impulsively hit a sibling when frustrated and then immediately feel tremendous remorse for doing so. Despite the awareness right after the event, these children resume their unthinking behavior immediately following an apology and do not learn from previous experience.

ADHD children also seem to live for the moment. If they see a toy they want, they will take it. If the paint is chocolate-colored and appealing, they may eat it. If the ball rolls into the street, they immediately run after it, and may suffer injury from not considering the consequences of their actions.

Impulsive children can also be disorganized and forgetful. The messy bedroom is a classic problem for families. Looking for something to wear, these youngsters will empty every drawer to find it. When that is done, the room is trashed, but they are on their way to the next activity. Even when cleanup is accomplished, ten minutes later it may be trashed anew when something else is missing. This is not a problem for the child, only the parents. Likewise with homework, an impulsive child can lose it somewhere between the kitchen table and the backpack. Or, once in the backpack, it is lost on the way to school.

Teachers commonly experience exasperation with ADHD children's behavior. Disorganization is a major problem at school. Their desks look like a tornado hit, or their lockers are in complete disarray.

For these children, impulsivity is the most difficult of the behaviors to cope with because it leads to trouble. They appear very aggressive if they hit others with little provocation. They break windows, have or give bloody noses, and destroy toys without a thought. Again, these children are remorseful, and actually seem to be more surprised at what they did than the children and adults around them.

Social Functioning

Poor Peer Relations

Important, and often overlooked, is the social consequence of having ADHD. It can interfere with interpersonal contacts just as dramatically as it does with a child's academic performance. To make friends, children have to be able to pay attention. To get along in a group, they have to be able to follow what is being said. Social cues are often subtle: the narrowing of eyes, the raising of eyebrows, a slight change in tone of voice, a tilting of the head. Often the child with ADHD does not pick up on these cues, which leads to real social gaffes or a general sense of being out of it. Particularly in childhood, social transactions happen rapidly and the transgressor of norms is dealt with without pity. A lapse in social awareness, due to the distractibility or impulsivity of an ADHD child, can preclude acceptance by a group or deny understanding from a friend. In many cases, these children experience complete failure with peers and are then left alone.

Children of all ages quickly become aware of the ADHD child's socialization difficulty and perceive him/her negatively (Milich et al. 1982). Milich and Landau (1981) suggest that rejection by peers is an important predictor of psychopathology. Pelham and Milich (1984) contend that ADHD children differ from other children in that they experience "behavioral excesses leading to rejection and social skill deficits leading to low acceptance" (p. 560).

During the preschool period, while most children are developing the basic foundations of social skills, ADHD preschoolers frequently do not. Although they may not yet have developed well-defined negative patterns of social interaction, they are unable to integrate affectively with their peers. Only one out of five non-ADHD children present with similar problems (Campbell and Cluss 1982). These authors also found that inattentive and hyperactive children demonstrated disproportionately high rates of aggressive interactions with their peers.

In middle childhood, ADHD children may be immature and incompetent, and even their best efforts fail. Their social skill deficits result in a pattern of high-incidence, low-impact behaviors. They may lack the ability to join an ongoing conversation or take turns. While these are not terribly aversive behaviors, they do result in the ADHD child being less popular with agemates. In contrast, some ADHD children exhibit a pattern of low-incidence, high-impact behaviors. Although acts of aggression may not occur with great frequency, ADHD children nevertheless are rejected and disliked by others (Pelham and Milich 1984). Hyperactive ADHD children spend less spare time with peers and more time alone or with younger children who will accept and look up to them. In other cases, these children may still have active fantasy play, while peers practice competitive sports.

Diminished self-esteem can become a severe consequence of poor peer relations. As Ross and Ross (1982) point out, children frequently judge their own self-worth in terms of the opinions of others. Inappropriate efforts and a lack of acceptance in the peer group lead to further rejection.

Skill Deficits

Children with ADHD experience a wide range of problems that interfere with peer acceptance: difficulty with staying on task, disruptiveness, impulsivity, immature or aggressive responses, a basic impediment in communication, and difficulty adapting behavior to different situational demands (Whalen et al. 1979). Possessing poor social problem-solving skills, they may be able to verbalize what they should do, but when observed in free-play periods they rarely follow through. By responding impulsively, they end up in difficult situations. Self-control eludes them unless incentive is provided.

Aggressiveness, a very stable trait that does not diminish with age (Loeber and Dishion 1983), is now recognized as a frequent component of the behavior problems of ADHD children. It appears that nonaggressive children have lower levels of peer rejection as they get older while their aggressive ADHD counterparts continue to be rejected (Ross and Ross 1982). Aggressiveness is more highly correlated with peer problems than hyperactivity (Pelham and Bender 1982).

Peer ratings indicate that ADHD females are more similar to normal females than ADHD males are to normal males. ADHD females appear to have fewer problems with aggression but more with mood and emotion than their ADHD male counterparts.

Academics

Observational studies of ADHD children have shown that they do not fit into the normal routines of the classroom. School is a major problem for them. Difficulty paying attention leads to unfinished work, impulsivity results in academic errors and social disruptions, and hyperactivity causes constant fidgeting and excessive talking. Underachievement is the all too common result. These children may spend a great deal of time studying for an examination, only to forget the information by the next day. They may complete the homework under duress, only to lose it on the way to school or forget to turn it in. They may know the answer, but respond impulsively before the teacher finishes the question and decrease their grades. Even those children with high intellectual functioning do not perform like their intellectual counterparts. ADHD children are aware that they have to work harder and get less in return. They finish the math test first and end up with "careless" errors. They disrupt other students by humming while they are thinking. All in all, their school experiences become negative ones.

ADHD children are admonished for not attending, not sitting still, being lazy, not working up to potential, being inattentive, and so on. Many parents have commented that the teacher's conference starts with "You have a very bright child, but . . ." Once again, this illustrates the frustration felt by parents, teachers, and, most importantly, students.

Russell Barkley has said that ADHD children get one "A" and we hold it against them for the rest of their lives. They are consistently inconsistent. Being supportive and understanding of the disorder helps, but in most cases, these children are ridiculed for not doing better.

Emotional

As a group, ADHD children suffer more symptoms of anxiety, depression, and low self-esteem than normal children or children with learning disabilities (Bohline 1985). While everyone is looking at the overt behaviors, very little attention is paid to the inner workings of the child. All of these deficits and problems lead to lower self-esteem, feelings of incompetence, feelings of failure, and depression. While clearly it is not one of the core symptoms of ADHD, depression might likely occur over time when a child has ongoing frustrating experiences with parents, teachers, and peers. Because the appearance of childhood depression differs from that of adults, it is sometimes overlooked.

Depression in young children may be manifested by high risk-taking, changes in eating habits, relatively high rates of overactivity, frequent loss of temper, and lack of pleasure. Treatment is necessary when there is a clear change in behavior, either abrupt or over time.

In addition to the depression that may be caused by ADHD, there are anxiety disorders that are more highly comorbid with ADHD. Specifically, many of these children experience fears that are not age appropriate. Adult ADHD clients have confirmed that at 10 to 12 years of age, they were still afraid of dinosaurs and monsters coming to their bedroom. These anxieties, sometimes managed by the child, severely interfere with normal functioning at other times. Parents classically say: "There is nothing to be afraid of," when the child, although unable to verbalize it, is certain that there is.

Physical Characteristics

Physical Anomalies

It has been shown that ADHD children have more minor physical anomalies than normal children (Firestone et al. 1976). Some of these are (1) an index finger longer than a middle finger; (2) a curved fifth finger; (3) third toe as long or longer than second toe; (4) adherent ear lobes; (5) a single transverse palmar crease; (6) furrowed brow; (7) greater than normal head circumference; (8) low-seated or soft, fleshy ears; (9) electric, fine hair; (10) two whorls of hair on back of head (Barkley 1990).

Health Problems

Chronic health problems, such as recurring upper respiratory problems, allergies, or asthma, have also been noted more often in hyperactive than in normal children (39 to 44 percent versus 8 to 25 percent). Some of these children are constantly irritated by a nagging stuffy nose or scratchy throat. In addition, colds are easily contracted, which may result in upper respiratory infections.

Enuresis, particularly nighttime bed-wetting, has been noted to occur in as many as 43 percent of ADHD children compared with 28 percent of normal children (Stewart et al. 1966). Hartsough and Lambert (1985) reported that ADHD children were more likely to have difficulties with bowel training than were normal children (10.1 percent versus 4.5 percent).

Sleep Problems

Studies have found children with ADHD to have a higher likelihood of sleep disturbance than normal children. As many as 56 percent of ADHD children have difficulty falling asleep, compared with 23 percent of normal children. Frequent night wakings occur in up to 39 percent of ADHD children (Kaplan et al. 1987). Since they seem to require less sleep than their peers, these children may go to sleep later and awaken earlier, leaving parents exhausted. Over 55 percent of ADHD children have been described by their parents as tired upon awakening compared with 27 percent of normal children (Trommer et al. 1988).

Positive Characteristics

One must not neglect the positive characteristics of ADHD, which are so often overlooked. These children have an unusually high level of energy. When this energy is channeled, it can produce wonderful athletes, successful business people, and in general, animated, vigorous, and productive adults. These children are often very affectionate and demonstrate their love effusively. They hug with enthusiasm, albeit very tightly, and it must be on their terms. But they certainly are emotional. In addition, ADHD children love to help. Given a bottle of glass cleaner, they will spray and wipe the entire house including the antique piano. With a strong desire for social contact, they make many mistakes, but still try to seek out friends most of the time. Creativity is another positive characteristic. Many of the children are excellent in music, dance, drama, or art and, if they are well-coordinated, excel in sports. Interestingly, some people consider ADHD children to be unusually empathetic. When someone cries, they tend to show an emotional response. When their impulsivity doesn't get in the way, they attempt to help. An overall focus on the positive attributes reframes the problems and allows parents to view this disorder as more manageable.

Etiology

Most investigators endorse the theory of a biological predisposition to ADHD, much like that of mental retardation. A variety of neurological etiologies can give rise to the disorder through disturbance in a final common pathway in the nervous system. In the case of ADHD, it would seem that hereditary factors play the largest role in the occurrence of these symptoms in children. Transmitted genetically may be a tendency toward dopamine depletion in, or at least underactivity of, the prefrontal-striatal-limbic regions and their rich interconnections. The condition can be exacerbated by pregnancy complications, exposure to toxins, or neurological disease, and by social factors, such as family dysfunction and educational problems. We know that ADHD does not come from bad parenting or food allergies. The latest findings of Zametkin et al. (1990) conclude that the brains of ADHD adults are different from their normal counterparts.

Treatment

The most common approaches to ADHD treatment are medication therapy, behavior modification, cognitive training, cognitive behavior therapy, and family systems therapy. In addition, play therapy is entering the field as a viable treatment alternative.

Medication Therapy

Psychostimulant medication, the most common treatment for children with ADHD, is given to more than 600,000 children annually. Primarily Ritalin or its generic form, methylphenidate, are prescribed for 1 to 2 percent of the school-age population, making ADHD the most medically treated childhood disorder (Safter and Krager 1983). Numerous studies clearly demonstrate medication-induced, short-term enhancement of the behavioral, academic, and social functioning of the majority of children being treated (Barkley 1990). While the drug is in use, such changes are seen. Many families, however, report behavior problems resulting in negative interactions during unmedicated after-school hours. Also, the side effects of these medications—insomnia, loss of appetite, increased anxiety, exacerbation of tics (Barkley 1990)—are sometimes difficult to deal with. Because the child may still experience low self-esteem, poor social skills, and depression, other approaches are necessary to supplement the treatment by medication. One issue that is frequently raised is whether stimulant medication, behavior therapy, or a combination is the best approach for ADHD (Abikoff and Gittelman 1985). Currently, most researchers in this area agree that the combination of two treatments is superior to either in isolation (Pelham and Murphy 1986).

Behavioral Approach

Cumulative evidence now attests to the effectiveness of behavior therapy techniques for a variety of problematic and nonfunctional behaviors such as inappropriate vocalization, aggression toward peers, talking out of turn, getting out of one's seat, and off-task behaviors (O'Leary and O'Leary 1972, Wolraich et al. 1978). Common interventions include (1) positive reinforcement and stimulus control (Mischel 1974), (2) reinforcement of competing responses (Kazdin 1975), (3) time-out (Forehand and Baumeister 1976), (4) prompting and fading (Craighead et al. 1981), and (5) modeling (Cohen and Przbycien 1974).

Compared with pharmacological approaches, behavior therapy has a number of advantages as a single treatment for ADHD children (Hersen and Barlow 1976, O'Leary and O'Leary 1976). It does not produce the negative side effects often found with pharmaceutical treatment (O'Leary and Dubey 1979). Furthermore, behavior therapy focuses on antecedent and consequent events, which results in a greater understanding of the elicitation and maintenance of problem behavior. Despite the abundance of evidence on the effectivensss of behavioral techniques, some studies have shown that behavior changes observed during treatment have tended not to persist, or do not generalize beyond conditions under which the contingencies have been operative (Kazdin 1975, Thoresen and Mahoney 1974).

Cognitive Approaches

The lack of generalization and maintenance evidenced by the behavioral approach prompted the development of alternative and more cognitively based treatment options. Many investigations have focused on problems associated with ADHD children (Camp et al. 1977, Douglas et al. 1976, Kendall and Finch 1978, Meichenbaum and Goodman 1971). Cognitively based techniques, such as self-instruction training and problem-solving skills training, constitute special procedures that may also be useful in maintaining and generalizing behavioral changes.

There is a growing body of research that explores the efficacy of self-instructional programs with children (Kendall and Hollon 1979, Mahoney 1977, Meichenbaum 1977). In the clinical setting, the use of cognitive-behavioral interventions that incorporate cognitive self-instruction techniques seem promising (Copeland 1981, Urbain and Kendall 1980). Within the cognitive-behavioral context, ADHD behaviors in children are, to an important extent, the result of cognitive deficiencies. Such children seemingly fail to engage in information-processing activities characteristic of an effective problem solver and fail to initiate the reflective thinking processes that govern behavior (Urbain and Kendall 1980). Cognitive interventions, therefore, emphasize skill building at the level of the cognitive processes that presumably mediate competent adjustment across a variety of situations.

In the treatment of ADHD children, cognitive training has more face validity than perhaps any other therapeutic modality. However, the belief that the development of internalized self-regulation skills facilitate generalization and maintenance effects over extended periods of time has not yet been realized (Abikoff 1991). While the children learn skills and perform them during the treatment, without continued intervention and reinforcement such skills disappear over time. Therefore, the implication that self-talk changes cognitions does not hold true.

Cognitive-Behavioral Approaches

With many successful specific treatment approaches in both the cognitive and behavioral therapies, an effort was made to investigate the efficacy of cognitive and behavioral interventions together. As with other therapeutic interventions, the goal of the cognitive-behavioral training is the reduction or elimination of maladaptive, inappropriate behaviors, and the establishment of more efficient, adaptive modes of response. Central to these goals is the development of self-control skills and reflective problem-solving strategies. It is assumed that the acquisition and internalization of these skills will provide the child with the means for self-regulation of behavior, thereby facilitating generalization and maintenance effects (Meichenbaum and Asarnow 1979).

While outcome studies of cognitive-behavioral treatment have generally provided support for this intervention strategy (Kendall 1981), some studies have resulted in contradictory findings (Friedling and O'Leary 1979, Higa et al. 1978, Palkes et al. 1972). Some researchers have found that traditional cognitive-behavioral programs may be less effective with children who exhibit severe behavior problems (Bugental et al. 1977, Sprafkin and Rubenstein 1982). It is quite common clinically to hear that ADHD children do not listen, fail to comply with instructions, or are unable to maintain instruction compliance over time, and do not follow directions associated with a task (Barkley 1990). Problems such as these could affect the efficacy of a traditional cognitive-behavioral approach because the child must be able to attend to instructions, must be motivated to comply with the instructions, and would need sufficient reinforcement for doing so. As the therapist attempts to train the child to use the necessary methods, the ADHD child may become bored and refuse to engage in the treatment. One way to overcome this difficulty is to present the training in a playful, nonthreatening environment.

Play Therapy Approach

There is a growing consensus about the common characteristics of play behaviors. First, play is intrinsically motivating. Children with ADHD have many impulsive behaviors and need help to attend and to stay on task. Activities performed for their own sake are intrinsically motivating because pleasure is inherent in the activity itself. Play seems to satisfy this inner desire in the child (Schaefer 1993).

The second characteristic of play is that the child is more concerned about the play activity itself than the outcome or successful completion of the activity (Schaefer 1993). Therefore, the play process is more important than the end result. During this play, the child is open to learn, to problem solve, to experience.

Positive feelings are the third characteristic that is inherent in play. The child player derives pleasurable feelings from play. ADHD children need to experience more positive feelings to counter the negative environmental impact of teachers, parents, siblings, and peers telling them to stop, to pay attention, and to behave.

The fourth characteristic, the child's active involvement in play, often is so engrossing that s/he becomes overfocused. A child with ADHD tends not to complete tasks, and goes from one activity to another. During a play period, s/he is able to stick to a task with the help of a therapist and experience a sense of accomplishment.

Play also has an "as if" quality, which means it is carried out as if it were real life. This fifth characteristic is extremely beneficial to an ADHD child who can work through problems, make mistakes, and see solutions, without the critical eye of others.

Play has the power not only to facilitate normal child development but also to alleviate abnormal behavior (Schaefer 1993). Schaefer (1993) has defined play therapy as "an interpersonal process wherein a trained therapist systematically applies the curative powers of play to help clients resolve their psychological difficulties" (p. 3). Several therapeutic factors facilitate the treatment of ADHD, most imperative of which is finding the right therapist to work with the child.

The Ideal Play Therapist

The ideal play therapist for an ADHD child should have the following characteristics:

1. Is thoroughly knowledgeable about ADHD and accepting of the legitmacy of the disorder.
2. Is tough as nails about rules, but always calm and positive.
3. Is ingenious about modifying therapy strategies and materials.
4. Tailors therapy strategies to meet child's needs.
5. Mixes high and low interest tasks in tune with child's predilections.
6. Knows to back off when child's level of frustration begins to peak.
7. Knows to back off when therapist's level of frustration begins to peak.
8. Speaks clearly in brief, understandable sentences.
9. Looks the child straight in the eye when communicating.
10. Has a very predictable and organized playroom.
11. Provides immediate and consistent feedback (consequences) regarding behavior.
12. Controls the playroom without being controlling; is willing to share control of the playroom with the child.
13. Develops a private signal system with child to gently notify him when he's acting inappropriately.
14. Maintains close physical proximity without being intrusive.
15. Ignores minor disruptions—knows how to choose battles.
16. Has no problem acting as an "auxiliary organizer" when appropriate and necessary—helps make sure child is organized for homework, parents are involved in play therapy process, and so on.
17. Maintains interest in the child as a person with interests, fears, and joys—even after a trying session.
18. Is willing to consult with parents frequently about parenting, personal problems, and their own problems with attention.

19. Has a great sense of humor.
(Adapted from ADHD/Hyperactivity: A Consumer's Guide [1991] by Michael Gordon and used with permission.)

Therapeutic Powers of Play

The play therapy process contains a limited number of elements that are differentiated from one another by their specific effects on the child. In determining a treatment program, the following mechanisms may be considered: communication, emotional regulation, relationship enhancement, stress management, ego boosting, cognitive problem solving, and preparation for life.

Communication

It is through play, the language of the child, that children can express their thoughts and feelings. Because it is nonverbal, the language is quite different from verbal language. A more fantastic, drive-dominated form of communication, play is full of images and emotions. Unlike the logical, sequential, and analytical thoughts expressed by words, apparently left-brain centered, it seems more right-brain oriented (Schaefer 1993). Perhaps it is for this reason that play enables ADHD children to communicate thoughts and feelings that they are aware of but cannot express in words. In addition, children's play helps to uncover unconscious wishes and conflicts, which may be the underlying reasons for the inappropriate behavioral patterns.

Emotional Regulation

Play has the ability to enhance a child's emotional repertoire. Through abreaction and catharsis, experiences can be relived with the appropriate release of affect and slowly digested and assimilated mentally. Catharsis, a core therapeutic technique shared by many schools of therapy (Greencavage and Norcross 1990), provides the child with comfort through the release of tension and affect on such inanimate objects such as pillows and bobo dolls. ADHD children need to be able to express the full range of emotions like other children. They are, however, stifled in that ability in their real life because of action impulsivity and fleeting thoughts. They receive mixed messages in the real world when their inappropriate, unthinking acts result in blame for "intentional" actions. They commonly feel tremendous remorse. In play, however, they can release true feelings and experience true emotions in a safe environment. By having toys relive the children's own unpleasant past experiences, they gain a sense of mastery over a world that they tend to experience passively in real life. Erikson (1940) stated that playing out troublesome situations is the most natural self-therapeutic process that childhood offers.

The significance of a child's active involvement in treatment may be understood from several perspectives. Developmentally, s/he has a need to demonstrate a sense of mastery and control over the environment. Through the use of cognitive-behavioral techniques, where the child with ADHD focuses on his or her own thoughts, feelings, fantasies, and environment, s/he begins to exhibit increased levels of self-management of his or her own behavior. It is then possible to focus on a combination of situation-specific factors as well as the child's feelings about the problem.

Relationship Enhancement

A close therapist–child relationship is crucial for the child to gain a more adequate acceptance of him/herself (Schaefer 1993). Play, by its very nature, facilitates positive interactions that are fun-filled and concerned with enjoyment rather than achievement. A pleasurable bond is formed that positively affects the child's trust in the therapist and treatment. Especially with children with ADHD, who have social problems with both peers and authorities, identifying with the therapist's behaviors and values is important. The therapist can then model appropriate behaviors, make contracts with the child, and follow through to enhance the child's positive self-concept.

Stress Management

Play therapy can provide a place for management of stress with "stress inoculation" and stress reduction. Through the use of play techniques, the child with ADHD, who may be plagued by anxiety and fears, can experience a threatening object in a miniature situation, and gain a sense of mastery, power, and control over it. Also, methods can be taught through play to inoculate the child against future stressful encounters.

Ego Boosting

Using games and other play techniques can help the child learn self-control. The competitive nature of games demands concentration, impulse control, and self-confidence. Games invoke the processes of the ego and superego to a greater extent than those of the id. The process of learning how to play, improving performance, and affecting outcome increases self-confidence and provides a sense of mastery for the ADHD child.

Cognitive Problem-Solving

For young children in therapy, strengths and limitations in the cognitive sphere are crucial issues in developing appropriate treatment. Through direct teaching, many ADHD children can repeat the problem-solving method, but still do not seem to use it. Play, particularly symbolic play, is preferable to direct instruction for promoting children's creative problem-solving abilities (Sawyers and Horm-Wingerd 1993). It appears that play and creativity may be linked by personality variables and cognitive processes that include internal locus of control, metaphoric thinking, imagery and fantasy, breadth of attention span, curiosity/exploration, and symbolic activity. It is through exploration and play that children gain basic knowledge and experience. This is necessary but not sufficient, in and of itself, for creative problem solving to take place.

Preparation for Life

Role play and behavior rehearsal, where children have an opportunity to try out alternative behaviors, can prepare children with ADHD for real-life situations. Sociodramatic play is widely regarded as an advanced form of pretend play. New behaviors are tried in therapy, and their pros and cons considered afterward. Role playing also develops empathy. Many ADHD children act impulsively and do not recognize their own actions or their effect on others. Through this type of role play, they can see themselves, while still remaining safe. Teachers rate social competence, peer popularity, and conflict resolution skills as having positive correlations with pretend play (Rubin et al. 1983).

Theoretical Approach

Cognitive-behavioral strategies use performance-based procedures as well as cognitive interventions to produce changes in thinking, feeling, and behavior (Hinshaw and Erhardt 1991). Treatment must include considerations of the child's internal and external environment (Meichenbaum 1977). The therapist places emphasis on the learning process, the influences of the contingencies, and models in the environment. This also provides a framework for the child's involvement in treatment by addressing issues of control, mastery, and responsibility for one's own behavior. By incorporating the cognitive components, the child becomes an active participant in change. For example, children who are helped to identify and modify irrational beliefs may experience a sense of personal understanding and empowerment.

One of the early influences on cognitive behavior therapy has been Rotter's (1954) social learning theory, which states that the potential or likelihood of a specific behavior being emitted by an individual is the result of situation-specific reinforcement values and of expectations that the reinforcement could be attained by engaging in a specific behavior. Rotter emphasized the situational specificity of these cognitive processes but recognized that cross-situational cognition also developed in the form of generalized expectations (e.g., loss of control) and reinforcement values (needs or goals). Bandura's

(1977) social learning theory added other cognitive factors, including an individual's expectations about competently enacting a given behavior (efficacy expectations), self-reinforcement, and the tendency to attend selectively to certain observed models. In addition, Meichenbaum's early application of cognitive behavior therapy to children (Meichenbaum and Goodman 1971) suggests that children's acquisition of behavioral self-control was due to their use of language and of cognitive controls. Children are seen as learning to regulate their behavior through experiences with significant others. Thus, they "learn-by-doing" (Brown 1987).

In this regard, children with ADHD can make use of cognitive-behavioral play therapy to deal with issues they are experiencing. (Parents are also engaged in the treatment but not in the actual play therapy session.) The child, using toys necessary to process his/her problems, may choose transformers or small figures (e.g., dinosaurs, Aliens, Power Rangers). Once the child makes the choice, it is that toy that symbolically represents him/her. The next step, to implement the necessary change using that symbolic toy involves the use of many interventions.

To Increase On-Task Behavior

A game, like Beat the Clock, can be played in order to increase on-task behavior. The therapist initiates the game at the beginning of the session and gives the child ten poker chips. The child is required to stay on a specific task for ten minutes (reading a book, making a Lego model, drawing, etc.). If s/he gets distracted by anything during that time, s/he must give a chip to the therapist. If s/he maintains his/her attention during the entire time, s/he earns five more chips. A goal is set in advance regarding the number of chips needed to win a prize or snack. This game, which can be played for all or part of a session, must stop before the child gets bored, shuts down, and won't work. When the time has been extended to the point of remaining on task (even a boring one) for twenty minutes, s/he has accomplished the much-required behavior for the classroom.

Enhancing Verbalization of Feelings

Many children with ADHD have trouble verbalizing feelings and are likely to say "I don't know" more than other children. Because they are in trouble a lot, it is also a good way to protect themselves. In the Feeling Word Game, the therapist sits with the child and asks what feelings a child of the same age might have. As the child states the feelings (e.g., happy, angry, sad), the therapist writes each one down on a 4- by 6-inch piece of paper and puts them in two columns in front of the child. If the child is unable to think of eight words, the therapist suggests some, and asks for confirmation. After eight words are obtained, the therapist says: "I have a box of poker chips here that I call feelings. I am going to tell a story and then put some of the chips on the words that represent what I would feel in this certain situation. I can put as many as I want to represent the amount of that particular feeling, and I can change the amounts as I think about what I would feel." A simple story is then told, and the therapist models the putting down of feelings on the paper, placing different amounts of the poker chips on different feelings at the same time. S/he then can change the amount of feelings as s/he thinks about it. After the child sees how it is done, the therapist tells another story to the child that relates to him in a nonthreatening way (e.g., kicking a soccer goal at the team game, but the team loses anyway). The child then takes the chip "feelings" and puts them down on the various paper feelings. Next it is the child's turn to tell a story to the therapist, so that the therapist can put her feelings down. This can continue with each story getting more reality-based for the child, thereby enhancing the verbalization of feelings.

To Increase Self-Control

The following games are used to teach self-control, something with which these children have a great deal of difficulty.

Pick-Up-Sticks

The therapist and child play this game according to the rules. The goal of the therapy is to model "stop and think" behavior. Problem-solving skills are also taught to figure out ways to get the most sticks. Since a coping model is preferable, the therapist will make mistakes and comment on them. If the child does something to figure out a better way, the therapist can then follow the child's lead and repeat that step.

Rebound

The ADHD child has to slide the ball-bearing markers along the board and bounce them off a rubberband so that they land on the scored part of the board. Most of the children throw the ball-bearing too hard. By using the term *self-control*, the therapist calms the child down and helps him/her control his/her behavior.

Biofeedback Racing Game

Created by this author for use in group format (Kaduson 1993), over time it has been used with ADHD children in individual sessions with the same success. The game utilizes an electromyograph (EMG) biofeedback machine attached to a car racing set through a Biofax machine. The child is taught relaxation

(Jacobsonian or progressive) and then hooked up to the EMG machine. The electrodes are placed on the frontalis muscles (which are reported to be tenser in these children than in others). The child's baseline microvolts are recorded. The machine is then placed one notch lower and the child is required to keep the EMG machine off in order to have the car race around the track. This provides the current necessary to run the car. The goal is eighty-five laps in two minutes. This reflects a totally relaxed state because the power is constantly running to the car. Once that is attained, the time is increased. The child is then helped to maintain that relaxed state and to read his/her body's signs in that state so that it can be recognized in other situations. After fifteen minutes of training at a set microvolt, the machine is once again lowered so that the child starts again at two-minute segments. This has been shown to increase self-control as well as self-esteem (Kaduson 1993).

Strategic Board Games

Strategy games have been shown to be useful in treating children with control problems (Dubow et al. 1987, Kaduson 1993) as well as those with weak egos. Playing decisions are based on a rational problem-solving process, awareness of alternative courses of action, evaluation of consequences, delay in immediate reaction in favor of longer-term strategies, and acceptance of personal responsibility for success or failure of the game (Serok and Blum 1983). Examples of strategic games are *Checkers*, *Trouble*, *Connect Four*, *Sorry*, and *Battleship*. Children can learn and practice self-control and frustration tolerance by taking turns, and modifying their own responses in order to improve their performance.

Case Illustration

Jason, age 7½, was referred for therapy after being diagnosed with attention-deficit hyperactivity disorder and oppositional defiant disorder. Having difficulty with friends at school and at home, Jason had the core symptoms of ADHD: hyperactivity, impulsivity, and inattention. He did not seem to take responsibility for any of his actions, and was beginning to be aggressive toward his parents, siblings, and friends.

Early Phase of Treatment

To engage Jason in the treatment process, cognitive behavior play therapy was utilized. Placing a strong emphasis on the child's involvement in treatment in a way that many other behavioral methods do not, this model provides a framework for his/her active participation by addressing issues of control, mastery, and responsibility for one's own behavior changes (Knell 1993). Play is used to teach skills and alternative behaviors, as well as to communicate to the child which behaviors are appropriate. From the spontaneous use of particular toys and activities, I was able to obtain information that was then used to structure play sessions geared specifically for Jason. It was obvious from the first session that he gravitated toward the transformers toys. His spontaneous play revealed that these toys represented the good he perceived in the world. One small transformer, he stated, was "just like me" because it was small and had a piece missing.

In cognitive behavior play therapy, therapeutic goals are established and intervention is based on direction toward them. In Jason's case, the goals were to challenge his dysfunctional cognitions, increase his self-esteem and change his behavior. Because of the limited nature of Jason's cognitive and verbal abilities, modeling was an important component of the play therapy. Research supports modeling as a treatment for impulsivity (Kendall and Braswell 1985). Transformers, used as the model for Jason in treatment, paralleled and enacted his impulsive responses in school, at home, and in peer situations. His negative behavior patterns were modeled by the transformer, and then together he and I problem-solved about how the transformer would resolve issues by choosing alternatives to an impulsive response. The transformer's impulsive-aggressive behaviors were ignored (extinction), and when appropriate behavior was shown the transformer was intensely praised. Through the use of the toy, Jason was able to understand how one could exhibit inappropriate behaviors and still be considered good and likable. Observing Jason's reactions to the model provided me with an important understanding of Jason's perceptions of his parents' reactions toward him: he would make the transformer very aggressive toward its "parents," and he would verbalize how, no matter what he did good, he was always yelled at.

In addition to toys, the Feeling Word Game was used to teach Jason the interrelationship of thoughts, behaviors, and emotions. Prompting was needed to help him create feeling words so that we could add *nervous, frightened, successful, jealous,* and *confused* to *happy, mad,* and *sad.* Presenting with a great deal of irrational beliefs about his world, Jason thought that he had to behave well at all times to be loved, that he always had to please people (he felt like a failure with this), and that he wasn't allowed to be angry. Before addressing his irrational beliefs, I decided that it was important to show him that modifications in his emotional state and behavior would be desirable (DiGiuseppe 1989). Although Jason viewed himself negatively, change was frightening; he had a sense of security from being able to predict responses related to his current behaviors. To help this transition, Jason's parents were engaged in treatment.

Parental Involvement

Simultaneous with Jason's treatment, Mr. and Mrs. K. were guided through a positive parenting training program. This approach explores the parents' beliefs and expectations about the child and his behavior, the role of the parents' attentional or perceptual capacities as they relate to the child's behavior, and what constitutes good parenting (Braswell 1991). An assessment indicated that Mr. and Mrs. K. focused on Jason's negative behaviors, were very involved in punishing him as remediation, and that their interventions were having the opposite effect. Jason thought that his parents were disappointed in him because he could not do anything right. As Stark and colleagues (1991) reported, it is important to make family members aware of the subtle and not so subtle messages that are communicated and the effect these messages have on the child. Therefore, initially Mr. and Mrs. K. were educated regarding ADHD and reasons why children misbehave (Barkley 1987). Because most of Jason's negative cognitions revolved around his behavior, this was important to focus on. The assessment revealed that when Jason was noncompliant, impulsive, or hyperactive, his parents would attend to him a lot. When his behavior was acceptable or desirable, little parental attention was received.

The initial step in the parenting program was to enlist the parents' help in creating a good behavior book, in which only Jason's good behaviors were listed. Specific ones were addressed, for example, getting out of bed, dressing, and brushing teeth. Mr. and Mrs. K. were instructed to praise the behavior and write it in the book. Much of this work was done by Mrs. K. in the morning and Mr. K. at night. When the family came to dinner, Mrs. K. bragged about Jason's good behavior to Mr. K. at the dinner table. Each day's positive behaviors were read to Jason at bedtime. By the second session, Mrs. K. stated that Jason would tell her appropriate things he was doing and ask her to write it in the book.

The next sessions were devoted to increasing the parents' positive interactions with Jason. They were told to conduct a special play period with him for fifteen minutes per day, during which time they would narrate his play and praise his behavior. Compliance training periods were used to increase parental attention to appropriate behaviors and improve Jason's compliance to commands and rules given by them. Furthermore, they were instructed about how to treat him when he was not bothering them. His motivation to act appropriately increased, for he was eager to recapture the attention he used to have by misbehaving.

Lastly, Jason's parents were to implement a token economy system, using poker chips as the secondary reinforcers. All appropriate behaviors were reinforced and he was eligible to trade poker chips for other rewards, such as ice cream, soda, snacks, alone time with Mom or Dad, or renting a movie. He could also save his chips for a larger reward, which helped to teach delay of gratification.

Middle Phase of Treatment

Through the use of cognitive behavior play therapy and the positive parenting approach, Jason began to change his thoughts and feelings about himself. This was evident in his behavior at home where he became more compliant, offered to help, smiled more, and began talking about his feelings of anger toward friends and school, "because it was so difficult." Play sessions revealed that while he thought he was "a better kid now," he still had trouble interacting with peers in school. Managing anger and negative emotions were Jason's most difficult challenges. He still felt he lacked control over his low frustration tolerance. As Beck and associates (1990) point out, steps needed to be taken to increase (Jason's) tolerance for negative emotions. This was done by using the transformers, playing out scenes from those areas that produced negative emotions (school interactions), and having him verbalize how he could continue to talk about these areas while understanding the underlying emotions. As more difficult transformers were introduced so that he could work through his feelings of frustration, I encouraged him to attend to and verbalize his negative feelings.

Self-control training was begun, using several methods. First, Jason was introduced to many transformers and was reinforced for staying on task and problem solving, when he persisted until completion. Second, he was introduced to strategic board games, such as Trouble, Sorry, and Connect Four, in which he was required to make decisions based on a rational problem-solving process, awareness of alternative courses of action, evaluation of consequences, delay in immediate reaction in favor of longer-term strategies, and acceptance of personal responsibility for success or failure in the game (Serok and Blum 1983). Third, he was introduced to the biofeedback racing game. Because Jason was acknowledging his desire to gain self-control, this was a positive addition to the treatment. He was taught progressive muscle relaxation, and found the racing game to be great fun. He was able to decrease his microvolts by 5 points in three weeks.

Social Skill Game Play

To generalize many of his newly learned behaviors and to teach social skills, Jason was put into a Social Skills Group that included four other children with ADHD. Such a group meets one hour each week for a ten-week period. At first, the therapist has the group accept three rules: (1) stay in your seat, (2) do not touch anybody's body, (3) do not interrupt. The rules and the names of group members are posted. The children are told that they will receive an "X" for breaking a rule. If they accumulate three "X's," they will not be permitted to have a snack.

The first ten minutes of the group is devoted to the children transitioning into the room, taking a piece of paper, and drawing whatever they choose. The children's discussion about subjects such as new toys or school is opened by the therapist and then left for them to follow. The therapist then leads the sharing of pictures, having each child hold up his/her drawing, explain what it is, and share it with the group. The other children, one at a time, compliment the "artist." The artist responds with a "Thank you." No putdowns or negative comments are permitted.

The next thirty minutes, devoted to game play, is particularly revelant to children over the age of 5, for whom concerns about competence and social interaction are very important. Game play in a therapy setting provides experiences of pleasure and fosters communication and self-expression, reality testing, and insight, and strengthens cognition, socialization, and self-control (Reid 1993).

Because playing games is fun, it is intrinsically motivating. Children play instinctively; one need not work at getting them involved. Play and games represent an educational and therapeutic medium that is naturally attractive and important in the overall development of children (Nickerson and O'Laughlin 1983).

Games appear to have a unique potential as a teaching tool. Crocker and Wroblewski (1975) delineated six helping functions of games:

1. Games may be used as a projective test. By playing a game, participants often become sensitized to behaviors of which they were not aware. Because of their impulsivity, children with ADHD typically are not aware of their inappropriate behavior until it is pointed out to them, or after it has occurred.

2. A game may set up a situation in which anxiety can be confronted and dealt with about a certain condition. A game that sets two people against a third may be helpful for someone who chronically complains that "everyone is against me." That person can be paired with someone in order to become aware of his/her own power. For many of these children, the lack of acceptance by peers is an anxiety-arousing situation, which often promotes positive change. In groups, they may withdraw or act inappropriately. Thus, for them the game situation can provide a format for working through anxieties.

3. Playing a game offers a player an opportunity to deal with the rules of the game as an analogy to living acceptable societal norms. This aspect may be useful in helping children with ADHD accept the reality of social rules and the consequent need for self-control.

4. A game situation temporarily allows a player's childlike playfulness to emerge and thus bypass some behaviors that have prevented other interventions from being helpful. For example, children with ADHD might oppose the rules governing behavior that they typically find so difficult, but might comply with the rules of the game because they are presented in a fun-like manner.

5. Games create a safe and permissive climate in which individuals can experiment with new behaviors. In a play format, alternative ways of

dealing with impulsivity and self-control can be tried without threatening consequences.

6. Game playing teaches coping behaviors, such as the effects that winning and losing have on feelings of self-worth. In addition, children can learn how to control their expression of those feelings.

Games provide an opportunity for the therapist to avoid the preachy instructional mode of cognitive behavior training and to produce a low-pressure method of learning skills. Rapport is easily established through game play. Games are also ideally suited to children's group therapy because they require interdependent interaction between two or more players.

Social skills training games teach some additional basic lessons: sharing, cooperation, turn-taking, joining a conversation, following directions, complimenting. The children play the game focusing on only one skill.

During the next ten minutes, the group members have snack and discuss the required weekly homework (e.g., sharing five times a day). If the child completes the assignment and returns the sheet indicating completion, s/he receives a small prize.

Jason was cautious in the beginning of group and remained somewhat quiet. During the second and third week sessions, he seemed more comfortable and was able to interact appropriately with the other children. He completed his assignments and was excited to receive the small token prize. By the fifth week, he was initiating conversations and connecting with one of the boys outside of group. It was clearly seen that Jason was feeling more confident about himself and being with others. He was proud of his accomplishments in the group.

As Jason became more comfortable acknowledging his feelings and interacting with others, he began to take responsibility for his actions. His mother reported that he had hit his brother again, but unlike the past, he went to her and said that he made a mistake. He became more comfortable with himself and began to work within the limitations of ADHD.

Conclusion

Because of its prevalence in the childhood population (3 to 5 percent), clinicians can expect to see many cases of ADHD in their practices. While there are several ways to treat this disorder, a multimodal approach seems to be most successful. Inherent in this approach is play therapy, a place to learn and experience, work through, and solve problems. Children with ADHD will engage more readily in treatment if they find it to be fun. In the safety of a play environment, they can practice and learn the skills necessary to help communicate their true feelings through play, the language of the child. Playing games with the therapist, they can identify and express happiness, sadness, anger, and frustration, perhaps for the first time. By employing positive feedback approaches as part of the treatment program, children with ADHD and their families can learn to reverse negative messages, negative attention-seeking, and negative responses. These children are then free to work in therapy toward modifying socially unacceptable behaviors. Learning to attend and gain self-control through play will help to eliminate the impulsivity that is so characteristic of children with ADHD. As therapists foster their ego strengths, ADHD youngsters learn to deal with a world that is very critical of who they are.

References

Abikoff, H. (1991). Cognitive training in ADHD children: less to it than meets the eye. *Journal of Learning Disabilities* 24:205–209.

Abikoff, H., and Gittelman, R. (1985). Does behavior therapy normalize the classroom behavior of hyperactive children? *Archives of General Psychiatry* 41:449–454.

American Psychiatric Association. (1994). *Diagnostic and Statistical Manual of Mental Disorders*, 4th ed. Washington, DC: APA.

Bandura, A. (1977). Self-efficacy: toward a unifying theory of behavioral change. *Psychological Review* 84:191–215.

Barkley, R. A. (1987). *Defiant Children: A Clinician's Manual for Parent Training.* New York: Guilford.

———— (1990). *Attention Deficit Hyperactivity Disorder: A Handbook for Diagnosis and Treatment.* New York: Guilford.

Barkley, R. A., Cunningham, C. E., and Karlsson, J. (1983). The speech of hyperactive children and their mothers: comparison with normal children and stimulant drug effects. *Journal of Learning Disabilities* 16:105–110.

Barkley, R. A., and Ullman, D. G. (1975). A comparison of objective measures of activity and distractibility in hyperactive and nonhyperactive children. *Journal of Abnormal Child Psychology* 3:213–244.

Beck, A. T., Freeman, A., and Associates (1990). *Cognitive Therapy of Personality Disorders.* New York: Guilford.

Bohline, D. S. (1985). Intellectual and effective characteristics of attention deficit disordered children. *Journal of Learning Disabilities* 18:604–608.

Braswell, L. (1991). Involving parents in cognitive-behavioral therapy with children and adolescents. In *Child and Adolescent Therapy: Cognitive-Behavioral Procedures*, ed P. C. Kendall, pp. 316–351. New York: Guilford.

Brown, J. (1987). A review of meta-analyses conducted on psychotherapy outcome research. *Clinical Psychology Review* 7:1–23.

Bugental, D. B., Whalen, C. K., and Henker, B. (1977). Causal attributions of hyperactive children and motivational assumptions of two behavior change approaches: evidence for an interactionist position. *Child Development* 48:874–884.

Camp, B., Bloom, G., Herbert, F., and van Doorninck, W. (1977). "Think aloud": a program for developing self-control in young aggressive boys. *Journal of Abnormal Child Psychology* 5:157-169.

Campbell, S. B., and Cluss, P. (1982). Peer relationships of young children with behavior problems. In *Peer Relationships and Social Skills in Childhood*, ed. K. H. Rubin and H. S. Ross, pp. 121-130. New York: Springer-Verlag.

Cohen, S., and Przbycien, C. (1974). Some effects of sociometrically selected peer models on the cognitive styles of impulsive children. *Journal of Genetic Psychology* 124:213-220.

Copeland, A. P. (1981). The relevance of subject variables in cognitive self-instructional programs for impulsive children. *Behavior Therapy* 12:520-529.

Copeland, E. D., and Love, V. L. (1991). *Attention, Please!* Atlanta, GA: SPI.

Craighead, W., Kazdin, A., and Mahoney, M. (1981). *Behavior Modification: Principles, Issues and Applications*, 2nd ed. Boston: Houghton Mifflin.

Crocker, J. W., and Wroblewski, M. (1975). Using recreational games in counseling. *Personnel and Guidance Journal* 53:453-458.

DiGiuseppe, R. (1989). Cognitive therapy with children. In *Comprehensive Handbook of Cognitive Therapy*, ed. A. Freeman, K. M. Simon, L. E. Beutler, and H. Arkowitz, pp. 515-533. New York: Plenum.

Douglas, V. I. (1972). Stop, look, and listen: the problem of sustained attention and impulse control in hyperactive and normal children. *Canadian Journal of Behavioral Science* 4:259-282.

———— (1983). Attention and cognitive problems. In *Developmental Neuropsychiatry*, ed. M. Rutter, pp. 280-329. New York: Guilford.

Douglas, V. I., Parry, P., Marton, P., and Garson, C. (1976). Assessment of a cognitive training program for hyperactive children. *Journal of Abnormal Child Psychology* 4:389-410.

Dubow, E. F., Huesman, L. R., and Eron, L. D. (1987). Mitigating aggression and promoting prosocial behavior in aggressive elementary schoolboys. *Behavior Research Therapy* 25:527-531.

Erikson, E. (1940). Studies in the interpretation of play. *Genetic Psychology Monographs* 22:559-671.

Firestone, P., Lewy, F., and Douglas, V. I. (1976). Hyperactivity and physical anomalies. *Canadian Psychiatric Association Journal* 21:23-26.

Forehand, R., and Baumeister, A. (1976). Deceleration of aberrant behavior among retarded individuals. In *Progress in Behavior Modification*, ed. M. Hersen, R. Eisler, and P. Miller, 2nd ed., pp. 112-123. New York: Academic Press.

Friedling, C., and O'Leary, S. C. (1979). Effects of self-instructional training on second and third grade hyperactive children: a failure to replicate. *Journal of Applied Behavior Analysis* 12:211-219.

Gordon, M. (1991). *ADHD/Hyperactivity: A Consumer's Guide*. DeWitt, NY: GSI.

Greencavage, L. M., and Norcross, J. C. (1990). Where are the commonalities among the therapeutic common factors? *Professional Psychology* 21:372–378.

Hale, G. A., and Lewis, M. (1979). *Attention and Cognitive Development*. New York: Plenum.

Hartsough, C. S., and Lambert, N. M. (1985). Medical factors in hyperactive and normal children: prenatal, developmental, and health history findings. *American Journal of Orthopsychiatry* 55:190–210.

Hersen, M., and Barlow, D. H. (1976). *Single Case Experimental Designs: Strategies for Studying Behavior Change*. New York: Pergamon.

Higa, W. K., Tharp, R., and Calkins, R. P. (1978). Developmental verbal control of behavior: implications for self-instructional training. *Journal of Experimental Child Psychology* 26:489–497.

Hinshaw, S. P., and Erhardt, D. (1991). Attention-deficit hyperactivity disorder. In *Child and Adolescent Therapy Cognitive-Behavioral Procedures*, ed. P. C. Kendall, pp. 98–128. New York: Guilford.

Kaduson, H. G. (1993). Self-control game interventions for attention-deficit hyperactivity disorder. *Dissertation Abstracts International*, vol. 54(3-A), 868.

Kaplan, B. J., McNichol, J., Conte, R. A., and Moghadam, H. K. (1987). Sleep disturbance in preschool-aged hyperactive and nonhyperactive children. *Pediatrics* 80:839–844.

Kazdin, A. E. (1975). Covert modelling, model similarity, and reduction of avoidance behavior. *Behavior Therapy* 5:325–340.

Kendall, P. C. (1981). Cognitive-behavioral interventions with children. In *Advances in Clinical Child Psychology*, vol. 4, ed. B. B. Lashey, and A. E. Kazdin, pp. 89–99. New York: Plenum.

Kendall, P. C., and Braswell, L. (1985). *Cognitive-Behavioral Therapy for Impulsive Children*. New York: Guilford.

Kendall, P. C., and Finch, A. J., Jr. (1978). A cognitive-behavioral treatment for impulsivity: a group comparison study. *Journal of Consulting and Clinical Psychology* 46:110–118.

Kendall, P. C., and Hollon, S. D. (1979). Cognitive-behavioral interventions: overview and current status. In *Cognitive-Behavioral Interventions: Theory, Research and Procedures*, ed. P. C. Kendall, and S. D. Hollon, pp. 5–23. New York: Academic Press.

Knell, S. M. (1993). *Cognitive-Behavioral Play Therapy*. Northvale, NJ: Jason Aronson.

Loeber, R., and Dishion, T. (1983). Early predictors of male delinquency: a review. *Psychological Bulletin* 94:68–99.

Mahoney, M. J. (1977). Reflection on the cognitive-learning trend in psychotherapy. *American Psychologist* 32:5–13.

Meichenbaum, D. H. (1977). *Cognitive Behavior Modification*. New York: Ple-

Heidi Gerard Kaduson 225

Meichenbaum, D. H., and Asarnow, J. (1979). Cognitive-behavioral modification and metacognitive development: implications for the classroom. In *Cognitive-Behavioral Interventions: Theory, Research and Procedures*, ed. P. C. Kendall, and S. D. Hollon, pp. 111–118. New York: Academic Press.

Meichenbaum, D. H., and Goodman, J. (1971). Training impulsive children to talk to themselves: a means of developing self-control. *Journal of Abnormal Psychology* 77:115–126.

Milich, R., S., and Kramer, J. (1985). Reflections on impulsivity: an empirical investigation of impulsivity as a construct. In *Advances in Learning and Behavioral Disabilities*, vol. 3, ed. K. D. Gadow, and I. Bialer, pp. 57–94. Greenwich, CT: JAI.

Milich, R. S., and Landau, S. (1981). Socialization and peer relations in the hyperactive child. In *Advances in Learning and Behavioral Disabilities*, vol. 3, ed. K. D. Gadow, and I. Ler, pp. 116–141. Greenwich, CT: JAI.

Milich, R. S., Landau, S., Kilby, G., and Whitten, P. (1982). Preschool peer perceptions of the behavior of hyperactive and aggressive children. *Journal of Abnormal Child Psychology* 10:497–510.

Mischel, W. (1974). Processes in delay of gratification. In *Advances in Experimental Social Psychology*, vol. 7, ed. L. Berkowitz, pp. 34–50. New York: Academic Press.

Nickerson, E. T., and O'Laughlin, K. B. (1983). It's fun, but will it work? The use of games as a therapeutic medium for children and adolescents. *Journal of Clinical Child Psychology* 12:78–81.

O'Leary, K. D., and O'Leary, S. G. (1972). *Classroom Management: The Successful Use of Behavior Modification*. New York: Pergamon.

——— (1976). Behavior modification in the school. In *Handbook of Behavior Modification and Behavior Therapy*, ed. H. Leitenberg, pp. 475–515. Englewood Cliffs, NJ: Prentice-Hall.

O'Leary, S. G., and Dubey, D. R. (1979). Applications of self-control procedures by children: a review. *Journal of Applied Behavior Analysis* 12:449–465.

Palkes, H., Stewart, M., and Kahana, B. (1972). Porteus maze performance of hyperactive boys after training in self-directed verbal commands. *Child Development* 39:817–826.

Pelham, W. E., and Bender, M. E. (1982). Peer relationships in hyperactive children: description and treatment. In *Advances in Learning and Behavioral Disabilities*, vol. 1, ed. K. Gadow and I. Bialer, pp. 365–436. Greenwich, CT: JAI.

Pelham, W. E., and Milich, R. (1984). Peer relations of children with hyperactivity/attention deficit disorder. *Journal of Learning Disabilities* 17:560–568.

Pelham, W. E., and Murphy, H. A. (1986). Attention deficit and conduct disorders. In *Pharmacological and Behavioral Treatments: An Integrative Approach*, ed. M. Hersen, pp. 108–148. New York: Wiley.

Reid, S. (1993). Game play. In *The Therapeutic Powers of Play*, ed. C. E. Schaefer, pp. 323–348. New York: Jason Aronson.

Ross, D. M., and Ross, S. A. (1982). *Hyperactivity: Current Issues, Research, and Theory*, 2nd ed. New York: Wiley.

Rotter, J. B. (1954). *Social Learning and Clinical Psychology*. Englewood Cliffs, NJ: Prentice-Hall.

Rubin, K. H., Fein, G. G., and Bandenberg, B. (1983). Play. In *Handbook of Child Development*, ed. E. Hetherington, pp. 67–90. New York: Wiley.

Safter, D.J., and Krager, J. M. (1983). A survey of medication treatment for hyperactive-inattentive students. *Journal of the American Medical Association* 260(15):2256–2258.

Sawyers, J. K., and Horm-Wingerd, D. M. (1993). Creative problem solving. In *Therapeutic Powers of Play*, ed. C. E. Schaefer, pp. 81–105. Northvale, NJ: Jason Aronson.

Schaefer, C. E. (1993). *The Therapeutic Powers of Play*. Northvale, NJ: Jason Aronson.

Serok, S., and Blum, A. (1983). Therapeutic uses of games. *Residential Group Care and Treatment* 1:3–14.

Sprafkin, J., and Rubenstein, E. A. (1982). Using television to improve the social behavior of institutionalized children. In *Prevention in Human Services: Rx Television: Enhancing the Preventive Impact of TV*, ed. J. Sprafkin, C. Swift, and R. H. Ross, pp. 5–16. New York: Haworth.

Stark, K. D., Rouse, L. W., and Livingston, R. (1991). Treatment of depression during childhood and adolescence: cognitive-behavioral procedures for the individual and family. In *Child and Adolescent Therapy: Cognitive-Behavioral Procedures*, ed. P. C. Kendall, pp. 165–206. New York: Guilford.

Stewart, M.A., Pitts, F. N., Craig, A. G., and Dieruf, W. (1966). The hyperactive child syndrome. *American Journal of Orthopsychiatry* 36:861–867.

Thoresen, C. E., and Mahoney, M. J. (1974). *Behavioral Self-Control*. New York: Holt, Rinehart & Winston.

Trommer, B. L., Hoeppner, J. B., Rosenberg, R. S., et al. (1988). Sleep disturbances in children with attention deficit disorder. *Annuals of Neurology* 24:325.

Urbain, E. S., and Kendall, P. C. (1980). Review of social cognitive problem-solving interventions with children. *Psychological Bulletin* 88:109–143.

Weiss, G., and Hechtman, L. T. (1986). *Hyperactive Children Grown Up: Empirical Findings and Theoretical Considerations*. New York: Guilford.

Wender, P. H. (1987). *Minimal Brain Dysfunction in Children*. New York: Wiley.

Whalen, C., Henker, B., Collins, B. E., et al. (1979). Peer interaction in structured communication task: comparisons of normal and hyperactive boys and of methylphenidate (Ritalin) and placebo effects. *Child Development* 50:388–401.

Wolraich, M., Drummond, D., Salomon, M., et al. (1978). Effects of methylphenidate alone and in combination with behavior modification procedures on the behavior and academic performance of hyperactive children. *Journal of Abnormal Child Psychology* 6:149–161.

Zametkin, A. J., Nordahl, T. E., Gross, M., et al. (1990). Cerebral glucose metabolism in adults with hyperactivity of childhood onset. *New England Journal of Medicine* 323:1361–1366.

Zentall, S. S. (1985). A context for hyperactivity. In *Advances in Learning and Behavioral Disabilities*, vol. 4, ed. K. D. Gadow, and I. Bialer, pp. 273–343. Greenwich, CT: JAI.

9

Conduct Disorder: Grounded Play Therapy

Neil Cabe

There was a child went forth every day,
And the first object he look'd upon, that object he became,
And that object became part of him for the day or a certain part of the day,
Or for many years or stretching cycles of years.

Walt Whitman

Background

For the conduct disordered and oppositional defiant child, the world into which he walks each day is not a particularly attractive one. The lives of these children are often filled with school problems, frequent contacts with the police, a chaotic family life, age-inappropriate sexuality, and somatizations. Often, the things these youngsters look upon are the things that they become. For years. Or stretching cycles of years. This chapter discusses a play therapy approach for breaking the cycle of conduct disorder and oppositional defiant behavior.

One of the real joys of working with children lies in the rebuilding of hope in the lives of families and youngsters in whom hope has almost died. That hope has emerged for me as one of the earliest foci of the therapeutic process. For parents, there is perhaps no more apparently hopeless child than the oppositional defiant or conduct disordered youngster. Most alarming to me are opinions such as this one:

> No psychotherapy has been found to help sociopaths. Anti-social personality disorder is ego-syntonic, sociopaths have no desire to change, consider insights excuses, have

no concept of the future, resent all authorities, including therapists, view the patient role as pitiful, detest being in a position of inferiority, deem therapy a joke and therapists as objects to be conned, threatened, seduced, or used. [Maxmen 1986, p. 319]

Description of Conduct Disorder Children

The male pronoun will be used throughout this chapter as there is evidence that the disorders are three times more prevalent in boys than in girls (Graham 1979). However, as social systems change, as the impact of the growing number of single parent/female headed households becomes more clear, and as women become more empowered in American society, I expect that dated statistic to change.

While children are not clinically sociopathic, the disruptive behavior disorders run a sort of developmental continuum from normal oppositional behaviors, through oppositional defiant disorder, to conduct disorder, and then to antisocial personality disorders. Defiant behaviors such as lying, stealing, cheating at games, aggression, and simple disobedience emerge temporarily in normal childhood development, whereas conduct disorder as a diagnosable entity emerges as an ongoing and stable pattern of antisocial behavior. The latter produces problems in the everyday life of the child and his family. As a result of this pattern of behavior, the child will come in contact with mental health professionals, police, school authorities, juvenile court, and perhaps clinicians treating substance abuse.

Along the continuum, oppositional defiant disorder (classification number 313.81 in DSM-IV) is a pattern of negative, hostile, and defiant behavior that occurs more frequently than in other people of the same mental age as the client. These children lose their temper, argue incessantly with adults, refuse adult requests, annoy others intentionally, and blame others for their own mistakes. They are touchy and easily annoyed, angry, resentful, spiteful, vindictive, and occasionally obscene. Conduct disordered children frequently present with problem behaviors such as stealing, running away from home, fire-setting, truancy, breaking and entering, deliberate destruction of property, and cruelty to animals. They may also force sexual activity, initiate physical fights, use weapons in some of those fights, and be physically cruel to people. To qualify for this diagnosis, such behaviors must be present for at least six months (American Psychiatric Association 1994).

Conduct disorder as a diagnostic entity (312.8 in DSM-IV) increases the ante. The child has developed a pattern of behavior that begins to violate the rights of others and societal norms. The pattern is persistent, frequent, chronic, severe, and causes major disruptions in the life of the child and his family. Further, the symptoms or behaviors do not occur in isolation from each other, but rather in clusters of behavioral patterns (American Psychiatric Association 1994).

As this child enters adulthood, in the absence of change, antisocial personality disorder (301.7 in *DSM-IV*) may be the result. That is, the pattern of behavior begun in early childhood, exacerbated in adolescence, and carried into adulthood continues many of the features mentioned above, and grows to potentially include failure to honor financial obligations, poor parenting, an inability to plan ahead, impulsiveness, inconsistent work behavior, arrest, harassment, and/or having an illegal occupation. Clients with antisocial personality disorder tend to get into many fights, may be involved in spouse or child abuse, are reckless, abandon responsibility, and are usually without remorse (American Psychiatric Association 1994).

It is not uncommon for conduct disorder children to be misdiagnosed. They often appear to be hyperactive, exhibit poor interpersonal relationships, and are socially ineffective. These youngsters commonly interpret the activities of others as hostile, and they regularly have academic problems. These children are less able to identify solutions in their lives, and are perhaps incapable of taking the perspective of others. They become resentful, suspicious, angry, acting out, hostile, and isolated – until they find other children just like themselves. Then, the behaviors crying out for therapeutic intervention will find reinforcement and praise within peer groups. At some point, I believe, the behaviors become their own reward and their own powerful reinforcer, making change doubly difficult.

The prognosis for these clients is notoriously poor. Among children for whom interventions were attempted, long-term studies have indicated that delinquents did not benefit from any intervention attempted. In some cases they appeared to be worse than those children who were left alone (Reid 1989). Even among those children who do not continue to evidence antisocial behaviors, most will have other social problems as adults, including frequent unemployment, divorce, and difficulty with law enforcement agencies.

Much of the literature on this population describes symptoms but seems light on etiology. That is, nobody knows where it comes from, in spite of the fact that a third to a half of the referrals to outpatient clinics are for aggression, conduct problems, and antisocial behaviors (Gilbert 1957). However, we are able to describe the systems influencing a child's life when he presents with antisocial behaviors.

One element, perhaps the primary one, in the development of oppositional-defiant behaviors is family discord. Many of these children present with a history of parental desertion, divorce, custody fights, and other family disruption. Frequent moves, early deaths of parents, and separations from significant others are common. Parental discipline is often harsh and inconsistent, and affection is doled out sparsely and intermittently. Maternal neglect and indifference, alcoholism in the family, and paternal sociopathy are often seen. One must wonder about the possibility of some genetic predisposition.

Chaos and poorly managed families are central to the development of conduct disorders, and may predict later delinquent behaviors in children (Loerber and Dishion 1983). Having experienced failure in almost every area of life, the child becomes unhappy and socially inept. Failure becomes the only thing at which the child may succeed. It is at this point, I believe, that the behavior becomes its own reward.

The etiology of the disorder itself is insidious. That is, shaping in an operant sense occurs in the family on a totally unintentional level, occurring outside the awareness of either the child or his parents. The inconsistent demands and affections of the family members cause the child to attempt to escape double-binding. This translates into problems with adults at school and in other settings. When the child is presented with a gestalt similar to the familial one, he resorts to the often violent and clearly dysfunctional behaviors he has learned at home. This is especially so in abusive homes. Parental roles are generalized to all authority figures and the child's responses to each become essentially identical. Home and school behaviors lead to ever more severe family dysfunction, arrested social skill development, and other problems. This process develops into a cycle. It is no wonder that early patterns of antisocial behavior in middle childhood become predictive of adolescent delinquency (Loerber and Dishion 1983), which can then perseverate as antisocial behavior in adulthood.

The root causes for conduct and oppositional defiant disorders are numerous, reinforced throughout childhood, and often occur outside the awareness of either the child or his parents. Historically, most interventions have ranged between ineffective and damaging. The prognosis for these children is abysmal, and they are at risk for other disorders including substance abuse, depression, and learning problems. They are at high risk for suicide due to impulsiveness coupled with an often intransient depression. What then might be done?

Traditional Treatment Strategies

Based on all of the above, it is clear that treatment for the conduct disordered youth is a difficult undertaking. In fact, it appears that no treatment protocol has been found to be especially effective in dealing with this difficult population (Kazdin 1991). It is almost as if the predisposing factors—family dysfunction, familial antisocial behaviors, paternal alcoholism, abandonment in early childhood, and social environment—form a psychosocial chain in the mind of the child from which escape becomes almost impossible.

I, for one, do not believe this to be so. As Eliana Gil (1991) so clearly states, "If given a nurturing, safe environment, the child will inevitably gravitate toward the reparative experience" (p. 53). Those environmental interventions that lead toward an improved family life, more appropriate social skills, educational support and academic achievement can be effective. Environments that emphasize consistency, fairness, clear boundaries, and realistic expectations will lead, I believe, to that reparative experience. The play therapy environment has the potential to give this experience to the child. However, play therapy alone will not accomplish this task. Family contacts, school cooperation, group home reinforcement, and play therapy should all be utilized, as will be demonstrated below in a case illustration. This multimodal treatment may be effective in treating children with conduct disorders.

Traditional treatment strategies have included a range of attempts at helping these children. None has proved to be particularly helpful, as noted above. For instance, individual psychotherapy has been previously utilized in every case of a conduct disorder child I have encountered. With its focus on the internal bases for antisocial behavior, especially along developmental lines, not a lot has been accomplished. Here, as in all interventions with this population, the relationship with the therapist is of paramount importance. The therapist is the single most important avenue of change for the client. In some sense, the individual therapist attempts to help guide the child to appropriate and socially effective interactions through the use of insight. But insight, unfortunately, is not one of the strong points in the conduct disordered youth's armamentarium. Role play techniques, discussion, talk therapy, empathy, and sympathy do not seem to be particularly helpful with this population, especially when used in isolation from other interventions.

Perhaps the most popular and enduring way of dealing with oppositional, defiant, and conduct-problem youths is a wide range of behavioral techniques. They meet with minimal but occasionally promising results (Kazdin 1989). After targeting particular behaviors for change, direct training takes place. Modeling as well as positive, negative, and aversive reinforcement is used. The techniques are to be put in place not only in the therapy sessions, but also in the home and school environments. Clearly, this approach insists on the cooperation of the family, if one exists, and of the schools, if school personnel are able and willing to help. Many of the children I have known scoff at paste-on stars, smiley-faced charts, and token economies. In fact, most of the behaviors of these youngsters, especially severely conduct-disordered children, are more influenced by avoiding police and court referrals than by any simple reward or punishment system. Unfortunately, even the threat of potentially lengthy incarceration offers no real threat to many of these youngsters. Many have been in detention for varying periods of time. In fact, I have treated some who vocally prefer juvenile detention to the home situation, to the point of breaking the law intentionally in order to be placed.

Psychopharmacology, especially the use of lithium carbonate and haloperidol for their antiaggressive effects, has been tried with many conduct-disordered children (Campbell et al. 1984). Working from a medical model, the theory is that underlying biological factors can be influenced to control antisocial behaviors. As with many of the other therapy techniques, none of these can be expected to operate in a vacuum. Each must be a part of a well-developed treatment plan.

Residential treatment offers the possibility of implementing a number of techniques within a controlled environment. Separation from parents, removal from the toxic environment, pharmacotherapy as appropriate, behavioral modification, reward and punishment schedules, controlled educational situations, may all be applied. While many children will benefit from the combination of approaches the residential treatment program offers, the unfortunate fact is that the child will in most cases be returned to the environment of origin. That is, he will go back to a neighborhood where the precipitating problems still exist. I have found that if families have been trained and modified, and if the environment of origin is somehow detoxified, residential treatment using a variety of techniques does hold some promise. My experience has been that the child will perform well while in the residential program with controls in place and nurturing available. When the controls and nurturing are removed, the old behaviors reappear. That is, the child's long-standing homeostasis, compensatory needs, and resultant acting out will reemerge.

Parent training and family therapy are necessary parts of any treatment plan for these children. Parenting skills are predictably poor or totally absent. In some cases, parents are so completely exasperated by the child's behavior that they are glad to have him placed somewhere. In a strict family therapy–based approach, the family becomes the identified patient rather than the child. Here, the focus is on roles, family dynamics, boundaries, interpersonal relationships, and family organization. Structure and communications may be emphasized, and the development of negotiating skills, compromise, and problem-solving skills becomes the focus of treatment. An additional element in this approach may be community programs and the establishment of appropriate and positive peer connections for the child. In theory, the child will generalize these prosocial behaviors and healing will occur.

Where then does play therapy enter this continuum? It is this topic that we will now address.

Rationale for Play Therapy

In considering a disorder with such a completely disheartening prognosis, one must wonder what powers there may be to affect outcome for these children. I do not find the prognosis as bleak as I have outlined above. With Ruth Hartley (Schaefer and Kaduson 1994), I believe that reading the language of play is reading the hearts and minds of children. Unfortunately, for many conduct disordered and oppositional defiant clients, no one has bothered to read. I believe it is a rare child whose heart and mind will not emerge in a safe and nurturing play environment.

I am convinced that most, if not all, mental health problems are the direct result of a breakdown in relationship: with self, with others, and existentially. That is, when a child is disconnected from his sense of self, when he has no person with whom he may connect in meaningful ways, and when he loses—or never gains—a sense of being connected to all of humanity, the confusion and heartache are enough that acting out is a natural outcome.

In normals, we assume that actions are mediated by cognition, which emanates from deep emotion. For children, the cognitive process is most often absent. Certainly for youngsters who have been deprived of a safe, nurturing, and appropriately stimulating environment, cognitive process addressing societal norms will be absent. Rather, the child will illustrate in his acting out the norm of his own life: disconnection, confusion, fear, anger, violence, and a crying need to separate himself from deep feelings too painful for his young life to bear. That is, for these children emotions lead directly to actions: they act out. In a way, it makes sense.

In an appropriate play environment, the child may experiment in a safe and nurturing milieu, with attachment formation and a safe relationship, at first with the therapist, then through transition and generalization with others in his life. Play provides the opportunity for the release of energy and deeply held emotions, for an awareness of sensation and affect and for the internal organization of previously disorganized affective and cognitive processes and events. He may engage in creative problem solving, and discover the verbal labeling of emotions, which may lead to the appropriate integration not only of affect but also of personality. What powers of play are there that may be involved in the treatment of disruptive behavior disorders?

Therapeutic Powers of Play Involved in Treating Disruptive Behaviors

One of the clear powers of the play process is the power of attachment formation. I use the term broadly here, to include attachment not only to others, but also to self and self-in-environment. Appropriately achieved, this "connectivity" leads to self-awareness, a more positive self-image, understanding, problem solving within the societal framework, and relationship enhancement. The play therapy environment provides the possibility for overcoming resistance, establishing communication and teaching communication skills, building self-confidence, and creating competencies with the child. It allows for metaphoric teaching, using nonthreatening media, and allows the expression of and practice with positive emotions. This idea forms the basis for a prescriptive approach to dealing with conduct disordered children and adolescents.

In this respect, it cannot be stated too strongly that the initial and primary goal of any treatment of these disconnected youngsters lies in relationship. The therapist must build positive regard and positive interaction with the client immediately, and that relationship must grow as the play process unfolds. In the absence of a positive therapist–client relationship, little will be accomplished.

What techniques then might a play therapist choose in order to help such clients? In what ways can we help the conduct disordered and oppositional defiant client to connect with himself, with others, and with his own place in the broad spectrum of society?

Approach

The Grounded Play Therapy Processing Approach

Lusebrink (1990) describes a continuum of expressive therapies and healing dimensions. Moving from most resistive to least resistive, he describes the properties of two-dimensional and three-dimensional media, with healing dimensions and emergent functions for each level of process. The levels include kinesthetic, sensory, perceptual, affective, cognitive, and symbolic.

At the kinesthetic level, motor movements and exploration allow the release of energy and help the child to better form perceptions and discover affect. The sensory level, dealing with tactile explorations and the realization of inner sensations, allows for the awareness of internal sensations and the expression of slow rhythm. These will further aid affect discovery and help the child to experience and express internal images. At the perceptual level, with its emphasis on form, concrete images, and formal elements, the organization of stimuli and the formation of healthy gestalts will lead to verbal labeling and a growing ability toward self-instruction. The expression of feelings and moods, with an emphasis on color, will lead to an awareness of appropriate affect, the verbal labeling of feelings, and the internalization of images. This occurs at the affective level. The cognitive level, with an emphasis on concept formulation, abstractions, and verbal self-instructions, will help develop the generalization of concrete experiences and lead to creative problem solving using verbal interaction. Finally, at the symbolic level, which is described as intuitive and self-oriented, the child learns concept formation and abstraction, and will learn to resolve symbols through personal meaning and to generalize to concrete personal experiences. This leads to insight and the discovery of new parts of the self.

In conjunction with the different levels of expressive therapies and the healing and emergent dimension of each, Lusebrink proposes that the media of play itself are integrally related to the healing process. This has proven to be so in my work with disruptive as well as traumatized clients.

Two- and three-dimensional media have properties of concretion emerging from the most resistive to the least resistive media within each class. For example, two-dimensional media such as art materials move from most resistive, such as a pencil, to the least resistive, such as finger paint. At the far end of the two-dimensional continuum and merging into the three-dimensional lies finger painting with pudding that has been colored with food coloring. In ascending order toward fluidity, between the pencil and pudding, lie magic markers, chalk, poster paints, watercoloring, and standard finger paint.

Early in the therapeutic process, pencils and ballpoint pens are most appropriate. While markers might be available, the more resistive media are most convenient for the client. For example, initial house-tree-person drawings will most likely be completed with a pencil, and only later involve poster paints. While the therapist should help the client select an appropriate medium, it is potentially damaging to insist on more fluid media before the child himself chooses them.

In three-dimensional media, the same process of movement from most resistive to least resistive product applies. Stone and wood will lead to sand, which will glide into the use of oil clay and water clay. At the least resistive end of this continuum may lie the processes of making play dough or making "gloop" using a mixture of school glue and starch.

Drawing on the work of Lusebrink (1990), Piaget, Maslow, and Moustakas (1992), grounded play therapy processing describes how a client may move in order to achieve healing, integration, and full functioning. Table 9-1 illustrates the processes described by each of these authors.

For each child presenting for therapy, there is a certain *homeostasis*. That is, there is an existing balance in his life, no matter how healthy or pathological that balance may be. For the conduct disordered child, the homeostasis consists of antisocial behaviors, contact with police, school truancy, family disruption, parental detachment, familial substance abuse issues, and harsh and inconsistent discipline.

The earliest part of the process for the therapist involves a thorough initial clinical assessment, any testing deemed necessary, a review of the history, and a summary of home and school functioning, and any other ecosystemic influences. Suggested activities for each of the stages in the grounded play therapy process are listed below, and the case illustration in this chapter describes the use of some of them.

Following the appraisal of homeostasis, *animation*, the least threatening

Table 9-1
The Therapeutic Process

Lusebrink	Maslow	Piaget	Moustakis
Symbolic	Self-actualization	Formal operational	Preservation
Cognitive	Esteem	Concrete operational	Ambivalence
Affective	Belonging	Preoperational	Focused hostility and fear
Perceptual	Safety	Sensorimotor	Generalized anxiety and fear
Sensory/ kinesthetic	Physiological needs		Diffuse and pervasive anxiety and fear

and perhaps most attractive process for the often hyperactive conduct disordered or oppositional defiant youngster, comes into play. Here, the child begins to understand and become aware of his own body process, and to develop physical awareness via his relationship to the therapist. This eventually generalizes to others. Perception and consciousness are paramount, and may be enhanced by any number of tactile activities. Kaleidoscopes, magnifying glasses, telescopes, photographs, and visual activities are useful. Rhythm exercises, puzzles, voice amplifiers such as Space Phones and telephones, bells and tone generators, chalk drawings if the child can tolerate them, games of catch, Silly Putty and play dough, and various methods of tactile energy release are appropriate.

Trust-building exercises are used next to develop a sense of sanctuary, self-assurance, and security in the child. Here, sensory and perceptual as opposed to motor activity exercises begin to come into play. As trust builds in the play environment and between the client and his therapist, the vesting process begins. As the child becomes more aware of himself, more trusting of his own perceptions of the world around him, and more able to manage and control the play environment, he becomes more vested not only in the process, but also in himself. Here, affective and cognitive activity will become more a part of the play process.

Then, as the child becomes ever more secure in himself, more connected to his sense of self, more connected to others in his life, and more able to manage his own emerging emotions, he develops a sense of potency. That is, he begins to see that effective interaction with the environment is a possibility. At this point, changes in the conduct disordered child's behaviors should become more obvious both to him and to those around him. Energy levels in appropriate ways will increase, hyperactivity for its own sake will decrease, concentration is easier, and the oppositional behaviors, while still experimented with occasionally, will continue to decrease.

Finally, preservation suggests that the lessons learned and ground gained in the play therapy process will persevere and generalize to the child's environment. It will require some time before the full effects of the preservation phase are clear, and even more to be sure that generalization has occurred. Table 9–2 illustrates the process involved in grounded play therapy.

It is wise for the therapist to realize that attempting to implement techniques and activities inappropriate to the phase of therapy within which the child emerges is not only futile, but also potentially damaging to the child and the child–therapist relationship. This must be handled delicately. There will be some overlap from phase to phase, and the child will return to certain activities until he has achieved closure on and mastery of each of his own symbols, whatever they are. Regularly, the child will participate with the therapist in externalizing his own behavior, discomfort, confusion, or dilemma, gaining symbolic mastery, and moving on.

Table 9-2
Grounded Play Therapy Processing

	Preservation: Client's appropriate behaviors persevere then
Symbolic, creative:	*Potency:* Effective interaction with the environment, energy then
Affective, cognitive:	*Vesting:* A sense of residence within the self; inherence then
Sensory, perceptual:	*Trust:* Some sense of sanctuary; assurance; security then
Kinesthetics:	*Animation:* Consciousness; perception then
	Homeostasis: Existing balance

Techniques

Play Therapy Suggestions Appropriate to Each Stage of the Grounded Play Therapy (GPT) Process

Homeostasis

A thorough initial clinical assessment is a part of the homeostasis stage, which may require several sessions to complete. The assessment process includes a family history, perhaps including a genogram, a behavioral checklist appropriate to conduct disordered youth, and an assessment of depression and anxiety. I have found the Childhood Depression Inventory (Kovacs 1992) and the Revised Childhood Manifest Anxiety Scale to be helpful, as each is time sensitive and may be used at some later date to assess progress for the client. The Adolescent Sexual Concerns Questionnaire (Hussey and Singer 1994) and the Behavioral True/False Inventory (Cabe 1994) have proven helpful in assessing childhood sexual and physical abuse, and a dissociative behavior checklist may help to examine the extent of dissociation in the client. A suicide interview guideline and noninjury contract if required are potentially important documents to include in the client file. At this point it is also helpful to contact the appropriate probation or parole officer, the client's family if possible, appropriate school personnel, and the contact person in the child's living situation. An understanding of all of the systems at work in the client's life is important to the therapeutic process, and cooperation among each of these systems is critical to healing.

Animation

In the animation stage of the GPT process, beginning disclosures of important life events occur. It is important to be able to offer the child play activities that will facilitate this and help with the integrative process. The GPT approach offers a symbol to the child for his behavior, embedded affect, or trauma, which allows the child to externalize that behavior, affect, or event and then to gain mastery over it.

To aid in this part of the process, puzzles will allow the integration of parts to a whole. Nondirective play will allow the child to gain some mastery over the play environment as well as allow for transition of life control to other areas in his life. Here, safety concerns both in and out of the play environment must be addressed, rules are rehearsed, and the child will probably test the limits of those rules. Consistency and fairness are critical. Systems interventions with police, children's services agencies, housing and other physical needs may be necessary. The "Space Phone," commercially available plastic funnels attached with wound wire that produce wonderful echoes and mysterious sounds, are fun and with other telephone-like toys will emphasize connection and communication for the child. Moving along the resistive/fluid continuum noted above, markers and chalk become appropriate, as do commercial play dough and Silly Putty, and Velcro paddles and balls facilitate conversation while separating from difficult behavior; crash dummies or large pillow-soft dolls may be used for anger ventilation. Where age appropriate, toy soldiers and dinosaurs facilitate reenactment and reconstruction, and puppets may be used for separation from and mastery over difficult life events.

Trust

Trust is an extremely difficult thing for the conduct disordered youth. The rehearsal and consistent application of play environment rules put boundaries on the client's life that tie him to reality and make the world a safer place. The same is true of school and living environments. As the child trusts his therapist more, deeper disclosures and self-examination become possible. One extremely effective technique is "Draw-A-Rose," first described by Violet Oaklander (1988). The child imagines a rose, draws it as he wishes, and then becomes it. For even deeper self-investigation, the child can imagine a lake, make a cross section of it, and become the lake. The "depths" of the lake magically become the deepest thoughts of the child. Some clients quickly realize that they are describing themselves, but I have yet to find an adolescent or adult who did not benefit from the experience. This is also a good point at which to reexperience the house-tree-person drawings; changes from the initial set can be dramatic.

Any exercise that reinforces boundaries and control over one's own body space is effective in the trust phase, as are family sessions and parent training if possible. Rhythm exercises, especially with real drums such as Native-American tom-toms, are not only fun but also healing for the child.

Vesting

In the vesting phase, the child becomes more vested not only in the therapeutic process but also in himself and himself-in-environment. Here, moving further toward least resistive media, the therapist and child may make play dough; some children will be able to tolerate making personal Silly Putty with two parts school glue mixed with one part household starch. The personal Silly Putty is a very sticky and messy activity. Poster paints are appropriate, as are mood drawings using only colors and shapes, beginning finger painting, feeling charts and checks, and trigger explanation and explorations. Artwork in the vesting phase can be helpful in cognitive reconstruction. If available, a sampling of the client's childhood photos can be helpful in noting growth, change, and self-in-environment, as well as serving to trigger memories.

At this point, the therapist may explain to and graph for the child the fact that levels of emotions common to all persons typically lead to cognition, with that cognition leading to action. We may explain that emotion leading only to action is called "acting out" and that such action needs to be understood, controlled, and appropriately expressed in order to be socially acceptable. Perhaps all conduct disordered youth have severe problems with understanding this concept, as well as the fact that actions have consequences. Making domino "topple-overs" provides a memorable symbol for the child that his actions have consequences, and that thinking ahead to consequences dramatically changes outcomes in most situations.

Potency

For the conduct disordered youth, believing that he is powerful enough to affect his own environment is often a foreign idea. The empowering process reinforces this concept. Simply making a list of strengths and weaknesses with the client may emphasize his positive qualities. Richard Gardner's (1973) "Talking, Feeling, Doing" game, storytelling cards, or Gardner's (1988) "Story Telling Card Game" may all be useful in the potency phase. Using any available resources, and perhaps allowing the client to redo activities of his own choosing, can be useful in essential abreaction of difficult or traumatic events as well as for reenactment and reframing. Reframing can be as simple as making a list of the child's presenting symptoms, tearing it up, and forcefully throwing it in the trash.

Anger management is an ongoing process for most disruptive behavior disordered clients. One technique I have found especially helpful is teaching the child to break a board, using a martial arts technique on one- by twelve-inch dry pine crosscut in three-inch sections. The concept of looking past present problems and through to a solution is clearly represented by striking through the board to a point where it is already broken. Any therapist untrained in the technique can be taught by a competent Tae Kwon Do or karate instructor in a matter of minutes. As anger management techniques, I also frequently use a life-size doll, foam blocks and balls, which can be thrown without injury, and the simple focus of anger and aggression on the pages of an old telephone book, later to be torn to shreds. All are relieving and healing techniques.

Preservation

Clearly, no matter how much is learned in the play therapy session, it is without value if preservation does not occur. I see this as an ongoing process throughout the GPT process. I regularly provide transitional objects for the child, which leads to transfer into other environments, and preservation of learned concepts. Feeling charts, strengths and weaknesses charts, homemade play dough, and Silly Putty and drawings regularly accompany the client back to his living environment. At termination, I often give the child a stamped envelope with my address on it so he maintains a connection with me and his own healing environment. Parental conferences, court follow-ups, and school checks during termination are important to the preservation process.

Case Illustration

The body language is perhaps typical. With a sort of saunter, one foot dragging behind and raising on his toes, Michael, a 13-year-old African American, ambled into my office. He threw himself into the overstuffed rocker, arms spread, legs apart, like he was ready for an attack or a quick exit, whichever the situation required. Eyes half-closed, he was quiet, although not quite sullen. He was in treatment by court order, and had recently entered a group home near my office. Michael was required to enter counseling in order for his probation officer to consider allowing him to return home. In fact, he could not go without my permission, and he knew this. While this is not ideal in dealing with the conduct disordered or oppositional defiant child, it is perhaps the norm.

Michael's background is perhaps as typical as his walk. Recently released from the Department of Youth Services for car theft and assault, he had also been charged with complicity to rape, but that charge was dismissed. His history was replete with referrals to the Department of Human Services, frequent contacts with the police, multiple suspensions and then expulsion from school, and counseling experiences that had proven to be largely ineffective. After four months in a juvenile detention center, his behavior was good enough for placement in the group home.

In this first session, my only aim was to establish something like rapport, and to gather as much personal history as the child could tolerate. In spite of his stance, nervousness rattled in his voice, and his fingers began to drum on the arm of the overstuffed chair. I had been careful not to touch him, as he offered no fist-pounding handshake, sneaking only furtive glances at me through eyes half-closed. Casually, I flipped a ball of putty over to him, asked him to try stretching it, noted to him that it would bounce. For the first time, he almost smiled, and for the first time he looked at me full in the eyes. This was only for a second, as if it weren't allowed. As he worked the putty in his small hands, he began to respond to the questions I asked, which were as nonleading as I could make them.

He was taught how to flip cars by this father, who was in jail for a long time. The child did not know why. When I asked him what "flipping cars" is, he was obviously pleased to explain it: repainting, changing the interiors, altering vehicle identification numbers, and reselling stolen vehicles. He explained in detail how to change the VIN under the left front fender without pulling the engine, and was proud that his father had taught him how to do this. At the age of 11 Michael could get an expensive automobile for anybody who wanted one, and make $200 a day doing it.

Michael's brother was incarcerated for robbery, another brother died at birth, and another was shot in the back and killed the previous year at the age of 17. Michael was 13 years old at the time of our initial session. He had been in trouble with the police at least fourteen times, by his own count. His mother had two more children at home, and there was a total of nine children in the family. He did not know all of their names. He was angry, feared for his future, felt as if he should be at home to take care of his mother and little sister, and felt as if the paternal role in the family was his own. Michael reacted with surprise when I pointed out to him that 13 was awfully young to be a husband and father.

The initial clinical interview was largely uneventful. The child was euthymic and friendly, albeit suspicious and guarded, with no unusual mannerisms. His affect was broad and appropriate to content, and at times a genuine smile was noted. There was no delusional behavior, he was oriented in three spheres, had minimal attention deficit, and his immediate memory was good, with some impairment of recent memory. Remote memory, perhaps predictably, was poor. There was no suicidal ideation. Michael was somewhat hypervigilant, which is common among inner-city youth. His startle response was somewhat exaggerated, and he reportedly slept very lightly but claimed never to have nightmares. He had no friends.

The Children's Depression Inventory (Kovacs 1992) was administered and suggested no pathological depression, but showed moderate to severe difficulty with interpersonal relationships. His feelings were deeply buried, and Michael felt there was little he could do to change his life situation. Quizzically, he asked, "Can you help me?" "We'll try," I said. The Revised Childhood Manifest Anxiety Scale (Reynolds and Richmond 1985) indicates this boy was at or below the mean on all scales. He claimed to have never used drugs, and that he had been intoxicated only once. As an afterthought, he mentioned to me that he just gotten over a bout of gonorrhea, which had led to an eye infection. He did not know how he got it. An informal sexual abuse interrogatory using the Adolescent Sexual Concerns Questionnaire (Hussey and Singer 1994) and *Woody and Willy Say It's O.K. to Tell* (Cabe 1990) revealed only one abusive event. Michael's reading ability was fairly low, so I chose to use *Woody and Willy Say It's O.K. to Tell*, a coloring book I developed that promotes disclosure in a nonthreatening and nonleading series of drawings. Michael noted that a neighbor's father once put a hand in Michael's pants, he told his mother, the mother called the police, and the perpetrator was incarcerated for ninety days. No other abusive events were described, and the sexually transmitted disease remains a mystery.

Developing The Treatment Plan

Of the criteria for conduct disorder (*DSM-IV*), Michael exhibited or had previously exhibited at least ten of the 15 primary criteria for classification number 312.8 (childhood onset type, severe). The predisposing factors in Michael's case seemed as typical as his walk: parental rejection, paternal antisocial behavior and substance abuse, maternal substance abuse, large family size, harsh and inconsistent discipline, and association with a delinquent subgroup—in this case a group of other adolescents connected with a pair of adult males who paid the boys for stealing cars. Michael had experienced multiple school suspensions, legal problems, an unexplained bout with a venereal disease, fights, and removal from the home for unruly behavior. He had been institutionalized for almost two years.

I was struck by the lack of human connections in Michael's young life. He admitted to only mild dissociative behaviors, which he enjoyed, and which lasted only moments at a time. They were described as more than daydreams, but less than clear dissociative episodes. Michael was disconnected from his family, not even knowing the names of all of his brothers and sisters, having one brother and his father in prison. Uncharacteristically for this population, he did not have grandparents available to him and he named no cousins, aunts, or uncles with whom he had contact. Never having been in school for more than short periods of time, he had no friends. In addition, Michael informed me that he was glad his counselor was a "white guy." In part, I believe he was simply differentiating himself from me, and with the lack of individual human connection in his life, Michael was also missing racial and cultural connections.

Michael was disconnected from himself, from family, from social relationships, and from his own racial identity. My feeling was that the powers of play would help this child reconnect. The child was placed in a group home with seven other African-American boys. The facility was headed by a strong-willed and very capable "house mother," and staffed by appropriate male role models. My hope was that in that setting social connections and appropriate cultural identity might evolve. The school had already been contacted by the group home, releases had been signed, and the school counselor would be in contact with me and the group home leader if problems arose. I would be in contact with Michael's mother.

The goal for this child was not only the diminution of his antisocial behaviors, but also to prepare Michael to return home. The optimum goal was for Michael to be able to identify his own tendencies to antisocial behavior, and to learn ways to mediate those behaviors before they occurred. Finally, it was hoped that he could learn to connect with himself, with some significant other, and in some sense existentially.

The Course of Treatment

First Session

Michael entered the playroom without hesitation and with some curiosity. My comments were minimal, but watching him I saw his reluctant curiosity arise. Since the problems in this child's life began quite early, I was aware of some regressive tendencies. I kept my distance from him, giving him a little more than arm's distance at all times, and gently I said, "It's OK to act a little younger than you really are here, Michael, if you want to."

His comments were equally sparse. "We can paint?" "Yes," I assured him, "we can." Whatever he would like to draw we could draw, using pencils, markers, poster paint, and even finger paint. He responded with a grunt and a nod. "You got clay?" "Yes," I said, "we have clay and play dough, and we can even make some play dough for you to take back home if you like." "Hmph," he said. "Wassat?" he said, pointing to the "slingshot," a homemade twelve-foot piece of surgical tubing covered in soft brushed velour. It stretches to roughly twice its length, and is very strong. I told Michael we could play with it if he liked. He fingered it curiously, dropped it back into the toy box, and continued to explore the play room, noting the trucks and blocks, the giant checkers and floor puzzles, and touching his nose with a scented marker.

At the end of the session, he timidly asked me to show him how to work the slingshot. In the hallway, as he took one end and I took the other, we stretched it to its full length. "You will hurt me if you let it loose," I told him. "How you know I won't?" he asked. I responded, "I trust you. That's how." He smiled at this, and walked haltingly back to me with it in his hands. As the session ended, he turned to me on leaving, and said, "You straight," smiling briefly as he left.

Sessions Two Through Six

On entering the second session, Michael went immediately to the toy box, retrieved the slingshot, and said, "Let's do this together." I agreed, and in the hallway we again stretched the toy to its limit. I decided to push a little toward our goal of connectivity. Each of us got inside the slingshot, Michael walked backward to the limit of its stretch, and then I asked him to "sling" himself right up to me. He hesitated only briefly, and then ran with a laugh right up to me, his hands flat against my chest. He asked to do this four more times.

The next step in the slingshot process is difficult for many clients, and especially so for boys like Michael. Stretching the toy to its limit once again, I asked him to run up to me and let me catch him as he jumped up into my arms. He did it! In fact, he asked to do the same exercise every time for the next four visits in a row, leaping with abandon, and throwing himself against me. At one point, he simply laid his head on my shoulder and laughed, with his arms around my neck. From that point on, our sessions became easier, gentler somehow, and the child began to invest himself more deeply in the play process.

Session Seven

This was another happy session with Michael. His behavior in school had improved dramatically, and there were no reports of behavior problems at the shelter where he was living. During this session, he asked if I was his friend. I told him that I was, but that as his counselor it was important for us to discuss even the hardest things in his life, so it was a special sort of friendship. We could not see each other outside the office, but we could be happy together while he was here.

In this session, we completed an art project first suggested by Violet Oaklander. The child is asked to draw a rose bush, with whatever he likes around it, any way he wants to draw it. Then, he is asked to "become" the rose, and tell me about himself. Michael's drawing was complex and rich in what it presented. It contained a hole, almost like the trauma scar so often seen in house-tree-person drawings. Michael said he "got the hole when his father left for prison." Also, he told me that when the rose was little, someone pulled at its stem and hurt it, and that we could talk about this. I made a mental note to myself to pursue the topic with the coloring book *Woody and Willy* (Cabe 1990), which walks a child through disclosure, and includes one page showing a picture of "Willy," a teddy bear, and asking the child to mark on the bear's body any place where the child had ever been hurt or made uncomfortable by anyone. On the drawing, Michael marked only the groin area as a place where he had been hurt, and described being fondled by an adult neighbor who eventually went to jail.

During this session, Michael was able to say that he never got to play as a child. He didn't even realize that at 13 he still was a child. He also shared that the time we spent together felt really good for him. The rose drawing included a child standing inside a fenced area, and on the other side a little girl, his sister, who was also fenced in. Above the flower was a cloud, which he said drifts in and out, and that this was a lot like his father who was in and out of his life before he went to prison. He noted that the fences were needed for protection. Next to the rose, Michael drew a tree with a big, strong trunk, also with a hole. In the hole was a squirrel. This, he said, would be like a dad, or someone he could depend on, who could be playful as well as strong. Here, the child made clear not only his relationship to his world, but also some of his deepest needs. He entered the process well, and was able to smile as he said, "I really told you a lot about me, didn't I?" "Yes," I said, "I suppose you did."

Session Eight

After two months of weekly sessions, Michael was ready to move further along the continuum toward even greater fluidity. He had negotiated drawings with scented markers, engaging his senses of smell, touch, and imagination. He continued to connect with me using the slingshot and even came directly up with a handshake at the beginning and ending of our sessions. His behavior at school and in the shelter was improving noticeably. Occasionally, as we simply talked, he asked for the putty, which brought him in contact with himself and allowed the release of tension while we discussed difficult topics.

I continued to emphasize Michael's own identity and sense of self. In this session we completed a listing of positive and negative traits about him. He was able to see himself as handsome, athletic, loyal, occasionally helpful, friendly with some people, kind to animals, usually cheerful, and brave. I noted the equivocal nature of each of his positive qualities, and he responded by saying it was hard to be that way all the time. Further, he noted that a lot of this was new for him. It was in this session that he announced happily that he had made a friend at the shelter with one of the other boys who was two years older. The other boy was stable and on his way home very soon. The older friend helped Michael with his homework, and consequently Michael's grades continued to improve.

In the negative column on his list, Michael first listed a number of the things he had done for which he had been arrested. I noted that what he had done is not who he "is"; Michael seemed to understand, and said to me sadly that it was still very hard for him to trust people. "They always let you down," he said, "and that hurts." Growing emotional sensitivity and even the beginnings of empathy were wonderful improvements in this child. As both a transitional object and as an effort at perseverating, the strengths and weaknesses list went home with him at the end of the session.

Session Nine

In this session, with the permission of his social worker and his mother, I had a colleague videotape the slingshot exercise with Michael, who clowned around for the camera and put his arm around my shoulder as he introduced us to the unseen audience. When we played back the tape, I emphasized for him how strong he was, how well he moved, and noted the grace with which he now carried himself. In some sense, my aim here was to continue to help the child establish a sense of himself in his own environment. Michael told me that he had never *seen himself* before (emphasis mine). According to Michael's social worker, the child had been having absolutely no problems at school or at the shelter. He was passing all of his classes for the first time in his life.

Session Ten

Michael had his first home visit over the weekend, and it went well. He made no connection with the old group of delinquents, although he had ample opportunity to do so. When I asked him about this, he said he was tired of being in trouble.

In this session, we played with play dough for the first time, spreading it out on a bright tablecloth that was illustrated with dinosaurs in brilliant colors, on the floor of the playroom. In part, all Michael did was mush the stuff around, letting his hands work the dough into shapes, smashing and reforming, rolling and pushing, using the kitchen instruments in our cabinet to make cookie shapes and people. These he later rolled into amorphous globs. We made "talking heads" by pushing thumbs into a ball of play dough, using two snakes for arms and legs, and pushing "hair" through a garlic press. The heads talked to each other about what it was like at home, and what it is like now, with each of us shifting roles, depending on the needs of the child's story. At the end of the session, there was a predictable war, and both of the heads ended up eating each other. Michael was delightful, and cleaned up the aftermath without a single word of encouragement.

It was an amazing thing to watch Michael as he realized that his present was a part of his past, that the two can become one, and the future depends on what he makes of them both. The present really can eat up the past if he is willing to do the work that the present requires. I do not believe this is a cognitive function on the part of the child; rather, it happened somewhere deep within, evolving out of the simple power of the play experience. Healing seemed to occur in the absence of verbal validation.

Sessions Eleven Through Sixteen

For the next several sessions with this growing boy, we focused on game play. Throughout this phase of the treatment process, I emphasized the need for rules, and the need for each of us to work within the boundaries of those rules if the games were to be any fun for either of us. He did well at checkers, won with grace, and accepted with only minimal complaint when he lost. Michael seemed to be enjoying the playing process more than being intent on either winning or losing and the boundaries that game play introduced were both healthy and healing for him.

The Talking, Feeling, Doing Game, and The Storytelling Card Game both revealed interesting and enlightening information about Michael. Further, it seemed as if Michael was actually enjoying the self-disclosure that each of these games required.

Michael enjoyed watching me dance across the room on one foot and decided that a tiger was the best animal for him to become if he were to become one. When questioned by the game about who in his life he loved, Michael was able to say his mother, his sister, and the shelter director, who he was sure loved him because she made him obey the rules. Michael then stated, "I don't know about you, about you loving me. You care about me. And you want me to be good and to do good. I guess that is a kind of love, isn't it? It's not like my mother, but it is kind of." "Yes," I said, "it is a kind of love." But I emphasized that he would be leaving me and the center, and going home before long. I would remember him. But his mother would love him forever.

For a child so starved for affection, this is a delicate issue. I dared not let the child misconstrue our relationship, but at the same time it was important for him to realize that I do care about him. He seemed satisfied with my answer.

Session Seventeen

Once again, we spread the dinosaur tablecloth on the floor and Michael happily asked me to choose our activity for the day. Unceremoniously, I pulled two complete sets of finger paint, and three large jars of it out of the cabinet. During this session we finger painted, something which Michael had never done before.

Many children from abusive or underprivileged homes are malnourished in terms of tactile activity. They are never given the opportunity to make cookies, play in backyard pools, squish their feet in mud puddles, or spend lazy time in bathtubs with tubes of soap or bottles of liquid bubbles. Part of the healing process and the power of play activity involves giving the child a chance to engage in a fluid activity in the context of a safe and supportive environment. To have attempted to introduce finger painting for Michael earlier in the therapeutic process would have been not only inappropriate, it could also have been damaging. Timing, which is largely an intuitive enterprise on the part of the therapist, is critical in working with all children, and especially so with youngsters like Michael.

Gingerly putting the tip of one finger in the paint, Michael began to draw a house with many rooms, clouds in bright blue, a glaring orange sun smiling from the sky, and green grass all along the well-grounded drawing. When I asked him to tell me a story based on his drawing, it was one filled with laughter, a happy family with a mom and a dad living with him and his sister. He added that no one was on drugs. Michael described an idealized situation far different from his family of origin. On some level, he was reconstructing his life, both cognitively and emotionally, even though he had at this time no clear idea that he was doing so.

As the session progressed, Michael and I rolled off another sheet of paper. He asked what would happen if we mixed all of the colors. I suggested he simply try it. He marveled at how the blue and yellow made green, the red and blue made purple, and then mixing all the remaining colors he encountered himself again. Using large amounts of the black and orange, in mixture with the other colors, Michael produced a lovely shade of chocolate brown. Curiously, he looked at it on the tip of his finger, looked at me, and put some on his own arm and then on mine.

"Mixing all the colors looks like me," he said. "If you look at it, I am everybody. Not on you it's not. But on me, all the colors is me! I'm everybody, Neil. Look!" The smile on this child's face brought tears to my eyes. For the first time in his life, he was completely proud of who he was, and he announced this eagerly to his social worker as they gathered their coats to leave.

I confess this was serendipitous for me. I had no idea the child would use the mixing of colors as he did, nor did I know what it meant for him to be "everybody." But I do know he loved the realization that the deep dark-chocolate brown of the paint and the velvet shade of his own skin were both beautiful things to see and to experience.

To end this session, we both got great globs of the dark brown mixture all over the palms of each of our hands, and put them down with a splat on sheets of computer paper. He took my hand then, and laced our fingers together, placing both of our hands on the same piece of paper. He asked to hang this one in the playroom where we spent time together. He took another with him as he left the session. As with the strengths and weaknesses chart, Michael again provided himself with a transitional object of personal meaning, which was part of the preservation process.

I saw Michael for a total of twenty-three sessions. During that time, his minimal depression mediated nicely, his behavior at school improved dramatically, and he experienced no recurrent behavior problems at the shelter. On one occasion, when an older boy threatened him at school, Michael went directly to the principal's office. The other boy was suspended and Michael was congratulated by the principal on his mature handling of the matter. On another occasion, one of the other boys at the shelter pestered Michael when Michael was attempting to do his homework. Michael went to the director and had his room changed to avoid the problem. For a conduct disordered client, in fact for any 13-year old, this is responsible behavior. His visits with his mother and sister continued to go well, and Michael was discharged from the shelter. He was referred for ongoing contact with a counselor near his home and his mother attended and finished a parenting skills training class. The child is presently behaving well in school and the last report I had on Michael indicated he continues to do well.

Conclusion

In terms of the ecosystems at work in his life, Michael was a typical conduct disordered client. Familial systems fit the pattern of parental detachment, paternal sociopathy and substance abuse, harsh and inconsistent discipline, divorce, large family size, and general family chaos. He had problems in school, including multiple suspensions and ultimately expulsion. He was part of a group of other children like himself, and was involved in activity that clearly deviated from the societal norm, including assault, assault with a weapon, car theft, petty theft, aggression, and fighting. Socially, he was isolated, hostile, and generally socially ineffective. These patterns of behavior had become consistent, frequent, chronic, and severe.

He was involved with social services on several occasions, due in part to family chaos, and in part to his own antisocial behaviors. And, he had reached a point where the only thing at which he was really competent was being bad. His involvement included juvenile court, various attempts at counseling, family services, a parole officer, school personnel, and the group home which was his most recent domicile.

In treating this conduct disordered client, it must be made abundantly clear that the play therapy techniques, while apparently both powerful and successful, were only a part of the entire treatment plan for the child. School counselors and teachers, group home personnel, parole officials, the counselor, and the mother were all involved in the process. Without the cooperation of each, the child's ultimate apparently successful discharge from the group home, release from parole, attendance at his home school, and reunification with his mother and sister would certainly have been impossible.

The goals of the therapeutic process included lessening the antisocial behaviors, helping the child to become aware of his own behavior and learn to think before acting, affirming racial and personal identity, and facilitating connection for the child with self, with others, and existentially. To accomplish this brazenly optimistic set of goals for this child, the grounded play therapy processing approach was adopted. In this case, as described above, the abundance of symptoms in this client had contributed to a pattern not only of antisocial behavior, but also to a severe loss of connection with self and others.

In the homeostasis phase the Childhood Depression Inventory, Revised Childhood Manifest Anxiety Scale, Adolescent Sexual Concerns Questionnaire, a thorough initial clinical assessment, contact with all parties attached to the child's case, and related investigative activity were implemented.

In the animation phase the child was exposed to a wide variety of materials and activities that encouraged simple awareness and kinesthetic interaction, evolving into trust. The slingshot was most effective for this client in this respect, helping him to achieve a sense of security and sanctuary. Vesting was most clearly accomplished in the finger painting exercise, which emphasized the child's connection not only to himself, but also to his own identity. The potency phase involved the child in practicing effective interaction with his own environment, and was best illustrated and facilitated by the use of therapeutic games. While preservation appears to be ongoing, only time will tell.

Based particularly on the dismal track record of previous treatment strategies with this young man, it appears that the grounded play therapy processing approach was an effective one. It clearly seems to hold promise for a conduct disordered client who regularly becomes what he encounters in the world around him, for years, and stretching into cycles of years.

Resources for Some Toys Mentioned in this Chapter

Silly Putty is used for hand rehabilitation. Contact: Smith + Nephew Rolyan, Inc. One Quality Drive, Germantown, WI 53022 (800-558-8633); $23.00 per pound; containers are ten for $4.50.

Super String, crayons, dinosaurs, play dough, and more are available from the Oriental Trading Company (800-228-0122 sales and 800-228-2269 orders). Great catalogue!

Elastic tubing: Kent Latex, Kent, OH (216) 673-1011. You'll have to buy a quantity. Cut it in about 12-foot lengths, cover with soft velour, tie it securely, and have fun!

Space phone: The Toy Box, 6036 Busch Blvd., Columbus, OH 43229. (614) 846-4340. $21.95 plus shipping.

Velcro-faced puppets with a supply of features (ears, noses, tongues, cheeks, eyes, teeth, etc.): about $25 plus shipping from Brian Grosvenor, 10 Oakland Avenue, Somerville, MA 02145. Phone (617) 628-6750. Extra "Critter Parts Packs" are $12.50 but worth it!

References

American Psychiatric Association (1994). *Diagnostic and Statistical Manual of Mental Disorders*, 4th ed. Washington, DC: American Psychiatric Association.

Cabe, N. (1990). *A Book for Boys: Woody and Willy Say It's O.K. to Tell*. Privately printed. Mantua, OH: Racin-Leslie Graphics.

———— (1994). *The Behavioral True/False Inventory*. Privately printed. Mantua, OH: Racin-Leslie Graphics.

Campbell, M., Snell, A. M., Green, W. H., et al. (1984). Behavioral efficacy of haloperidol and lithium carbonate: a comparison in hospitalized aggressive children with conduct disorder. *Archives of General Psychiatry* 41(7):650–656.

Gardner, R. (1973). *The Talking, Feeling, and Doing Game*. Cresskill, NJ: Creative Therapeutics.

———— (1988). *The Story Telling Card Game*. Cresskill, NJ: Creative Therapeutics.

Gil, E. (1991). *The Healing Power of Play: Working with Abused Children*. New York: Guilford.

Gilbert, G. M. (1957). A survey of "referral problems" in metropolitan child guidance centers. *Journal of Clinical Psychology* 13(1):37–42.

Graham, P. (1979). Epidemiological studies. In *Psychopathological Disorders of Childhood*, ed. H. C. Quay and J. S. Wentz, 2nd ed., pp. 185–109. New York: Wiley.

Hussey, D. and Singer, M. (1994). The adolescent sexual concerns questionnaire. In *Handbook for Screening Adolescents at Psychosocial Risk*, ed. M. I. Singer, L. T. Singer, and T. M. Anglin, pp. 131–163. New York: Lexington.

Kazdin, A. E. (1989). *Behavior Modification in Applied Settings*, 4th ed. Pacific Grove, CA: Brooks/Cole.

———— (1991). Aggressive behavior and conduct disorder. In *The Practice of Child Therapy*, ed. T. R. Kratochwill and R. J. Morris, pp. 174–271. New York: Pergamon.

Kovacs, M. (1992). *The Childhood Depression Inventory*. North Tonawanda, NY: Multi-Health Systems.

Loerber, R., and Dishion, T. J. (1983). Early predictors of male delinquency: a review. *Psychological Bulletin* 94(1):68–99.

Lusebrink, V. B. (1990). *Imagery and Visual Expression in Therapy*. New York: Plenum.

Maxmen, J. (1986). *Essential Psychopathology*. New York: Norton.

Moustakas, C. E. (1992). *Psychotherapy with Children: The Living Relationship*. Greeley, CO: Carron.

Oaklander, V. (1988). *Windows to Our Children*. Highland, NJ: Center for Gestalt Development.

Reid, W. H. (1989). *The Treatment of Psychiatric Disorders*. New York: Brunner/Mazel.

Reynolds, C., and Richmond, B. (1985). *The Revised Childhood Manifest Anxiety Scale*. Los Angeles: Western Psychological Services.

Schaefer, C., and Kaduson, H., eds. (1994). *The Quotable Play Therapist*. Northvale, NJ: Jason Aronson.

10

Release Play Therapy for the Treatment of Sibling Rivalry

Heidi Gerard Kaduson

Sibling rivalry is defined as competition between siblings for the love, affection, and attention of one or both parents, or for other recognition or gain. Found in the bible with such characters as Cain and Abel, Jacob and Esau, and Joseph and his brothers, this phenomenon is universal. When handled properly, healthy competition between siblings will lead to the acquisition of social, interpersonal, and cognitive skills that are important to the development of the child. Mismanagement may lead to psychological problems, such as feelings of inadequacy or serious abuse of siblings (Bakwin and Bakwin 1972). In spite of its frequency and potential associated complications, sibling rivalry has received little attention in the pediatric literature.

Over 80 percent of the families in the United States have more than one child. Functioning of siblings is influenced by the number, sex, and age spacing. These factors must be considered not only in view of their effects on parent–child interaction, but also in terms of the influence siblings have on each other.

Sibling relations are also affected by birth order. The older child is frequently expected to assume some responsibility and self-control toward the younger sibling who has displaced him/her in family position. When the older child shows jealousy or hostility and is restrained or punished by his/her parents, the younger one is likely to be protected and defended. On the other hand, the older child is more dominant, competent, and able to dominate, or, conversely, to assist and teach the younger offspring. It is therefore not surprising that older children have been found to show both more antagonistic behavior, such as hitting, kicking, and biting, and more nurturing prosocial behavior toward their younger siblings (Abramovitch et al. 1982). Also, something about the relationship with young, same-sex siblings pairs tends to intensify the negative aspects of interaction. Aggression, dominance, and cheating are more likely to occur with a same-sex sibling than with one of the opposite sex (Minnett et al. 1983). Difficulties with peers and teachers during elementary school (Richman et al. 1982) may result from poor sibling connections during the preschool years.

Etiology

Jealousy, a normal reaction that children experience, is found in virtually all families and considered fundamental to family life (Dunn 1983). The firstborn may react to the birth of a sibling by showing signs of disturbance in sleep, frequent crying, toilet training breakdown, an inability to concentrate on play, and, above all, exhibiting difficult and demanding behavior (Dunn 1983). These problems reflect the heavy emotional impact that the sibling's arrival has on a young child.

When threatened by the loss of parental love and attention, children may react by rejecting or "hating" the new sibling, perceived as an intruder. This is more common if the child feels insecure as a result of the parents' overprotection, domination, impatience, or excessive discipline.

Sibling rivalry is more common with a firstborn child, who has lived through a solo period without the necessity of sharing his/her parents with a sibling (Dunn and Kendrick 1982). With the birth of a new baby, the older child usually feels supplanted by the parents' preoccupation with the newcomer and the relative lack of attention for him/her. Sibling rivalry may be aggravated by moving him/her to make room for the new baby. When friends and relatives visit, they tend to pay more attention to the newborn and leave the older child feeling neglected. Legg and colleagues (1974) interviewed the parents of twenty-one children during the period surrounding a second child's birth and found that sibling rivalry in the form of regressive behavior was present in most of the firstborn children. Similarly, Trause and colleagues (1978) discovered an increase in behavioral problems in 92 percent of the thirty-one firstborn subjects.

Although sibling rivalry exists in large families, it is less intense than in smaller families (Bakwin and Bakwin 1972). As the family grows, the intensity of the rivalry tends to decrease. This occurs because children in large families have more opportunity to comprehend the division of parental love and attention that occurs with each new child. Exclusive parental devotion to any given child is less likely and the children become more dependent on each other for friendship, affection, and sympathy.

Sibling rivalry is more common in same-sex siblings because their common desires and attributes create more room for competition (Bakwin and Bakwin 1972). It is also more common in girls than in boys.

Problems of sibling rivalry appear more severe in children between 2 and 4 years of age (Dunn and Kendrick 1982). The smaller the age difference between the children, the more likely rivalrous feelings will occur (Illingworth 1987). Such emotions are less common in children over the age of 8 because they tend to have a better understanding of their position in the family. Also, as they grow older, the home situation becomes relatively less important than do friends, school, and outside interests.

Levy (1938) found that the closer the relationship between the existing child and the parents, the greater was the disturbance and the demonstration of hostility toward the new baby. Sibling rivalry is more common in children of divorced families because "the stock of parental investment has been reduced" (Shapiro and Wallace 1987, p. 101). In a divorced family, there is only one parent at a time giving the love and attention to the child. Therefore, more attention is drawn to the differences between the children.

An older child may be jealous of a younger sibling who appears to be more protected and better loved, and who has usurped privileges that were previously bestowed upon him/her. Conversely, the younger child may be jealous of the older sibling who seems to have more privileges, such as being the first to go to school, staying up later, and having new books.

Sibling rivalry is more common in rejected children. If parents show favoritism, the unpreferred child will feel hurt and may antagonize his/her sibling. Even in the absence of outright favoritism, comparisons are a common cause of ill feeling. If one child is more talented than another, sibling rivalry may occur. In general, competition for prestige and accomplishment usually comes later than competition for the love and affection of parents. In older children, the school and community often become the forum for social comparison and sibling rivalry. Pfouts (1976) found that the child who suffered from the comparison experienced resentment and ill will toward the successful sibling. The more able child, although not resentful of the less able, may report feelings of discomfort and ambivalence in the sibling relationship (Pfouts 1976).

Children from lower socioeconomic groups are more likely to show conflicts over the possession of material objects than are more socioeconomically advantaged children. These feelings of jealousy and resentment can build and explode into clinical manifestations of sibling rivalry.

Clinical Manifestations

With the birth of a sibling, the older child may show hostility even to the point of denying the newborn's birth. Aggressive feelings are sometimes exhibited openly through direct verbal or physical attacks on the infant. One mother told me of her son's repeated pushing and pinching of the new baby whenever she held the child. Some children suggest taking the baby back to the hospital, giving it away, flushing it down the toilet, or requesting that it go back into

Mommy's tummy. Others display frustration or demand attention when the newcomer is picked up by or otherwise occupied with the parent. The older child may hit, punch, push, kick, or bite the younger one (Bakwin and Bakwin 1972). Green (1984) discusses five children who inflicted serious injuries, out of jealousy, on their younger siblings.

Deliberately causing irritation or distress to the baby by throwing its pacifier across the room or banging the crib until the baby awakens and cries, are other examples of negative reactions.

Children may show ambivalence toward the newcomer through outward expression. For instance:

Jennifer (to baby): All right, Baby (hugs him gently). (to mother): Smack him!

Mark: My baby. My baby. (hugs). Monster. Monster.
Mother: She's not a monster.
Mark: Monster head.

Sometimes children clearly express their dislike of the baby, and find that they are not allowed to do so:

Mary (pushing stroller fast): Time to send you far, far, far away.
Mother: Now, you don't mean that. That's a mean thing to say.

Regressive phenomena are common in sibling rivalry and may take the form of bed-wetting, encopresis, demanding to be fed, baby talk, asking to be carried, thumb sucking, head banging, temper tantrums, refusing to go to bed, crying excessively, or remaining extremely quiet (Leung 1986, Leung and Robson 1990).

Play Behavior

What happens to sibling rivalry during pretend games? The frequency of play, which varies greatly from family to family, can sometimes fill almost all of the child's time. In the case of 2-year-olds and older siblings, roughly 60 percent of the 2-year-olds' pretend play episodes involved the mother, or the sibling, or both (Dunn and Dale 1984). If we compare the make-believe games that such young children play with their siblings and their mother, some striking differences become apparent. While all different kinds of pretend play, from the simplest to the most elaborate, were engaged in, the way in which children cooperated with their siblings differed greatly from the way in which they played with their mothers. Mothers tended to act as spectators in the make believe, offering suggestions or comments but not entering the games as full participants. Their suggestions were usually concerned with rendering it as close as possible to the real-life situation that was the focus of the play.

By contrast, in sibling make believe without the mother's input, both children usually cooperated as partners in the fantasy. This collaboration between siblings was very striking in one respect: about one-quarter of the 2-year-olds in the studies joined their brothers and sisters in games that involved their taking on a pretend identity or playing at being in a pretend place (Dunn and Dale 1984). Sibling rivalry gave way to cohesiveness between the children.

Traditional Treatment Strategies

Family Therapy

Research on sibling therapy has been less prevalent than that on whole family therapy involving young children (Kahn and Lewis 1988). Minuchin and Whitaker are probably the best known family therapists specifically attending to young children, although neither of them sees children exclusively. Minuchin primarily focuses on siblings for the purpose of shifting triangles and restructuring the family (Minuchin 1974, Minuchin and Fishman 1981), although the sibling relationship itself does not seem primary. He may have parents move to another side of the room or sit behind a one-way mirror when he wishes to work with the sibling subsystem.

Whitaker, who joins the family through the children, is noted for sitting on the floor and playing with infants or play fighting with young children. He may ignore parents while interacting with the children as he sees offspring as speakers of the real issues in the family and as a barometer for the family's strength and affect (Whitaker 1967, Whitaker and Keith 1981). Contact is made directly with each child, rather than encouraging sibling interactions.

Family therapists are beginning to look at the sibling subgroup as a target for intervention in times of family disruption, when the whole nuclear group is not available, or when the sibling relationship (sibship) is troubled.

There are several ways in which sibling conflict comes to the therapist's attention. On occasion, a mother will make a specific call, asking for therapy because of rivalry between children. More often, when the entire family is being seen, the embittered relationship between the siblings is mentioned or becomes apparent in a therapy session. If the therapist is seeing only one child, the problems with other siblings may be mentioned.

Children are not born hating their brothers and sisters. Something happens to turn normal sibling squabbling into a destructive process. Preferential and intrusive parenting are two common contributing factors to sibling friction. Another is rigid transgenerational roles placed on siblings, leaving them in open conflict. Replays of unresolved sibling issues from the parents' own childhoods can be present. When a triangulated or parentified child is overinvolved with one or both parents, brothers and sisters may resent the sibling who has crossed into the adult hierarchy. They may scapegoat or abandon that child. Another cause of sibling conflict may be related to unequal distribution of natural abilities, for example, one child excels in many areas (Pfouts 1976).

Family treatment can consist of the therapist's seeing siblings together for a one-time assessment, for periodic meetings in the midst of ongoing family therapy, or for time-limited or ongoing sibling therapy. A meeting may be recommended to evaluate the style or quality of the sibling relationship or to give the children some privacy to address a specific topic.

Periodic sessions with the siblings can then be beneficial when they repeatedly get stuck around a particular problem, when there is generalized dyadic or triadic tensions, or when parental upheavals are creating disturbances among the siblings. In these meetings, the children can learn to separate their feelings toward one another from loyalty to their parents.

At times, the treatment of choice is ongoing or time-limited sibling therapy. This is most often recommended for children without a stable family structure, and for children living in foster homes or families where the parental system is inadequate and the siblings need to pull together to take care of themselves (Kahn and Lewis 1988). In such circumstances, sibling therapy can focus directly on the effect of the family problems on each child as an individual and on the sibship.

Once the decision is made to have a family therapist see the siblings, toys are employed to enable the children to "talk." These toys need not be elaborate and are usually basic office equipment, such as paper and pencil or magic markers. Other inexpensive toys include puppets, clay, soft material for hitting or throwing, a lightweight punching bag, scissors, and paste. One goal of the therapist is to have the children talk about the issues that create the sibling rivalry. Another goal is to allow the conflict to occur within the session, and to help them to express their (range of) feelings and find less destructive ways to deal with tension. If the children learn to understand the underlying problem, they may be better able to generalize from one conflict to another.

Behavior Therapy

Verbal and physical sibling aggression can result in most aversive behaviors stemming from sibling rivalry. Competition for toys or attention, lack of turn taking, and verbal teasing are examples of provocateurs (Sloane 1976). When a sibling rivalry situation becomes too intense to handle by parental intervention using behavior modification techniques, a therapist may be contacted.

Because of its demonstrated efficacy, time-out is the treatment of choice for common behavior problems in children, including sibling aggression (Allison and Allison 1971, O'Leary et al. 1967, Olson and Roberts 1987). Time-out, combined with positive attention for appropriate play, was also found to be effective (Allison and Allison 1971, O'Leary et al. 1967). Olson and Roberts (1987) compared three treatments for sibling aggression: time-out, social skills training, and a combination of the two. Again time-out was the most useful remediation as long as excessive use did not spoil its value.

Another effective strategy is overcorrection. Two types have been described: restitution and positive practice (Matson et al. 1979). Restitution requires that the individual overcorrect environmental disturbances caused by the misbehavior. Positive practice utilizes repetitive use of positive behaviors, which are physically incompatible with the misbehavior. Adams and Kelley (1992) concluded that overcorrection was a socially valid, viable alternative to time-out for managing sibling aggression.

In addition, parents can be trained to attend to positive behaviors of the child, with specific emphasis on the appropriate interactions with his/her sibling. This type of attention will increase the amount of positive time spent with the child. A sticker system could also be implemented to reward him/her for positive behavior with the sibling during specified times. For example, the day could be broken into periods: before school, after school until dinner, and dinner until bedtime. For each segment of time that the child does not hit, tease, or instigate other negative action toward the sibling, s/he would receive a sticker. After accumulating a total of fifteen, the child could receive a reward. This helps the parents and child focus on positive behaviors, while encouraging a better relationship to be developed between the siblings.

Cognitive and Social Therapy

Understanding, leading to a change in cognitive and social forces governing their actions, is central to effective work with children (Barth et al. 1986). For this reason, techniques should not be limited to one-on-one interviews with children. Social and cognitive methods can be taught by caregivers through instruction and ongoing consultation.

Like their social counterparts, cognitive interventions for aggression and sibling rivalry are most effective when they are long lasting and include occasional refresher courses (Camp and Ray 1984). Cognitive interventions show promise when combined with social contingencies for angry behavior. The primary uses of cognitive training in social interventions are to increase children's ability to control their impulses, to help children obtain available rewards for nonaggressive behavior, and to help caregivers consistently apply behavioral treatments.

Cognitive therapy can be effective for children who experience sibling rivalry by helping to regulate their performance. The therapist recommends techniques for promoting positive behavior before those for reducing negative behavior. The child helper uses competency-building techniques first.

Camp and Bash (1981) have a well-tested method for teaching aggressive children self-management. Their think-aloud program is designed to teach aggressive boys both interpersonal problem-solving skills and self-management. Their manual provides material for forty half-hour sessions in which children are instructed to use self-talk to guide social problem solving. The program includes activities to increase coping skills, to generate alternative responses, to understand cause and effect, to evaluate possible actions, and to understand the feelings of others (that is, social perspective-taking).

While self-instruction and self-talk may be very helpful, the mere knowledge of what competencies are and how to use them does not ensure their performance. Likewise, there is no guarantee that such knowledge will be put to timely or appropriate skill use. Thus, there are limitations to the use of cognitive therapies.

The therapist, who must be mindful of the cognitive level of anyone in treatment, needs a special awareness of this most critical issue when working with young children. For the very young, developing appropriate treatment modalities depends on strengths and limitations in the cognitive sphere. Also, the intensity of feelings and consequent strong defenses in sibling rivalry, make such feelings somewhat inaccessible within the treatment session. Therefore, it is better to work through the child's own language, that of play.

Rationale for Play Therapy

Mental health practitioners from various theoretical backgrounds have developed innovative structured strategies for use in the diagnosis and treatment of children (Halpern and Kissel 1976, Nickerson 1973, Prout 1977). Examples of clinical child intervention techniques include Gardner's (1971) use of storytelling, board games; Gittelman's (1965) behavior rehearsal, Marcus's (1979) use of costumes in play therapy, Meichenbaum and Goodman's (1971) self-instructional training techniques for impulsive children, and Winnicott's (1971) squiggle technique.

The use of structured interventions in play therapy has increased over time. Many child therapists have found that selecting one or two critical issues can serve them well. They can then determine particular tasks, games, books, or toys that be useful to present and to use in response to the child's material. The therapy endeavor thus has greater direction and is facilitated (Brooks 1993).

When we focus on the issue of sibling rivalry, the therapeutic powers of play can be used to help the child resolve his/her issues. In play therapy, the child is free to confront, experience, and master feelings that cannot be expressed verbally, which indeed may be underlying the behaviors that result in sibling rivalry. Specific mechanisms include communication, abreaction, catharsis, role play, and behavioral rehearsal.

Communication

When children use play to express themselves, their efforts are facilitated by the use of toys as their words and play as their language (Landreth 1993). Play provides an unrestricted forum in which they can play out fantasies of love and hate. In the case of sibling rivalry, it is permissible to simulate the killing of a sibling, and act out regressions of a toddler and the issues that perplex them about sharing their world with another child. Play enables children to uncover their feelings completely; nothing is held back. The self the child is can be aired safely through the natural facilitative dimensions of play. There is no required translation from one language to another or from one mind to another; it simply is self-expression (Landreth 1993).

Both conscious and unconscious material comes out in play. The child's wish to be the only child again and his/her feelings of competition all show themselves in the safe environment of fantasy and play. With the help of a knowledgeable therapist, the child is guided through these fantasies and helped to resolve them.

Abreaction

Sigmund Freud (1924) first used the concept of abreaction to explain how trauma victims resolve an experience they encountered. It is a mental process in which repressed memories are brought to consciousness and relived with appropriate release of affect. When Freud applied this concept to children, he noted that play offers young children a unique opportunity to work through traumatic events. By reiterating events that made a great impression on them in real life, they abreact the strength of these impressions and empower themselves as masters of the situation.

Through the use of repetition, children can re-create play situations related to the original event (e.g., birth of a sibling). Every new repetition in play seems to weaken the negative effect associated with the event and strengthens the child's sense of control over it. In addition, Erikson (1950) reports that children in play reconstruct, reenact, and reinvent their stressful experiences in order to understand them, assimilate their reality, and achieve mastery. Through play, children can adopt roles that were not part of real experiences, transform passivity into activity, and thus, master difficult life situations (Schaefer 1994).

Catharsis

The importance of emotional expression and release are acknowledged by most psychotherapists as essential ingredients in psychotherapy. From the time of Freud to the present, theories and perspectives on catharsis vary from approach to approach. According to Nichols and Zax (1977), catharsis is generally understood as a process in which unexpressed, unconscious, or hidden emotions are released to relieve tension and anxiety. Breuer and Freud (1893–1895) have influenced the present concept of catharsis and emotional release. The basic premise is that the failure to express emotions is responsible for maladaptive attitudes and behavior. Releasing the repressed feelings that relate to the event frees the child from those emotions. As a result, the child's behavior improves. A new baby in a family creates ambivalence in most children. The child feeds on parental excitement. When the actual event occurs, the child's feelings may go "underground." Initial feelings of being left out, no longer the "special one," and having to share the parents' attention may not be tolerated. Therefore, the child cannot act out his/her wishes of returning to life before the sibling was born. Through the use of play, the child can release the emotions that are buried within him/her.

Role Play and Behavior Rehearsal

Most children experiencing sibling rivalry will deny the fact that they have any behavior problem, or externalize the blame to the infant, the parents, or whomever. They would certainly have trouble explaining their thoughts and feelings on the subject to their therapist. An acceptable way for many children to begin a dialogue is through symbolic play activities. This mode of expression is natural and comfortable for most, providing the safety of a disguise along with the pleasure of play.

In this context, children develop patterns of role playing. They may take the part of the mother, the child, or the baby. When used in a play session, role play can be a teaching tool or a way to sharpen skills, to problem solve, to try on new behaviors, or to take another's point of view.

When patterns of behavior are unconsciously determined or removed from awareness, roles are more often implicit. These express personality attributes that originate in early internalizations and identifications and become enduring psychological patterns. They are the outgrowth of countless interactions between the growing child and his caregivers (Irwin and Curry 1993). Through the scenes that they depict and the roles that they assume, children can tell us a great deal about their feelings and underlying issues.

Research frequently emphasizes the use of role play to foster altruism and to facilitate empathy with another's point of view. Through the use of play, the therapist enters the child's world under the child's direction and encourages communication and problem solving by modeling playfulness. Gardner (1971) does this in his mutual storytelling technique. The therapist may change the story line to help the child see that there are other ways to view the situation. In doing this, the therapist gradually focuses on the repressed feelings of the child that has been projected onto others.

Release Play Therapy

There is a sound basis for treating the child's problems by employing his or her own methods. This is done in release therapy. A child uses imaginative play as an important way of getting rid of tensions arising from anxiety. To allow this process to unfold, the therapist provides the necessary materials and directs the play so that the problem is the center of the play situation. It remains non-threatening because the following aspects of play are included:

1. it is symbolic;
2. it is as if the situations were real;
3. conditions are miniaturized; and
4. it is intrinsically fun.

Release play therapy has been used currently with post-trauma cases, where the child is presented with a miniaturization of the real situation and allowed to play freely with it. To be effective, this therapy necessitates direct handling of the play objects by the child, and the subject becoming so absorbed that s/he becomes oblivious to the surroundings and plays out fears fully by repetition of the trauma. The repetition of the play allows piecemeal assimilation of the trauma and subsequent mastery of the situation. This same approach can be modified to deal with sibling rivalry.

David Levy (1933) described a series of three experiments with children in standardized situations for the study of sibling rivalry. In the first, mother, baby, and brother or sister dolls were presented, with no suggestion as to the direction of the activity. In the second series, the hostility of the child was activated after exposure to the situation under the conditions of the first series. This was done by showing the mother and infant in a nursing situation, and telling the child that the brother sees the baby for the first time. "What does he (or she) do?" the experimenter asks. After one or more trials, usually three, activity was stimulated by the words: "When the sister (or brother) saw the baby, she thought, 'The nerve, at my mother's breast.' " A third series was described in which an amputation doll alone was used as a direct substitute for the rival sibling. Over time, the third series was eliminated, and the first and second were repeated. Following the experiments, the play activity was allowed to take a free form.

It is important to utilize this experimental procedure at the beginning of therapy because it is simpler to let the child proceed from the controlled situation into free play than the reverse. However, the controlled situation may be returned to at any appropriate time to stimulate activity in free play therapy.

The child is told that you and s/he are going to play a game that will need a mother, a baby, and an older sister (brother). The therapist uses an amputation doll (which has no breasts) to represent the mother, a celluloid baby doll, and a larger doll for the older sibling.

> *Therapist*: The mother must feed the baby. (Pointing to the chest of the doll) But she has no breasts. Let's make some.

The therapist makes one breast, the child, the other. This procedure is employed to facilitate the intervention since some children are hesitant about making breasts yet feel free to do so if the therapist goes first. After the breasts are placed in position on the mother doll, the baby doll is put in the nursing position with the mother's arms encircling it. The child is asked to name the baby and the sister (brother).

> *Therapist*: Now this is the game. The sister (brother) comes and sees a new baby at the mother's breast. She (or he) sees it for the first time. Now what does she (or he) do? Do whatever you think.

The child is encouraged with such phrases as "Go ahead," "Don't be afraid."

After the controlled situation has been augmented, the therapist may stimulate activity in various ways. The original cases (Levy 1933) describe in detail how the rivalry is released. In essence, the therapist encourages the child with phrases such as "When the sister (or brother) saw the baby she thought, 'The nerve, at my mother's breast!' "

Throughout the experiment, encouraging remarks are made to overcome anxiety and facilitate behaviors. Every device is used to smooth the path into a display of primitive feelings. It is important that the child not view the therapist as pushing for s/he may withdraw, the technique may boomerang and its purposes will be defeated.

Gauging time and pressure for remarks by the therapist can be more easily felt during the session. Simple interjections of: "Go ahead," "Don't be afraid," "Let the brother (brother doll) do what he wants" should not prove too disturbing. If the child wants the therapist to join in the activity, s/he does so.

Levy (1933) presents an example of this joining with a 3-year-old boy. The child said in the sixth session: "Now we must have dinner," and enumerated the parts of the meal, which consisted of parts of the baby doll. The child handed over a glass containing the parts. The therapist took some and they both put the parts in their mouths. While some children hesitate to attack the objects, and may need some prompting, others go into the material rapidly, then recoil, as indicated by increasing inhibition of movement.

Levy states that the less the need for therapist intervention, the better. Err on the side of omission, rather than commission. This is especially true when it comes to asking questions of the child to clarify meaning of an act, where this meaning is not apparent through overt behavior or spontaneous expression. A question may deflect activity, may be regarded by the child as an accusation, may increase the child's opposition, and can alter what appeared to be a natural process of activity. On the other hand, the child's answer may give a very significant clue to the meaning of his or her behavior, and when not questioned at a particular moment, may be lost. An example would be a 4-year-old girl's first attack on the sister doll, saying: "She was bad, now she's good." When the question was presented: "Why was she bad?" the reply was, "She wanted to take the baby away." This made it clear that the meaning of the act was self-punishment because of a hostile impulse. The question clarified it and, in keeping with the method, helped in making the reasoning more direct and less inferential. Questions may, however, defeat their purpose. The rule of the matter should be that if there is doubt about the effect of a question on the flow of the activity, it is best to forgo it. Levy's (1933) experiments were done with children who had younger siblings and ranged in age from 5 to 13 years. The main referral problems were rebellious behaviors: negativism, disobedience, temper tantrums, and the like.

Hambridge (1955) followed this lead by creating structured play situations such as: "New baby at mother's breast (sibling rivalry play)." This is the standard stimulus situation used by Levy in his experiments on sibling rivalry and hostilities. The therapist provides a mother doll, a baby doll, preferably easily destructible and replaceable, and a self doll, which is called Brother or Sister, depending on the sex of the patient. The therapist asks the child if s/he knows what breasts are for, simultaneously modeling a clay breast and placing it in position on the mother doll. If necessary, the child is told briefly about the milk-giving function of the breast. S/he is then asked to make, and place in position, the mother doll's other breast. Then, while placing the mother doll in the chair and the baby in her lap, sucking at the breast, the therapist says: "This is the mother and this is the baby. The brother (or sister) comes in and sees the baby for the first time. He sees the baby nursing at his mother's breast. What happens?" A further stimulus to the expression of hostility can be added by saying: "He sees that bad, bad baby nursing at his mother's breast." This play situation is useful not only to facilitate the abreaction and working through of sibling rivalry and dependency conflicts, but also to check on a patient's progress during treatment. Thus, for comparative purposes, it is advantageous to use it in the standard form, so that one may compare the patient's handling of this situation from time to time.

268 The Playing Cure

Solomon (1938) advocated an even more directive and active approach for the therapist. He developed active play therapy because he concluded that child therapists tend to be too passive and wait too long for things to happen with traumatized children. To move things along he suggested the following:

1. The therapist should be active and keep the conversation in the third person to provide anonymity and reduce defensiveness.
2. The therapist should actively play out the scene with the child. Having a partner may help him/her master the stress and make it less frightening.
3. The therapist should actively direct the child's play, thus helping to uncover the child's inner fantasy life.

Anxiety created by this approach can be reduced by introducing a therapist doll. The child can then release his/her feelings with the doll.

Case Illustration

Aaron, age 4, was referred to me because of soiling, oppositional behavior at home, and hitting, tripping, and pinching a younger brother. A major dynamic was that Aaron's 2-year-old brother was mild mannered and favored by their parents. While there were intermittent outbursts of anger toward his brother, Aaron would not discuss these feelings or the experience of deprivation and neglect that was associated with his younger sibling. The soiling and oppositional behavior could have been approached behaviorally, but I felt that the sibling rivalry was a main source of Aaron's discomfort and acting out.

At the onset of treatment, I had Aaron draw a picture of himself and his family, and he drew the family without his brother. When I questioned him about whether this was his whole family, he said "Yes." I then presented him with four dolls: a mother, father, baby, and brother doll. I had clay available to mold into breasts. He acknowledged that he knew breasts were for feeding babies. (If a child is known to have been fed by a bottle instead of breast, this play is modified to depict that situation with a miniature bottle.) I molded a breast, put it on the mother doll, and asked him to make the other. He made a much larger one and then attached it. Next, the baby doll was placed in the mother's arms and the head was put at the breast to suckle. When I then asked him to place the father and boy doll in the setting, he put the father on the bed sleeping, and had the little boy outside playing.

> *Therapist:* Okay, this game begins with the little boy coming into the house and seeing the baby for the first time. Then what happens?
> *Aaron:* I don't know.
> *Therapist:* Go ahead.

Aaron (moving his hand closer to the baby doll, almost touching it): I
   guess . . . (starts to play with something else in the playroom).
Therapist: Aaron, what do you think would happen? Go ahead and show me.
Aaron (taking the brother doll and banging its head again and again): Bad,
   bad boy wants to take the baby and now he's good.

Then Aaron removes the baby from the mother's breast and drops it on the
floor. He picks up the baby doll and then throws it harder to the floor. He picks
up the doll one more time and then steps on it.

Aaron: Well, he's gone. Now what?

At that moment, he goes to squeeze the breasts and, inhibiting his movement,
stops. Then he amputates the mother doll, taking both breasts off her and
making them into hamburgers.

Aaron: The baby likes hamburgers (while he squashes the hamburgers into
   the baby's face). Eat it all up!

Aaron then takes the boy doll and plays in another corner of the room. He has
become distracted from his activity with me, but continues to play with the boy
doll for the remainder of the time.

   In the next two sessions, similar trials were seen. For the most part, there
was a free release of hostility and less self-punishing behavior. Aaron began to
attack the baby in the first moment, even before I gave the instructions.

   In the fourth session, he immediately removed the baby from the breast.
He then stepped on it over and over again until parts of the doll fell off. He
picked up the crushed parts and pulled them to bits. Aaron then proceeded to
scratch at the mother doll and pull her arms.

Aaron: I'm just checking to see how this is made (pulling at the legs and arms
   together).

Aaron then removed one of the arms of the mother and dropped it on the floor.
He continued the attack on the baby doll by piling up all the parts.

Aaron: This just needs to be a little more (stepping on the parts again). The
   baby said to put the head on, but no, I can't do that. (He tries to fix the
   head, and then piles up the baby parts again and steps on them.)

At this point, there is an elimination of his blocked and inhibited movements,
and an increase in the number and intensity of his attacks. There is more release

of primitive hostility. This exemplifies Aaron's ability to become sufficiently free of anxiety to achieve direct release of hostility toward the objects.

Similar play took place in the next two sessions. At the same time, his mother had commented that there was beneficial change in the sibling rivalry relationship. He was actually hugging his brother without crushing him, had stopped the pinching behavior, and seemed more relaxed.

Restitution, the activities that restore or attempt to restore objects to their original state, is also part of the process that is seen in this type of therapy. Aaron attempted restitution in the fourth session, but then stepped on the baby anyway. At another point, he said, "The baby is all right again," and put the baby to the mother's breast.

Restoring acts occur more frequently than self-retaliatory acts and may occur at that point in a sequence where self-punishment takes place. Although giving an impression of being more satisfying than self-punishment, in some cases the restitution starts more hostility.

There is abundant evidence that the behavior of children in play therapy, more specifically in an activity with dolls representing mother and baby, affects the relationship with the real mother and baby (Levy 1938). A general observation made in Aaron's case was that there was a functional change in the sibling relationship when the primitive hostility emerged, and was generally unhampered by preventing, self-punishing, restoring, or defensive behavior. The permission to release the hostile feelings in a safe environment gave Aaron the freedom to feel. He then was able to have a more gentle relationship with his sibling and behave less oppositionally with his parents. This, in turn, helped to balance the attention the younger sibling was getting. Both parents, in fact, showed Aaron more attention when he attended more easily and got along better with his brother. His mother commented that Aaron and his brother now ask for each other and like to include one another in their play.

Conclusion

The unleashing of hostile and aggressive urges through play therapy can help turn a destructive real-life relationship between an older and younger child into one of constructive promise. While there is no guarantee of its lasting effect, encouraging a child to ventilate primitive feelings without restriction or negative feedback, can create changes in behavior. When the rivalry is prolonged and bitter, the child's constricted view of the intruder supersedes any area of pleasure that may be derived from the relationship. Aggressive and possessive responses may be the only ones available to the child. Treatment methods that explore various outlets and restructuring techniques can be beneficial. In cases where the hostility is unacknowledged by the child, play provides the safety of a disguise as well as pleasure. Adopting roles that were not part of the real-life experience can often transfer passivity into activity, necessary for problem solving and mastery.

It is clearly seen that children's feelings can be revealed through play sessions that are structured around the actual event. In those constructed to release feelings of sibling rivalry, the child's hostile responses are elicited through the mother–baby combination. Felt chiefly as an urge to destroy by such acts as crushing or tearing, sibling rivalry involves impulses the child had been able to check by blocking or allowing only partial release. Once the hostile behavior is set in motion, however, it runs its own course. Every new repetition in play seems to weaken the negative effect and serves to strengthen the child's sense of mastery. Following the release of hostile feelings in play therapy sessions, the child's behavior toward the object of rivalry is changed in a beneficial way. Presumably, when anger toward the sibling is reduced, it will no longer monopolize the relationship. This allows positive components to grow.

References

Abramovitch, R., Pepler, D., and Corter, C. (1982). Patterns of sibling interactions among preschool-age children. In Sibling Relationships, ed. M. E. Lamb, and B. Sutton-Smith, pp. 76–92. Hillsdale, NJ: Lawrence Erlbaum.

Adams, C. D., and Kelley, M. L. (1992). Managing sibling aggression: overcorrection as an alternative to time-out. Behavior Therapy 23:707–717.

Allison, T. S., and Allison, S. L. (1971). Time-out from reinforcement. Effect on sibling aggression. Psychological Record 21:81–86.

Bakwin, H., and Bakwin, R.M. (1972). Behavior Disorders in Children, 4th ed. Philadelphia: W.B. Saunders.

Barth, R. P., Blythe, B. J., Schinke, S. P., et al. (1983). Self-control training with maltreated parents. Child Welfare 62:313–324.

Breuer, J., and Freud, S. (1893–1895). Studies on Hysteria. New York: Basic Books, 1957.

Brooks, R. (1993). Creative characters. In Play Therapy Techniques, ed. C. E. Schaefer and D. M. Cangelosi, pp. 211–224. Northvale, NJ: Jason Aronson.

Camp, B. W., and Bash, M. A. S. (1981). Think Aloud: Increasing Social and Cognitive Skills—A Problem-Solving Program for Children (Primary Level). Champaign, IL: Research Press.

Camp, B. W., and Ray, R. S. (1984). Aggression. In Cognitive Behavior Therapy with Children, ed. A. W. Meyers, and W. E. Craighead, pp. 126–138. New York: Plenum.

Dunn, J. (1983). Sibling rivalry in early childhood. Child Development 54:787–811.

Dunn, J., and Dale, N. (1984). I a daddy: two-year-olds' collaboration in their pretend play with sibling and mother. In Symbolic Play: The Development of

Social Understanding, ed. I. Bretherton, pp. 43–66. New York: Academic Press.

Dunn, J., and Kendrick, C. (1982). *Siblings: Love, Envy and Understanding.* London: Grant McIntyre.

Erikson, E. H. (1950). *Childhood and Society.* New York: Norton.

Freud, S. (1924). *Beyond the Pleasure Principle.* New York: Boni and Liveright.

Gardner, R. A. (1971). *Therapeutic Communication with Children: The Mutual Storytelling Technique.* New York: Science House.

Gittelman, R. (1965). *Anxiety Disorders in Childhood.* New York: Guilford.

Green, A. H. (1984). Child abuse by siblings. *Child Abuse and Neglect* 8:31–37.

Halpern, W., and Kissel, S. (1976). *Human Resources for Troubled Children.* New York: Wiley.

Hambridge, G., Jr. (1955). Structured play therapy. *American Journal of Orthopsychiatry* 25:601–617.

Illingworth, R. S. (1987). *The Normal Child*, 9th ed. Edinburgh: Churchill-Livingstone.

Irwin, E. C., and Curry, N. E. (1993). Role play. In *The Therapeutic Powers of Play*, ed. C. E. Schaefer, pp. 167–187. Northvale, NJ: Jason Aronson.

Kahn, M.D., and Lewis, K. G. (1988). *Siblings in Therapy.* New York: Norton.

Landreth, G. (1993). Self-expressive communication. In *The Therapeutic Powers of Play*, ed. C. E. Schaefer, pp. 41–63. Northvale, NJ: Jason Aronson.

Legg, C., Sherich, Z., and Wadland, W. (1974). Reaction of pre-school children to the birth of a sibling. *Child Psychiatry and Human Development* 5:3–39.

Leung, A. K. (1986). Encopresis. *Contemporary Pediatrics* 2:20–25.

Leung, A. K., and Robson, W. L. (1990). Head banging. *Journal of Singapore Paediatric Society* 32:14–17.

Levy, D. M. (1933). The use of play technique as experimental procedure. *American Journal of Orthopsychiatry* 3:266–275.

———— (1934). Rivalry between children of the same family. *Child Study* 11:233–61.

———— (1938). Release therapy in young children. *Psychiatry* 1:387–390.

Marcus, I. M. (1979). Costume play therapy. In *The Therapeutic Use of Child's Play*, ed. C. Schaefer, pp. 373–382. Northvale, NJ: Jason Aronson.

Matson, J. L., Horne, A. M., Ollendick, D. G., and Ollendick, T. H. (1979). Overcorrection: a further evaluation of restitution and positive practice. *Journal of Behavior Therapy and Experimental Psychiatry* 10:295–298.

Meichenbaum, D. H., and Goodman, J. (1971). Training impulsive children to talk to themselves: a means of developing self-control. *Journal of Abnormal Psychology* 77:115–126.

Minnett, A. M., Vandell, D. L., and Santrock, J. W. (1983). The effects of sibling status on sibling interaction: influences of birth order, age spacing, sex of child and sex of sibling. *Child Development* 54:1064–1072.

Minuchin, S. (1974). *Families and Family Therapy.* Cambridge: Harvard University Press.

Minuchin, S., and Fishman, C. (1981). *Techniques in Family Therapy*. Cambridge: Harvard University Press.

Nichols, M. P., and Zax, M. (1977). *Catharsis in Psychotherapy*. New York: Gardner.

Nickerson, E. T. (1973). Recent trends and innovations in play therapy. *International Journal of Child Psychotherapy* 2:53–70.

O'Leary, K. D., O'Leary, S., and Becker, W. C. (1967). Modification of a deviant sibling interaction pattern in the home. *Behavior Research and Therapy* 5:113–120.

Olson, R. L., and Roberts, M. W. (1987). Alternative treatments for sibling aggression. *Behavior Therapy* 18:243–250.

Pfouts, J. H. (1976). The sibling relationship: a forgotten dimension. *Social Work* 21:200–204.

Prout, H. (1977). Behavioral intervention with hyperactive children: a review. *Journal of Learning Disabilities* 10:141–146.

Richman, N., Graham, P., and Stevenson, J. (1982). *Preschool to School: A Behavioral Study*. London: Academic Press.

Schaefer, C. E. (1994). Play therapy for psychic trauma in children. In *Handbook of Play Therapy*, vol. 2, ed. K. O'Connor, and C. E. Schaefer, pp. 297–318. New York: Wiley.

Shapiro, E. K., and Wallace, D. B. (1987). Siblings and parents in one-parent families. In *Practical Concerns About Siblings: Bridging the Research-Practice Gap*, ed. F. F. Schachter, and R. F. Stone, pp. 91–114. New York: Haworth.

Sloane, H. N., Jr. (1976). *The Good Kid Book*. Champaign, IL: Research Press.

Solomon, J. C. (1938). Active play therapy. *American Journal of Orthopsychiatry* 8:479–498.

Trause, M. A., Boslett, M., and Voos, D. (1978). A birth in the hospital: the effect on the sibling. *Birth Family Journal* 5:207–210.

Whitaker, C. (1967). The growing edge—an interview with Carl Whitaker. In *Techniques in Family Therapy*, ed. J. Haley, and L. Hoffman, pp. 16–42. New York: Basic Books.

Whitaker, C., and Keith, D. (1981). Symbolic-experiential family therapy. In *Handbook of Family Therapy*, ed. A. Gurman, and D. Kniskern, pp. 48–60. New York: Brunner/Mazel.

Winnicott, D. W. (1971). *Therapeutic Consultation in Child Psychiatry*. New York: Grune & Stratton.

Part IV

OTHER

11

Thematic Play Therapy: An Approach to Treatment of Attachment Disorders in Young Children

Helen E. Benedict and Lisa Binz Mongoven

In recent years, play therapy has emerged as a treatment of choice for children who have experienced a wide range of maltreatment, trauma, and inadequate caregiving (James 1989, Terr 1990). One significant clinical group needing effective intervention is children with attachment disorders. This chapter describes a model of play therapy designed with this population in mind. Thematic Play Therapy, based on attachment theory, especially the work of John Bowlby, and object relations theory, combines an emphasis on the child's relationship to the therapist with focused intervention around the themes presented in the child's play. Using the combined therapeutic factors of metaphor, role play, communication, fantasy, catharsis, and abreaction in addition to the working alliance and attachment to the therapist, this model enables the child to change his inner model of relationships and enter into healthy attachment relationships more easily (Schaefer 1993). We have found Thematic Play Therapy, especially when combined with clinical work with the caregiver, to be effective with children who suffer from attachment disorders.

Background of the Disorder

Description of Attachment Disorders

Attachment is the bond or emotional tie between an infant and "some other differentiated and preferred individual, who is usually conceived [by the infant] as stronger and/or wiser" (Bowlby 1979, p. 129). Attachment is characterized by strong emotional components such as joy, security, love, anxiety, anger, and grief. Behaviors have been identified that are indicative of attachment; these attachment behaviors include but are not limited to clinging, crying, smiling, crawling, walking, reaching, and vocalizing (Ainsworth 1982). Infants vary in the degree to which they display these different attachment behaviors and researchers have used this variance to identify different types of attachment (Ainsworth et al. 1978, Main and Solomon 1986). Infants and toddlers who have been able to develop strong emotional ties with their caregivers are considered to be securely attached. A secure attachment tends to develop when a caregiver is warm, available, and capable of meeting the child's needs for safety and nurturance (Cicchetti et al. 1995). Anxious attachments, on the other hand, have behavioral ramifications. Sroufe (1986) acknowledges that children with anxious attachment histories tend to lack persistence, self-confidence, cooperation, positive affect, enthusiasm, empathy, curiosity, and ego-resilience when compared with children with secure attachment histories. Insecurely attached children have been characterized as having low self-reliance, low resilience, and difficulty integrating into structured environments (Kraemer 1992).

The process of attachment can go awry and pathology can develop. Lieberman and Pawl (1988) suggest that disorders of attachment are defined as "distortions in the parent–child relationship that result in the baby's inability to experience the parent as emotionally available and as a reliable protector from external danger or internal distress" (pp. 328–329). Similarly, McMillen (1992) suggests that pathology is prone to develop "when a child's primary caregivers are unresponsive to the child's needs" (p. 207). While both researchers and clinicians agree that disorders of attachment exist and that they are typically accompanied by some degree of inappropriate or absent caregiving, these disorders differ markedly in terms of both specific symptoms and subtypes.

Much of the research has focused on the Ainsworth subtypes of attachment relationships in intact mother–child pairs and largely nonclinical samples. Types A and C, and in later research type D, have been associated with later social development (Sroufe 1983, 1989), child maltreatment (e.g., Crittenden 1988), maternal depression (e.g., Cummings and Cicchetti 1990), maternal substance abuse (Rodning et al. 1991), and conduct problems and oppositional behavior in children (see Cicchetti et al. 1995 for a review). Clinicians have focused more on clinical cases and the patterns of symptoms seen in children who would meet the criteria for a reactive attachment disorder of infancy and childhood, although much of the work of clinicians predates the recent revisions within the *Diagnostic and Statistical Manual of Mental Disorders*, fourth edition (*DSM-IV*; American Psychiatric Association 1994), which includes attachment disorders as a reactive attachment disorder of infancy and childhood that can be expressed in either an inhibited or disinhibited subtype. This definition focuses on "markedly disturbed and developmentally inappropriate social relationships" associated with grossly pathological care, and beginning before age 5 (APA 1994, p. 116). In the inhibited type the child is hypervigilant, excessively inhibited, and shows ambivalent responses such as resistance to comfort and frozen watchfulness. In contrast, in the disinhibited type the child shows a lack of selectivity in choice of attachment figures with indiscriminate sociability as the predominant feature.

Lieberman and Pawl (1988) suggest three major categories of attachment disorders: nonattachment, anxious attachment, and disrupted attachment. James (1994), focusing more on those instances when attachment disorders are accompanied by additional trauma, proposes five categories: good enough attachment relationship with trauma-related attachment problems, maladaptive attachment relationship without potential for change with attachment trauma, maladaptive relationship with potential for change with disturbed attachment, new primary attachment relationship with attachment trauma, and nonprimary supplemental relationship with trauma-related attachment problems.

Zeanah and his colleagues (1993) more recently have proposed a five-category classification of attachment disorders that focuses on patterns of child symptoms rather than causative factors. According to these authors, all disorders of attachment represent "profound and pervasive disturbances in the child's feelings of safety and security" (p. 337) but the disorders proposed differ with respect to the overt behavior of the children. These five categories are nonattached attachment disorder, indiscriminate attachment disorder, inhibited attachment disorder, aggressive attachment disorder, and role-reversed attachment disorder. This system seems to match best the kinds of attachment disorders seen in our clinical practice where a variety of causative factors have been found with each of the child patterns seen. It will be used as the basic definition of the disorder for purposes of this discussion.

The first two of Zeanah and colleagues' attachment disorder categories, nonattachment and indiscriminate attachment, appear to be associated with disrupted attachment rather than insecure attachment, which is the focus of much of the literature. A disrupted attachment typically results from a separation or a permanent loss. Separation is defined as the premature and prolonged removal of a child from his/her attachment figure, whereas loss is a permanent separation (Lieberman and Pawl 1988). In everyday life, a child may experience a wide variety of separations, which vary in their psychological impact on the child. Depending on the specific factors involved, a separation from a caregiver may encourage psychological growth. A separation, particularly a prolonged one of longer than two to three weeks, may also trigger such intense anxiety that it has long-term, negative consequences on the child's personality development and on his/her ability to form enduring, trusting relationships (Lieberman and Pawl 1988). Separations and maternal deprivation have been associated with acute distress syndrome, inappropriate anxiety states, aggression, conduct disorders, pathological mourning, depression, affectionless psychopathy, and intellectual retardation (Bowlby 1969, Kraemer 1992, Rutter 1979). According to Bowlby, the experience of loss may also make the child more vulnerable and more likely to encounter adverse experiences later in life.

Nonattached Attachment Disorder

This type of disorder occurs when infants are reared with minimal opportunity for forming emotional connections with other human beings. Disorders of nonattachment may be found in institutionally raised children who have several anonymous caregivers, or in youngsters who have been severely neglected. These children show impairment in interpersonal relationships, cognitive functioning, and impulse control (Lieberman and Pawl 1988). According to Paterson and Morgan (1988), a young child whose needs frequently go unmet may come to believe that he/she is unworthy of attention and incapable of influencing others. Furthermore, this child may perceive relationships as unrewarding and come to view others as withholding or unavailable. These perceptions are believed to contribute to pathological functioning. Thus, these children fail to develop a preferred attachment figure even under conditions of stress, fail to show specific separation protest (either showing no protest or indiscriminate protest as separation from any adult), and are either asocial or indiscriminately social (Zeanah et al. 1993).

Indiscriminate Attachment Disorder

This type appears quite similar to the *DSM-IV* reactive attachment disorder in infancy and childhood: disinhibited type. Clinical presentation of this disorder is associated with institutional care or multiple early caregivers. Zeanah and his colleagues (1993) propose two subtypes of this disorder: socially promiscuous and reckless/accident-prone/risk taking. These children fail to use the caregiver as a "secure base" by neither checking back in unfamiliar settings nor retreating to the caregiver in times of stress. In addition, they appear to show "indiscriminate and promiscuous use of others for comfort and nurturance" (p. 340).

The remaining three attachment disorders involve distortions in the attachment bond rather than loss per se. These children have formed an attachment bond, but it is insecure, characterized by such deviations from a secure attachment as excessive inhibition, excessive aggression, or hypervigilance coupled with a need for the child to care for the caregiver.

Inhibited Attachment Disorder

When an infant has been able to bond with his/her caregiver, but the attachment relationship is characterized by an unusual amount of anxiety, then the child is said to have an anxious attachment. Disturbances in this relationship generally revolve around the perceived availability (physical or emotional) of the caregiver. Sroufe (1986) suggests that an infant who is anxiously preoccupied with the accessibility of his/her caregiver has probably experienced inconsistent care. An anxious attachment can therefore be viewed as an adaptive defense that serves to protect the child from anxiety about the caregiver's availability (Lieberman and Pawl 1988). Zeanah and his colleagues (1993) suggest that one form this anxious attachment takes, when it becomes severe enough to be considered psychopathology, is inhibition. This form includes two subtypes: excessive clinging and compulsive compliance. The children showing excessive clinging appear unwilling to venture away from the caregiver to explore their environment at a level beyond initial shyness or slowness to warm up. Compulsively compliant children seem to have "learned to comply immediately and unquestioningly, in order to avoid physical abuse" (p. 342) and show behavior characterized by hypervigilance, subdued affect, wariness, and lack of spontaneity. This subtype most closely matches the inhibited type of reactive attachment disorder of infancy and childhood in *DSM-IV*.

Aggressive Attachment Disorder

Some attachment relationships differ quite markedly from those discussed above in that they are characterized by anger and aggression. Young children with this type of disordered attachment tend to view the world as less available and more threatening or hostile than children with secure attachments (Suess et al. 1992). Having experienced others as hostile or rejecting, some children come to expect hostility and to view even unintentional mishaps as aggressive. These children behave as though others are malevolent, which contributes to their own rejection. Crittenden (1992a) describes a similar pattern for preschoolers called "coercive" strategy. The strategy of the "coercive" child consists of forcing the caregiver, through threats, bribes, and noncooperation, to attend to him/her. These children show attachment to the caregiver, but this is accompanied by angry outbursts toward both the caregiver and the self, and, at times, others as well (Zeanah et al. 1993). While they may be anxious, the anxiety is secondary to the problems with aggression. Similarly, Speltz (1990) argues that conduct problems in preschoolers are often an attempt by the child to regulate the proximity and sensitivity of a caregiver where there is a history of unresponsive parental care. Delaney (1991), focusing on attachment disordered foster children in middle and late childhood, describes such symptoms in this latter population as sadism and violence, disordered eating, counterfeit emotionality, compulsive lying or stealing, sexual obsessions (when there is co-occurring sexual abuse), passive-aggressive behavior, and defective conscience. While there are no data to establish the relationship between these symptoms and the early childhood manifestation of aggressive attachment disorder, these children would appear to be from the same group.

Role-Reversed Attachment Disorder

This disorder involves a role reversal in which the child assumes roles and responsibilities ordinarily belonging to the parent. These children are often bossy and controlling with the caregiver, and typically exhibit great concern about the caregiver's well-being. These children often seem parentified in their assumption of adult roles. At times, these children actually provide caregiving to the adult, comforting the adult when distressed (Zeanah et al. 1993). While this pattern of relationship has long been observed clinically, only recently has the centrality of the attachment relationship to this dynamic been emphasized (Lieberman and Pawl 1988).

These five categories, while differing markedly in their manifestation in children, share several key features with implications for intervention. First, these children all have an insecure or undeveloped attachment and therefore find it difficult to trust adults. They share common concerns about safety and the availability of adults to provide the necessary environmental and emotional supports to sustain that sense of safety. Furthermore, the problems in the attachment relationship tend to parallel difficulties in social relationships in general by the preschool years (Cicchetti et al. 1995). Finally, these difficulties will be reflected in the internal working models (Bowlby 1988) of the self and others that should emerge developmentally by the third year of life, and which serve to direct relationships with others.

While the *DSM-IV* asserts that attachment disorders are rare, clinical experience with young children suggests that attachment disorders of the types described above are distressingly frequent. Today's social conditions seem to foster poor attachments. A large number of preschoolers appear to develop no attachments; these children live in foster care or are victims of severe abuse or neglect. Many other preschoolers have anxious attachments. For example, Crittenden (1988) found that about 90 percent of the maltreated children she assessed using the strange situation paradigm were insecurely attached. They come from homes where caregivers are inconsistently available and therefore do not have a secure base from which to explore the world. Still others have disrupted attachments. These youngsters suffer losses through parental divorce, foster care placement, parental death, or parental mental illness. Effective treatment strategies are urgently needed for these children and play therapy holds tremendous promise for effective intervention.

Traditional Treatment Strategies with Attachment Disorders

Several approaches to treatment of attachment disorders have been proposed in the literature. One major approach is parent–infant psychotherapy, first developed by Selma Fraiberg and her colleagues (1974). Generally initiated in the first two to three years of life, these approaches primarily focus on the caregiver, usually the mother (Erickson et al. 1992, Lieberman 1992, Lieberman and Pawl 1988). These approaches propose that attachment disorders at this age largely derive from problems encountered by the mother in being an effective caregiver and that intervention therefore should be aimed primarily at the mother and her interactions with the infant. Furthermore, the mother's difficulties are rooted in her early relationship with her caregiver. While the infant is typically included in the interventions with the mother, intervention is not directed at the child; the child instead serves as a transference object. Lieberman and her associates have developed a model based on psychoanalytic theory with particular emphasis on projective identification by the mother and the infant's response to those projections. Erickson and colleagues (1992) use a program they developed called STEEP (Steps Toward Effective, Enjoyable Parenting) to modify the mother's internal working model of relationships.

A quite different approach is presented by Speltz (1990), who incorporates attachment concepts into a behavioral program for parent training. After first describing how many of the conduct problems seen in preschool children can be understood as expressions of the child's attempt to control the caregiver's proximity, especially at times of transition, Speltz elaborates a treatment for attachment disorders in preschool children. In this treatment, Speltz augments a behavioral parent management program with several elements focused on attachment. Specifically, the program begins with an educational component that addresses the development and importance of the attachment relationship. After presenting behavioral management procedures, Speltz adds a unit on parent–child communication training incorporating problem solving and communication techniques to enable the parent and child to develop a "goal-corrected partnership" (p. 415).

James (1994) proposes a treatment model for children who have experienced attachment problems related to other trauma. While the model is too complex to present fully here, the central structure of her approach is to use "therapeutic parenting" on the part of the caregiver (whether this is the original attachment figure, foster parents, or a new caregiver) to address the attachment problems while the therapist works with the child on the trauma issues. James's model for working with the child also addresses attachment issues in that the therapist must first establish a safe and protective environment for therapy to proceed. James proposes four issues as central to children suffering from attachment trauma: self-identity, relationship building, affect tolerance and modulation, and behavior mastery. As the child deals with these issues in the protective environment, explores the trauma, and mourns losses, consolidation emerges.

Two other models for addressing attachment disorders have developed with significant similarities to each other: Jernberg's (1979, 1993) theraplay and Brody's (1993) developmental play therapy. Jernberg proposes to replicate the early parent–infant relationship in the relationship between the child and the therapist. She focuses on four dimensions of the relationship—structuring, challenging, intrusion, and nurturing—that the therapist addresses through structured activities. These activities involve touching, singing, talking, and moving in a playful manner. At times the activity is intrusive, at times it structures space and time, at times it nurtures and soothes, and at times it challenges the child to be a partner. Through these therapist-directed and -initiated activities, the child's internal organization develops and a sense of trust in the caregiver emerges. Brody (1993) also utilizes therapist-initiated touch as the central feature of her approach. She believes that the therapist's touching of the child provides an environment where the child's needs are experienced by the therapist. She believes that this develops the child's sense of self and his/her attachment to the therapist. These two models are similar in a number of ways. Both share an emphasis on touching, both use the therapist rather than the caregiver to foster attachment, both rely on therapist–child activities rather than play with toys, and both expect that the therapist initiates and controls the activities. In addition, both models of treatment are regarded as effective with a wide range of problems of childhood rather than focusing primarily on attachment problems.

Delaney (1991) works with foster children using an approach based on Bowlby's theory. Specifically, Delaney argues that foster children, who have typically experienced neglect or abuse and who have often had multiple caregivers, have developed negative working models of the self, the caregiver, and their relationships. There is a cycle wherein the negative working model leads to conduct problems, which lead to reenactment (the re-creation of old relationships with new people), which produces a negative response from the foster parent, which then reinforces the negative working model. Therapy is directed at changing this negative working model by working both with the child and the foster parent. When working with both the child and the parent, Delaney proposes four components of treatment. He begins by containing conduct problems. He then works toward increasing verbalization of the negative working model, fostering communication of needs and negotiating differences, and promoting positive encounters. Therapy sessions include behavioral training, verbal confrontations with therapist and/or foster parents, and direct work on negotiating skills.

Crittenden (1992b) developed a treatment model for anxious attachments based on an integration of the "work of Stern on affect regulation, Ainsworth on quality of attachment, Piaget on cognitive development, Tulving on memory systems, and Bowlby on internal working models" (p. 575). The primary treatment goal for preschoolers involves changing each child's internal procedural model to help him/her deal effectively with complex interpersonal situations. She describes this rather complex model in general terms, looking both at interventions with the caregiver and interventions with the child. With the caregiver, intervention centers on enhancing the caregiver's attunement and affective resonance with the child through modifying the semantic and episodic representations that the caregiver provides the child. Intervention with the child is similar. The therapist's goal is to be sensitive to the child, to accept the child with his/her painful experiences, to identify the nuances in the child's experiences, and to create semantic models for the child that are accurate and supportive. While the theoretical underpinnings of this approach are well articulated, it is difficult to translate the model into actual behaviors by the therapist.

This chapter proposes a model for therapy that differs in several ways from the treatment strategies described above. This model, while including the caregiver in the treatment when available, focuses on the child. Based theoretically on the works of Bowlby and Tulving, this approach uses play therapy as the primary agent of therapeutic change. This approach contrasts with many of the approaches above (e.g., parent–infant psychotherapy, Speltz's approach, and James's work), which assume that the primary intervention for amelioration of attachment disturbances should come through an attachment figure. The other approaches, which focus on the child in treatment (e.g., theraplay, developmental play therapy, and therapy with foster children) utilize the play in a very directive way. They either do not use play as a primary therapeutic medium (Delaney 1991), use play only in the sense that the touch used is playful (Brody 1993), or limit the play to structured activities selected by the therapist (Jernberg 1979). Crittenden, whose theoretical model is similar to the model presented here, presents goals rather than techniques by which the goals could be attained.

Rationale for Play Therapy

Therapeutic Powers of Play Involved

Many authors have argued that the use of play in a therapy setting serves a number functions. For example, O'Connor (1991) suggests that play is a major medium for learning for children. It helps children expend energy while also helping them gain physical and psychological mastery. At times, play facilitates relaxation. At other times, it provides children with kinesthetic stimulation or "something to do." Play is also a major means of communication. Although a child's play may be communicative, the child's message may not always be explicit. Landreth (1993) asserts that children frequently communicate through the use of symbols. According to Landreth, symbolic play "provides a safe or controlled way for children to express emotions, since the emotion itself or the target of the emotion is disguised through the symbolism" (p. 49).

In 1993 Schaefer elaborated several "therapeutic powers" of play, each of which contributes to the therapeutic process in ways that effect change. The therapeutic factors are combined in various ways to make play therapy an effective intervention for a host of problems encountered by children. Schaefer's work represents an important step in examining systematically what components contribute to the therapeutic change seen in play therapy. Articulation of the range of therapeutic factors operating in play therapy provides an essential base to the endeavor of matching therapeutic factors to the particular problems of the child.

In the past several years, numerous theoretical approaches to play therapy have been elaborated, ranging from familiar models based on familiar theories, such as client-centered (Landreth 1993), psychoanalytic (Cangelosi 1993), and Gestalt (Oaklander 1988), to more recent developments such as Jungian (Allen 1988, Allen and Bertoia 1992); metaphorical play therapy (Mills and Crowley 1986), and ecosystemic play therapy (O'Connor 1994), to various technical, innovative, and disorder-specific approaches (e.g., O'Connor and Schaefer 1994, Schaefer 1988, Schaefer and O'Connor 1983). Each of these various approaches tends to incorporate only some of the therapeutic factors listed by Schaefer. The process of matching play therapy approaches, each with its own combination of therapeutic factors, to those children who will respond best to them remains to be done.

Thematic Play Therapy for children with attachment disorders employs several of the therapeutic factors of play outlined by Schaefer (1993). Thematic Play Therapy attempts to translate Bowlby's (1988) five therapeutic tasks into the medium of therapeutic play. Bowlby's tasks begin with the establishment of a secure base for the child that will enable him/her to explore painful aspects of present and past relationships. Another task proposed by Bowlby that also particularly focuses on the child–therapist relationship consists of the therapist helping the child use the relationship between the child and therapist to examine the internal working models and the expectations the child brings to the relationship. The remaining tasks outlined by Bowlby focus on the child's internal working model of self and other in relationship. These tasks include assisting the child in exploring and understanding his/her expectations, feelings, and behaviors in current relationships. He also proposed that the therapist must assist the child in considering how current relationships and behavior may have been influenced by past events. Finally, he proposed that the therapist must help the child recognize when old governing images or internal working models are not accurate and help the child modify those models toward healthier working models of relationships with others.

Thematic Play Therapy, through several of the therapeutic powers of play, addresses these tasks within play therapy. This therapy initially focuses on the relationship with the therapist. In Thematic Play Therapy, the relationship is pivotal in two ways. First, the relationship enables the therapist to provide the child with a secure base, which is the first of Bowlby's therapeutic tasks. Second, as the relationship becomes important to the child, the child will bring to the relationship all the expectations, feelings, and internal models characteristic of the child's relationships with others where they can be examined, thus addressing another of the tasks specified by Bowlby. The therapeutic powers necessary for this component of play therapy to be effective include aspects of attachment formation (Jernberg 1993), relationship enhancement (Guerney 1993), and overcoming resistance to build a therapeutic alliance (Bow 1993).

The development of a secure base through play depends initially on what Jernberg (1993) calls attunement, or the therapist's efforts to become connected with the child. The four dimensions of play enumerated by Jernberg—structuring, challenging, intrusion, and nurturing—when employed sensitively by the therapist foster in the child the secure base necessary for therapy to proceed. For older attachment-disordered children, resistance to forming a relationship may be quite noticeable in the early phases of treatment. At this point, a deliberate effort on the part of the therapist to use play to overcome resistance is needed (Bow 1993). Bow suggests that an attitude of playfulness and humor can help overcome resistance. He also suggests using puppets, drawing, and other play activities to help the resistant child. The power of play to overcome resistance can be crucial in establishing a secure base with the older child.

The child's relationship with the caregiver is postulated as pivotal in the development of attachment disorders. In the same way, the relationship with the therapist plays a central role in providing the child with information to change his/her negative working model. This aspect of the therapeutic relationship shows clearly the power of play for relationship enhancement (Guerney 1993). Playing together seems to facilitate an especially strong bond between the child and the therapist. Guerney (1993) suggests this bond may be due to several factors including the shared pleasure of playing, the therapist's acceptance and encouragement of fantasy, which creates a safe haven in the play setting for feelings, and the very different role the therapist enacts, which includes joining in the child's play with a level of understanding not typically found in most of the child's adult relationships. In our view, the power of the therapeutic relationship to enable the child to change both internal conceptions of the world and relationships with others outside of the therapy setting cannot be overestimated.

Thematic Play Therapy, once the relationship is formed, centers on the child's play themes and the therapist's reactions to those play themes. Through this aspect of Thematic Play Therapy, the remaining tasks outlined by Bowlby

(1988) can be met. In attempting to carry out these tasks to help the child understand current working models and then modify the child's maladaptive internal working models, role play is central (Irwin and Curry 1993). Through the roles the child assigns to himself and to the therapist, the therapist can assist the child in understanding current roles and relationships. Through the child-responsive and invitational response of the therapist, alternatives to the initial child–caregiver relationship can be acted out. The child can experience new kinds of interactions that contrast with his/her previous experiences. Thus, role play is a very powerful tool within play therapy to facilitate change.

As suggested above, the therapist's response to the role play or thematic play of the child is pivotal to our model. While the child-responsive model we propose will be described in more detail later, the ways thematic play therapy effects change depend on two additional powers of play. First, play for the child is a means of self-expressive communication (Landreth 1993). The therapist must sensitively and accurately understand this communication by the child both to maintain the relationship and to determine where the child's current understanding (internal working model) is incomplete or inaccurate and needs modification. Child-responsive play therapy always begins with the themes introduced to therapy by the child, as the child uses play to communicate his/her needs and concerns. Thematic Play Therapy also relies partially on the power of deliberate use of metaphor by the therapist (Frey 1993), particularly on elaborating and modifying the child's metaphors when responding to the child's play themes.

Many children with attachment disorders have experienced inadequate parenting or interruptions to attachment that were traumatic and painful for the child. Bowlby (1988) recognizes this in his therapeutic tasks by calling on the therapist to help the child work through the painful process of discovering how current expectations, feelings, and relationship patterns may derive from past experiences. For those attachment-disordered children who have traumatic or painful pasts, two final powers of play become important. Catharsis, or emotional release, and its closely related power, abreaction, the "process by which children resolve passively experienced traumatic events of the real world by actively repeating them in the microcosmic play world" (Oremland 1993, p. 143) work together to enable children to heal past trauma (Ginsberg 1993). In Thematic Play Therapy, the therapist provides the child with a secure base and a trusting relationship within which it becomes safe to use these therapeutic powers of play to express intense feelings (catharsis) and reenact through play a previous traumatic event (abreaction). In so doing, the child begins the process of healing the trauma. The response of the therapist, which includes acceptance of feelings, child-responsive role play, and use of metaphor to present alternative outcomes of the trauma for the child, helps the child then begin to consider different understandings of the trauma that will ultimately enable the child to form new working models for future relationships.

Approach

Description

The treatment model proposed for attachment disorders in young children has two components. The first component, Thematic Play Therapy, involves individual play therapy with children who have had disturbed attachments. Centered on the child's relationship to the therapist and the therapist's responses to the child's play themes, Thematic Play Therapy provides a general model of play therapy that must be individualized to address the specific problems encountered in a particular child or type of disorder, in this case attachment disorders. When treating attachment-disordered children, the therapist needs to adopt two general goals. First, the therapist needs to provide the child with a secure base from which the child can explore the world. Second, the therapist needs to give the child an opportunity to experience a positive relationship and to help the child see the contrasts between this positive relationship and earlier largely negative relationships. Therapy is effective because it provides the child with an experience that does not meet his/her negative expectations. The child learns that relationships can be rewarding, and uses this information to alter his/her internal model. Once the internal model has been changed, behavioral changes tend to follow.

The second component involves the child's caregivers. Caregivers are included in this approach to attachment disorders because interventions with young children are most effective when concerned adults become involved. Interventions with caregivers include increasing support, providing education, and helping them deal with their own attachment issues (Mongoven 1995). Because this chapter focuses on the healing aspects of the play therapy component, detailed description of the caregiver component will not be included here.

The Play Therapy Component

Thematic Play Therapy is based on object relations theories, especially Mahler and Winnicott, and Bowlby's theory of attachment, integrated with current research knowledge of social, emotional, and cognitive development in children. This model places central emphasis on the relationship between the therapist and the child as well as the therapist's use of child-responsive techniques to respond to and interpret the child's play themes (Benedict and Grigoryev 1995). When applied to children with attachment disorders as is illustrated here, Thematic Play Therapy must be particularly sensitive to the issues and themes central to the development of attachment disorders.

According to Karen (1990), what is now called attachment theory was born in the early 1950s of three unlikely parents: ethology, developmental psychology, and psychoanalysis. These different approaches to psychology were brought together and integrated into a theoretical model by Bowlby, who has produced several volumes over the last three decades outlining his views on attachment and the major role attachment plays in psychological disorder (Bowlby 1969, 1979, 1988). Central to Bowlby's theory is his belief that human infants, like other animal newborns, are predisposed to develop attachments to their primary caregivers. Bowlby believes that attachment behavior is biologically rooted and that it serves to protect the infant (McMillen 1992). From this perspective, all infants, however treated, will become attached to the available caregiver (Sroufe 1986).

Two of Bowlby's concepts are particularly important to the application of Thematic Play Therapy to treatment of attachment-disordered children. The first concept centers around what Bowlby calls the *secure base*. The second concept relates to what Bowlby calls the *internal working model*. The concept of the secure base refers to the infant's tendency to use the caregiver as a safe haven from which to explore and learn about the world. A secure base is typically provided for an infant by a responsive caregiver. The infant feels protected while he/she is close to the caregiver. This arrangement fosters a sense of security, self-confidence, and courage in the child. As the child becomes more experienced, he/she becomes increasingly more comfortable venturing away from the caregiver. When sick, tired, frightened, or injured, the youngster returns to the caregiver for comforting. When the child feels threatened (because of increased distance, lapsed time, or apparent danger), he/she attempts to reestablish contact with the caregiver by emitting attachment behaviors. Once the child is reassured of the presence and availability of the secure base, he/she is able to resume his/her explorations.

Bowlby suggests that once an infant becomes attached, he/she uses the caregiver as a secure base. Although this idea is not entirely new (previous theorists have postulated that children derive "security" from being near their parents; see Karen 1990), Bowlby's contribution comes from his ability to integrate the concept of a secure base into his understandings of attachment. Bowlby postulates that it is through the establishment and use of the secure base that a child develops the skills necessary for dealing with his/her world.

Bowlby suggests that an internal working model is a type of cognitive prototype of the self and others, and of how the two relate. It is believed that an infant develops his/her internal working model between the ages of birth and 3 years. This model is generally developed from the child's experience with his/her caregivers. The model develops when "aspects of what is initially a relationship are internalized by the child as the self, or personality, emerges" (Suess et al. 1992, p. 44). Once internalized, this model guides interactions not only with the primary caregivers, but with others as well. Bowlby (1988) considers the internal working model to be pivotal in determining the quality of future relationships because it contains beliefs about how others tend to behave. Theoretically, once the model is established it becomes increasingly resistant to change over time (Bretherton 1991).

Bowlby (1988) suggests that "the working models a child builds of his mother and her ways of communicating and behaving towards him, and comparable models[s] of his father, together with the complementary models of himself in interaction with each, are being built by a child during the first few years of his life and, it is postulated, soon become established as *influential cognitive structures*" (p. 129, italics added). How this occurs can be better understood by looking at the works of Endel Tulving.

Tulving (1985) postulates that there are three different memory systems (i.e., episodic, semantic, and procedural). According to Tulving, each memory system has special functions. Procedural memory enables a person to retain learned stimulus-response connections and helps him/her respond in an adaptive way to the environment. Semantic memory is characterized by the individual's capacity to internally represent states of the world that are not perceptually present. Episodic memory gives the individual the capacity to acquire and retain personal types of knowledge.

In addition to having different functions, each of the three memory systems differs in its method of acquisition and in its representation of knowledge (Tulving 1985). For example, entry into the procedural system requires overt behavioral responding. This contrasts with the methods of acquisition for the semantic and episodic systems, which are able to acquire information by more covert means (e.g., by cognitive activity or observation). Within the procedural system, Tulving (1985) suggests that information is represented in "prescriptive" rather than "descriptive" form. In essence, the information is stored as a blueprint for future action. In contrast, the representations in the semantic system are strictly descriptive while those in the episodic system simply carry detailed information about personal history. Neither semantic nor episodic memories are believed to guide future behavior.

An integration between Bowlby's attachment concepts and Tulving's theory of memory systems is particularly helpful to the development of a treatment model for attachment disordered children. The concept of the internal working model proposed by Bowlby and adopted by other attachment theorists (e.g., Mills and Allan 1991) is similar to Tulving's procedural memory system. According to Bowlby (1988), as elaborated by Crittenden (1992a), the child develops "several separate memory systems, each with an internal working model" (p. 212) and proceeds to interact with the world based on these models. From Tulving's perspective, when a child interacts with the world, he/she builds memories. Of particular interest are the memories that serve a prescriptive function (and guide future interactions as postulated by Bowlby). These memories are believed to be a part of the procedural memory system.

The integration of these two theories has implications for treatment.

The Playing Cure

Working from Bowlby's model, Crittenden (1992a) suggests that children frequently have skewed perceptions of the world, which stem from their internal working models. According to Crittenden, a child's internalized model restricts his/her range of perception while also influencing interpretations of what is seen. Ultimately, the child develops expectations about interactions based on his/her internal working model and these expectations lead to future interactions that fulfill these expectations in a cyclical way. For a child to make new predictions about the world, he/she needs to learn new information about human interactions (i.e., acquire new procedural memories). Psychotherapy is viewed as a way to help the child create some of these new procedural memories. Play therapy is believed to be a particularly effective intervention for children because it involves overt responding, which has immediate access to the procedural memory system.

While agreeing with Crittenden that the child's internalized model can create a type of tunnel vision, we believe that it is unlikely that it causes complete blindness. If the child's expectations are not fulfilled during an interaction, the child's internalized model is believed to shift in a way that accommodates the new information. This position is consistent with the work of Mills and Allan (1991). When the child experiences a new situation, he/she creates a revised model that is believed to consist of both the old internal working model and additional, adaptive alternatives. A young child's internal working model is believed to be less firmly established than an adult's because of his/her relatively smaller number of life experiences. The young child's understanding of the world is limited and can easily be affected by brief encounters. This makes a young child an especially good candidate for treatment.

Thematic Play Therapy builds on these concepts in two ways. First, therapy begins by establishing a trusting relationship between the therapist and the child. This relationship, once formed, serves as a secure base for the child to explore the world. This exploration, through the therapist's responses to the child's play themes, provides interactions that do not fit with the child's expectations. These interactions are instrumental in modifying the child's internal working model. Therapy is effective because it provides the child with a new kind of experience. Once an attachment-disordered child has a positive, therapeutic relationship, he/she begins to develop memories that do not fit into the original model. The child must integrate this new information into his/her understanding of the world. When the new information is integrated, the child is faced with new possibilities. Future encounters may be hurtful (like some of the child's earliest relationships), or they may be rewarding. The possibility of having rewarding interactions in the future increases as the child modifies his/her internal working model.

According to McMillen (1992), "Persons with unchanged internal working models of self and others will continue to elicit behavior which confirms their working models" (p. 208). From our perspective, these individuals do not know that there are alternative ways of viewing the world. This is particularly likely for young children who are limited cognitively in their abilities to comprehend things that have not yet happened. Early intervention is particularly helpful in decreasing the chances that these children will continue to elicit behaviors that confirm their negative impressions of the world.

Before discussing the model in detail, it should be noted that the ability to appropriately apply this model is based on the therapist's ability to effectively assess the child and confirm that the child has an attachment disorder. To get an accurate picture of the child's problems, the therapist must be able to integrate his/her findings from such sources as the child's history, group observations, individual play assessment, and possible assessment-specific techniques (see Cicchetti et al. 1995). While discussion of the assessment of attachment disorders is beyond the scope of this chapter, careful assessment is obviously crucial if an effective match between the child's problems and the treatment approach is to be made.

Initiating Therapy

The first and most important element of treatment is the development of a therapeutic relationship. Therapy will not progress until the therapist has established a trusting relationship with the child. Unfortunately, establishing such a relationship can be very difficult. Attachment-disordered children have relied on others in the past, only to be disappointed or violated or hurt. These children expect that future relationships will also be hurtful. In an effort to protect themselves, they are reluctant to trust. As a result of these serious difficulties trusting others, they may appear avoidant or withdrawn or they (or their play figures) may act somewhat suspicious, reluctant, or resistant in their social interactions.

The attachment-disordered child has developed an internal working model of others as unreliable. Even after several sessions, the child may feel uncertain about future interactions with the therapist. The goal of therapy is to help the child begin to trust others. Therapy provides the child (and his/her play figures) with a positive, reliable, and trustworthy relationship. When the child experiences this type of relationship, his/her internal working model is challenged. The child is faced with new options and is forced to recognize that all relationships are not alike.

Once the child's internal working model has shifted to accommodate the idea that some people can be trusted, the therapist's treatment goal is altered to accommodate the child's learning. During the later stages of therapy, the treatment goal is to help the child learn to discriminate between people who can be trusted and those who are not trustworthy. The therapist also supports the child as he/she attempts to develop positive relationships outside of the therapy environment.

There are several ways that a therapist can foster the development of a trusting relationship. According to Petrick (1994), "Consistency on the part of the therapist will facilitate the development of a child–therapist relationship that feels safe to the child" (p. 49). Therapeutic consistency takes many forms. It is most helpful if therapy is scheduled at regular intervals. Weekly or biweekly appointments work best with preschoolers because of their inability to comprehend longer spans of time. It is also best if therapy is consistently conducted in the same office, at the same time of day. Consistent routines such as these help the child develop expectations about his/her therapy appointments.

The therapist's attitude toward the child will also influence the development of a trusting relationship. A therapist who is warm and who exhibits positive regard toward the child is likely to be trusted more quickly than a therapist who is less affirming. An attachment-disordered child needs to feel accepted by his/her therapist before he/she can begin to trust.

For trust to develop, the therapist must be sensitive to the child's needs. He/she must strive to understand the child's current situation as well as anticipate future concerns. Attending to the child's mood and affect in various situations can be particularly helpful when attempting to ascertain current needs. The therapist must also attempt to help the child meet his/her needs whenever possible.

One way that the therapist can demonstrate sensitivity toward the child is through the use of child-responsive therapy (Benedict 1994), an approach to treatment that depends heavily on the child. The child sets the theme and the activity level of each session. The therapist's job is to consistently follow the child's lead in an effort to create a secure base. By using a child-responsive treatment approach, the therapist conveys that he/she is open to the child's communications. The therapist is able to be sensitive to all modes of communications including verbal, nonverbal, and metaphorical. The therapist is also able to listen to the child for as long as it takes the child to convey a particular message.

Child-responsive therapy is neither *directive* or *nondirective* as the terms are traditionally used (Axline 1947). It does, however, contain elements of both of these approaches. A metaphor might help to exemplify this approach. Child-responsive therapy allows the child to choose his/her route into the forest. However, once inside, the therapist, who knows the child's ultimate destination, is able to effectively guide the trip.

Even if the therapist has managed to be consistent, accepting, and sensitive to his/her young client, the child will not begin to trust the therapist unless the child feels safe. The therapeutic environment must be a safe place for the child, both physically and psychologically. Attachment-disordered preschoolers frequently play dangerously. As mentioned earlier, they take risks and are accident-prone because they lack an internalized concern for self-preservation. The therapist must therefore take explicit measures to ensure the child's physical safety. Three basic rules are routinely adopted: (1) the child is not allowed to harm himself/herself, (2) the child is not allowed to harm the therapist, and (3) the child is not allowed to destroy the playroom or the toys. The therapist may choose to expand on these rules or create additional rules as needed. To increase the child's feeling of safety, all rules need to be clearly communicated and upheld at all times.

Psychological safety is a by-product of consistency, affirmation, sensitivity, and physical safety. If the therapist has successfully created all of these conditions, then the child will feel safe to explore his/her thoughts and feelings within the context of therapy. Once the child feels psychologically safe, he/she begins to trust the therapist. It is from within this context that the next phase of treatment begins.

The following case exemplifies how a child might communicate his/her inability to trust.

A 3-year-old girl named Jenny arrives for her second play therapy session. Although she has been brought to her session by her mother, she is reluctant to enter the play therapy room. Jenny walks into the room slowly, watching the therapist the whole time as if to keep her distance. She is relatively quiet and talks very little. When the therapist hands Jenny a toy and offers to play collaboratively with her, Jenny shows no interest. Jenny seems most comfortable when she is playing alone.

Jenny has developed her own way of dealing with the world. She expects that others will be unreliable and she, therefore, withdraws as a way to protect herself from disappointment. Unfortunately, by withdrawing, Jenny will never have the opportunity to test out her assumptions. She will always behave as if others are not trustworthy.

Jenny's therapist might choose to intervene in a number of ways: (1) The therapist may choose to say very little, interact only minimally, and not "intervene" in any dramatic way. By taking this approach, the therapist allows Jenny to adjust to the presence of the therapist at her own pace. (2) The therapist may acknowledge how difficult it is for Jenny to trust others and may give her permission to have her feelings. (3) The therapist may acquire a specific toy that Jenny wants (e.g., a particular doll) as a way to encourage interaction. If the therapist routinely plays with the intriguing toy, then it is likely that the child will become less avoidant and more inclined to interact as a way to also play with the toy. (4) The therapist must be trustworthy. When he/she makes a promise to the child, he/she needs to do everything in his/her power to make sure that the promise is kept. The child needs to know that the therapist is dependable.

These interventions are believed to be helpful because they allow the therapist to circumvent the child's efforts to avoid and withdraw. The child is provided with a secure base where he/she can experience a trusting relationship. This experience will open up new possibilities for future relationships.

Experiential Phase of Treatment

Once trust is firmly established, therapy enters an "experiential" phase. It is during this time that the child begins to encounter a new kind of interaction with the therapist. The child learns that interpersonal relationships are not all the same. The child also starts to question his/her own internal model of relationships.

The therapist is able to witness the child's confusion about relationships by observing his/her play. As the child struggles to understand interpersonal relationships, particular play themes become apparent. These themes represent the issues that the child is struggling with internally (Petrick 1994). The therapist's awareness of these themes is central to effective interventions. Once the play themes become apparent to the therapist, he/she can work from within them to offer new options or resolutions to the child. The therapist's response attempts to expand upon the child's theme in a way that helps the child establish a more appropriate and flexible model of the world.

Thematic interventions are particularly appropriate for young children. As mentioned earlier, young children tend to have difficulty differentiating between their own and others' perspectives due to their limited cognitive development. For this reason, it is relatively safe to assume that the play themes of young children are related to their own issues. For example, if a child tells a story of a baby lion, and the baby lion is reportedly scared, then it is likely that the child is also struggling with similar feelings. Because young children have difficulty adopting others' perspectives, they will as a matter of course share their own perspectives through their play. The knowledgeable play therapist will be able to recognize these play themes and use them to make appropriate interventions.

Each attachment-disordered child has his/her own unique history and equally unique issues. It is therefore impossible for any treatment model to present exact instructions for addressing all possible scenarios. The model presented here does not attempt to provide a therapist with specific steps for modifying a child's internal working model. Indeed, providing a "paint by numbers" approach to therapy for attachment-disordered children seems counter to the goal of providing a secure base. To truly provide a secure base, the therapist needs to be keenly aware of and responsive to the child's individual needs. A "paint by numbers" approach would force the therapist to ignore individual differences and treat the child in a prescribed way. Such an approach would not be helpful to the child.

Techniques Used

The model presented here provides a unique way to understand attachment disorders in children. The model addresses (1) issues that an attachment-disordered child might struggle with, (2) ways these issues might relate to the child's attachment history, and (3) goals that might be appropriate for dealing with presented issues.

There are five general themes that attachment-disordered children present in their play: safety, anger, nurturance, constancy, and loss. These themes reflect the predominant issues of these youngsters. In our experience, these themes are not equally salient to all children. Some children are most focused on safety and anger issues while others are most concerned with nurturance and constancy issues. Also, over the course of therapy, the child may work on several of the themes, either simultaneously or sequentially. These individual differences depend on many factors such as the predominant type of attachment disorder the child shows, the nature of the child's initial attachment relationship (e.g., was the child nonattached or did the child lose an attachment figure following an adequate attachment relationship), and the co-occurrence of abuse or other trauma. These themes, however, have appeared consistently in the attachment-disordered children we have treated. The importance of these themes lies in their usefulness within play therapy. Each theme represents an unresolved issue that either prevents the child from being able to use an adult as a secure base or prevents the development of an internal working model that sees the self as good and valuable and sees others as potential positive relationships. Thus, each theme can be the basis of an effective intervention.

Many attachment-disordered children struggle with issues related to safety. The child who is grappling with safety issues will demonstrate this struggle through his/her play. He/she may play in an aggressive, destructive, or dangerous manner to test the limits within the therapy room. He/she may also behave carelessly. Symbolic play in which a central character is injured or in danger may suggest that the child feels unsafe. The child may also report that his/her play figures feel vulnerable or scared of something (e.g., monsters, wild animals, or "bad people").

The child's concerns about safety parallel his/her inability to find a secure base from which to explore the world. To the young child who has not experienced a secure base, the world feels quite threatening. The therapeutic goal within this context is to increase the child's internal sense of safety. The therapist does this by creating a safe environment for the child (and for the child's play figures). In this way, the child experiences safety and learns that it is possible to create safety for him-/herself.

The following play scenario exemplifies the play theme of safety.

During his third therapy session, a 3-year-old boy named Larry enters the playroom. He is very quiet and withdrawn. He explores the toys minimally before showing an interest in several brightly colored cars. The therapist encourages Larry to play with whatever interests him and, therefore, he proceeds to get the cars out of storage. As Larry dumps the cars onto the table where he is playing, one of the cars falls off the table and crashes onto the floor next to the therapist. Larry appears noticeably upset.

While there are several possible interpretations of the above exchange, one possible interpretation is that Larry had a strong affective response because his therapist (i.e., the only available adult) failed to keep his figure (i.e., the car) safe. This was particularly difficult for Larry because adults had failed to protect him from abusive situations in the past.

Based on the above interpretation of the interaction, the therapist might choose to address Larry's safety issues in a number of ways. (1) The therapist may acknowledge the strong feelings exhibited by Larry and may give him permission to express these feelings openly. (2) The therapist may apologize to Larry for his/her failure to protect the child's figure. (3) The therapist may decide to take additional, possibly even extreme, precautions to ensure the future safety of Larry's figure. For example, the therapist could develop new rules specifically for getting the toys out of storage. The therapist could also build a wall around the edge of the table to "prevent other cars from falling and getting hurt." (4) The therapist may introduce a "helping figure" that could assist Larry's figure in times of need (e.g., the therapist may introduce an car mechanic into Larry's play to help "fix" the car after the wreck).

These interventions are believed to be helpful for a number of reasons. They acknowledge the child's veiled communications and help to create a secure base for the child. They are also helpful because they are counter to the child's internal working model. The presented alternatives communicate that others can be sensitive to the child's needs and provide safety and security to the child.

A second play theme that is frequently presented by attachment-disordered children is anger. Children who have experienced neglect, abuse, a nonresponsive, detached caregiver, or loss of a caregiver are fundamentally angry, even enraged at the caregiver and often other adults as well. Anger is a natural, healthy response of an infant when its needs are not met and it feels unsafe. Expression of angry feelings alerts the caregiver and elicits the nurturance or safety the child needs. In a healthy relationship, the infant learns that it is acceptable to have needs and to express those needs. The infant learns that anger does not destroy either the infant or the caregiver. Over time, the infant learns appropriate ways to express anger, ways to elicit caregiving, ways to self-comfort, and learns that he/she can be loved and cared for even if angry.

Attachment-disordered children, in contrast, typically have difficulties with anger. Some have learned that it is dangerous to express anger. They may fear abandonment if they express anger at the caregiver. Alternatively, the child may have learned that the parent responds to anger with anger and possibly abuse. In other cases, the anger receives no response from the caregiver (through neglect or personal preoccupation on the part of the caregiver), which leads the child to fear abandonment has already occurred. Also, some children, especially those who show inhibited attachment disorder, may have developed excessive compliance and stop expressing any anger. Finally, some attachment-disordered children, rather than being inhibited about anger, seem to be perpetually angry, showing aggression and oppositionality to the caregiver as a way of at least engaging the caregiver's attention (Speltz 1990).

The therapist is often presented with extremes around the issue of anger. Some attachment-disordered children appear aggressive and angry with generally strong and unmodulated feelings that frequently elicit negative responses from the caregiver and other adults. Some attachment-disordered children present angry feelings rarely, and when they do they present them in disguised form or very indirectly. Some children show both types of behaviors, often in alternation. While the presentation is very different, some of the underlying concerns may be quite similar for the different groups of children. Some of the key issues that must be considered in intervening effectively around feelings of anger include underlying fears of abandonment; the belief that anger is "bad" and the child is therefore "bad" for having angry feelings; the belief that it is "bad" to have needs, often expressed in views that babies are bad if they cry or poop and that is why they don't get taken care of; fear of anger itself; and a belief that its expression will somehow destroy the child or the caregiver.

Intervention around anger occurs at many levels in play therapy with an attachment-disordered child. The response of the therapist when anger is expressed is critical. The therapist must both accept the anger without withdrawing from the child (and thus fueling the child's fear of abandonment) and without being angered or frightened by the anger (and thus fueling the child's fear that the attachment figure will be destroyed by the anger). At the same time, the therapist must provide safety to the child so that the child does not frighten him/herself, get hurt, or hurt the therapist or the playroom. By calmly and warmly accepting the child's anger while maintaining the safe base, the therapist provides the child with an experience of healthy anger.

The following play scenario exemplifies the play theme of anger.

Colton is a 5-year-old boy with an insecure attachment with his mother. He had very infrequent and rather unhappy contact with his father following a divorce when he was 3. After a few months of therapy, Colton began playing that he was a baby with the therapist playing the father figure using a male puppet. For several sessions, Colton had the father come to visit the baby who was very excited to see him and on these visits the father would feed the baby. When the daddy puppet "went home" after the visit, Colton would crawl under the table and pretend to cry until the daddy came to visit again. This session, when the father came to visit, Colton wouldn't play with him and began shooting the father puppet. The father puppet (therapist) says he's sorry he made the baby mad. Colton says he wasn't mad and tells the therapist to have daddy come visit again. On this second visit, Colton hides and then suddenly, unpredictably, comes out and yells, scaring the daddy, and he does this over and over. Finally he comes out from hiding, grabs the daddy puppet off the therapist's hand, chokes it, stomps it and yells "I hate him," finally throwing the puppet across the room into the wall.

There are several possible interpretations of the above play. Colton over the sessions described had shown a wide range of affect toward the father figure from affection and a longing for contact to the rage of the last session described. Much of this clear ambivalence may trace back to one of Colton's first overnight visits with his father following the divorce. Colton at 3 was active and boisterous and upon returning him home, the father yelled at the mother, stating that she had not disciplined Colton and he had misbehaved all weekend. The father did not visit Colton again for eight months. One interpretation is that Colton believed his misbehavior caused the father to reject him. Colton intensely desires visits with the father and at the same time is angry because his father rejected him.

Based on the above interpretation of the interaction, the therapist might choose to address Colton's anger issues in a number of ways. (1) The therapist may acknowledge the strong feelings exhibited by Colton and may give him permission to express these feelings openly. (2) The therapist (as father) may reassure Colton that he is a good boy. (3) The therapist may decide to interpret more directly some of the confusing past history for Colton. For example, the father (therapist) could tell the baby (Colton) that he has to go home because he and the mother could not get along and so he lives in a different house. Over several reenactments the father (therapist) could explain the various aspects of Colton's history to him in ways that are understandable to a 5-year-old and that counter some of Colton's distorted cognition about why his father doesn't visit him.

These interventions help in several ways. By providing the child with an experience of healthy anger, the therapist enables the child to modify his/her internal working model to include the understanding that relationships can continue despite the presence of anger. In addition, the therapist's interpretations within role play may counter some of the unhealthy cognitions about anger that the child might have. For example, when a child punishes a baby for crying for food, the therapist can say, "Babies aren't bad when they cry. Babies need to cry to let their mommy know what they need. Babies need to be fed and taken care of." Thus, the therapist can use role play to offer alternative ways for the child to understand relationships.

Nurturance is another theme frequently seen in play of attachment-disordered children. This theme appears to be related to the child's experience of unmet needs. These needs may be of a physical or a psychological nature. Children who are struggling with nurturance issues may appear very demanding. They may behave in ways that get them the attention they need. They may appear clingy, tearful, or whiny. They may also have weight problems or eating disorders.

Children who have been unable to get their physical and/or emotional needs met by caregivers develop internal working models based on their experiences. They continue to have needs, but they do not believe that others will satisfy these needs. Therapy is therefore based on helping these children experience others as giving, nurturing, and satisfying.

Children can present unmet needs for nurturance in many ways. They may seem particularly interested in the act of feeding, having play figures (i.e., babies) who are quite needy. Such children also indicate their needs by taking on the role of a baby (e.g., vigorously sucking on the baby bottle).

The therapist working with a child presenting such themes might choose to intervene in the following ways: (1) The therapist may support the child's attempts to provide for their needy play figures by verbally acknowledging what *all* babies (or other figures) need. (2) The therapist may model good caregiving of the babies. (3) The therapist may take on the role of a caregiver and provide nurturance to the child as if he/she were an infant. The therapist may feed, hold, rock, or read to him/her as a way to provide the nurturance that he/she needs.

Interventions such as these are believed to be helpful to attachment-disordered children for a number of reasons. They gratify some of the child's unmet needs. They foster the development of a secure base. They also allow the child to experience others as helpful and nurturing. This experience challenges the child's internal working model and, therefore, introduces new possibilities for the future.

Attachment-disordered children frequently struggle with issues related to constancy and consistency. Given that these children have only recently developed the ability to cognitively represent missing important attachment figures (i.e., object constancy), it is not surprising that to them, the world can seem unpredictable, confusing, and out of their control. In addition to having difficulties comprehending consistency due to their limited development, many attachment-disordered children also have caregivers who are indeed quite unpredictable. These children frequently live in environments that are confusing and chaotic. This, no doubt, contributes to their deep concerns about consistency.

Children may demonstrate consistency play themes through games such as hide and seek. They may ask questions repeatedly in an effort to see if others' expectations have changed. They may insist on controlling interpersonal interactions so that they can create consistency for themselves. They may also test limits constantly in an effort to understand the stability of the situation. They may hide a toy or rearrange some part of the playroom to see if it stays constant between visits. In this case, it is imperative that the therapist either maintain the changes, or tell the child from the beginning that they will have to put it back, giving a reason such as the fact that other people use the room.

The following scenario will help to exemplify how a child might demonstrate play themes of consistency.

A 4-year-old boy named Jose enters his fourth play therapy session. He explores the toys and asks about the whereabouts of specific items. He examines the guns, puzzles, binoculars, and dish set. What is most striking is that Jose seems more interested in accounting for the toys than playing with them. He finally acknowledges that the toys are "all there" and begins to play. Toward the end of the session, Jose asks the therapist if he can take the binoculars home with him. The therapist explains that the toys must stay in the therapy room and that he will be able to see them during his next visit.

One interpretation of the above exchange is that Jose is struggling with consistency issues. He is concerned about the stability of his environment as well as the stability of the therapeutic relationship. Although it is not practical for the therapist to give away his/her toys, Jose's request makes a great deal of sense given his issues. Some type of transitional object would increase Jose's sense of stability because it would serve to remind him of the therapeutic relationship in its absence.

The therapist might choose to address consistency issues in a number of ways: (1) The therapist may acknowledge and talk about Jose's need for consistency. (2) The therapist may use crayons and paper to make a drawing that Jose can take with him. (3) The therapist may obtain a camera (preferably a Polaroid or Instamatic) and allow Jose to take photographs of the toys, the playroom, and the therapist. Once again, Jose may be allowed to keep these pictures and to take them home.

These interventions are effective for various reasons. Some help to establish the therapeutic relationship as a secure base by meeting the child's developmental needs. Other interventions provide the child with transitional objects (e.g., crayon drawings or photographs) that facilitate the development of object constancy. These interventions also provide the child with symbols of the therapeutic relationship. The more the child is exposed to this relationship (or to symbols of this relationship), the more he/she can integrate it into his/her internal working model.

The final theme that is seen in the play of attachment-disordered children is loss. This theme is believed to be related to the child's life experiences. Many attachment-disordered children have experienced losses, some of them life changing, but few have had the opportunity to openly deal with their pain. There are two common reasons for this situation: (1) Frequently, losses that affect a young child also affect his/her family. Caregivers may be doing all that they can to deal with their own feelings and may not be emotionally available to the child. (2) Whether the loss is a death, divorce, or a new job, the young child is often thought to be "too young" to be involved. Caregivers may believe that if they do not talk with the child about the loss, then he/she is somehow protected. This belief causes caregivers to be less available to the child than they might be otherwise.

Themes of loss will often be evident in the play of attachment-disordered children. These children may appear sad or even angry when reminded of their pain. They may seem to be withdrawn or avoidant in interpersonal situations. They may harbor fantasies about their own power and believe that they are responsible for their losses. These children may obsess about reunion fantasies. They may also engage in symbolic play in which the central figure dies or is destroyed. It seems particularly difficult to predict how a child might communicate issues of loss. How a child expresses this theme is largely dependent on the type of loss, the extent of the loss, and the child's developmental level.

The following interventions might be used when a child is expressing play themes of loss: (1) The therapist may encourage the child to talk about his/her feelings and concerns. This approach is probably the most helpful given that many young children have limited opportunities to talk with uninvolved adults. (2) While the therapist is in a good position to point out the attractive qualities of the child, this should only be done if the therapist has clearly communicated that the child's concerns have been heard.

These interventions are instrumental in establishing a secure base for the child. The therapist is available to the child in a way that others have not been accessible. From the secure base, the child is able to begin processing his/her feelings of loss and pain.

During any given session, an attachment-disordered child may express one or more of these themes through his/her play. It is the job of the play therapist to recognize these play themes, singularly or in combination, and to respond to them appropriately. In summary, appropriate responses are those that provide a secure base and challenge existing internal working models.

Termination

There are several ways to know that a child's internal working model has shifted and that it is time for therapy to end. One might look for a decrease in symptomatology, an increase in positive affect, or a shift in play themes. These are not considered to be rigid criteria for assessing progress but rather rules of thumb that can be adopted as appropriate.

Termination may be more important than any other phase of treatment.

How therapy ends (e.g., the feelings that the child has when he/she stops therapy), can color his/her perceptions of the entire therapeutic relationship. Furthermore, for many children, the termination of therapy means that the child is losing a very significant relationship. How this is handled can greatly affect the outcome of treatment.

It is crucial for the therapist to remember that the child has experienced previous losses. For therapy to have a beneficial effect, the losses associated with termination need to be distinctly different. There are several ways that the therapist can ensure that this experience is unique for the child. For example, the therapist can work with the child's caregiver to plan a date for the final session. The therapist can then introduce the idea to the child in a timely way. It is often helpful to give the child something tangible, like a special calendar, to help him/her count the days until the last session. This approach is particularly beneficial with preschoolers given their limited ability to comprehend time. Once the plan has been shared with the child, it is very important that the therapist and the caregiver follow it as closely as possible.

Most children are able to prepare emotionally for an upcoming termination if they are told about the event several weeks in advance. Counting the sessions remaining gives the child a sense of control as well as a sense of safety because he/she is able to predict the future. The child is also able to see that the planned termination is not a punitive response to his/her behavior. Many therapists choose to reframe the termination in a way that emphasizes the child's treatment success. The upcoming termination is presented as a kind of "graduation" and as a sign of growth.

The termination may be less difficult if the child is given something tangible to take with him/her. This can be done in a number of ways: (1) The therapist and the child may choose to make something together that the child could keep. (2) The therapist may give the child a special toy to take home. (3) The therapist may offer the child a camera and allow him/her to take photographs of the last session. (4) The therapist might write a short, developmentally appropriate book about the child's history and his/her therapy experience and give it to the child. Regardless of the approach used, the child is given a tangible object that symbolizes the therapeutic relationship. The object helps the child deal with the loss of the therapist by serving as a constant reminder of this positive encounter.

During the termination sessions, the child needs to be given permission to talk about his/her feelings. This may be particularly difficult for some children to do. Regardless of the child's ability to verbalize his/her feelings, it is especially important for the therapist to acknowledge that the child might be dealing with difficult feelings. The therapist can normalize these feelings and share his/her own feelings of loss as a way to model appropriate emotional expression. Such openness leaves the child with an image of the therapist that is unique and caring. If the therapist is able to make the termination a "different kind of loss," then he/she has once again challenged the child's internal working model and given the child new options for the future.

Case Illustration

Background Information

Antonio, age 4 years, 3 months, and Maria, age 3 years, 2 months, were accompanied by their 5-year-old sister when they were brought to the Department of Protective and Regulatory Services (DPRS) office by their biological mother. The mother, a relatively young Mexican-American woman, reported that she needed the agency to find a home for her children. The mother had been living with her children on the streets; the father's whereabouts were unknown. Although the mother stated she hated to terminate her parental rights, she recognized that she was unable to care for her children properly. The DPRS caseworker reported that the mother's rights were legally terminated because of "neglect of supervision" as well as a "failure to protect."

Very little is known about the children's early history. When they arrived at the DPRS office in early July, the children were poorly groomed and inappropriately dressed. The caseworker suspected that all three had been the victims of physical abuse, emotional abuse, and neglect. The children were immediately placed with an experienced foster care family in a rural community. The arrangement was meant to be temporary as their caseworker hoped to find the children an adoptive home within the year. In the fall, the oldest child was enrolled in the local public school for educational services. The younger two children were enrolled in the local Head Start program.

Presenting Problems

Within the first two weeks of classes at Head Start, the teacher reported concerns about Antonio's behavior. Antonio would routinely hit and kick other children, throw toys, and resist group activities. He would refuse to follow directions. His moods seemed to shift quickly, from cheerful to angry, and then to "spaced out." He also had speech problems that made him difficult to understand. Initially, Antonio exhibited most of his aggressive behavior at school. However, over time, Antonio became increasing aggressive in his foster home placement. Antonio's behavior suggested that he matched the description of aggressive attachment disorder.

While Maria was occasionally aggressive toward other children, her behavior in the classroom was quite different than her brother's. Maria was generally quiet and withdrawn in the classroom. She did not participate in group activities and, even during individual free play she spent much of her time just watching the other children. She was overly sensitive to others' comments and tended to cry easily. Like her brother, she had serious speech problems that made her almost impossible to understand. Because Maria was not acting out aggressively in the classroom, she was not identified for psychological services as quickly as her brother. Maria was first brought to the attention of the mental health team when her DPRS caseworker expressed a concern about her adjustment to foster care. Her behavior suggested an inhibited attachment disorder.

Treatment Plan

The DPRS caseworker agreed that Head Start could provide psychotherapeutic services to both Antonio and Maria. Each of the children was met individually for weekly play therapy appointments; joint therapy sessions were not conducted for several reasons. At the time the children were removed from their biological mother, they were at very different developmental levels. Each was dealing with the loss of their mother in his or her own way. Antonio was also becoming increasingly demanding and aggressive, and on one occasion verbalized feelings of "hatred" toward his sister. It would have been countertherapeutic to include Maria in sessions where she would have had to compete for attention and where she could have become the victim of aggression. For these reasons, it was decided that each of the children would benefit most from individual treatment.

Individual play therapy with Antonio was designed to address four major areas of concern: (1) Antonio's oppositional and aggressive behaviors, (2) his feelings of low self-esteem, (3) his feelings about being removed from his mother and placed in foster care, and (4) his difficulty in expressing his feelings appropriately. Maria's individual play therapy addressed the following areas: (1) Maria's withdrawn behaviors, (2) her difficulty adjusting to the loss of her mother, (3) her difficulty expressing her feelings appropriately, (4) her needs for nurturance, and (5) her parentified sense of responsibility.

Attaching to the Therapist

Antonio and Maria needed different kinds of assurances before they would allow themselves to develop a relationship with a therapist. Their different needs were reflected in the way they each approached therapy. When Antonio arrived for his first therapy session, he exhibited a great deal of energy. He entered the playroom without hesitation and immediately found a container of large plastic animals. He proceeded to take two of the adult animals and hit them together rather dramatically. He repeated this with two baby animals and stated, "They're fighting." Antonio left the animals and explored the other toys in the room. He found a pair of binoculars that he used to look at the therapist. He then found a gun set. He put on the belt and holster containing the gun and used the gun to shoot things in the room, including the therapist. The therapist interpreted Antonio's behavior as a sign that he did not feel safe. She shared her belief that Antonio was trying to shoot "bad people" and hypothesized that he might be shooting her because he thought she "might be bad." Antonio accepted this interpretation and continued shooting the gun.

In this session, Antonio entered the playroom with a statement about what he expected from the relationship (i.e., conflict) and seemed genuinely surprised when what transpired did not fit his expectations. Antonio spent several weeks checking out the therapist, as if through binoculars, before he began to trust her. During the fourth session, Antonio asked his therapist if she would be his "new mother." This request was the first outward sign that Antonio was actually starting to trust his therapist.

Maria became attached to her therapist much more quickly than her brother. For her first session, Maria was awakened from her afternoon nap. She walked into the therapy room, appearing rather drowsy, and started to play with the therapist's dolls. She hugged them, kissed them, and used bottles to feed them. The feeding ritual continued for quite some time; it appeared that the "babies" were very hungry. After feeding the dolls, Maria took one of the bottles and pretended to feed herself. The therapist recognized Maria's interest in the bottle and offered her a larger bottle "of her very own." Maria appeared very excited and immediately began to suck on her bottle vigorously.

Maria's extreme neediness as well as the therapist's sensitivity to her needs seemed to speed up the formation of the therapeutic relationship. By the end of the first therapy session, Maria seemed very interested in the attention of her therapist. One week later, when the therapist came to get Maria for her second session, she was lying awake on her cot. She had refused to take her nap that afternoon because she did not want to miss her appointment. It soon became clear that Maria had already begun to develop a trusting relationship with her therapist.

Attachment Themes Seen During Treatment

Attachment-disordered children typically exhibit a combination of play themes while in therapy. The themes of safety, anger, nurturance, consistency, and loss as described earlier seem to be particularly relevant for this population. While a combination of play themes is commonplace (across sessions or even within one session), it is also typical for these children to exhibit one or two predominant themes in their play. These predominant themes serve an important role in the therapy process as they tell the therapist where the client needs the most help. The therapist must be aware of the child's predominant theme in order to develop an appropriate treatment strategy.

Although Antonio and Maria had very similar histories, their presentations during therapy were dramatically different. Each presented with predominant play themes that were characteristic of their individual concerns. Antonio's therapy, for the most part, centered around themes of anger, safety, and loss. Maria, on the other hand, seemed to be most focused on issues of nurturance.

Antonio was seen for a total of twenty-five therapy sessions. Over one-third of Antonio's therapy sessions revolved around issues of safety. Early in therapy, Antonio tended to use the plastic animals to act out scenarios in which someone or something was in danger. The therapist's role during this play was to be the protector; the therapist was responsible for keeping the "babies" safe in a dangerous environment. As therapy progressed, there was a gradual shift in Antonio's safety play. Antonio began to use role play more routinely. He also began to take on the protector role himself. On several occasions, the babies and the therapist were in danger and Antonio came to their rescue. It was believed that this change reflected a shift in Antonio's perceptions about his place in the world.

The following scenario exemplifies how Antonio addressed safety themes during the middle phase of his treatment. During his fourteenth session, Antonio entered the therapy room and immediately picked up the bag of plastic animals. He got out two of the animals, threw them against the floor, and stated, "I don't like them. They bite." Antonio then got out the lions and tigers and made them fight among themselves. After quite a bit of fighting, the felines ganged up on a rather helpless turkey. During the conflict, one of the baby lions was injured. The therapist talked about how all babies needed to be safe, and Antonio responded by giving the therapist the injured cub. The therapist cared for the cub with the assistance of one of the adult lions while the fighting continued nearby. The injured cub watched the fighting along with several of the other lion cubs. One of the cubs, according to Antonio, did not want to watch the fighting. Almost impulsively, Antonio picked up the lion cubs and climbed inside a large box that was stored in the playroom. The box had been used as a "safe place" in earlier sessions and Antonio decided to use it again to keep himself and the babies safe from the fighting. The therapist acknowledged how important it was for all of them to be safe. Upon Antonio's request, the therapist covered the opening of the box with a large towel, so that "everyone was safe." She then read to Antonio until he appeared to feel safe once again.

In the above scenario, the therapist protected the "babies" while Antonio acted out the danger in the world. As the session progressed, Antonio began to experience strong emotions about his play, emotions that made him feel unsafe. Fortunately, Antonio had learned from previous sessions that he could increase his own sense of safety by retreating to a safe place. The irony of this situation was that Antonio needed a safe place (i.e., the box) within his safe place (i.e., the therapy room).

In addition to issues of safety, Antonio struggled with feelings related both to anger and to the loss of his mother. This was demonstrated in his fifth play therapy session. Antonio used the plastic animals as he had done in previous sessions. However, in this session he specifically stated that the plastic tigers were "boys" and that the gorilla was a "girl." Antonio began the session with the animals fighting. The therapist watched for a few minutes before intervening. The therapist suggested that the fighting could mean that the animals were "angry" and, moreover, that the animals could be angry because they wanted to see their mothers. The therapist asked Antonio if he ever thought about or wished to see his mother. Antonio acknowledged that he did think about his mother and proceeded to tell the therapist about some of his memories. The therapist told Antonio that sometimes children get angry when they cannot see their mothers and suggested that Antonio might feel this way at times. In response to the therapist's comment, Antonio took out the guns and began shooting the gorilla (the only female animal in the room). The therapist suggested that, while some guns might want to shoot the gorilla, other ones might not want to do so. The therapist then helped the guns argue about whether or not to shoot the gorilla. Antonio seemed particularly fond of this intervention. He made the guns argue until the end of the session.

Antonio struggled with his issues of loss by displaying anger frequently. In this session, Antonio's feelings about the loss of this mother became clear when he allowed the guns to argue about shooting the gorilla. While Antonio was angry at his mother for abandoning him, he also had positive feelings for her. Ambivalence characterized his experience of loss.

To help Antonio deal with his loss issues, the therapist introduced Antonio to the book, *Zachary's New Home* (Blomquist and Blomquist 1990). This book was specifically written to help children who were placed in foster care understand and deal with their losses. From its introduction, Antonio showed a great deal of interest in the book. At times, Antonio would gather all the animals around him and have his therapist read the story to the entire group. On other occasions, the animals would become angry and would fight in order to prevent the book from being read. Antonio would have the animals fight among themselves as a way to show some of the anger he felt because of the loss of his mother. The book, when it was read, seemed to help Antonio understand his situation more clearly.

Antonio's sister, Maria, was seen for a total of twenty-three individual therapy visits. Her therapy sessions were very different than her brother's as they typically centered around different themes. The most prominent theme in Maria's play was nurturance; Maria frequently played with dolls and bottles as a way of addressing these issues. Early in therapy, Maria indicated that her babies were very needy. Not only did they need food, but they also needed emotional support (i.e., hugs and kisses). Maria spent a great deal of time and energy tending to "my babies." She also put effort into tending to herself. During this time, Maria adopted one of the baby bottles as her "very own." She would routinely fill her bottle and keep it close to her throughout the session. Maria would also drink from her own bottle regularly while tending to her doll's needs. The babies' needs seemed to parallel Maria's own needs.

As therapy progressed, Maria's behaviors toward the dolls changed. At times, she was nurturing and caring, and at other times, she was neglectful and harsh. On one occasion, she even refused to feed her babies. It was believed that Maria was continuing to express the theme of nurturance in yet a different form. For Maria, her needs were directly tied to her experience of abuse and neglect. Maria used her therapy time to deal with these issues both directly and symbolically. When Maria was mistreating her babies, the therapist emphasized the babies' needs for food, clothing, positive attention, and safety. The therapist also acknowledged the reality that some babies do not get the things they need. Maria became increasing more attentive of her babies with these types of interventions.

The following scenario exemplifies Maria's play themes of nurturance. At the beginning of her fourteenth session, Maria announced that the therapist had been "naughty" and, as her punishment, she had to stand in the corner. Maria proceeded to surround the therapist with chairs to keep her from leaving the corner. When the therapist "cried," as instructed to do, Maria insisted that she stop crying. When the therapist did not stop, Maria became outwardly agitated and began hitting her until she did stop. At that point, the role play changed dramatically and Maria got out the dolls. The therapist was told to be the "mommy" while Maria played the role of the "big sister." Maria got out a book and read to the baby while the therapist did household chores. When the "mommy" had to change the baby's diapers, Maria helped. Maria then laid down to take a nap while the therapist prepared "snacks" for her two children. When Maria awoke from her pretend nap, she was very excited about the prepared snack and seemed to enjoyed it until the session ended.

The play theme of nurturance was clearly predominant during the above scenario. Maria demonstrated her concerns about nurturance from the position of a harsh disciplinarian as well as from the position of a caring older sister. While Maria continued to struggle with issues of nurturance throughout she therapy, she became increasingly less harsh and less abusive as therapy progressed. This change was attributed to the belief that Maria was able to address some of her needs for nurturance over the course of treatment.

Conclusion

Attachment-disordered children present many and varied challenges to the play therapist. We believe that Thematic Play Therapy offers an effective approach to helping these children. The initial challenge is to develop a trusting therapeutic relationship with the child and thus provide a secure base for the child. Thematic Play Therapy does this by using aspects of attachment formation, relationship enhancement, and overcoming resistance to build a therapeutic relationship. Specifically, the therapist provides consistency, warmth, and acceptance, sensitivity to the child's needs, and safety, both physical and psychological. Following the development of a trusting relationship, the therapist works to modify the child's internal working model of relationship with the caregiver (and others) and the child's internal working model of the self. The therapist uses role play, metaphor, catharsis, and when relevant, abreaction, as well as the relationship itself to provide experiences that contradict the child's working model and thus enables the child to modify that model. Five themes are particularly important to attachment-disordered children: safety, anger, consistency, nurturance, and loss. Resolution of the issues the child has around these themes within the context of the secure base provided by the relationship with the therapist is the heart of the therapeutic process. Thus, Thematic Play Therapy uses a variety of therapeutic factors within a framework based on attachment theory and object relations theory to provide a healing experience for those children whose early life history failed to supply a vitally needed secure, healthy attachment.

References

Ainsworth, M. D. S. (1982). Attachment: retrospect and prospect. In *The Place of Attachment in Human Behavior*, ed. C. M. Parkes, and J. Stevenson-Hinde, pp. 3–30. New York: Basic Books.

Ainsworth, M. D. S., Blehar, M. C., Waters, W., and Wall, S. (1978). *Patterns of Attachment*. Hillsdale, NJ: Lawrence Erlbaum.

Allen, J. (1988). *Inscapes of the Child's World*. Dallas, TX: Spring.

Allen, J., and Bertoia, J. (1992). *Written Paths to Healing: Education and Jungian Child Counseling*. Dallas, TX: Spring.

American Psychiatric Association. (1994). *Diagnostic and Statistical Manual of Mental Disorders*, 4th ed. Washington, DC: APA.

Axline, V. M. (1947). *Play Therapy*. New York: Ballantine.

Benedict, H. E. (1994). *Play assessment of young children*. Paper presented at the Eleventh Annual International Play Therapy Conference, San Antonio, TX, October.

Benedict, H. E., and Grigoryev, P. B. (1995). *Practical Application of Object Relations Theory to Play Therapy Techniques*. Paper presented at the Twelfth Annual International Play Therapy Conference, San Francisco, October.

Blomquist, G. M., and Blomquist, P. B. (1990). *Zachary's New Home*. New York: Magination.

Bow, J. N. (1993). Overcoming resistance. In *The Therapeutic Powers of Play*, ed. C. E. Schaefer, pp 17–40. Northvale, NJ: Jason Aronson.

Bowlby, J. (1969). *Attachment and Loss*, vol. 1. New York: Basic Books.

———— (1979). *The Making and Breaking of Affectional Bonds*. London: Tavistock.

_____ (1988). *A Secure Base: Parent–Child Attachment and Healthy Human Development.* New York: Basic Books.

Bretherton, I. (1991). Pouring new wine into old bottles: the social self as internal working model. In *Self Processes and Development: vol. 23. The Minnesota Symposia on Child Development,* ed. M. R. Gunnar, and L. A. Sroufe, pp. 1–41. Hillsdale, NJ: Lawrence Erlbaum.

Brody, V. A. (1993). *The Dialogue of Touch: The Developmental Play Therapy.* Treasure Island, FL: Developmental Play Training.

Cangelosi, D. M, (1993). Internal and external wars: Psychodynamic play therapy. In *Play Therapy in Action,* ed. T. Kottman, and C. Schaefer, pp. 347–370. Northvale, NJ: Jason Aronson.

Cicchetti, D., Toth, S. L., and Lynch, M. (1995). Bowlby's dream comes full circle: the application of attachment theory to risk and psychopathology. In *Advances in Clinical Child Psychology,* vol. 17, ed. T. H. Ollendick, and R. J. Prinz, pp. 1–75. New York: Plenum.

Crittenden, P. M. (1988). Relationships at risk. In *Clinical Implications of Attachment,* ed. J. Belsky, and T. Nezworski, pp. 136–174. Hillsdale, NJ: Lawrence Erlbaum.

_____ (1992a). Quality of attachment in the preschool years. *Development and Psychopathology* 4:209–241.

_____ (1992b). Treatment of anxious attachment in infancy and early childhood. *Development and Psychopathology* 4:575–602.

Cummings, E. M., and Cicchetti, D. (1990). Toward a transactional model of relations between attachment and depression. In *Attachment in the Preschool Years,* ed. M. T. Greenberg, D. Cicchetti, and E. M. Cummings, pp. 339–372. Chicago: University of Chicago Press.

Delaney, R. J. (1991). *Fostering Changes: Treating Attachment-Disordered Foster Children.* Fort Collins, CO: Corbett.

Egeland, B., Jacobvitz, D., and Sroufe, L. A. (1988). Breaking the cycle of abuse. *Child Development* 59:1080–1088.

Erickson, M. F., Korfmacher, J., and Egeland, B. R. (1992). Attachments past and present: implications for therapeutic intervention with mother–infant dyads. *Development and Psychopathology* 4:495–507.

Fraiberg, S., Adelson, E., and Shapiro, V. (1974). Ghosts in the nursery: a psychoanalytic approach to the problems of impaired infant-mother relationships. In *Clinical Studies in Infant Mental Health: The First Year of Life,* ed. S. Fraiberg, pp. 164–196. New York: Basic Books.

Frey, D. E. (1993). Learning by metaphor. In *The Therapeutic Powers of Play,* ed. C. E. Schaefer, pp. 223–240. Northvale: NJ: Jason Aronson.

Ginsberg, B. G. (1993). Catharsis. In *The Therapeutic Powers of Play,* ed. C. E. Schaefer, pp. 107–142. Northvale: NJ: Jason Aronson.

Guerney, L. F. (1993). Relationship enhancement. In *The Therapeutic Powers of*

Play, ed. C. E. Schaefer, pp. 267–290. Northvale: NJ: Jason Aronson.

Irwin, E. C., and Curry, N. E. (1993). Role play. In *The Therapeutic Powers of Play*, ed. C. E. Schaefer, pp. 167–188. Northvale: NJ: Jason Aronson.

James, B. (1989). *Treating Traumatized Children: New Insights and Creative Interventions*. Lexington, MA: Lexington.

————— (1994). *Handbook for Treatment of Attachment-Trauma Problems in Children*. New York: Lexington.

Jernberg, A. M. (1979). *Theraplay: A New Treatment Using Structured Play for Problem Children and Their Families*. San Francisco: Jossey-Bass.

————— (1993). Attachment formation. In *The Therapeutic Powers of Play*, ed. C. E. Schaefer, pp. 241–266. Northvale: NJ: Jason Aronson.

Karen, R. (1990). Becoming attached. *The Atlantic Monthly*, February, pp. 35–70.

Kraemer, G. W. (1992). A psychobiological theory of attachment. *Behavioral and Brain Sciences* 15:493–541.

Landreth, G. L. (1993). Self-expressive communication. In *The Therapeutic Powers of Play*, ed. C. E. Schaefer. Northvale, New Jersey: Jason Aronson.

Lieberman, A. F. (1992). Infant–parent psychotherapy with toddlers. *Development and Psychopathology* 4:559–574.

Lieberman, A. F., and Pawl, J, H. (1988). Clinical applications of attachment theory. In *Clinical Implications of Attachment*, ed. J. Belsky, and T. Nezworski, pp. 327–351. Hillsdale, NJ: Lawrence Erlbaum.

Main, M., and Solomon, J. (1986). Discovery of a disorganized/disoriented attachment pattern. In *Affective Development in Infancy*, ed. T. B. Brazelton, and M. W. Yogman, pp. 95–124. Norwood, NJ: Ablex.

McMillen, J. C. (1992). Attachment theory and clinical social work. *Clinical Social Work Journal* 20(2):205–218.

Mills, B., and Allan, J. (1991). *Play therapy with the maltreated child*. Paper presented at the meeting of the Association for Play Therapy, Breckenridge, CO, October.

Mills, J. C., and Crowley, R. J. (1986). *Therapeutic Metaphors for Children and the Child Within*. New York: Brunner/Mazel.

Mongoven, L. B. (1995). *Disorders of attachment: theoretical issues and the treatment of preschoolers*. Unpublished Doctoral Project, Baylor University, Waco, TX.

Nezworski, T., Tolan, W. J., and Belsky, J. (1988). Intervention in insecure infant attachment. In *Clinical Implications of Attachment*, ed. J. Belsky, and T. Nezworski, pp. 352–386. Hillsdale, NJ: Lawrence Erlbaum.

Oaklander, V. (1988). *Windows to Our Children: A Gestalt Therapy Approach to Children and Adolescents*. Highland, NY: Center for Gestalt Development.

O'Connor, K. J. (1991). *The Play Therapy Primer*. New York: Wiley.

————— (1994). Ecosystemic play therapy. In *Handbook of Play Therapy*, vol. 2, ed. K. J. O'Connor, and C. E. Schaefer, pp. 61–84. New York: Wiley.

O'Connor, K. J., and Schaefer, C. E., eds. (1994). *Handbook of Play Therapy*, vol. 2. New York: Wiley.

Oremland, E. K. (1993). Abreaction. In *The Therapeutic Powers of Play*, ed. C. E. Schaefer, pp. 143–166. Northvale: NJ: Jason Aronson.

Paterson, R. J., and Morgan, G. (1988). Attachment theory, personality, development, and psychotherapy. *Clinical Psychology Review* 8:611–636.

Petrick, C. (1994). *Implications of the object relations theories of Mahler and Winnicott for play therapy*. Unpublished doctoral clinical project, Baylor University, Waco, TX.

Rodning, C., Beckwith, L., and Howard, J. (1991). Quality of attachment and home environment in children prenatally exposed to PCP and cocaine. *Development and Psychopathology* 3:351–366.

Rutter, M. (1979). Maternal deprivation, 1972–1979: new findings, new concepts, new approaches. *Child Development* 55:305–314.

Schaefer, C. E., ed. (1988). *Innovative Interventions in Child and Adolescent Therapy*. New York: Wiley.

Schaefer, C. E. (1993). What is play and why is it therapeutic? In *The Therapeutic Powers of Play*, pp. 1–15. Northvale, NJ: Jason Aronson.

Schaefer, C. E., and O'Connor, K. J., eds. (1983). *Handbook of Play Therapy*. New York: Wiley.

Speltz, M. L. (1990). The treatment of preschool conduct problems: an integration of behavioral and attachment concepts. In *Attachment in the Preschool Years*, ed. M. T. Greenberg, D. Cicchetti, and E. M. Cummings, pp. 399–426. Chicago: University of Chicago Press.

Sroufe, L. A. (1983). Infant-caregiver attachment and patterns of adaptation in preschool: the roots of maladaptation and competence. In *Minnesota Symposium in Child Psychology*, ed. M. Perlmutter, pp. 41–83. Hillsdale, NJ: Lawrence Erlbaum.

——— (1986). Appraisal: Bowlby's contribution to psychoanalytic theory and developmental psychology; attachment: separation: loss. *Journal of Child Psychology and Psychiatry and Allied Disciplines* 27(6):841–849.

——— (1988). The role of infant–caregiver attachment in development. In *Clinical Implications of Attachment*, ed. J. Belsky, and T. Nezworski, pp. 18–38. Hillsdale, NJ: Lawrence Erlbaum.

——— (1989). Relationships and relationship disturbance. In *Relationship Disturbance in Early Childhood*, ed. A. Sameroff, and R. Emde, pp. 97–124. New York: Basic Books.

Suess, G. J., Grossmann, K. E., and Sroufe, L. A. (1992). Effects of infant attachment to mother and father on quality of adaptation in preschool: from dyad to individual organization of self. *International Journal of Behavioral Development* 15(1):43–65.

Terr, L. (1990). *Too Scared to Cry: How Trauma Affects Children and Ultimately Us All*. New York: Basic Books.

Tulving, E. (1985). How many memory systems are there? *American Psychologist* 40:385–398.

Zeanah, C. H. Jr., Mammen, O. K., and Lieberman, A. F. (1993). Disorders of attachment. In *Handbook of Infant Mental Health*, ed. C. H. Zeanah, Jr., pp. 322–349. New York: Guilford.

12

Play Therapy with the Resistant Child

James N. Bow

Developing and maintaining a psychotherapeutic relationship with children is a major challenge. Therapists are often frustrated by their attempts to engage children so that therapeutic progress can be made. Each therapist can recollect stories of the Quiet Mary, Withdrawn Tom, Hostile Harry, Tornado John, and Stealing Melissa, who challenged his/her therapeutic skills and knowledge. Such cases often cause bewilderment and despair among therapists. In this chapter the concept of resistance is reviewed and examples of how it surfaces in various phases of treatment are discussed. The curative powers of therapeutic play for overcoming resistance are discussed, along with specific intervention techniques. Lastly, case examples are provided.

Background

Resistance is defined as any behavior, thought, or feeling that hinders or interferes with the development and maintenance of a working alliance and the child's progress in therapy. Resistance may surface in any phase of treatment. It can present as overt or covert and may vary in intensity from mild to severe. Resistance presents in various stages of treatment with different underlying dynamics in each situation.

Play therapy is often divided into four stages: initial, acting out/regressive, growth, and termination. Each stage is unique and reflects different aspects of the treatment process. During the initial stage, children are introduced to play therapy. They explore the playroom and toys. Trust is established in the therapist, which facilitates the development of a treatment alliance. Resistance at this stage of treatment may be manifested as a refusal to enter the therapist's office, temper tantrums, hiding behind furniture, running uncontrollably about the office, destroying toys, and/or refusing to talk or listen.

Many different dynamics may underlie the child's resistance during this initial stage. First, children do not usually initiate treatment (Gardner 1979). Referrals are usually made by their parent(s), teacher, or the court. Therefore, motivation and commitment is usually lacking in the child client. Second, children are sometimes provided with misinformation by the parent about the purpose and intent of therapy prior to the initial session. This leads to distrust of the whole process because the child perceives the parent and therapist as aligned. Another dynamic is that children often perceive therapy as punishment. They view themselves as being singled out and blamed for family/school problems (Bow 1988). An extension of this dynamic is the fear of being labeled as different and needing help, which therapy infers. Children tend to view their behavior as ego syntonic. They usually lack insight into their problems. Furthermore, they are concerned that others will find out that they are in treatment. A fourth dynamic is that children are often fearful and scared (Markowitz 1959) of the initial therapeutic encounter. It is an unfamiliar setting that is confusing and anxiety provoking (Gabel et al. 1988). This difficulty is further complicated when children have been abused and/or neglected (Mann and McDermott 1983). Such children often feel vulnerable and powerless and fear further harm. Therapeutic involvement may be avoided by these children because it is a threat to their sense of security. Lastly, loyalty issues surface in divorce situations when one parent pursues treatment for the child over the wishes of the other parent. The child will often act out the wishes of the parent who opposes treatment as a means of showing loyalty to that parent. These loyalty issues also arise in court-ordered abuse/neglect treatment cases in which the parent(s) oppose therapy (Bow 1988).

During the acting-out/regressive stage of play therapy, limit testing begins and unresolved conflicts surface during play. Due to the trusting, safe, and protective relationship the child has developed with the therapist, ego defenses are reduced and thus the ego regresses. Resistance may be manifested as limit testing, infantile behavior, and/or acting-out behavior. Limit testing may include challenging the therapist's authority, violating therapy rules, cheating during games, or avoiding sessions. Infantile behavior is characterized by whining, clinging, demanding, tantrums, and/or silliness. Baby talk or mutism may also be present. Acting-out behavior is usually seen as aggression toward self or others, destroying toys, and/or stealing toys. In terms of play, avoidance or minimal involvement with toys or the therapist may reflect resistance. Erratic and disorganized or inhibited and rigid play may also suggest resistance. Defensiveness toward therapeutic interventions further suggests resistance.

In terms of dynamics, children commonly reenact past patterns of behavior and identify with the aggressor (Mordock 1994). Children's interactions with their therapists directly reflect past ways of relating to adult figures. When interaction patterns have been dysfunctional they are magnified in the therapy setting. For instance, children will have difficulty accepting attention from a caring adult who views them in a positive way if they have rarely been treated that way (Gabel et al. 1988). Another factor that can contribute to resistance is when children are overwhelmed by strong feelings that threaten their sense of self-control (Dodds 1987). Gardner (1979) notes that resistance also surfaces as protection against facing inadequacies. In most cases, children view their symptoms in an ego-syntonic manner and they have little insight into their difficulties. As therapy progresses, they gain insight into the dysfunctional nature of their symptoms. This is threatening and they attempt to protect themselves from feelings of inadequacy. The dependence/independence dynamic also surfaces during this stage. Children will attempt to deny their reliance and dependency on others through opposing controls and rules.

During the growth stage of play therapy, children integrate and work through past trauma or negative experiences (O'Connor 1991). Interpretations are widely used by the therapist. A sense of mastery and competency is attained. Conflicts are gradually resolved. Resistance may be manifested during this stage as difficulty leaving sessions, testing the therapist's degree of concern and trust, and jealousy toward other clients. Dynamics may revolve around dependence/independence issues and ownership of the therapist. During this stage, children become very attached to the therapist. They often demand additional time or request to take home office toys. It is a way of gaining more contact or connectedness. Furthermore, they show jealousy toward other clients and may ask their therapist who he/she likes better or request that other children not play with certain toys or projects.

In the termination stage, children consolidate their therapeutic gains and work through feelings surrounding the closure of therapy. Symptoms are reduced or eliminated and therapeutic goals are attained. Play may symbolically reveal themes of independence, autonomy from adult figures, leaving home, and control of interpersonal connections (Dodds 1987). Resistance commonly takes the form of missed sessions or abrupt termination, destroying toys, a regression in functioning, angry outbursts, avoidance of therapeutic material, and wanting to take home personal items or toys. Dynamics may revolve around perceived abandonment and loss (Gabel et al. 1988). Termination often re-creates painful memories of loss. This process is exacerbated when children have experienced major and recent losses. Termination also creates feelings of rejection. Anger and sadness surface as a reaction to the loss of a valued relationship (Dodds 1987). Separation anxiety and difficulty detaching are other dynamics underlying resistance. Children may experience fear and panic once the therapeutic relationship is terminated. Their special time with an accepting, supportive adult is no longer available. Now problems and concerns have to be addressed without the input of this valued individual—the therapist.

Resistance is an expectable occurrence in the course of therapy, but varies in type, quantity, and intensity. Resistance can be broadly categorized as externalizing or internalizing behaviors. Externalizing behaviors include aggression, destruction, noncompliance, and/or negativism, whereas, avoidance, mutism, passive-aggressive traits, and fearfulness are internalizing behaviors. The type of resistance reveals valuable information about how the child copes and reacts to psychic conflict and distress. However, it is even more crucial to analyze the amount and intensity of the resistance. As noted by Moustakas (1982), disturbed children present negative attitudes, such as anger, anxiety, hostility, and fear, more frequently and intensely. Also, the attitudes are less focused and less directed. Through assessing these factors, therapists will better understand the degree of disturbance.

It is also critical to evaluate possible factors underlying children's resistance. Through understanding motives, feelings, and attitudes underlying resistant behavior the therapist is better able to deal with resistance and choose appropriate therapeutic interventions. The next section will discuss traditional treatment strategies with resistant children, followed by the rationale for using play.

Traditional Treatment Strategies

A variety of psychotherapy approaches have been tried in dealing with resistance. Traditional talk therapy, that is, individual therapy focusing on the child talking about his/her feelings and thoughts, is probably the most common. The major drawback with this approach is that children are action oriented and often lack the necessary verbal skills to make this approach highly effective. Family therapy has also been used to address resistance. Again though, it relies heavily on verbalization. It also focuses more on family dynamics than individual issues. A third approach is group therapy, which is based on group members confronting each others' resistance. Much reliance is placed on verbalization and adequate social skills, which limits its use with child clients. Music/art therapy is another approach. Although effective with some resistant children, its use is less universal than play.

Rationale for Play

Purpose

Play is effective with children for a variety of reasons. Play is a natural way for children to communicate (Landreth 1993). Children are action oriented and play is an ideal way for them to express their feelings and thoughts. It is a symbolic language for expressing unconscious and conscious conflicts and allows children to play out their experiences (Amster 1982).

Children also have very rich fantasy lives, which they can utilize in play. Children lack the defensive structure seen in adults (Amster 1982). Therefore, their egos can easily regress. Through reenacting past negative events or experiences in play, children can search for new solutions and develop a sense of mastery (O'Connor 1991).

Play also acts as a bridge between the child and therapist (Carek 1972) and creates a comfort barrier (Dodds 1987). As a result, it is less threatening than other forms of therapy.

Analyzing a child's play provides valuable information about his/her cognitive, language, motoric, and social development (Schaefer 1993). Play is helpful for identifying problem areas or psychic conflicts that need to be addressed in therapy. Play also helps children work through conflicts and gain mastery, which gives them a sense of control and competency.

Therapeutic Powers of Play That Apply to Resistant Children

Schaefer (1993) outlines fourteen therapeutic factors of play. The first factor, overcoming resistance and thereby developing a working alliance, is the focus of this chapter. Little can be accomplished in therapy without a working alliance. However, all the other factors play a critical role, too. Communication, creative thinking, and fantasy help resistant children develop self-understanding, identify solutions to problems, and learn imagery techniques. Role playing, game play, and metaphoric teaching encourage children to practice and acquire new behavior, develop appropriate social skills, and gain insight in a nonthreatening and fun way. Attachment formation and relationship enhancement, although initially difficult for resistant children to develop, happen later in treatment and promote closeness to others and a sense of bonding. Catharsis, abreaction, and positive emotions help resistant children release negative emotions, work through trauma, and express positive emotions. Lastly, mastering developmental fears and gaining a sense of competency in resistant children assists them in resolving psychic conflicts.

Approaches

Description

Gaining a child's involvement and commitment to treatment can be a major challenge. Four important aspects in this process will be discussed: the therapist's personality, establishing the relationship, toy selection, and initial contact.

The Therapist's Personality

The therapist's personality is probably the most important and critical variable in this process. A sensitive and caring attitude is necessary, along with inner warmth (Gabel et al. 1988). These attributes help create an atmosphere of concern and support. The therapist also needs to convey acceptance and an ability to self-project. The latter refers to the therapist's ability to place him/ herself in the child's situation and understand what he is experiencing (Gardner 1975). The therapist should also be trustworthy and create a sense of safety and protection for the child. Flexibility is another crucial factor in dealing with children. The therapist must be able to adapt and adjust because each child is unique and has ever-changing needs. Furthermore, a sense of humor is helpful (Salameh 1986).

Therapists also need to understand child culture, with an awareness of current interests and trends. However, therapists should not try to imitate the clothing or jargon used by children because it would interfere with the up-coming separation and individuation process. The child's expression of his culture reveals significant information about self-identity.

Patience is another important characteristic for therapists. Children progress at different rates. Among resistant children, the development of a therapeutic alliance is a gradual and difficult process. Also, resistance surfaces during other stages of treatment. During these times the therapist must play the role of a model and educator and patiently handle difficult situations.

Therapists must also have insight into personal issues that may have an impact on treatment. By doing this, therapists can avoid antitherapeutic roles such as the perfect parent, rescuer, or enabler.

Establishing the Relationship

The second step in engaging children in therapy involves establishing a relation-ship. A consistent time together with a therapist makes the child feel important and valued. A comfortable, safe, and nonthreatening environment also en-hances the relationship. Proper expectations in the cognitive and social-emotional areas are also important to the relationship. The child's cognitive abilities, along with strengths and weaknesses need to be considered. Social-emotional functioning varies widely among children and can have important implications for therapy. For example, a child with an attention deficit hyper-activity disorder (ADHD) would have difficulty sitting and attending for 45 minutes. Therefore, the type of strategies and play activities vary depending on the child's specific problems and level of functioning.

It is important for children to understand that the role of a therapist is to help them, not control them. Power struggles should be avoided. Providing choices is one way of avoiding power struggles and simultaneously increasing the child's sense of control.

When parents schedule the first therapy appointment it is important to give them suggestions about how to inform the child about the initial play therapy session. The following are helpful suggestions for parents (Bow 1993). First, be honest and open. Second, prepare the child a few days before the appointment. Don't wait until the morning of the appointment. Third, discuss the reason for the appointment, such as, "We have been yelling and arguing a lot. Maybe this person can help us get along better." Fourth, explain that the therapist helps children and families deal with worries and concerns and that both talking and playing are involved. Lastly, stress that no medical procedures will be performed such as blood work or shots. A good book for parents and children about this subject matter is *A Child's First Book About Play Therapy* (Nemiroff and Annunziata 1990).

It is critical to clarify confidentiality issues during the first session. Children and parents need to understand the boundaries and limits of confidentiality. There are three instances in which confidentiality should be violated: danger to self, danger to others, and suspicion of abuse/neglect. Through clarifying these issues future controversies and ethical dilemmas can be avoided.

Toy Selection

The selection of toys for play therapy has specific diagnostic and therapeutic purposes. The type of toys available determines the form and extent of play exhibited by the child (Landreth 1993). Ginott (1982a) recommends toys that permit reality testing, allow children to express their need symbolically, and encourage catharsis and insight. In addition, toys should have a variety of uses and allow exploration. They should allow the child to tap into difficult feelings, such as aggression and dependency (Ginott 1982a). They should encourage interaction between the child and therapist. And lastly, toys must be durable and safe, especially when working with aggressive and destructive children.

Carek (1972) categorizes play things into three classes. In the first class are toys that facilitate self-expression, such as crayons, pencils, puppets, play house(s), and cars. Toys in the second class facilitate regression, such as clay, sand, water, and finger paints. The third class includes board and card games that involve competition between the child and therapist.

Landreth (1993) defines three broad groups of toys. Real-life toys consists of dollhouse and family, puppets, and nondescript figures that can represent the child's family. Cars, trucks, boats, and cash register can symbolize other real-life situations. A second group is acting-out aggressive-release toys. Bop bag, toy soldiers, guns, wild toy animals, pounding pegboard, and rubber knife are in this group and allow the expression of anger and hostility. The last group involves toys for creative expression and emotional release. Sand, water, and clay are in this group. Therefore, a wide variety of toys from the above categories should be available to address diagnostic and therapeutic issues.

In terms of diagnostic issues, play allows the therapist to analyze intrapersonal and interpersonal features of behavioral expression. The child's reaction to the playroom is the first important area to assess. Is he fearful and scared or stimulated and aroused? This response pattern reveals information about the child's adjustment to new situations. A second area to assess is the degree of self-control shown. Is the child driven, moving quickly from activity to activity, or reserved and inhibited, with a cautious and deliberate style of playing? The state of the ego is revealed, spontaneous versus rigid, along with the balance between impulses/drives and ego material. The age-appropriateness of toys/activities is determined by the developmental line of play, which is another important area to assess. Representational play allows children to express their feelings and desires through action. This type of play is usually present until age 2. After age 2, symbolic or pretend play starts. Fantasy predominates, with puppets and toys taking a variety of "as if" stances. Around age 6, games with rules begin, with strong competitive and interpersonal components. The specific type of toys, activities, and fantasy material that the child chooses should be assessed. Each has symbolic meaning. Furthermore, it is important to assess the type of themes that surface during play, which provides information about the child's fantasies and the nature of his/her psychic conflicts. The quantity and intensity of each theme provides valuable information about the degree of disturbance (Schaefer 1979).

Initial Contact

Agencies vary in their intake procedures. Some child agencies gather intake information from the parent(s) during the first session without the child being present, with the therapist meeting the child during the second session. Other agencies perform the intake during the first session with both the parent(s) and child present. Irregardless of the intake procedure, it is important that the following be gathered or assessed: comprehensive psychosocial history; identification of major problem areas and treatment goals; and observation of the parent–child interaction style. The latter should occur in both the waiting room and therapy office and include observations of both verbal and nonverbal interactions.

During the initial contact with the child, the therapist needs to present as friendly, self-assured, and competent. A sense of control needs to be portrayed. However, the therapist shouldn't act in an intimidating or overbearing manner. Bending down to the child's level, with an awareness of interpersonal space, will create a comfortable and caring atmosphere. Asking the child what name he/she would like to be called is another way of showing the child you are sensitive to his/her needs. Often during the first meeting it is best to see young children with their parents, at least for a portion of the play session. This reduces the child's anxiety, allows an opportunity to watch the parent–child interaction, and affords an opportunity to clarify the purpose and intent of play therapy. After about 20 minutes, the child is usually comfortable enough for the parent to return to the waiting room. At that point, the child can be introduced to play materials and activities.

How play develops during the session is very important to assess. Normal children have a smooth unfolding of play, whereas the play of disturbed children is often disjointed. Another area to assess is how closely the play represents the specific area of conflict. A moderate degree of displacement is healthy. Psychotic children show little visible connection, while the play of conduct disordered children is transparent (Bow 1993). The emotional reaction exhibited by the child is also important to analyze because it reflects the child's perception of the world. Is the child frightened/anxious, indifferent, hyperaroused, or happy? Healthy play is characterized by the latter. Furthermore, the ability to suspend reality is another area to explore. Normal play involves the ability to move between internal and external reality, while maintaining clear reality ties. Psychotic children become overconsumed with fantasy and lose external ties, whereas obsessive-compulsive children cling to external reality and avoid fantasy.

The amount of talking during the play sessions reveals valuable information about the child's style of interacting. Some children play with no talk, while at the other extreme some children talk and avoid play. For play therapy purposes, it is best for children to both play and talk. Another area to assess is the child's reaction to the therapist and interventions. Does the child view the therapist as an authority figure, playmate, or source of unconditional acceptance? In terms of interventions, does the child ignore them, become overly defensive/resistant, or stop playing?

The level of social play is also critical to assess. Partin (1932) outlines six stages of play: unoccupied behavior, onlooker, solitary, parallel, associative, and cooperative. Unoccupied behavior involves looking around the room. Some simple movements may occur, but they are not goal directed. The onlooker watches others, but doesn't join in. In solitary play, the child plays alone, showing no interest in the activities of others. Parallel play occurs when the child is playing in the close vicinity of other children, with similar toys, but without any direct interaction. Associative play consists of interacting with other children in a play setting, but without a common goal. It usually appears during the early preschool years. Cooperative play happens when children socialize and play together with a common goal. This begins in the late preschool years.

Through analyzing these different aspects of play, the therapist is better able to understand the child's resistance and dynamics, degree of disturbance, and type of psychopathology. This will assist in making treatment plans and developing appropriate interventions. The next section focuses on specific intervention techniques to use with resistant children.

Techniques for Overcoming Resistance

Structuring the Session

Resistant children vary in the type and amount of structure they need during play therapy sessions. Play therapy sessions can vary on a continuum from unstructured to structured. The following factors determine the degree of structure: type of setting, therapist's role, type of psychopathology presented by the child, and specific type of toys and play materials available.

Play therapy can occur in a variety of settings, such as the therapist's office, playroom, or activity room. Sessions in the therapist's office usually need to be much more structured due to the presence of nonplay materials. Play and activity rooms allow greater freedom and less structure.

The therapist's role can vary from nondirective to directive. In the nondirective approach, the therapist observes the child's play, with a focus on the child's frame of reference, and a belief that the children are able to resolve their own conflicts. Reflection is commonly used. Therapists with a directive orientation attempt to facilitate play to address specific issues or concerns. They are also more assertive with interventions. In general, the directive approach is considered structured, while the nondirective is viewed as unstructured.

Kissel (1990) selects toys/materials according to the type of psychopathology exhibited by the child. He places children into two categories, too loose or too tight. Children in the too loose category display poor self-control and conduct-related problems, while the too tight category is composed of fearful, anxious, depressed, and inhibited children. Loosening toys/materials include clay/dough, crayons, paper, finger paints, blocks, punching bag, and sandbox. These toys/materials create a free and spontaneous setting, which relaxes the child's defenses. Tightening toys/materials involve models, board games, checkers, video recorders, and cards. These toys/materials provide structure and contain impulses and drives. Play activities are planned accordingly, with too loose children having structured activities (e.g., board games, models, and cards) and too tight children having unstructured activities (e.g., crayons, blocks, clay, and punching bag). Therefore, play materials and activities are planned depending on the type of psychopathology and type of resistance, along with the need for structure.

Furthermore, Bow (1988, 1993) discusses a variety of innovative play activities with resistant children, including the hidden puppet, storytelling, family word association game, and affective coloring tasks. These techniques gain the attention and involvement of children, break down resistance, and are goal oriented.

All these factors need to be considered in dealing with resistant children in play therapy. Acting-out, impulsive children will need a small playroom, with a directive approach, and a toy selection that contains impulses and drives. A nondirective approach, with greater freedom in the playroom, and toys that allow spontaneous expression, are best for withdrawn and quiet children.

Limits in Therapy

Resistant children frequently test limits. This occurs for a variety of reasons. It is important for therapists to explore the dynamics underlying limit testing and attempt to understand the rationale for limits. Ginott (1982b) outlines the following reasons for limits: (1) to encourage acting out of feelings through symbolic channels; (2) to allow therapists to maintain an empathic and accepting attitude; (3) to assure a safe environment for the child and therapist; and (4) to increase the child's ego control by providing structure.

The following limit setting techniques are recommended by Ginott (1982b). First, recognize the child's feelings and help him/her identify them, such as anger or disappointment. Second, clearly state the limit, for example, "No hitting is allowed." Third, point out alternative channels that the child can use to express feelings, such as, "You can't hit me, but you may hit the punching bag." Fourth, help the child discuss feelings that arise from the limit, for example, frustration. Throughout this process, the therapist must remain calm, focused, and matter-of-fact. Limits should not be given in a threatening or punitive manner.

When setting rules or limits it is important to prioritize them, especially with resistant children. Most rules and limits focus on safety, protection of play materials, and socially unacceptable behavior (e.g., spitting and chronic profanity). When dealing with externalizing or too loose resistant children, it is best to outline basic expectations and rules at the beginning of the session.

Modeling

Kissel (1990) and Gardner (1975) discuss the importance of modeling. A therapist acts as a role model for interpersonal relationships. His/her ability to relate and interact in a positive manner has a direct impact on the child's ability to develop such skills. Also, the therapist's ability to deal with frustration and other negative feelings during the session is a positive learning experience for the child. By a therapist modeling anger control and problem-solving strategies, the child sees how these techniques are used properly. In addition, a therapist's ability to deal with secrets or confidential information teaches the child the importance of personal boundaries and proper information exchange. Overall, it is hoped that children will view their therapists as ego-ideals and attempt to emulate their behavior.

Joining Techniques

Marshall (1982) describes a variety of intervention techniques that he groups under the label of joining. Affirmation refers to accepting and valuing the child's communication. It implies that the defense-resistance will not be challenged, opposed, or removed until the child feels ready. A second technique is satiation. This involves the therapist creating a situation so that the child sees the inappropriateness of his/her resistant response. This allows underlying affect, conflicts, and concerns to surface. For example, if a child is tapping the table with a pencil and refuses to listen, the therapist would request that the child continue that behavior for 15 minutes. Prescribing the resistance is another technique, which is best with oppositional or negatively suggestible children. It consists of creating paradoxical situations by prescribing the child to exercise the resistance. A classic example of this is a child who refuses to talk and the therapist prescribes that he not talk for the remainder of the session. A fourth joining technique mentioned is mirroring. It involves imitating the child's verbal and nonverbal actions.

Other Intervention Techniques

Lewis (1974) outlines five different levels of interventions. The first is attention statements, in which the therapist's comments make the child aware of his actions. For example, "I see you're hitting the mother doll." Reductive statements tie together unnoticed and dissimilar patterns of behavior into common form, such as "I notice that when you make up play situations you like to be the strong hero." Situational statements attempt to make the child aware of those situations that give raise to certain feelings or behaviors. For example, "Whenever you play with the mother doll you become very angry." Transference interpretations attempt to show how the child's conflicts surface in the therapeutic relationship, such as "You seem very worried that I'll get mad at you and leave you, like your father left you and your mother." Etiology statements attempt to link current behavior with past developmental events. For example, "It seems that remembering how helpless you were as a very young child makes you want to be very tough now."

In terms of interpretations, Harter (1983) identifies four levels. The first level involves interpreting through a toy/object that has some meaning to the child, such as "Casper (puppet) is angry at his father for working all the time." The next level consists of interpreting through a toy/object, but making a connection to the child. For example, "Do you ever feel like Casper?" The third level involves indirect interpretation. The therapist discusses a similar problem experienced by an anonymous client or friend, but makes no connection to the child. "Johnny started stealing because he was angry at his father for working too much" would be an example of this type of interpretation. The fourth level consists of direct interpretations, such as "Your stealing appears related to your anger toward your father for never being available."

Two prerequisites are important before making interpretations, especially with resistant children. First, a relationship between the therapist and child must be established. The therapist must know the child fairly well to make valid interpretations, and a degree of trust needs to be developed. Second, the child must be psychologically ready to accept an interpretation. This is dependent on the type of psychological defenses utilized by the child, along with the child's potential for self-observation and insight.

When a child is distressed by an interpretation or intervention it may surface in the following ways: the child stops playing; the child moves away from the therapist; the child quickly changes play activities; the child asks to leave the room (e.g., to go to the bathroom, join mother in the lobby); or the child becomes anxious, agitated, unfocused, or restless.

Case Illustrations

The following cases illustrate the concepts and techniques discussed in dealing with resistant children with different types of social-emotional problems. The first case focuses on an angry firesetter from a dysfunctional/abusive family. The second case is about a quiet, sad, and withdrawn girl who has difficulty separating from her mother. The last case discusses a conduct-disordered boy, with strong oppositional-defiant traits.

Case 1

David, a 7-year-old, was referred for inpatient hospitalization because of firesetting. He had set a fire in his bedroom, which burned the house down. The psychosocial history revealed a very dysfunctional family, with a chronic history of physical abuse by the stepfather. David readily entered the playroom, but seemed detached from the therapist. Some basic expectations were reviewed, along with issues of confidentiality. David moved quickly around the playroom, exploring one activity after another. He talked to himself ("Boy, is this cool!"), but avoided direct interaction with the therapist. He finally pulled the dollhouse off the shelf and asked, "Where are the people?" This was his first direct interaction with the therapist. Assistance was provided and the figures were found in the back room of the dollhouse. As he played with the dollhouse his play was very transparent, with little displacement from actual life events. He said, "Did you know I burned my house down?" The therapist acknowledged that he knew this fact and explored David's feelings and thoughts about the incident. He expressed sadness over losing his dog in the fire, but noted that nobody else was hurt. David also expressed an interest in seeing where his house used to be located, noting he currently resides in a trailer. Toward the end of the session, David started playing with the puppets. He chose the big bad wolf and moved about the room ordering the other puppets and therapist around in an intimidating and threatening manner. Themes of power/control, loss, and trust surfaced during this session. At this stage, attention and affirmation statements were used.

During the next few sessions, repetitive play patterns continued over the firesetting. David talked more about his feelings and anger toward family members, especially his stepfather. As the therapeutic alliance was established, an increase in acting-out behavior was evident. His play became more aggressive and destructive. He seemed to have difficulty accepting a warm, caring adult. Furthermore, he was reenacting past patterns of interacting with his stepfather. Therefore, limits were reviewed, along with ways to appropriately channel negative feelings. Situational statements were also used, such as "When you talk about your stepfather you become very upset and angry," in order to help increase David's self-awareness. Emphasis was also given to increasing David's emotional vocabulary through identifying and labeling feelings. Greater structure was required to contain and control drives and impulses and to provide a safe and protective environment.

Dynamics were directly addressed as he moved into the growth stage of play therapy. A variety of intervention techniques were utilized, including transference interpretation (e.g., "You fear that I will treat you like your stepfather treated you"), etiological statements (e.g., "Remembering how you were abused as a very young child makes you want to be tough and in control at this time"). Harter's (1983) different levels of interpretations were also used (e.g., level 1 – "The big bad wolf was so angry he wanted to strike out at those that have hurt him"; level 2 – "Did you ever feel like the big bad wolf?"; and level 3 – "Some children are so angry about being hurt that they want to destroy or hurt others. Have you ever felt like that?"). The focus was on linking understanding with feelings and reducing troublesome feelings. There was also an emphasis on finding more acceptable ways of expressing needs and negative feelings. In addition, anger control techniques were taught through puppet play.

During the growth stage David showed increased attachment to the therapist. He showed jealousy toward other clients, often asking questions about them. He also experienced difficulty leaving the session if another client was scheduled after his session. Reframing comments and interpretations were utilized to address these ownership issues.

As David entered the termination phase and discharge from the hospital approached, some acting-out behavior resurfaced. However, he responded well to ego support and interpretations. Therapy focused on consolidating his gains, working through issues surrounding termination (e.g., loss), and helping him accept aftercare plans (i.e., residential placement). The patient's play showed increased themes of independence and more adaptable coping strategies. A drawing/picture book was also compiled by David of his experiences and accomplishments at the hospital, which assisted him in reviewing his progress and providing therapeutic closure.

This case illustrates the effectiveness of play therapy with an angry, resistant child. It shows how play assisted in the development of a therapeutic alliance, identified psychic conflicts, allowed opportunities for therapeutic intervention, and helped resolve conflict. David was discharged to a residential treatment setting because of an unsafe home environment. Family therapy was also used throughout the treatment process as a means of addressing and working through family issues.

Case 2

Sue, a 6-year-old, was brought by her mother for outpatient treatment. The mother was concerned because Sue had become increasingly quiet, sad, and withdrawn since the parents' divorce three months earlier. As the therapist approached the lobby area, he saw Sue sitting on her mother's lap. He bent down to Sue's level for introductions, and then requested they both accompany him to his office. Sue clung to her mother, who carried her to the office. Sue continued to sit on her mother's lap while in the office. The purpose of the session was reviewed, along with specific areas of concern. Confidentiality issues were briefly reviewed at an age-appropriate level. The mother was requested to leave the session after 25 minutes, but Sue clung to her and started crying. The remainder of the session was spent showing Sue and the mother toys/activities available in the office and explaining the role of play therapy. At the end of the session, it was mentioned that a big playroom was available, but only kids and therapists were allowed in the room. On the way to the lobby, the therapist showed Sue and the mother the big playroom. For the first time, Sue showed some positive emotion and wandered into the room as the mother and therapist remained in the doorway.

During the next session, Sue again had difficulty separating from her mother. Both she and the mother were seen in the therapist's office. Sue again sat on her mother's lap. She was reserved and inhibited, but seemed fascinated by some of the toys pointed out by the therapist. The mother and therapist engaged in some puppet play, describing how the rabbit puppet was scared about meeting a new person (e.g., therapist) and talking about worries and concerns. At the end of the session, Sue whispered in her mother's ear that she wanted to go by the big playroom. Her mother appropriately told her to ask the therapist. In a soft voice, Sue asked. The therapist responded that they would pass the room on the way out, but time wouldn't allow them to play in the room. Plus, she was reminded about the kids only, no parent rule. We passed the big playroom on the way to the lobby and Sue again seemed fascinated.

When the therapist went to the lobby to greet Sue for the third session, her mother mentioned that Sue wanted to go to the big playroom. Sue reluctantly left her mother and accompanied the therapist to the room. She was quiet and anxious. Once in the big playroom, she slowly moved around the room, examining different toys in a deliberate manner. She always asked for permission before taking toys out of the cabinet or off the shelves. Sue wanted the therapist close by, but said little. She seemed most interested in structured type of activities, such as puzzles, books, and simple games (e.g., Candy Land). At the end of the session, Sue was praised for coming to the big playroom by herself and encouraged to do so again next week.

During the next and ensuing sessions, Sue separated from her mother with less anxiety as the therapeutic alliance solidified. As this occurred, some regressive behavior was evident (e.g., thumbsucking and whining). Ego support was provided, along with affirmation statements (e.g., "You worry about your mom"), situational statements (e.g., "When you're away from mom it can be scary"), and reductive statements (e.g., "You like to keep different parts of your life in order because it makes you feel in control").

As therapy progressed into the growth stage, less structured activities were encouraged, such as painting, drawing, puppets, and sandbox. Gradually Sue became more spontaneous and free. Play revealed themes of family conflict, loss, and negative feelings (e.g., sadness, fear, and anxiety). Puppet skits enacted by Sue revealed ongoing conflict over the divorce and feelings of abandonment by the father. Issues surrounding the divorce were addressed through play, such as self-blame, reunification fantasies, shame, absent father, and fears of losing Mom. Interpretations during play were used to increase self-observation, link understanding with feelings, and develop mastery over conflicts.

After fifteen sessions, Sue had made significant progress. Home and school reports indicated less sadness, greater assertiveness, and less separation anxiety. As termination was discussed, regressive behavior reappeared. The loss of a male therapist through termination re-created feelings and thoughts of losing her father. It also raised dependency issues again. The final five play sessions focused on dealing with termination issues, consolidating therapeutic gains, and age-appropriate dependency. Puppet skits, drawing/painting, storytelling, and costumes were used to work through these issues. Themes revealed a mastery of loss issues and an increased sense of competency.

This case illustrates the use of play therapy with a quiet, sad, and withdrawn child. It emphasizes the need to create a comfortable, secure, and supportive environment for these types of children, while encouraging spontaneous and free play. Parent guidance was also used to help the mother deal with Sue's separation anxiety and feelings/thoughts about the divorce.

Case 3

Leon, a 9-year-old, was referred by his school because of oppositional-defiant behavior. His mother was overwhelmed by Leon's problematic behavior, which included lying, stealing, and cruelty to the family dog. When the therapist approached the lobby he noticed the mother, but Leon was absent. When asked about Leon, the mother said he was sitting on a bench in front of the clinic. When Leon was approached by the therapist a series of profanities came out of his mouth. He adamantly stated he was not crazy and did not need help. Affirmation was shown for his feelings and thoughts, along with providing clarification about the purpose of the session. It was noted that initially most kids don't like attending therapy, but once in the playroom they don't mind it. He was then given the choice of joining the therapist and his mother or staying on the bench, noting the former would be best because the therapist would like his side of the story. He agreed to go inside and walked to the playroom, but sat a good distance from his mother. The therapist reviewed what the mother had told Leon about the session. Leon angrily interrupted, stating she told him he was going bowling. A bowling alley was behind the clinic. Once in the parking lot, she told him they had to meet someone in the clinic, at which point they had a verbal altercation in the car. Affirmation was again shown for Leon's feelings. Clarification was attempted in regards to the purpose and nature of treatment. However, Leon put his fingers in his ears, acting like he didn't want to hear what was being said. The therapist used a paradoxical technique, telling the child it was probably best for him not to hear what was being discussed because it was private. At that point, the child immediately removed his fingers from his ears. The reasons for the referral were then reviewed and confidentiality issues were explained. In addition, basic limits in the playroom were covered. After twenty minutes, the mother was asked to return to the lobby. Leon continued his dictatorial attitude, demanding to play in the sandbox and then dumping sand on the floor. He moved to the water area and used the water gun to squirt the therapist. A brief break was taken to review rules and expectations. It was decided to review the different toys and activities in the playroom in a structured way rather than allowing him total freedom to explore on his own.

Leon and his mother arrived promptly for the second session. However, the receptionist called the therapist complaining that Leon was cursing at his mother in the lobby. The therapist brought Leon to his office and explored what was happening in the lobby. Leon expressed anger at his mother because she wouldn't allow him to buy something from the candy machine. Proper expectations for lobby behavior were reviewed, along with ways of controlling angry feelings. Leon was then taken to the playroom. His play had a driven and impulsive quality. Aggressive toys, such as guns, knives, and soldiers, were his primary play objects. His play was also transparent and erratic. He ignored most interventions. Play themes involved aggression, loneliness, power, and control. He saw the world as chaotic and disorganized and identified with the aggressor as a way of controlling his environment. It was apparent that Leon was a very disturbed child, with poor self-control and little respect for authority.

Gradually a treatment alliance was established. Modeling was utilized to show appropriate interpersonal interactions and limit setting. Choices were provided about play activities to give Leon a sense of control and provide greater structure. Satiation and paradoxical intervention techniques were used, such as requesting that Leon say no to everything I suggested.

During the growth stage, interpretations were made regarding his identification with the aggressor and the need for control. Alternative ways of gaining control were discussed, along with anger control techniques. Leon's play gradually became more focused, organized, and less violent. He developed some insight into his dynamics, such as rage toward his mother for inadequate parenting, lack of limits within the home, and low self-esteem due to a learning disability.

Special education services were pursued for Leon to address his emotional and learning problems. He was placed in a day treatment program, which provided both educational and therapeutic services. As a result, he was transferred to a therapist at the day treatment center. Four sessions were planned to prepare Leon for the transfer, but he missed two of the sessions. His play revealed themes of abandonment and rejection. Reframing and interpretations were made, along with much support.

This case illustrates a defiant, resistant child, who needed a great deal of structure and supervision within the therapy setting. Play was effective at identifying and addressing many of Leon's dynamics. Parent guidance was also used to assist the mother with management skills. As noted above, day treatment services were also pursued.

Conclusion

Resistance is defined as any behavior, thought, or feeling that hinders or interferes with the development and maintenance of a therapeutic alliance and the child's progress in therapy. It surfaces in all stages of treatment and may vary in type, quantity, and intensity. Resistance reveals valuable information about how the child deals with conflict and distress. Therefore, it is critical to analyze factors underlying its presence.

Play is highly effective for analyzing and dealing with resistance and for building a treatment alliance. Play allows therapists to assess intrapersonal and interpersonal aspects of behavior in a natural, nonthreatening manner. It also permits children to symbolically express their inner feelings and thoughts. Through understanding each child's dynamics, the therapist is better able to choose appropriate intervention techniques to address the resistance.

In terms of specific intervention techniques for resistant children, engaging them in treatment is the first step. Important factors such as the therapist's personality, establishing the relationship, toy selection, and the initial contact all facilitate this process. Next, the therapist must determine the type and amount of structure required. The degree of structure varies depending on the setting, type of toys available, therapist's role, and type of psychopathology (e.g., internalizing versus externalizing). Acting-out, impulsive children require greater structure, while withdrawn, shy, and sad children need encouragement to act more free and spontaneous. Limits are another important intervention technique, especially with children who exhibit poor impulse control. A safe, protective environment must be maintained.

Joining techniques, such as affirmation statements, satiation, paradoxical situations, and mirroring were presented. Their usefulness with resistant children, especially during the initial stages of therapy, were described. Different types and levels of interpretations were reviewed. Their usefulness is dependent on the establishment of a solid therapeutic relationship and the child's readiness to hear and accept them. In general, interpretations should be saved for later stages of therapy.

References

Amster, F. (1982). Differential uses of play in treatment of young children. In *Play Therapy: Dynamics of the Process of Counseling with Children*, ed. G. Landreth, pp. 33–42. Springfield, IL: Charles C Thomas.

Bow, J. N. (1988). Treating resistant children. *Child and Adolescent Social Work* 5:3–15.

———— (1993). Overcoming resistance. In *The Therapeutic Powers of Play*, ed. C. E. Schaefer, pp. 17–40. Northvale, NJ: Jason Aronson.

Carek, D. (1972). *Principles of Child Psychotherapy*. Springfield, IL: Charles C Thomas.

Dodds, J. B. (1987). *A Child Psychotherapy Primer*. New York: Human Sciences.

Gabel, S., Oster, G., and Pfeffer, C. R. (1988). *Difficult Moments in Child Psychotherapy*. New York: Plenum.

Gardner, R. A. (1975). *Psychotherapeutic Approaches to the Resistant Child*. New York: Jason Aronson.

———— (1979). Helping children cooperate in therapy. In *Basic Handbook of Child Psychiatry*, vol. 2, ed. J. D. Noshpitz, pp. 414–433. New York: Basic Books.

Ginott, H. G. (1982a). A rationale for selecting toys in play therapy. In *Play Therapy: Dynamic of the Process of Counseling with Children*, ed. G. L. Landreth, pp. 145–159. Springfield, IL: Charles C Thomas.

———— (1982b). Therapeutic intervention in child treatment. In *Play Therapy: Dynamics of the Process of Counseling with Children*, ed. G. L. Landreth, pp.

160–172. Springfield, IL: Charles C Thomas.

Harter, S. (1983). Cognitive-developmental considerations in the conduct of play therapy. In *Handbook of Play Therapy*, ed. C. E. Schaefer, and K. J. O'Connor, pp. 95–127. New York: Wiley.

Kissel, S. (1990). *Play Therapy: A Strategic Approach*. Springfield, IL: Charles C Thomas.

Landreth, G. L. (1993). Self-expressive communication. In *The Therapeutic Powers of Play*, ed. C. E. Schaefer, pp. 41–63. Northvale, NJ: Jason Aronson.

Lewis, M. (1974). Interpretations in child analysis: developmental considerations. *Journal of the American Academy of Child Psychiatry* 13:32–53.

Mann, E., and McDermott, J. F. (1983). Play therapy for victims of child abuse and neglect. In *Handbook of Play Therapy*, ed. C. E. Schaefer, and K. J. O'Connor, pp. 283–307. New York: Wiley.

Markowitz, J. A. (1959). The nature of the child's initial resistance to psychotherapy. *Social Work* 4:46–51.

Marshall, R. J. (1982). *Resistant Interactions: Child, Family, and Psychotherapist*. New York: Human Science.

Mordock, J. B. (1994). *Counseling the Defiant Child: A Basic Guide to Helping Troubled and Aggressive Youth*. New York: Crossroads.

Moustakas, C. E. (1982). Emotional adjustment and the play therapy process. In *Play Therapy: Dynamics of the Process of Counseling with Children*, ed. G. L. Landreth, pp. 217–230. Springfield, IL: Charles C Thomas.

Nemiroff, M. A., and Annunziata, J. (1990). *A Child's First Book About Play Therapy*. Washington, DC: American Psychological Association.

O'Connor, K. J. (1991). *The Play Therapy Primer: An Integration of Theories and Techniques*. New York: Wiley.

Partin, M. B. (1932). Social participation among preschool children. *Journal of Abnormal and Social Psychology* 27:243–269.

Salameh, W. A. (1986). The effective use of humor in psychotherapy. In *Innovations in Clinical Practice: A Source Book*, vol. 5, ed. P. A. Keller, and L. G. Ritt, pp. 157–175. Sarasota, FL: Professional Resource.

Schaefer, C. E., ed. (1979). *The Therapeutic Use of Child's Play*. New York: Jason Aronson.

———— (1993). What is play and why is it therapeutic? In *The Therapeutic Powers of Play*, pp. 1–15. Northvale, NJ: Jason Aronson.

13

Building a Family: Play Therapy with Adopted Children and Their Parents

Terry Kottman

Background

"Adoption is common in our society and is of interest to many researchers and practitioners because of its potential positive and negative effects on child development and family process" (Berry 1992, p. 525). Every year, 1 to 2 percent of the families in the United States will adopt a child who is not related by birth to the members of the family (Bachrach et al. 1990, Berry 1992, LeVine and Sallee 1990, Smith and Brodzinsky 1994). Among these nonrelative adoptions, older child (age 3 and older) adoptions account for approximately 14 percent and infant adoptions account for approximately 76 percent (Bachrach et al. 1990).

Description of the Population

The majority of adopted children seem to be well adjusted and their families seem to be balanced and mentally healthy (Brodzinsky 1987, Groze 1992, Kadushin 1980, Smith and Brodzinsky 1994). Eighty-four percent of the adoptions studied by researchers have been labeled "successful" by professionals (Kadushin 1980). Despite the fact that most children and their families "do not experience psychological problems" (Wierzbicki 1993, p. 452), a disproportionately high percentage of adopted children and their families struggle with psychological, behavioral, interpersonal, and educational difficulties. This population is overrepresented in outpatient mental health facilities (5 percent of the referrals), inpatient psychiatric facilities and residential treatment centers (between 10 and 15 percent of the referrals) (LeVine and Sallee 1990, Smith and Brodzinsky 1994), and special education classes (Brodzinsky and Steiger 1991).

Research studies with adopted children have shown a pattern of disproportionate rates of externalizing behavior difficulties; personality problems; and conduct problems, including hyperactivity, defiance, aggression, lying, stealing, running away and other inappropriate negative behaviors (Austad and Simmons 1978, Brodzinsky et al. 1993, Brodzinsky et al. 1987, Cohen et al. 1993, Fullerton et al. 1986, Grotevant et al. 1988, Kotsopoulos et al. 1988, Lindholm and Touliatos 1980, Wierzbicki 1993). Brodzinsky and colleagues (1987) found that girls who were adopted exhibited a higher rate of clinically significant depression than girls who were not adopted and that boys who were adopted exhibited a higher rate of uncommunicative behavior than boys who were not adopted. Adopted children also seem to have more school-related problems and lower school achievement and social competence than nonadopted children (Brodzinsky, Schechter et al. 1984).

There is disagreement in the literature about whether the differences between adoptees and nonadoptees are related to age at adoption. Some researchers strongly suggest that the older a child is at the time of adoption, the more likely her or she is to have problems (Berry 1992, Valdez and McNamara 1994). However, in a meta-analysis of sixty-six published studies comparing the psychological adjustment of adoptees and nonadoptees, Wierzbicki (1993) concluded that the differences between these two groups was not related to age at adoption, even though "clinical experience suggests that early adoptions are likely to be the most successful and that children adopted at later ages are especially at risk for psychological problems" (p. 452). The difficulties experienced by children adopted at a later age may be more closely related to their experiences before adoption than their age at their adoption. The number of placements prior to the adoptive placement has been found to influence adoption disruption (Barth et al. 1988, Valdez and McNamara 1994). Verhulst and colleagues (1992) found that abuse, early neglect, and the number of changes of caregivers and living environments increased the probability that children will experience later maladjustment. Since the older children are at the age adoption the more likely it is that they have experienced some of these traumas, it is a logical conclusion that older adoptees are more likely to have difficulties than infant adoptees.

While the research strongly supports the idea that adoptees, regardless of their age when adopted, experience elevated rates of emotional, behavioral, and educational difficulties, there have been few research studies designed to explain exactly how and why these problems evolve (Wierzbicki 1993). Most of the explanations of etiology are theoretical and clinical, rather than empirical. One of the few empirical studies in this area was conducted by Groze (1992). His findings suggested that adopted children, especially those who have been maltreated by their birth parents, foster parents, or other caregivers, may have difficulty forming attachments with adoptive parents or other adults. This seems to be due to a "lack of confidence in the parent or parent figure to be available, responsive and helpful to meet his/her needs, or to comfort him/her should the child encounter adverse of frightening situations" (p. 175).

Alternate explanations of the etiology of these problems include (1) environmental risk factors, such as poor prenatal care and institutionalization before adoptive placement, and (2) genetic risk factors, such as biological parents with psychological disorders and educational handicaps (Wierzbicki 1993). Still other theories about the etiology of the unusually high levels of problems in adoptees relate to negative interpersonal experiences, including feelings of rejection, loss, separation, and "differentness" (Wierzbicki 1993). Brodzinsky (1987, 1990) has suggested that the adjustment of adoptees is directly related to how their adoptive families cope with the stressors connected with the adoption processes.

Key Issues that Affect Adoptive Families

To be able to help these children, it is essential to understand the important issues that seem to have an impact on all adopted children and their adoptive families, whether or not they exhibit behavior or psychological difficulties. Reitz and Watson (1992) listed seven key issues that affect adopted children and their families: (1) entitlement; (2) claiming; (3) unmatched expectations; (4) shifts in the family system; (5) separation, loss, and grief; (6) bonding and attachment; and (7) identity formation. The author of this chapter has noted in her clinical experience that power and control are also frequently issues for this population. A play therapist working with this population must assess the impact of each of these issues on the adopted child and on each member of the adoptive family, especially the parents, in order to design an intervention that meets the needs of the child and the family.

Entitlement

Entitlement "refers to the adopted parents' sense that they have both the legal and emotional right to be parents to their child" (Reitz and Watson 1992, p. 125). While the court system confers the legal right to the child, the development of the sense of emotional right to parent is more complex. As parents begin to feel more comfortable with their roles as father or mother to their children, their sense of emotional entitlement grows.

A weak sense of entitlement can sabotage the growth of a loving and supportive relationship between the parent(s) and the child. Parents who are uncertain about their right to develop an emotional attachment with their children may stifle the process of claiming and attachment. The resulting instability in the parent–child relationship could have debilitating effects on the children's sense of self-worth and identity formation, resulting in behavioral, emotional, and educational difficulties. A strong sense of entitlement by the adoptive parent(s) will result in clear and powerful communication to the children that the adoptive arrangements are "right" for all parties involved. Adoptive parents must work to develop this belief in their right to raise their children in order to clear the way to deal with the other issues involved in adoption.

Claiming

Claiming is "the mutual process by which an adoptive family and an adopted child come to feel that they *belong* to each other" (Reitz and Watson 1992, pp. 126–127). The beginning of this process occurs when adoptive parents identify similarities between children's behavior or appearance and their own behavior or appearance or that of other family members. Other ways of claiming a child include using a family name for an unnamed infant or using a family name as a nickname or a middle name. Taking many photographs of the child with the new family unit and with members of the extended family is also important.

The claiming process with older children must also include ways for the children to claim the family as well as for the family to claim the children—a kind of reciprocal claiming. Some experts (Melina 1986, Reitz and Watson 1992) suggest that life books (scrapbooks in which children can chronicle the story of their lives, including events, reactions, feelings, and plans) are an invaluable resource in helping older adopted children claim their new families.

Reciprocal claiming is an important process for adopted children so that they can feel as though they are an integral part of their adoptive families. Children who do not experience adequate reciprocal claiming may feel almost invisible (Partridge 1991), since they do not receive as much parental feedback on their physical attributes as nonadoptees. They also lack the "kind of mirroring that comes from constantly being able to see and take in what others look like who have similar features, similar coloring, identical toes, and so on" (p. 204).

Parents must be careful not to overcompensate during the claiming process and begin ignoring or rejecting the differences between their families and other biologically based families (Howe 1992). There are three ways for adoptive parents to deal with the parental role and the process of claiming their adopted children—"rejection of difference," "insistance of difference," and "acknowledgment of difference" (Brodzinsky 1987, Kirk 1981).

In the rejection of difference strategy, parents deny that their family and their situation as parents is different from biological parents. This strategy has potential for harming children, as it does not allow them to explore their biological origins or to feel secure in being different from their adoptive parents.

Rejecting the difference also prevents an accepting and trusting family atmosphere from developing (Brodzinsky 1987). The resulting family atmosphere may inhibit open and honest communication and exploration of the many issues that confront adoptive families. Denial of the differences between adoptive and biological families can give children the idea that being different is unacceptable, which will "accentuate feelings of isolation and disconnectedness from the family. It also is likely to foster feelings of guilt concerning their thoughts and fantasies dealing with birth parents and origins" (Brodzinsky 1987, p. 41).

Insistence of difference can also cause difficulties in the claiming process.

> Parents in these families not only acknowledge differences, but they emphasize the differences to the point where they become a, if not *the*, major focus of the family. Moreover, the differences are often seen as explanations for family disconnectedness and disharmony. Parents may have difficulty seeing their adopted child as an integral part of the family . . . children too sometimes adopt this coping style. They may see themselves as so different from their parents and siblings that they feel totally alien within the family; they may be unable to find anything within the adoptive parents with which to identify; they may feel psychologically rejected and abandoned in the midst of their own family. [Brodzinsky 1987, p. 42]

Using the third coping style, acknowledging the difference, parents can convey that they claim the child as a part of themselves and their families and that they also respect the child's uniqueness. The best way for families to cope with this issue seems to be a combination of using the strategies described for facilitating the claiming process and remaining open and honest about the fact that their family has been formed in a way that is not the "usual" way of forming a family.

Unmatched Expectations

When a family adopts a child, all of the members of the family have fantasies about how the child will fit into the family. With an older child, the child also has fantasies about the adoption. Quite frequently, the anticipatory expectations of both parties do not match the reality of family life (Reitz and Watson 1992). Quite frequently both parties also have reservations about whether the adoption will work out. Unmatched expectations and unexplored reservations can both sabotage the adoptive process before it has even begun.

It is essential that both parties discuss their fantasies and fears even before the child moves in with the family, in order to prevent unmatched expectations and unspoken reservations from permanently ruining communication between family members. Parents should receive all available information about the child's developmental history and experiences prior to the adoption to help them form reasonable and realistic expectations.

Shifts in Family Systems

Any time an additional member joins a family, a shift in the family system occurs. There is a changed structure in the family—the balance between members and the roles clearly defined before the adoption will be affected by the addition of a new family member. "An adoptive family is more vulnerable to these shifts, because the tie between the adopted child and the family is more tentative" (Reitz and Watson 1992, p. 130).

The older adopted child will bring his or her role from the previous placement into the new family. This can cause difficulty if another member of the new family system already plays that role. In other cases, the role the child has played in the past may not be syntonic in the new family system or it may be a "role the child has practiced in a prior dysfunctional family as a means of protection or control—one that is inappropriate in a functional family system" (Reitz and Watson 1992, p. 130). The family will have to renegotiate the power structure and roles in the family.

In many cases, the disruption in the family system is exacerbated by the child's behavior. The child, believing that he or she is unlovable, may try to sabotage a placement in order to avoid the "inevitable" pain of rejection when things do not work out with the adoptive family (Helwig and Ruthven 1990). The child may also sabotage the placement because he or she is struggling with divided loyalties—in order to belong to the new family, the child must usually give up the old family.

To cope with the impact an adopted child may have on the family system, parents must explore how the family works—power, roles, definitions of appropriate behavior—even before the child is placed. By having a picture of how the family is structured prior to placement, the parent(s) can form a clear understanding of the effects of the addition of a new member. Family members can then clearly discuss the changes in the family and negotiate new arrangements concerning roles and distribution of power. Parents must watch for potential sabotage by the new member of the family and communicate their love and acceptance at the same time they establish structure and limits. They should also clearly define their perception of appropriate and inappropriate behavior and develop a plan for teaching the adopted child how to fit into their family.

Separation, Loss, and Grief

Both the adoptive parents and the adopted child have issues related to grief and loss. If adoptive parents are infertile, they must deal with the sense of loss connected to their inability to produce a biological child.

First, there is the loss brought on by the infertility itself. The biggest factor in this loss is the realization of how much you wanted a loving relationship with a birth child. Second, deciding to adopt, for many people, symbolizes abandoning all hope of having a birth child. [Van Gulden and Bartels-Rabb 1993, p. 35]

Before coming to the adoption route, adoptive parents may have also lost (1) their image of themselves as having healthy reproductive systems, (2) their sense of competency in having attained their goals for their lives, (3) status in their families of origin or with their peers, and (4) a feeling of control over their lives and their destinies (Reitz and Watson 1992). So that they can get on with building a relationship with the adopted child and with their lives, infertile adoptive parents must recognize and resolve their feelings about their infertility.

The adopted child must also deal with feelings of loss and grief (Reitz and Watson 1992). The child has lost his or her birth parents, self-identity, and a genetic tie to the birth family (Van Gulden and Bartels-Rabb 1993). Older adopted children may have lost foster families or siblings, which will contribute to their sense of separation and loss. Grief reactions to separation and feelings of loss may occur both at the time of the separation and on subsequent occasions when they are reminded of those losses. An additional source of sadness would be feeling "different" from other children, which the child may translate as being "not as good" as other children.

Children adopted as infants may have delayed grief reactions that do not affect them until they are in grade school, because until the age of 6 they do not really understand the difference between birth and adoption as alternative methods of forming a family (Brodzinsky, Singer, and Braff 1984). By the age of 8, these children begin to develop an awareness of the reasons for adoption, as opposed to biological production of children. Between the ages of 8 and 11, these children start to understand the uniqueness of their status as adoptive members of their families, and they may begin to experience feelings of being different in a negative sense. At this point in their development, they may feel a sense of loss and bereavement.

While it is important for adoptive parents to be aware of the potential for feelings of grief and loss in their children, not all adopted children experience intrusive feelings of sadness. Parents must be careful not to overreact or make more of loss issues than is necessary. With children who are affected by grief issues, adoptive parents will need to help them express their bereavement and help them move through the stages of grief without taking the sadness and anger of the children personally.

Bonding and Attachment

Since bonding is a function of the biological connection between a birth mother and a child, adoptive parents cannot experience this connection with their children (Watson 1989–1990). However, they can and do experience attachment, which is the psychological process between two people of making connections and establishing significance for one another (Reitz and Watson 1992). Attachment usually occurs during the first three years of life, through a series of nurturing interactions between parents and their infants. This process occurs successfully in most infant adoptions.

However, with many older adopted children, children may have experienced parental maltreatment or neglect, which frequently results in difficulties in making and maintaining attachments (Barth and Berry 1988). These children must learn to become attached to others, starting with their adoptive parents. "This means teaching these older children how to become attached to others by providing them with the consistent nurturing they missed, in ways that symbolically relate to their early years but that do not infantilize the children" (Reitz and Watson 1992, p. 133).

Identity Formation

All adopted children struggle with the formation of their identities.

> Identity formation is harder for adopted children, because they may not have complete or accurate information about their genes and birth family history; because they may not feel full membership in their adoptive family; and because as they establish their "boundaries," they must cope with the ultimate attack on self-worth— "abandonment" by their birth families. [Reitz and Watson 1992, p. 134]

Many children may focus on negative interpretations of why they were placed for adoption or negative experiences that occurred before they were placed for adoption (Van Gulden and Bartels-Rabb 1993).

This struggle with identity formation is complicated by the fact that many adoptees feel that they have two different identities—one as part of their birth families and one as part of their adoptive families (Partridge 1991). This divided identity may lead to questions of loyalty for adopted children—if they learn to attach to members of their adoptive families, will they have to give up their connection and belongingness in their birth families?

Parents can foster positive identity formation in their adopted children by helping the children balance positive self-esteem and negative messages from self and from others. Van Gulden and Bartels-Rabb (1993) suggested the following strategies for accomplishing this balance: (1) accepting children's feelings, even when they seem to be at odds with the parent(s)' interpretations; (2) teaching children how to "filter" negative inputs from other people; (3) teaching children to accept positive inputs even if they do not really believe them; (4) teaching children to express feelings, especially anger in socially appropriate ways; (5) providing children with honest and abundant encouragement; (6) accepting children's goals and abilities, even when these goals are not congruent with parent(s)' goals and abilities; (7) developing an awareness of children's interpretations of their own personal, genetic, and cultural histories, even if these are not congruent with the parent(s)' interpretations; (8) helping children come to terms with past situations and traumas; (9) teaching children to appreciate their own assets, realistically evaluate their weaknesses, and make plans for developing strategies to capitalize on assets and compensate for weaknesses.

Power and Control

Many adopted children, especially those who were adopted at older ages, struggle with needing to be in control of situations and other people. They seem to feel afraid or powerless unless they have power over themselves and their environments. To acquire this power, these children may throw temper tantrums, exhibit disrespectful and inappropriate behavior, refuse to comply with requests or commands, display passive aggressive behavior, or any number of other strategies for "stealing" power from other people (Kottman 1995). Children who engage in repeated power struggles because of their excessive need for control seem to fall into three distinct categories: (1) those who have too much power; (2) those who have too little power; and (3) those who come from chaotic, out-of-control backgrounds (Kottman 1995).

Some older adopted children come from families in which they had too much power. Frequently, due to circumstances in their birth families, these children have effectively been the parent, which would give them the idea that they should always be in charge of every situation. Some older adopted children come from families in which they have too little power. They have no age-appropriate responsibilities or control. Many older adopted children come from chaotic environments, in which they may have experienced abuse, neglect, the death of one or both of their parents, or other situations that they perceived as being unsafe and out of control. Children who have been in the child welfare system a long time, moving from placement to placement, frequently fit into this category.

Older children who have moved from one family to another may have extremely complicated backgrounds, since families deal with power in different ways. A child might move from a family in which she felt powerless and out of control because of its disorganized environment, to a family in which she had too little power because the parents were tyrants, to a family in which she had too much power because the parents felt pity for her and pampered her. This type of switching from one type of background to another can totally confuse a child; at the same time it reinforces the idea that the only way she can be safe and happy is to be in control of herself and others in her environment.

Parents can help children with issues in the area of power and control by being consistent, setting up logical consequences for inappropriate behavior, and having reasonable expectations for self-care and self-responsibility. By establishing a democratic family atmosphere, in which children have a say in what happens in the family, but also have structure, routines, and consistent discipline, parents can teach children who try to "steal" power to feel safer sharing control with others (Bettner and Lew 1989, Kottman 1995). It is also important for the adoptive parents of these children not to take power struggles personally and to learn to appropriately set limits and withdraw from power struggles gracefully.

Traditional Treatment Strategies

Most traditional treatment strategies with adopted children involved family therapy, group therapy with either the children or the parents, and/or individual counseling with the children (Helwig and Ruthven 1990). In family therapy, intervention strategies have included structural approaches (Minuchin 1974), family sculpting (Euster et al. 1982, Satir 1972), role playing and psychodrama (Euster et al. 1992), brief solution focused techniques (Schaffer and Lindstrom 1990), telling and retelling the adoption story (Hartman and Laird 1990), developing rituals (Melina 1990), and expressive arts therapies (Harvey 1991).

Group therapy, especially with adolescents, has proven effective with adoptees and their parents (Helwig and Ruthven 1990). Group therapy helps adopted children and their parents realize that they are not alone in their feelings and situations. The support and encouragement available in a group help clients to develop self-confidence, enhance feelings of self-worth, and learn communication and problem-solving skills.

A search of the literature related to individual counseling with adopted children yielded few descriptions of interventions with this population. Some techniques traditionally applied to this population have been strategic interventions, redefinition, and the use of paradox (Helwig and Ruthven 1990, Katz 1980); cognitive strategies (LeVine and Sallee 1990); behavioral interventions (Levine and Sallee 1990, Melina 1986); storytelling and art techniques (Jarratt 1994, Levine and Sallee 1990); and individual "life books" (Backhaus 1984). Several authors (Jernberg 1979, Remkus 1991) described using play therapy techniques with adopted or foster children, and Van Fleet (1994) outlined a method for using filial therapy with adopted children and their parents.

The author believes that family play therapy, which is a combination of play therapy and family therapy, specifically tailored to the issues of adopted children and their families may be the most appropriate intervention strategy for work with this population, especially those adopted at an older age. By incorporating important elements of these two intervention strategies, the play therapist can provide encouragement and support for the adopted child, the adoptive parents, and any other member of the family in working through their issues.

Rationale for Play Therapy

Schaefer (1993) described fourteen therapeutic factors of play, along with the benefits that children can gain from each of these factors. These therapeutic powers are (1) overcoming resistance, (2) communication, (3) competence, (4) creative thinking, (5) catharsis, (6) abreaction, (7) role play, (8) fantasy/ visualization, (9) metaphoric teaching, (10) attachment formation, (11) relationship enhancement, (12) positive emotion, (13) mastering developmental fears, and (14) game play. Play therapists working with adopted children and their families can use all of these therapeutic factors to help the children, their parents, and other family members deal with the issues related to being adopted. The therapeutic powers that would probably be most helpful with this population, especially with children adopted past infancy and their adoptive parents, are overcoming resistance, abreaction, attachment formation, relationship enhancement, and positive emotion.

Overcoming Resistance

Because many adopted children, especially those who were adopted at a later age, have difficulty forming relationships, the therapeutic power of overcoming resistance can be extremely helpful in building a relationship between the play therapist and the child. By using play to build a working alliance with these children, the play therapist can begin to gain their trust, the first step in making a therapeutic connection. In family play therapy, the therapist can teach the adoptive parent(s) to play with their children. They, too, can use play to start forming a relationship and overcoming children's fear and distrust. By developing a special repertoire of play with their children, parents can extend the claiming process and the attachment between parents and their children.

Communication

Communication is a key component in the play therapist's enterprise of conveying empathy, genuineness, and warmth to the child. These therapeutic elements foster the growth of the relationship between the child and the play therapist, an essential component of the play therapy process, no matter what the theory of the play therapist. Communication is also necessary to parents' continuing efforts in building a relationship with the adopted child and in preventing problems from sabotaging the assimilation of an adopted child into his or her new family. In family play therapy, all of the participants use the child's natural language, play, to communicate. This honoring of the child's mode of communication conveys a great deal of respect to the child.

By teaching parents to use "entitling language" (Reitz and Watson 1992, p. 125), such as "our son," the play therapist can help adoptive parents begin to feel emotional entitlement to their parental role. By telling stories about the child's life before he or she came to live with the adoptive family, stories about the family's life before the child came to live with them, and stories about how the parents decided to adopt the child and about the process of the adoption can build a shared history that will make claiming occur more smoothly.

Communication is a key to helping adopted children and their families explore their expectations and to help them work out which of their fantasies can be realized and which are unrealistic. It can also be helpful in considering shifts in the family system and plans for coping with those shifts, with expressing grief and loss, in developing attachment between parents and children, and in forming an identity.

Competence

Poor self-concept is evident in adopted children who evidence negative behavior patterns (Groze 1992). These children can benefit from developing a sense of competence through the process of play. By mastering tasks in the play room, children can experience pride in themselves and their accomplishments. Because the parents are included in the play therapy and in parent consultations, the play therapist can teach parents how to build a sense of competence into family interactions and activities through encouragement (Kottman 1995). A generalization of this sense of competence can serve adopted children well, especially in the area of identity formation. The resultant boost in feelings of self-worth can potentially counter negative perceptions of self and negative input from others about their status. A sense of self-efficacy can also build children's confidence in establishing a positive role in the adoptive family and encourage them to feel in control in at least one area of their lives. Successful loving and fun interactions between parents and children can also build parents' confidence in their own ability to communicate with their children.

Creative Thinking

Children constantly use creative thinking in the playroom, which results in their generating innovative solutions to problems and increasing their confidence in their ability to solve their own problems. By incorporating this therapeutic power into the process of play therapy with adopted children, the play therapist can help children and their parents develop coping strategies for dealing with unmatched expectations, shifts in family systems, and grief and loss. As they develop a belief about themselves that includes confidence in their own ability to think creatively about problems, children's identities will evolve in a positive, proactive direction. By teaching parents to encourage creative thinking and problem-solving skills during parent consultation sessions, modeling these strategies in the play sessions with the various members of the family, and providing a safe play for parents to practice, the play therapist can increase the likelihood of beneficial outcomes from this therapeutic factor.

Catharsis

The process of catharsis involves the expression of strong feelings, resulting in emotional release. In play therapy, children quite frequently take advantage of the freedom of the play arena and the accepting nature of the therapeutic relationship with the play therapist to release strong negative (and occasionally positive) emotions. Adopted children, especially those adopted at a later age, have many strong feelings related to their adoption and to events that occurred to them before placement. They need a place to express their fears about the adoption, their anger about unmatched expectations, their sense of loss and sadness about their birth parents and siblings, and their joy as the claiming and attachment process develops. The playroom can be a safe place for them to do this and be heard—both by a supportive therapist and by loving parents and siblings. Adoptive parents may also need a relationship in which they can feel comfortable expressing and releasing their fears, grief, and elation. Parent consultation can provide them with an outlet for venting strong negative feelings without damaging their growing relationship with their children.

Abreaction

Since many older adopted children have experienced trauma, the therapeutic power of abreaction is essential to coping with their pasts. These children can use the play to help them process their traumatic or painful experiences. By playing out relationships from the past, adopted children may release some of the negative feelings and cognitions associated with those interactions and events. This will allow them to proceed through the stages of grief and to facilitate the development of attachment to the members of their new family and the growth of a positive identity. By witnessing and perhaps participating in their children's working through feelings about traumatic events they have experienced, adoptive parents can come to a much more powerful understanding of how these traumatic events have affected the children.

Role Play

Older adopted children may lack the social skills and interactional experience to understand how to fit into their new families. Role play can provide them with a vehicle for learning and practicing new skills, especially those related to attaining a new balance in the family system. Since various members of the family will participate in the family play therapy, different individuals can participate in roleplays with one another—sometimes playing themselves and sometimes playing other family members. They can use this therapeutic factor to help work out new ways of sharing power in an appropriate fashion.

Fantasy/Visualization

A resourceful play therapist will use positive, proactive fantasy/visualization as a way of helping adopted children and their families deal with unmatched expectations and grief and loss issues. By drawing out the participants in the family play therapy about their expectations about their ideal lives, the play therapist can help participants grieve for loss of their unrealistic or unfulfilled fantasies and substitute attainable fantasies. Having members of the family hear one another's fantasies can help create a sense of empathy and warmth among family members, which fosters attachment.

Metaphoric Teaching

To help adopted children and their parents gain insight into their own ways of interacting with others, quite frequently the play therapist will decide to use metaphoric teaching (Kottman 1995). With some families, confronting negative patterns directly and attempting to teach family members to substitute positive behaviors and attitudes simply evokes a defensive reaction. By using storytelling and art techniques in a metaphoric way, the play therapist can help clients explore their own issues and alternative solutions in an indirect fashion. With adopted children and their families, this strategy could be helpful in dealing with claiming, unmatched expectations, shifts in the family system, grief and loss, and power and control. The play therapist could also use metaphoric teaching to help the child with his or her identity formation, especially by telling stories about various adopted individuals who have been happy and successful in their lives.

Attachment Formation

The attachment formation therapeutic power of play can be useful in therapy with adopted children in two different ways. By establishing a bond with the play therapist, many children who have never felt attached to any other human being begin to learn the skills necessary for developing connection to other people (Kottman 1995). The play therapist can then help the child to generalize that connection, so that the child gradually learns to apply these skills to relationships with the other important people in his or her life.

In family play therapy, the therapist can also foster attachment between the child and various members of the adoptive family. Starting with one or both of the parents, the child can develop, through a sharing of playful and fun experiences, an attachment to them. In the playroom, the child can regress to an earlier stage of development in which he or she did not receive the consistent and appropriate parenting necessary for attachment to occur. Parents, under the guidance of the play therapist, can use the play experience to provide nurturing symbolically through the play.

Relationship Enhancement

In many cases, children adopted at an older age have not learned or practiced the skills necessary to start or maintain relationships. The therapeutic power of relationship enhancement can facilitate the claiming process, overcome unmatched expectations, and positively influence identity formation. The play therapist will use his or her relationship with children to help them practice social skills and other strategies for enhancing relationships as a prelude for helping children enhance their relationships with other members of their families through the process of family play therapy. By strengthening the relationships within the family, the various family members will also enhance their abilities to cope with other issues confronting them.

Positive Emotion

Play therapy is fun, and family play therapy is even more fun! By sharing fun times and laughter, by jointly experiencing situations that generate reminiscing and storytelling, adopted children and the members of their families can grow closer together and build a sense of connection that defines a group of people as a family. Sharing positive emotions together can make claiming easier, counter feelings of grief and loss, enhance attachment, add an element of humor and fun to identity formation and smooth struggles for power and control.

Mastering Developmental Fears

Adopted children have all of the same developmental fears as birth children, plus an entire set of fears that are distinctive to them. They are afraid that they are unlovable because their birth parents gave them up, they are afraid their adoptive parents will stop loving them and send them back to the agency, they are afraid they will always feel different from other people and never find a place to fit, they are afraid their birth parents will come back to get them, and they are afraid they may never get to meet their birth parents. By providing a venue for expressing and working through these fears—directly and indirectly—the play therapist can help children master them, enhancing their positive identity formation.

Game Play

Some adopted children, especially those who have experienced great trauma and loss, have relatively limited imaginations and weak social skills. With these children, fantasy play is usually lacking in the playroom. By providing structure and forcing children to take turns and communicate about specific topics, game play can help children learn valuable interactional skills. Game play, particularly in the context of family play therapy, can help children and their families work out role definitions and power structures within the family. Specific therapeutic games, such as the UnGame, Feelings Bingo, and the Talking, Thinking, and Doing Game, can help facilitate family members' communication about attachment, grief and loss, and power and control.

Family Play Therapy Applied to Adopted Children and Their Families

Description of the Approach

In working with adopted children and their family, the author believes the most effective strategy is an application of family play therapy. To optimize the therapeutic powers of play to help adopted children and their parents and siblings cope with the specific issues that seem to cause these families difficulties, it is important to tailor the specific application of play therapy to the family. Since there are as many different configurations of adoptive families and their issues as there are adoptive families, the play therapist must organize the process of play therapy—who comes to each session, which techniques to use, which issues to highlight—around that particular family.

The play therapist must also base his or her intervention strategies on his or her beliefs about people and how they change. Family play therapy is not yet clearly defined, so practitioners must apply their own theoretical orientations to the planning and the process. The author of this chapter is an Adlerian play therapist (Kottman 1993, 1994, 1995), so most of the specific aspects of the conceptualization and the techniques described in this chapter will evolve from an Adlerian perspective. This does not mean that the practitioner must be Adlerian to apply these ideas and strategies with adopted children. He or she may simply transfer an understanding of the issues inherent in working with adopted children and adapt the basics involved in family play therapy to his or her particular theoretical orientation.

Family play therapy (Anderson 1993, Gil 1994) is simply the process of combining the two different approaches—play therapy and family therapy—in order to use play and toys as a mode of communication between family members. This integration allows children to communicate in their natural language, which is play, and encourages parents to learn to "talk in play." It also provides parents a safe venue for expressing some of their own childlike feelings and attitudes-either directly or indirectly. Family play therapy builds connections—between the therapist and the family and among family members—with fun and laughter.

In family play therapy, just as in traditional family therapy, the family, rather than a specified member, is the unit of intervention. In family play therapy with adopted children, the entire family, rather than the child, is the client. The focus in this intervention strategy is on using the play therapy process to enhance communication about the specific issues related to adoption and how those issues are manifested in this particular family.

The therapist decides how to configure the sessions based on the current needs of the family. Sometimes the entire family comes to a session, sometimes one or both children come, sometimes individual parents come, and sometimes various combinations of children and parents come. The therapist can involve the family in making decisions about who is going to come to the next session, but should ultimately base this decision on his or her understanding of the unfolding process and the needs of the individual family members. For instance, if the father seems to have a positive alliance with the child that excludes the mother, the therapist would point out this pattern in a session with the entire family. After getting input from the family members, the therapist might decide to include all three of these family members in a session in order for them to work on balancing this relationship, or he or she might decide to just have the child and the mother attend a session or two to enhance the attachment.

The therapist must also decide how directive to be in the sessions. Some degree of structure is necessary in family play therapy sessions—while the therapist may choose to let the members of the family play freely with little direction in some sessions, this would probably not be appropriate for every single session. Many of the techniques appropriate for helping adopted children and their families work through their issues are relatively structured. Others are not so structured, but the family members will need some direction about what they are to do with one another during the session. Given this requirement, some degree of directiveness is necessary, but in determining how much structure to provide each therapist must consider his or her own comfort level and theoretical orientation.

Techniques Used

In addition to the usual techniques used by the play therapist, such as tracking, restating content, reflecting feelings, returning responsibility back to the child, and limiting (Kottman 1995), the family play therapist also can choose any techniques traditionally used by family therapists or therapists who work with children using talk therapy. This gives the family play therapist a wide array of therapeutic tools, far too vast for the space available in this chapter. The author has chosen the following techniques as representative samples of the available intervention strategies because, in her clinical experience with adopted children and their families, these techniques have proven particularly useful. These selected techniques include free play, directed cooperative play, nurturing play, power sharing, storytelling, life books, individually designed rituals, and assorted art therapy strategies.

Free Play

It is very helpful in family play therapy to have the entire family and selected subgroups of family members simply play. While the members of the family are playing, the therapist uses basic play therapy responses—tracking, restating content, reflecting feelings—and observes the patterns. The family members, after a brief time of being uncomfortable, will almost always "play" out the themes and patterns typical of their daily interactions. They will act out the roles they usually occupy in the family and display the power structure as it exists in the family. The play therapist can also assess how attachment is developing between the adopted child and the other members of the family and how the various members of the family are dealing with grief and loss. If members of the family are struggling with any of these issues, the therapist can shift the focus of future sessions to those areas.

Directed Cooperative Play

One of the best ways to assess attachment, unmet expectations, shifts in family structure, and power and control issues is to ask selected members of the family to make or build something together or play a cooperative game. The author usually uses the assignment to build a house or a tower out of pillows, Legos, or Lincoln Logs. Therapists can also use commercially available cooperative games, such as Sleeping Grump or Save the Princess, in which participants must cooperate to successfully complete the game.

For families in which the attachment is already strong, cooperative play can be fun and exciting. People who have formed attachments with one another do not usually have difficulty cooperating with one another. For families in which the attachment is tentative, cooperative play can be a struggle because it is difficult to form an alliance with someone without a certain level of attachment. One way of beginning to build a connection is to work together on a project.

In families with continuing unmet expectations, the members will also have difficulty cooperating with one another. Their play quite frequently manifests a pattern that reflects their unsatisfied desires in the relationship—the parents may have unrealistically high, developmentally inappropriate expectations of the child. The child may assume that the parents do not really want her help in the process, and so forth. The play therapist can make guesses to the family members about the meaning of such patterns and facilitate discussion about unmatched expectations. The cooperative play format can provide an avenue for work on continued honest communication about expectations and desires.

Cooperative play is also a useful tool for assessing shifts in family structure and promoting realignment of family structure. The various members of the family will rely upon their usual roles in the process of the play—the oldest child will try to tell the other children about the best way of making a tower, the youngest child will expect the other children to take care of him, and so forth. If the newly adopted child has had an impact on this interactional pattern, it will be obvious in the play.

In families struggling with issues of power and control, one or two members will always try to be in control of the project. By observing this pattern, the play therapist can gain an understanding of who wants power and how they go about getting it. The therapist can then make guesses about the various members' need for power, hoping to help them gain insight into their own dynamics and to rethink their position. The therapist can also make "rules" about who has power and about the necessity of sharing power or taking turns being in control. This strategy can teach adopted children who come from chaotic backgrounds or who have had too much power that they can be safe with their adoptive parents and siblings even when they are not in control. It can also teach parents who do not allow their children age-appropriate power and responsibility ways of sharing power with their children.

Nurturing Play

Many older adopted children had little nurturing in their lives before they were adopted. Children adopted as infants may not believe that they deserve to receive nurturing due to their basic convictions about the reason their birth parents gave them up for adoption. These factors may contribute to difficulties in forming attachments, and they may negatively affect children's identity formation.

One method of repairing the damage in this area is to encourage nurturing play between the adopted child and his or her parent(s) in the playroom. This play would include making "food" and feeding one another, taking care of dolls together, a parent rocking the child or singing songs to the "baby," a parent stroking the child's hair or back, and any other activities that a parent would typically do with a baby or a very small child.

It is important to be respectful of the child in setting up this type of play,

since there are many children who are not comfortable being this vulnerable.
But with talking about the possible activities and letting the child have a voice
in whether and how nurturing play proceeds, the therapist can avoid causing
any more damage in this area. The play therapist should also work to prepare
parents for this type of play in a parent consultation prior to proposing it to the
child, since many parents are not comfortable with regressive play and adoptive
parents (who may have never been around babies or very small children) may
not know how to provide the concrete nurturing activities necessary for this
intervention.

Power Sharing

Children with issues of power and control need help in learning to be comfortable with letting go of control and not trying to "steal" power from others. In
family play therapy, the therapist sets up interactions in which various family
members take turns being in control. This might be as simple as playing
"Mother, May I?" or Red Light, Green Light, taking turns being "it." Fantasy
play or storytelling in which family members must metaphorically share power
by taking turns being the "king" or by switching back and forth in narrating a
story are also helpful. During these interactions, the therapist makes guesses
about how each member feels about sharing power. This process helps family
members gain insight into their own thoughts, feelings, attitudes, and behaviors, which can increase their potential options in future situations.

Storytelling

Telling family stories is essential for beginning the process of entitlement and
claiming and for encouraging attachment and positive identity formation. The
story should include descriptions of (1) the decision-making process the family
went through in deciding whether to adopt a child, (2) the decision-making
process the birth parents went through in deciding whether to give their child up
(if this information is available), (3) the feelings and thoughts of the child during
this process (if the child was old enough to know what they were), (4) the
fantasies of the adoptive parents about the child, (5) the day the parents met the
child for the first time, (6) the day the adoption became final, and (7) any other
information about thoughts, feelings, and behaviors that might contribute to a
positive story of the adoption. By telling and retelling the story of how the
adopted child came to be a part of the current family, family members can form
a lasting bond with one another.

Life Books

A similar approach to the family story is the life book, which is an individually made book covering the child's life from birth to present, written in the child's own words. It generally includes a narrative describing what has happened to the child, when, and why, as well as what the child's feelings are about what has happened. The book may also incorporate photos, drawings, report cards, awards and certificates, letters from previous foster or adoptive parents and birth parents, a birth certificate, a genogram, and anything else a particular child might want to include. [Bakhaus 1984, p. 551]

The primary purpose of the life book is to help the child integrate the past, present, and future in order to facilitate a positive identity formation. The process of constructing the life book can also provide the child with an avenue for exploring feelings of loss and for exploring fantasies and expectations. In family play therapy, the life book can be an invaluable vehicle for communication between the adopted child and the rest of the family. By helping the child with the construction of the life book, various family members can increase their awareness and understanding of how the adopted child perceives his or her life — both before and after the adoption.

Although life books are usually done in individual talk therapy with a child, they can be equally helpful in family play therapy. The play therapist can invite all of the members of the family to contribute to the adopted child's life book, or the family members can combine their efforts and use their family storytelling to make a family life book. Writing and illustrating a book together that combines all of the different family members' perspectives on the story can build a sense of shared goals and responsibilities. The family can take the book home and share the story of the adoption process over and over — this will help to extend their sense of connection with one another from the setting of the playroom to the setting of their home.

Individually Designed Rituals

"Rituals not only celebrate what is, but help people get where they want to be" (Melina 1990, p. 1). Melina (1990) suggests that rituals can be used therapeutically with adopted children and their families to commemorate transitions and promote healing. Family play therapists can help family members create transition rituals to celebrate children's birthdays, adoptive placements, final adoptions, naturalization ceremonies, and other dates that are important to the family. These rituals can assist the family with entitlement, claiming, attachment, and identity formation. Rituals can help family members create healing rituals to say "good-bye" to the losses in their lives, to express their continued love for birth parents and love for adoptive parents, to bury traumatic events from the past, or demonstrate to a child that he or she is not "bad." These rituals can assist the family with unmatched expectations, shifts in the family system, grief and loss issues, and attachment.

In designing therapeutic rituals, the therapist must guide the family to consider place, actions, words, symbolism, and participants (Melina 1990). The family members should choose a place that is meaningful to the members of the family—they can conduct the ritual in the playroom or in any other special place. The actions and words that comprise the ceremony must be suited to the interests and priorities of the family. Family members can use time in the play session to generate the actions and words for the ritual even if it is going to be conducted elsewhere. It is essential for the actions and words to have some kind of symbolism—meaning beyond the actions and words themselves—such as lighting a candle that represents love, planting a tree that represents growth and nurturing, burying a belt that was used for beatings, and so forth. The family members must also decide who they would like to participate in their ritual. Some rituals are only appropriate for the immediate family, and others require participation from members of the extended family, friends, and members of the community.

Art Therapy Strategies

There are many art therapy strategies that are appropriate for use within the context of family play therapy with adopted children. Because of space considerations, the author will limit her descriptions to two such techniques: body outline drawings (Muro and Kottman 1995, Steinhardt 1985) and feeling art (Gerler 1982, Muro and Kottman 1995). Other art therapy strategies that would be especially appropriate in family play therapy with this population would be the kinetic family drawing (Burns and Kaufman 1970, 1972, Gil 1994), family self-portraits (Gil 1994); and family art assessments (Landgarten 1981).

Using body outline drawings (Muro and Kottman 1995, Steinhardt 1985) in family play therapy would involve having the adopted child lie on large pieces of paper while the parent or a sibling traces around his or her body. They would then collaborate on coloring the figure. The therapist can help the child and the other members of the family make a list of the physical, emotional, and mental traits the child inherited from his or her birth family and a list of the traits the child has learned from his or her adopted family. This can help the child examine and celebrate both his or her biological and environmental heritage.

Feelings drawings can be helpful in exploring many of the issues confronting adopted children and their families. The therapist can choose specific feelings for family members to draw, depending on the circumstances of the family. By watching how other members of the family see certain feelings, family members can increase their understanding of one another and their ability to provide support and encouragement to one another.

The preceeding description is a mere sampling of possible intervention techniques for use in family play therapy. The play therapist is only limited by his or her own imagination. Be creative; have fun.

Case Illustration

In my initial telephone conversation with Rita Sumner about her daughter, Kaitlin, I asked her what kinds of difficulties she had been experiencing, and it was as if a dam broke: "We've only had her for seven months, but I'm afraid that we made a terrible mistake. She won't mind us, and she tells us all the time that we're not her real parents. She seems to like my husband, James, but sometimes it feels as though she just hates me. Not only that, she fights with our son, Jeremy, constantly. Jeremy keeps saying that he wishes we would send Kaitlin back to the adoption agency. We've already done the final adoption and even if we hadn't, neither James nor I want to send Kaitlin back. We just don't know what to do."

I asked Rita and James to come in for a parent consultation so that I could gather more information about Kaitlin and the other members of the Sumner family. The following data is summarized from that session and from information gathered in subsequent parent consultations and in family play therapy sessions. The Sumners were in their late thirties. They had married soon after they had completed college and had waited six or seven years before attempting to conceive. Their attempts at conception failed, and after many tests and medical interventions, they had determined that if they wanted to have children they would need to adopt. They applied at an adoption agency and after waiting two years, they got their first child, Jeremy. He was only a month old when he came into their family, and his development and adjustment had been without problems.

When Jeremy was 5 years old, Rita and James applied for a second child. By this time, they decided that they wanted to adopt an older child—partly because they had heard that getting a healthy baby was increasingly difficult, partly because they did not want to go through the "hassles of having a tiny baby again." Over the next two years, Rita and James had been "offered" several children, but had waited for "just the right one"—Kaitlin. When I asked the Sumners to tell me about they ways that they knew Kaitlin was "the right one," they were at a loss and could not answer this question.

Kaitlin was 5 years old when she became part of the Sumner family. According to the information the social worker gave to Rita and James, Kaitlin had been abandoned at age 3 by her birth mother, who had simply dropped her off at the child welfare office, refusing to stay to talk about her reasons. Consequently, the social worker knew little about Kaitlin's birth parents and their interactions with Kaitlin. When she was abandoned, she was relatively well nourished and had no scars or other evidence of physical or sexual abuse.

Kaitlin was placed in a series of foster homes. None of these placements lasted more than six months. In each of these placements, Kaitlin's behavior had gotten progressively worse. However, in her last placement before the Sumners had adopted her, she had settled down and seemed to be adjusting well.

During the first four months of living with the Sumners, Kaitlin "was wonderful. She was so happy to be part of our family that she just smiled all the time. Jeremy had more of a hard time since he was used to being an only child and now he wasn't anymore. Kaitlin also gets attention from friends and relatives because she is a girl, and Jeremy seems kind of resentful about that. Kaitlin did kind of miss her last foster parents, but after about two months she didn't ask to see them anymore." At the end of this four month "honeymoon" period, Kaitlin started testing the limits set in the family. She got progressively less cooperative and seemed to be "just miserable, like nothing we could do would please her. Jeremy seemed to feel a bit better though. It was as if both of them couldn't be happy at the same time."

Although Rita and James really wanted me to do individual play therapy with Kaitlin, I explained to them that I thought it would be better for the entire family to participate in family play therapy. This would avoid identifying Kaitlin as "the problem" and encourage them to continue to form their new family in a proactive, positive way, rather than in a reactive, negative way. I introduced my initial analysis to them that the family needed to work on seven of the issues that affect adoptive families: entitlement; claiming; unmatched expectations; shifts in the family system; separation, loss, and grief; attachment, and power and control. I also discussed my belief that eventually Kaitlin would need to work individually on identity formation, with some additional support from the rest of the family.

Over the next six months, I worked with the Sumner family—sometimes with the entire family, sometimes with different pairs, and sometimes with individuals—to help them learn better ways of coping with these key issues. The session after my initial parent consultation, I asked the entire family to come in, and I used free play to give myself an idea of how the family usually interacted. Although at first the members of the family were extremely uncomfortable with my tracking their behavior, restating content, and reflecting their feelings, they seemed to forget I was there after about 15 minutes. At first, Jeremy tried to tell Kaitlin what to do, as Rita and James wandered around the playroom, picking things up and putting them back down. Kaitlin ignored Jeremy and started to paint a picture of a house. Eventually, Jeremy wound up playing "catch" with James, while Rita watched and Kaitlin continued to paint by herself.

I used directed cooperative play for the second session with the entire family, asking the family to build a tower of pipe cleaners. While Kaitlin watched, refusing to share her pipe cleaners with the other family members, everyone else in the family cooperated building a tower. James and Jeremy carried on a conversation as they worked, with Rita occasionally adding comments. After they were done, Kaitlin told them that it was a stupid tower and that they really didn't know what they were doing. Then, Kaitlin stood on a chair so that she could add her pipe cleaners to the top of the tower.

At the end of this session, I asked the entire family to tell me what they thought they had learned about the family and each other during our first two sessions. Rita said that she had noticed that the rest of the family worked together and Kaitlin kept to herself. She said that she thought that was so Kaitlin wouldn't have to be part of the family. James said that he had noticed that he and Jeremy seemed to work very well together, but that Rita helped a lot.

After encouraging Rita and James for the thought they had given to these questions, I added some other ideas of my own. I suggested that they might need to do more claiming. To facilitate this, I gave them a homework assignment for the entire family to brainstorm about ways that Kaitlin fit into the family and which traits she shared with various members of their extended families.

I also suggested that it seemed to me that while Jeremy knew just exactly how he fit into the family (being cooperative, making conversation, and so forth), that Kaitlin was not yet sure how she fit into the family. Since she seemed to feel as though the rest of the family was not including her and she felt powerless in this situation, Kaitlin "stole" power by refusing to cooperate with everyone else. I told them that we would work on this in the future.

For the next session (session 3), I wanted Kaitlin and Jeremy to come for the bulk of the session, but I also wanted to do a parent consultation with James and Rita. I asked both Kaitlin and Jeremy to do a kinetic family drawing by drawing a picture of everyone in their family doing something. Kaitlin drew Jeremy as a large figure who was helping James and Rita, and she drew herself very small in a corner of the page. Jeremy drew himself playing ball with James and drew Rita cooking dinner. He left Kaitlin out of his picture. When I asked him where she was, he told me that she was out of the house, "visiting friends." I made some guesses about Kaitlin not being sure how she could fit into the family and about Jeremy sometimes wishing that he were an only child again. They both acknowledged that these hypotheses were true.

I then asked them to do a variation on the family art assessment and cooperate on a picture of their family. I asked them to brainstorm and generate a list of four things each person in the family could be doing and to take turns drawing them. This was an attempt to engage both Jeremy and Kaitlin in thinking about ideas for how Kaitlin could fit into the family in a way that would not totally displace Jeremy.

In my parent consultation with Rita and James, I encouraged them to talk about their sense of entitlement, which was rather weak because their social worker had not been able to give them much information about Kaitlin's birth parents and the social worker had not been emphatic about their "right" to parent Kaitlin. I also talked with them about continuing to work on the claiming process, verbalizing about their own families and how both Kaitlin and Jeremy shared traits with various members of their extended family. I also suggested that they try and find one particular relative who would be willing to "sponsor" Kaitlin so that she could have a special nurturing relationship with another adult member of their family in order to further build the claiming process.

I used directive techniques in sessions 4 and 5 to help me understand the shifts in the family and any potential mismatched expectations. In session 4, I continued to work with Jeremy and Kaitlin in the playroom, asking them to do a "show" using the dollhouse telling me a story about a typical day in their family—things like when they got up, who fixed breakfast, who took care of the animals, and so forth. As they talked, I realized that James and Rita were probably doing too much for these children that they could do themselves. I speculated that was because of their desire to make up to the children for the fact that they were adopted. During my parent consultation, I suggested that James and Rita give more power and responsibility to the children—that they must stop doing things for the children that they could do for themselves.

In that same session, I also used directed cooperative play to ask them to do a puppet show for me. I wanted to see how the children perceived and communicated about the shifts in the family system. Interestingly enough, the two stories they told together were of a family in which some member was the boss and some member was left out. My analysis of this metaphor was that the children thought that their parents' love was finite—that they could not both be loved and lovable. They both also seemed to want power so that they would not feel helpless. I decided that the relationship with the children was not yet strong enough for me to do a mutual storytelling, but that I would use this strategy later in the relationship.

In session 5, I had the entire family in the session and asked each one to draw me a picture of what he or she had thought life was going to be like after the adoption and a picture of what life really was like after the adoption. All four members of the family drew extremely idealistic pictures of how they had thought things would be after Kaitlin was adopted and extremely gloomy and negative pictures about the current situation in the family. We used this exercise to begin to discuss what each family member had expected from the adoption. All of the members of the family had harbored very unrealistic expectations about how the placement would proceed and about the impact that the adoption would have on their lives. This theme of unmatched expectation cropped up many times during the subsequent ten weeks, with all of the family members struggling with what their expectations were and whether they could possibly be met in a practical, rational way. As time passed, each family member realized that the "pipe dreams" that each of them had generated were actually keeping them from seeing one another as they really were and that this process was hurting their ability to do what they called "make a family."

To help facilitate this process, I asked the entire family to come to sessions 6 and 7 as well. During session 6, I asked them to make feeling drawings to express their feelings about the gap between their fantasies and the reality. As they shared their feeling pictures, they realized that even though they might not share the same fantasy about how the family was going to interact, they were all disappointed at their discovery that relationships among family members were not always going to be happy and cooperative.

During session 7, I asked them to brainstorm a list of assets for each family member. We then designed a ritual for acknowledging these assets, using a crown and a "magic wand." They took turns standing in the middle of the group, wearing the crown and listening to the list of assets described by the person who had the "magic wand."

During these first six or seven sessions, I had noticed that Kaitlin sometimes struggled with wanting to be in control of everything in her life. To begin dealing with this situation, I asked that only Kaitlin come to play therapy for the next several sessions. I believed that her difficulty with control stemmed from making a switch from a chaotic out-of-control family of origin to a series of too strict or too lax parents in her foster homes. She presented an unusual combination of the backgrounds that contribute to problem with power and control. I decided that the underlying theme in Kaitlin's life, up to the point she came to live with the Sumners, was chaos, and I wanted to provide some calming experiences, so I started inundating her with power in the playroom over the next several sessions. I used the "whisper" technique (Kottman 1995, Landreth personal communication 1995) to return responsibility to her. For example, when Kaitlin would ask me to do something for her in the playroom, like deciding on the color of paint she should use on her picture, I would whisper, "What do you want me to say?" This strategy lets the child make decisions and be powerful in a positive way.

In parent consultations, I encouraged Rita and James not to pamper Kaitlin and to give her age-appropriate power and control whenever she was not whining or otherwise asking for it in a manipulative way. I wanted to teach them to share power with the children in a democratic parenting style, and I felt that this power-sharing process would be a logical first step.

Due to the shifts the Sumners were able to make in their parenting and her experience in her individual play therapy sessions with me, Kaitlin learned to be more comfortable in not always being in control. She also learned to ask directly for power, rather than trying to get it passively with her refusal to do things that other people wanted her to do, since I would never let her have her way that way and I would insist that she ask for power in appropriate assertive ways, rather than passive-aggressive ways.

By session 10, Jeremy's struggle with giving up his position as only child and Kaitlin's search for how to fit into the family was obvious. These shifts in the family structure were rather difficult to deal with since Jeremy was having to give up a role (the only child) that he liked and replace it with a role that he was not sure that he would like (the big brother). Working with Jeremy alone in sessions 10 and 11, I used mutual storytelling to work on ways of reframing this shift. This was a struggle, though. Initially, I asked Jeremy to tell me a story using the dolls in the dollhouse. He refused, telling me that the dolls were "girlish—something Kaitlin would use." I then asked him to use the animals or the puppets to tell me a story. He told a story about a lion who had been king of the jungle, but then a new animal—a dragon—came into the jungle and took over the job. I retold the story, using the same characters, and made up a new ending in which the lion and dragon took turns being king of the jungle. In the process, I also suggested that one of the things that the king was supposed to do was to look after and take care of the other animals who live in the jungle. My purpose in this story was to introduce the idea that Jeremy could be powerful and nurturing at the same time.

During these two sessions, I noticed that some of the problem with the shift in the family structure was related to Jeremy's feelings of loss and grief about his "old" position and the "old" family. I realized that I had not been working enough with grief and loss with the entire family, so I once again saw the whole family together for sessions 12 and 13 so we could talk about things that they had each lost. While Jeremy and Kaitlin were both willing to talk about things they felt sad about, Rita and James were not comfortable discussing their fertility problems in front of the children. I scheduled two sessions (14 and 15) with them by themselves to begin the discussion of this issue, and I encouraged them to continue these discussions with one another on their own. In session 16, I asked them to share a little of this information with Jeremy and Kaitlin so that the children were not left thinking that they were the only members of the family with grief and loss issues. We designed a candle lighting ritual so that each member of the family could begin the process of healing those feelings of loss and grief. At the beginning of each subsequent session, we lit a candle for one thing that each of them missed or which was sad for them.

In session 17 we started doing a life book for the entire family, beginning when Rita and James were children and moving up to the present day. In the next four sessions, the family worked on constructing the book, using some photographs and making other pictures for the pages. When the book was finished, we spent an entire session (22) going through the book, telling the story of each part of the life of the family. The Sumners brought the book home so that they could continue to share it with one another and with family friends and relatives.

The process of doing the life book as a group project further aided the attachment process between Kaitlin and the other members of the family, but by session 23 it was obvious that she and Rita were still rather distant, so I arranged to have just the two of them come by themselves for the next four sessions. During these sessions, I had them doing a lot of free play, directed cooperative play, and nurturing play together, emphasizing the fact that they could share power, nurture each other, and have fun with one another. They began to develop some personal rituals, such as nicknames for one another and some "special times"—activities that they shared in the playroom that they could also share at home, things like cooking together (pretend in the playroom, but real at home), brushing one another's hair, and so forth. These nurturing experiences helped to strengthen the attachment between the two women in the family.

By this time in the family play therapy process, the entire family was reporting that they were getting along much better and feeling good about their ability to "make a family." Everyone reported that Kaitlin was much happier and that she was getting along with the other members of the family. Jeremy was also much more content with his place in the family and his relationships with the other family members. Although Rita and James continued to struggle somewhat with their unresolved feelings of loss related to their infertility and their own control issues related to parenting, they felt much more relaxed and comfortable in their parenting role with Kaitlin. They had resolved their reservations about entitlement and naturally made many claiming comments about both children. The entire family was much more clear about what they could reasonably expect from one another and what they could reasonably expect in the way of family relationships. While there would continue to be shifts in the family structure as the family members developed, all of them seemed more comfortable with the possibility of changes and their own abilities to cope with whatever the future would bring them. Although the grief and loss issues of the family members were not completely resolved, they had all at least acknowledged that these issues could be a problem and they were somewhat better able to accept and support each other in their separate grieving processes. The attachment among the members of the family had grown much stronger and more secure. They completely stopped discussing the possibility of sending Kaitlin back to the adoption agency, and they seemed bemused that they had once considered that action as an option for handling their family difficulties.

I suggested that they might want to have some "booster" sessions occasionally in the future to keep progressing in the positive direction they had begun. It seemed especially important for them to consider some more family play therapy when Kaitlin was 8 or 9, since that is the age at which many adopted children realize that there might be negative implications of being adopted. I also suggested that it might be helpful for the family to come to counseling for several sessions when Jeremy and Kaitlin entered their adolescent years, since that would be another essential time in the formation of their identities and they might need extra support and nurturing during those times.

Conclusions

Although most adopted children have positive outlooks and are mentally healthy, this group has disproportionately high rates of emotional, mental health, and educational problems. While there is no clear empirical evidence about the etiology of these difficulties, there is strong support for the idea that adopted children and their family struggle with eight key issues: entitlement, claiming, unmatched expectations, shifts in the family system, grief and loss, attachment, identity formation, and power and control.

Play therapy—especially play therapy that involves the entire family—seems to be an ideal intervention strategy for helping adopted children and their families cope with these issues. All fourteen of the therapeutic factors delineated by Schaefer (1993) apply to this population, which would make play therapy the treatment of choice for young children who have been adopted—especially those who were adopted after infancy and who are struggling with how being adopted affects their lives and their relationships with others.

References

Anderson, R. (1993). As the child plays, so grows the family tree: family play therapy. In *Play Therapy in Action: A Casebook for Practitioners*, ed. T. Kottman, and C. Schaefer, pp. 457–484. Northvale, NJ: Jason Aronson.

Austad, C., and Simmons, T. (1978). Symptoms of adopted children presenting to a large mental health clinic. *Child Psychiatry and Human Development* 9:20–27.

Bachrach, C. A., Adams, P. F., Sambrano, S., and London, K. A. (1990). Adoptions in the 1980s. In *Advance Data from Vital and Health Statistics*, pp. 1–12. Hyattsville, MD: National Center for Health Statistics.

Backhaus, K. (1984). Life books: tool for working with children in placement. *Social Work* 29:551–554.

Barth, R., and Berry, M. (1988). *Adoption and Disruption*. New York: Aldine De Gruyter.

Barth, R., Berry, M., Yoshikami, R., et al. (1988). Prediction of adoption disruption. *Social Work* 33:227–233.

Berry, M. (1992). Contributors to adjustment problems of adoptees: a review of the longitudinal research. *Child and Adolescent Social Work Journal* 9:525–540.

Bettner, B. L., and Lew, A. (1989). *Raising Kids Who Can*. New York: Harper/Row.

Brodzinsky, D. M. (1987). Adjustment to adoption: a psychosocial perspective. *Clinical Psychology Review* 7:25–47.

———— (1990). A stress and coping model of adoption adjustment. In *The Psychology of Adoption*, ed. D. M. Brodzinsky, and M. D. Schechter, pp. 3–24. New York: Oxford University Press.

Brodzinsky, D. M., Hitt, J. C., and Smith, D. (1993). Impact of parental separation and divorce on adopted and nonadopted children. *American Journal of Orthopsychiatry* 63:451–461.

Brodzinsky, D. M., Radice, C., Huffman, L., and Merkler, K. (1987). Prevalence of clinically significant symptomatology in a non-clinical sample of adopted and nonadopted children. *Journal of Clinical Child Psychology*

16:350–356.

Brodzinsky, D. M., Schechter, D., Braff, A., and Singer, L. (1984). Psychological and academic adjustment in adopted children. *Journal of Consulting and Clinical Psychology* 52:582–590.

Brodzinsky, D. M., Singer, L., and Braff, A. (1984). Children's understanding of adoption. *Child Development* 55:869–878.

Brodzinsky, D. M., and Steiger, C. (1991). Prevalence of adoptees among special education populations. *Journal of Learning Disabilities* 24:484–489.

Burns, R., and Kaufman, S. (1970). *Kinetic Family Drawing (K-F-D): Research and Application*. New York: Brunner/Mazel.

_____ (1972). *Actions, Styles and Symbols in Kinetic Family Drawings: An Interpretive Manual*. New York: Brunner/Mazel.

Cohen, N., Coyne, J., and Duvall, J. (1993). Adopted and biological children in the clinic: family, parental, and child characteristics. *Journal of Child Psychology and Psychiatry* 34:545–562.

Euster, S., Ward, V., and Varner, J. (1982). Adapting counseling techniques to foster parent training. *Child Welfare* 61:375–382.

Fullerton, C., Goodrich, W., and Berman, L. (1986). Adoption predicts treatment resistances in hospitalized adolescents. *Journal of the American Academy of Child and Adolescent Psychiatry* 25:542–551.

Gerler, E. (1982). *Counseling the Young Learner*. Englewood Cliffs, NJ: Prentice Hall.

Gil, E. (1994). *Play in Family Therapy*. New York: Guilford.

Grotevant, H., McRoy, R., and Jenkins, V. (1988). Emotionally disturbed, adopted adolescents: early patterns of family adaptation. *Family Process* 27:439–457.

Groze, V. (1992). Adoption, attachment and self-concept. *Child and Adolescent Social Work Journal* 9:169–191.

Hartman, A., and Laird, J. (1990). Family treatment after adoption: common themes. In *The Psychology of Adoption*, ed. D. Brodzinsky, and M. Schechter, pp. 221–239. New York: Oxford University Press.

Harvey, S. (1991). Creating a family: an integrated expressive approach to adoption. *The Arts in Psychotherapy* 18:213–222.

Helwig, A., and Ruthven, D. (1990). Psychological ramifications of adoptions and implications for counseling. *Journal of Mental Health Counseling* 12:24–37.

Howe, D. (1992). Assessing adoptions in difficulty. *British Journal of Social Work* 22:1–15.

Jarratt, C. (1994). *Helping Children Cope with Separation and Loss*, rev. ed.. Boston: Harvard Common Press.

Jernberg, A. (1979). *Theraplay*. San Francisco, CA: Jossey-Bass.

Kadushin, A. (1980). *Child Welfare Services*, 3rd ed. New York: Macmillan.

Katz, L. (1980). Adoption counseling as a preventive mental health specialty.

Child Welfare 56:165–171.

Kirk, H. (1981). *Adoptive Kinship.* Toronto: Butterworth.

Kotsopoulos, S., Cote, A., Joseph, L., et al. (1988). Psychiatric disorders in adopted children: a controlled study. *American Journal of Orthopsychiatry* 58:608–621.

Kottman, T. (1993). The king of rock and roll: an application of Adlerian play therapy. In *Play Therapy in Action: A Casebook for Practitioners*, ed. T. Kottman, and C. Schaefer, pp. 133–167. Northvale, NJ: Jason Aronson.

———— (1994). Adlerian play therapy. In *Handbook of Play Therapy*, vol. 2, ed. K. O'Connor, and C. Schaefer, pp. 3–26. New York: Wiley.

———— (1995). *Partners in Play: An Adlerian Approach to Play Therapy.* Alexandria, VA: American Counseling Association.

Landgarten, H. (1981). *Clinical Art Therapy: A Comprehensive Guide.* New York: Brunner/Mazel.

LeVine, E., and Sallee, A. (1990). Critical phases among adoptees and their families: implications for therapy. *Child and Adolescent Social Work* 7:217–232.

Lindholm, B., and Touliatos, J. (1980). Psychological adjustment of adopted and nonadopted children. *Psychological Reports* 46:307–310.

Melina, L. (1986). *Raising Adopted Children.* New York: Harper & Row.

———— (1990). Adoption ritual needed to enhance sense of "family." *Adopted Child* 9(3):1–4.

Minuchin, S. (1974). *Families and Family Therapy.* Cambridge, MA: Harvard University Press.

Muro, J., and Kottman, T. (1995). *Guidance and Counseling in the Elementary and Middle School: A Practical Approach.* Dubuque, IA: Wm. C. Brown.

Partridge, P. (1991). The particular challenges of being adopted. *Smith College– Studies in Social Work* 61:197–208.

Reitz, M., and Watson, K. (1992). *Adoption and the Family System: Strategies for Treatment.* New York: Guilford.

Remkus, J. (1991). Repeated foster placements and attachment failure: case of Joseph, age 3. In *Play Therapy with Children in Crisis: A Casebook for Practitioners*, ed. N. Webb, pp. 143–163. New York: Guilford.

Satir, V. (1972). *Peoplemaking.* Palo Alto, CA: Science and Behavior Books.

Schaefer, C., ed. (1993). *The Therapeutic Powers of Play.* Northvale, NJ: Jason Aronson.

Schaefer, J., and Lindstrom, C. (1990). Brief solution-focused therapy with adoptive families. In *The Psychology of Adoption*, ed. D. Brodzinsky, and M. Schechter, pp. 240–252. New York: Oxford University Press.

Smith, D., and Brodzinsky, D.M. (1994). Stress and coping in adopted children: a developmental study. *Journal of Clinical Child Psychology* 23:91–99.

Steinhardt, L. (1985). Freedom within boundaries: body outline drawings in art therapy with children. *The Arts in Psychotherapy* 12:25–34.

Valdez, G., and McNamara, J. R. (1994). Matching to prevent adoption disruption. *Child and Adolescent Social Work Journal* 11:391–403.

VanFleet, R. (1994). Filial therapy for adoptive children and parents. In *Handbook of Play Therapy, vol. 2: Advances and Innovations*, ed. K. O'Connor, and C. Schaefer, pp. 371–386. New York: Wiley.

Van Gulden, H., and Bartels-Rabb, L. (1993). *Real Parents, Real Children: Parenting the Adopted Child*. New York: Crossroad.

Verhulst, F., Althaus, M., and Beiman, H. (1992). Damaging background: later adjustment of international adoptees. *Journal of American Academy of Child and Adolescent Psychiatry* 31:518–524.

Watson, K. (1989–1990). Infant bonding and attachment: a helpful distinction. *Stepping Stones*, December-January, pp. 2–9.

Wierzbicki, M. (1993). Psychological adjustment of adoptees: a meta-analysis. *Journal of Clinical Child Psychology* 22:447–454.

Index